DATE DUE

10-22-05			
11-10-05			
10-12-09			

home guide to
trees,
shrubs,
wild flowers

home guide to
trees, shrubs, and wild flowers

William Carey Grimm

STACKPOLE BOOKS

1. Trees   2. Shrubs
3. Wild Flowers

Home Guide to Trees, Shrubs, and Wildflowers
Copyright © 1970 by
THE STACKPOLE COMPANY
Published by
STACKPOLE BOOKS
Cameron and Kelker Streets
Harrisburg, Pa. 17105

Standard Book Number 8117-0806-3
Library of Congress Catalog Card Number 76-100348

PRINTED IN U.S.A.

CONTENTS

PREFACE

Here—for the first time—in one popular-style book is a guide to both woody plants and wildflowers. It is a book for the novice rather than the more serious or advanced student; for all who have at least a casual interest in the plant life of field and forest, and would like to become better acquainted. These are the wild plants most likely to attract one's attention in various parts of eastern North America, with the exception of semi-tropical and tropical Florida. Should this introduction open the door to a richer enjoyment of days spent in the outdoors, the purpose of this guide book will have been adequately fulfilled.

The plants in this book are not arranged as the professional botanist would arrange them: by families, genera, and species. First of all they are arranged according to habitat—the kind of place where you will find them—and then by other quite obvious characteristics. Many of these plants will be found growing from Canada deep into the South. Others are distinctly northern but are often found southward in the cool highlands of the southern Appalachians. Still others are typically southern or even may be limited to the coastal region of the Deep South. In the case of wideranging species the time of flowering and fruiting given in the book pertains to the whole range. Naturally it will be much earlier southward than at the northern extremity of the range. It will also be earlier at lower altitudes than at high elevations in the mountains.

Part I of the book introduces the woody plants—the native trees, shrubs, and woody vines—most frequently found in the various parts of eastern North America. With few exceptions these woody plants bloom in the spring and their flowers persist but a short time. Their leaves and often their fruits are therefore most useful in identifying them. Usually only those with especially showy or attractive flowers have their flowers shown in the illustrations.

Part II is an introduction to what we most often think of as being wild flowers. These are herbaceous plants or ones which are not conspicuously woody. Here are the flowers you are most likely to see on rambles through the spring woodlands. Here, too, are those you will most often find while on camping trips during the summer; and the flowers which add color to fields and waysides during the summer and fall. In this book they are arranged by seasons and the places where they usually grow: woodlands, wet places, or fields and waysides.

The material in this book has been taken from, or adapted from, three popular but much more complete books by the author—*The Book of Trees, Recognizing Native Shrubs,* and *Recognizing Flowering Wild Plants*—all previously published by The Stackpole Company.

GETTING ACQUAINTED WITH PLANTS

Many who would like to know more about trees, shrubs, and wildflowers and be able to recognize them have had little or no training in the subject of botany. For this reason a brief introduction to the types and arrangement of leaves and the structure and arrangement of flowers is presented here.

The plants presented in this book belong to two divisions of the plant world known as the seed plants, or plants which produce seeds. The first group, represented by the pine trees and their relatives, are what the botanist calls the *gymnosperms* or naked-seeded plants. They do not have really true flowers or true fruits. Trees such as pines, spruces, and firs simply produce two kinds of cones. In the spring they produce a great many stamen-bearing or male cones which produce a great abundance of dusty wind-borne pollen. After their pollen is shed, these cones quickly dry up and drop off the trees. On the same tree are a lesser number of female or ovule-bearing cones. These cones have pairs of ovules lying exposed on the upper surface of the scales—they are naked-seeded. After the ovules are fertilized by pollen from the male cones, they develop into seeds. The pistil-bearing cones develop into the familiar "pine cones" with their pairs of usually winged seeds.

Gymnosperms are primitive seed plants. They appeared on the earth many millions of years before the *angiosperms* or plants which have true flowers and fruits. Angiosperm flowers produce ovules inside the ovary portion of a pistil, and after fertilization of its ovules it develops into a fruit containing seeds. Aside from the pines and their relatives and the yew, all of the plants included in this book are angiosperms, or plants which have true flowers.

The flowers that most of us recognize as flowers are usually more or less showy. Usually, too, they are what botanists call *complete flowers:* flowers which have four sets of parts or organs—sepals, petals, stamens, and at least one pistil.

The *sepals* are the outermost organs of the flower. Commonly they are green in color and they protect the other parts of the flower in the bud stage. Collectively the sepals are known as the *calyx* of the flower. Sometimes the sepals are more or less joined together and may form what is called a *calyx tube*. Usually there are teeth on the rim of such a tube and they indicate the number of sepals united to form it.

FLOWER PARTS AND STRUCTURE

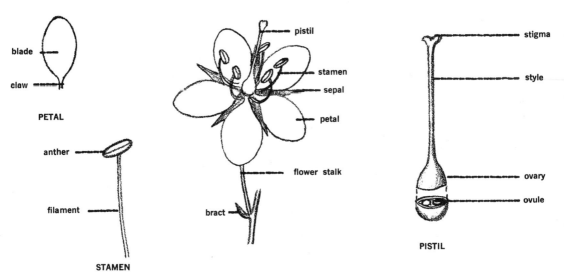

blade

claw

PETAL

anther

filament

STAMEN

pistil

stamen

sepal

petal

flower stalk

bract

stigma

style

ovary

ovule

PISTIL

PARTS OF A COMPLETE FLOWER

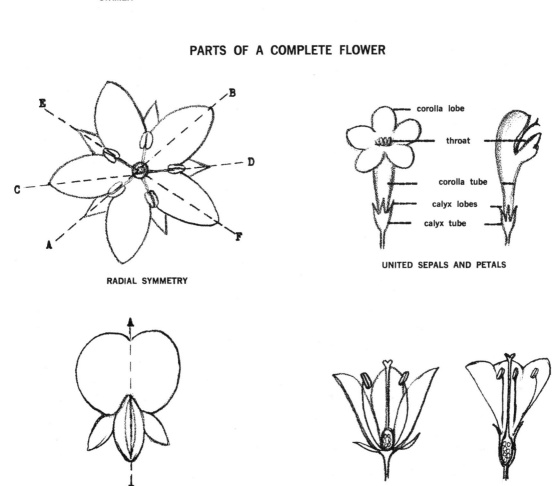

E

B

C

D

A

F

RADIAL SYMMETRY

corolla lobe

throat

corolla tube

calyx lobes

calyx tube

UNITED SEPALS AND PETALS

B

B

BILATERAL SYMMETRY

OVARY SUPERIOR

OVARY INFERIOR

TYPES OF INFLORESCENCES

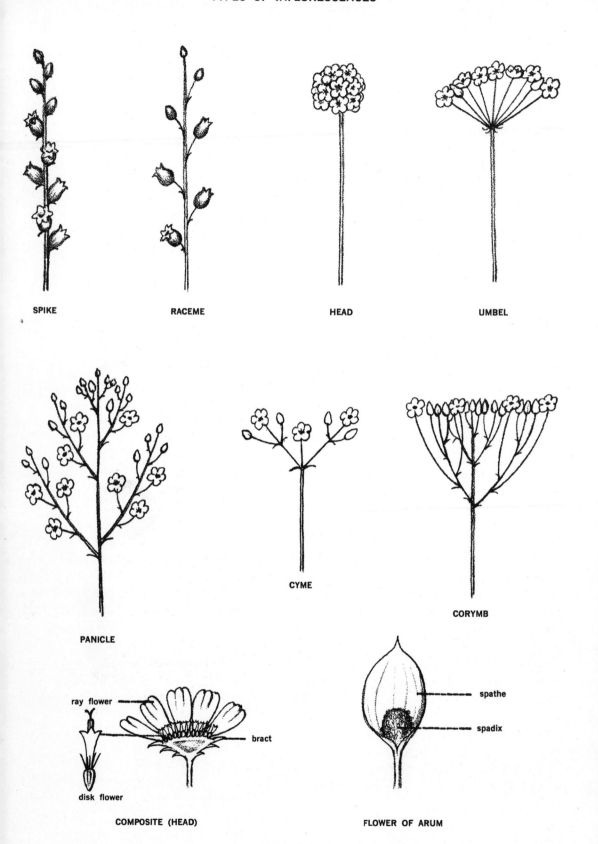

SPIKE

RACEME

HEAD

UMBEL

PANICLE

CYME

CORYMB

ray flower

disk flower

bract

COMPOSITE (HEAD)

spathe

spadix

FLOWER OF ARUM

The next series of flower parts are the *petals*. They are usually the white or colored parts that make the flower showy. Collectively the petals are known as the *corolla* of a flower. Like the sepals, the petals may be joined together and form a *corolla tube,* and usually lobes on its rim indicate the number of petals united to form it. At the bases of the petals there are often glands which secrete a sweet substance called nectar, from which bees make their honey. Petals, alluring odors, and nectar all serve to attract insects such as bees to flowers.

Stamens are the male organs of flowers. Usually they have two parts, a stalk called the *filament* and a boxlike compartment at the top called the *anther*. Pollen is produced in the anthers of the stamens.

In the center most flowers have one or more organs called *pistils*. The pistil is the female organ of a flower. At its base is the *ovary* within which are one or more bodies called *ovules*. At the summit is the *stigma* which receives the pollen. Between the ovary and the stigma there is commonly a stalk-like portion called the *style*.

Many people do not realize that trees such as oaks and ashes have flowers. They do not even remotely resemble the flowers of a magnolia or a rose yet they are really flowers. Stamens and pistils are the only parts of flowers that are actually needed for the production of fruits and seeds, but in order for them to develop a transfer of pollen from the stamens to the pistils must first take place. Plants which have showy flowers depend upon insects to effect such a transfer. Oaks and ashes, however, are among the plants which rely upon winds to transfer their dusty pollen. They have no need for showy petals, nectar, or alluring odors to attract insects. Their flowers are stripped to the barest essentials.

Flowers may either be solitary or arranged in a cluster or *inflorescence*, as shown diagrammatically on page 9. A *spike* is a simple inflorescence in which stalkless flowers are arranged along a common stalk. The *raceme* is similar to a spike except the individual flowers all have a stalk. The *panicle* is a branched flower cluster, each branch of which is similar to a raceme. A *cyme* is a more or less flat-topped cluster in which the central flowers open first while a *corymb* is a flat-topped cluster in which the outer or marginal flowers are first to open. A *head* is a dense cluster of stalkless or nearly stalkless flowers grouped at the tip of a common stalk while the *umbel* has stalked flowers arising from the tip of a stem.

What is often taken to be a flower may in reality be a whole cluster of flowers. Flowering Dogwood "blossoms" are one example. Each "blossom" is really a head of small flowers which is surrounded by four petal-like leaves or *bracts*. The familiar Jack-in-the-pulpit and other members of the Arum Family have tiny flowers seated on a thick and often club-like stalk called a *spadix*. Usually the spadix is more or less surrounded by a large and often colorful bract which is called a *spathe*.

Sunflowers, daisies, asters and other members of the Composite Family are real "foolers", too. What seems to be a single blossom is really a

11

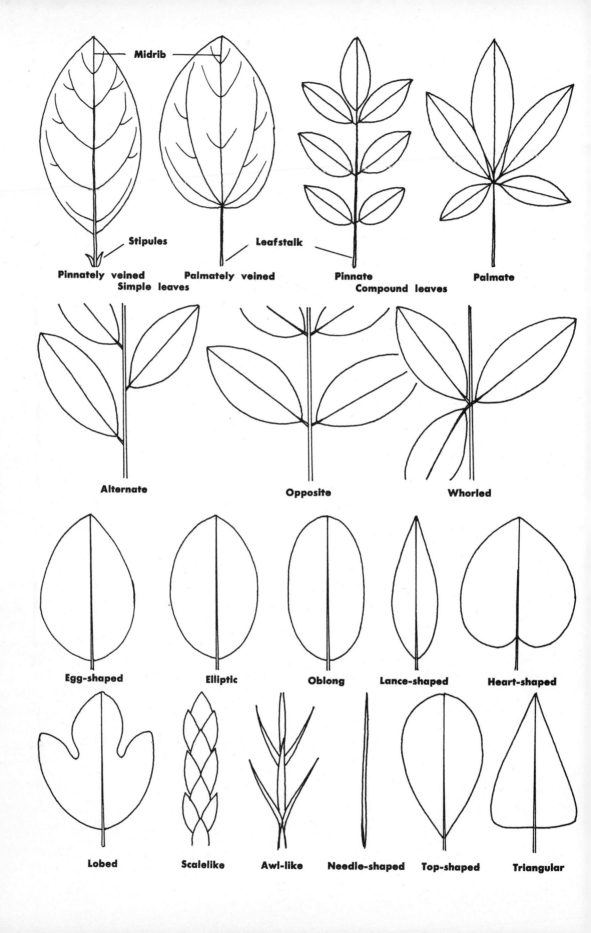

Midrib

Stipules

Leafstalk

Pinnately veined   Palmately veined   Pinnate   Palmate
    Simple leaves   Compound leaves

Alternate   Opposite   Whorled

Egg-shaped   Elliptic   Oblong   Lance-shaped   Heart-shaped

Lobed   Scalelike   Awl-like   Needle-shaped   Top-shaped   Triangular

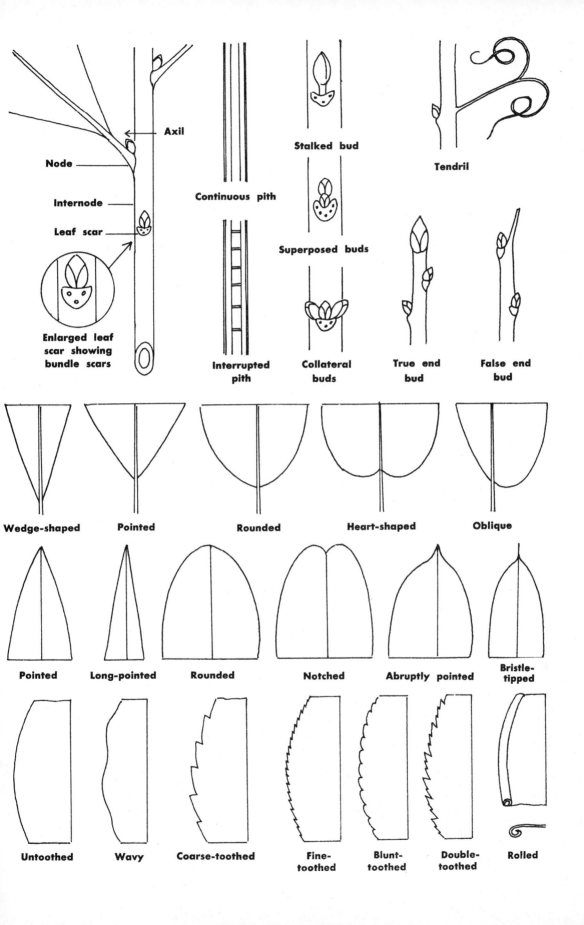

Axil

Node

Internode

Leaf scar

Enlarged leaf
scar showing
bundle scars

Continuous pith

Interrupted
pith

Stalked bud

Superposed buds

Collateral
buds

Tendril

True end
bud

False end
bud

Wedge-shaped   Pointed   Rounded   Heart-shaped   Oblique

Pointed   Long-pointed   Rounded   Notched   Abruptly pointed   Bristle-tipped

Untoothed   Wavy   Coarse-toothed   Fine-toothed   Blunt-toothed   Double-toothed   Rolled

head of flowers. Some composites, like those we have mentioned, have flowers with strap-shaped corollas around the margin of the head and they are often mistaken for petals. These are called *ray flowers*. The center of the head is a prominent disk on which are crowded small flowers which have tubular corollas. They are called *disk flowers*. The entire head is surrounded by an *involucre* which is made up of usually greenish bracts. Some composites, such as the dandelion, have heads composed entirely of flowers with strap-shaped corollas. Others, like the thistles, have only flowers with tubular corollas in their heads.

Types and arrangements of leaves

Leaves of plants vary greatly in size, shape, and in their arrangement on the stems. Often leaves are so distinctive that a plant may be recognized by its leaves alone. Most of the outstanding features of leaves are shown on pages 12 and 13 in this book. It would be well to become familiar with them.

Most leaves have a flattened and more or less broad portion which is called the *blade*. Often there is a prominent central vein or *midrib* from which veins branch off like the barbs from the shaft of a feather. Such a leaf is said to be *pinnately-veined,* or feather-veined. Other leaves have several main veins which radiate from the base of the leaf or the summit of the leaf stalk. This type of leaf is said to be *palmately-veined.*

The majority of the plants which we usually see have what are called *simple leaves*. A simple leaf is one which has a one-piece blade. The leaves of some plants, however, have the blades of their leaves divided into smaller leaf-like parts which are called *leaflets*. These are called *compound leaves*. Especially in the case of woody plants, it is usually quite easy to tell whether a leaf is simple or compound. Look for a bud. During the summer buds form in the axils of the leaves but they are never found in the axils of the leaflets of a compound leaf.

Often leaves or leaflets have teeth on their margins, and they are often much like the teeth on a saw. The teeth may be very fine or they may be large and coarse. Sometimes the larger teeth have smaller teeth on them and such leaves are said to be *double-toothed*. Quite often the blades of leaves or leaflets are more deeply cut, or cleft, and have projections called *lobes*. Many oaks and most maples have such *lobed leaves*. If a leaf or leaflet is neither lobed nor toothed on the margin it is said to be an *entire leaf*.

The manner in which leaves are arranged on the stem should always be noted. Most often leaves are *alternate* or scattered singly along the stem. Sometimes they are *opposite,* or arranged in pairs on opposite sides of the stem. Oaks, for instance, always have alternate leaves while those of the maples are always opposite. In some plants three or more leaves are arranged about a point on the stem and radiate like the spokes of a wheel. Such leaves are said to be *whorled*.

14

PART I
Trees, Shrubs, and Woody Vines

EVERGREEN TREES WITH NEEDLE-LIKE LEAVES IN BUNDLES
Northern and Mountain Pines

EASTERN WHITE PINE *Pinus strobus* L. Pine Family

FIELD MARKS: A large tree often 80 feet or more tall. *Leaves* needle-like, soft, flexible, bluish-green, 3 to 5 inches long, in bundles of 5's. *Cones* narrowly cylindrical, stalked, usually curved, 4 to 8 inches long; the cone scales thin at tip and unarmed, commonly with droplets of fragrant and sticky resin which becomes white and crusted.

RANGE: Newfoundland west to Manitoba; south to Pennsylvania, northern Ohio and southeastern Iowa, and in the Appalachian region to northern Georgia.

Valuable timber tree and often planted for ornamental purposes. Inner bark was used by the Indians as food and is used medicinally in cough remedies.

PITCH PINE *Pinus rigida* Miller Pine Family

FIELD MARKS: A medium-sized tree usually 40 to 60 feet tall but sometimes taller; usually found on dry, rocky ridges. *Leaves* needle-like, stout, stiff, usually twisted, yellowish-green, 2 to 5 inches long, in bundles of 3's. *Cones* broadly egg-shaped when closed, nearly stalkless, 1½ to 3 inches long, often persisting on the branches for several years; the cone scales thickened at tip and with a small hooked prickle.

RANGE: New Brunswick west to Ontario; south to Virginia, northern Georgia and eastern Tennessee.

RED PINE *Pinus resinosa* Ait. Pine Family

FIELD MARKS: A large tree 50 to 75 feet or more tall, native to the Northeast and Great Lakes regions. *Leaves* needle-like, straight, slender, soft, flexible, dark green, 4 to 6 inches long, in bundles of 2's. *Cones* egg-shaped when closed, stalkless, 1½ to 2½ inches long; the cone scales thickened at tip but unarmed.

RANGE: Nova Scotia west to Manitoba; south to Massachusetts, West Virginia, Michigan and Minnesota.

Valuable timber and ornamental tree. Often called Norway Pine although it is a New World species.

JACK PINE *Pinus banksiana* Lamb. Pine Family

FIELD MARKS: Usually a small tree 20 to 30 feet tall but occasionally 60 feet or more in height; growing on light sandy soils in the North. *Leaves* needle-like, stout, stiff, twisted, yellowish-green, mostly 1 to 1½ inches long, in bundles of 2's. *Cones* egg-shaped when closed, stalkless, curving toward the tips of the branchlets, 1½ to 2 inches long, often remaining closed for many years; the cone scales thickened at tip and often with a minute prickle.

RANGE: Nova Scotia west to region of the Mackenzie River; south to New England, northeastern New York, Michigan, Minnesota and northern Alberta.

Often forms pure stands on burned-over areas. Heat from fires causes the cones to open and release the seeds.

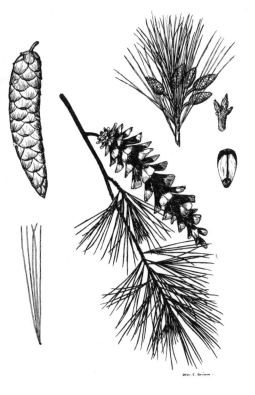

Eastern White Pine

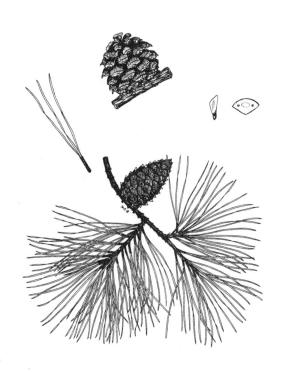

Pitch Pine

Red Pine

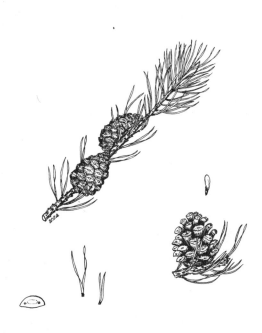

Jack Pine

Shortleaf Pine

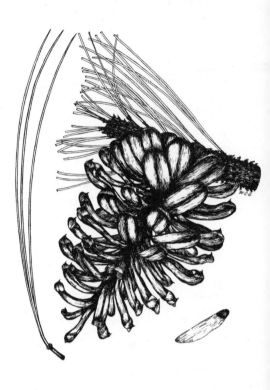

Longleaf Pine

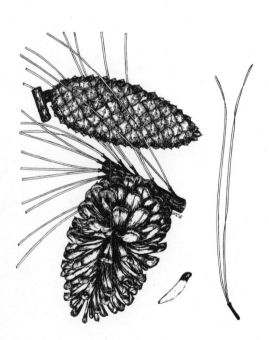

Slash Pine

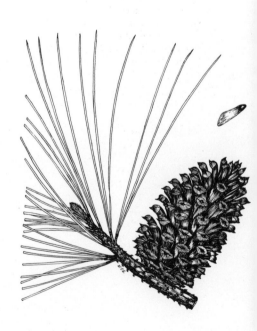

Loblolly Pine

SHORTLEAF PINE *Pinus echinata* Mill.   Pine Family,
FIELD MARKS: A large tree 80 to 100 feet or more tall; usually found on well-drained to dry, sandy or gravelly soils. *Leaves* needle-like, slender, flexible, dark green, 3 to 5 inches long, in bundles of 2's and 3's. *Cones* narrowly egg-shaped when closed, nearly stalkless, 1½ to 2½ inches long, often persisting for several years; the cone scales quite thin at tip and usually armed with a small prickle.
RANGE: Southeastern New York and southern Pennsylvania west to Missouri and Oklahoma; south to northern Florida and eastern Texas.

LONGLEAF PINE *Pinus palustris* Mill.   Pine Family
FIELD MARKS: A large tree 80 to 100 feet or more tall; growing naturally in usually dry sandy soils of the southern coastal plains. *Leaves* needle-like, slender, flexible, dark green, 8 to about 18 inches long, in bundles of 3's. *Cones* cylindrical egg-shaped, nearly stalkless, dull reddish-brown, 6 to 10 inches long; the cone scales thickened at tip and with a small hooked prickle; cones usually leave lowermost scales attached to branchlets upon falling. *Buds* at tips of stout branchlets are silvery-white.
RANGE: Southeastern Virginia south to central Florida; west to eastern Texas.
Seedling trees remain as a grass-like tuft of long needles for several years then rapidly grow upward. Valuable timber and naval stores tree.

SLASH PINE *Pinus elliottii*   Pine Family
FIELD MARKS: A large tree 80 to 100 feet tall; growing naturally in low wet places in the southern coastal plain but widely planted elsewhere. *Leaves* needle-like, dark green, shiny, slender, 6 to 10 inches long, in bundles of 2's and 3's. *Cones* egg-shaped when closed, stalked, shiny brown, 3 to 6 inches long, soon falling; the cone scales thickened at tip and with a short and slender prickle.
RANGE: Southeastern South Carolina south to Florida; west to southern Louisiana.
Valuable timber and naval stores tree.

LOBLOLLY PINE *Pinus taeda* L.   Pine Family
FIELD MARKS: A large tree 80 to 100 feet or more tall; growing in the southern coastal plains and Piedmont. *Leaves* needle-like, slender, stiff, yellowish-green, 6 to 9 inches long, in bundles of 3's. *Cones* oblong egg-shaped when closed, stalkless, dull brown, 3 to 6 inches long, soon falling; the cone scales thickened at tip and with a sharp stout prickle.
RANGE: Southern New Jersey south to central Florida; west to eastern Texas; north in Mississippi Valley to southern Tennessee, Arkansas and Oklahoma.
Valuable timber tree.

EVERGREEN TREES OR SHRUBS WITH SOLITARY NEEDLE-LIKE LEAVES

WHITE SPRUCE *Picea glauca* (Moench.) Voss. Pine Family
FIELD MARKS: A tree often 70 feet or more tall; growing in damp places, along shores of lakes and banks of streams. *Branchlets* usually smooth, orange-brown. *Leaves* needle-like, 4-sided, pointed at tip, stiff, bluish-green but often whitened with a bloom, ½ to ¾ inch long, attached to persistent short, woody stalks that roughen the branchlets. *Cones* narrowly egg-shaped, light reddish-brown, 1 to 2½ inches long, soon falling; the cone scales thin, flexible, and with smooth rounded edges.
RANGE: Labrador west to Alaska; south to Maine, northern New York, Michigan, South Dakota, Wyoming and British Columbia.

BLACK SPRUCE *Picea mariana* (Mill.) B.S.P. Pine Family
FIELD MARKS: A tree 30 to sometimes 80 feet tall; growing on dry barren slopes northward but southward in cold swamps and bogs. *Branchlets* minutely rusty-hairy. *Leaves* needle-like, 4-sided, blunt at tip, stiff, bluish-green, ¼ to ½ inch long, attached to persistent woody stalks that roughen the branchlets. *Cones* roundish or egg-shaped, dull grayish-brown, ½ to about 1 inch long, remaining on branches for many years; the cone scales brittle and with minutely ragged edges.
RANGE: Labrador west to Alaska; south to Saskatchewan, Manitoba, Minnesota, Michigan, West Virginia and Virginia.

RED SPRUCE *Picea rubens* Sarg. Pine Family
FIELD MARKS: A tree commonly 40 to 80 feet tall; growing in cool, moist places. *Branchlets* slightly hairy the first year. *Leaves* needle-like, 4-sided, usually pointed at tip, stiff, yellowish-green, about ½ inch long, attached to persistent woody stalks that roughen the branchlets. *Cones* narrowly egg-shaped, reddish-brown, 1 to 2 inches long, soon falling; the cone scales with smooth rounded edges.
RANGE: Nova Scotia and Ontario; south to northeastern Pennsylvania and along the higher Appalachians to western North Carolina and eastern Tennessee.
This and preceding spruces are much used for Christmas trees, lumber and pulpwood. In the southern mountains this spruce is known to the mountain people as the "He-Balsam".

BALSAM FIR *Abies balsamea* (L.) Mill. Pine Family
A tree often 40 feet or more tall; growing in cool moist places. *Leaves* flattened, rounded or notched at tip, dark green above but with 2 whitish bands beneath, ¾ to 1½ inches long, arranged feather-like on the branchlets or often curving upward, stalkless and leaving roundish scars on the branchlets upon falling. *Cones* erect, barrel-shaped, dark purple, 2 to 4 inches long; breaking up in fall leaving the central stalks on the branchlets.
RANGE: Labrador west to Alberta; south to New England, western Virginia, Michigan and northeastern Iowa.

FRASER FIR *Abies fraseri* (Pursh) Poir. Pine Family
This is the balsam fir of the higher Appalachians from southwestern Virginia to western North Carolina and eastern Tennessee. It differs from the preceding in having long bracts entending well beyond the cone scales. Mountain people call it the "She-Balsam". Balsam firs make excellent Christmas trees. Canada balsam is the sticky resin obtained from the blisters on the trunks.

20

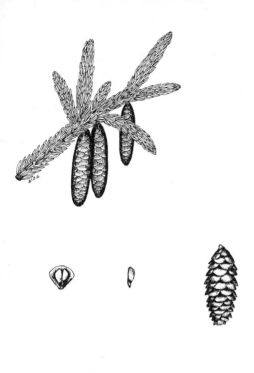

White Spruce

Black Spruce

Red Spruce

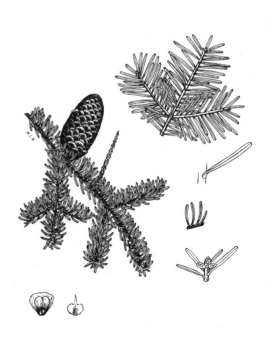

Balsam Fir

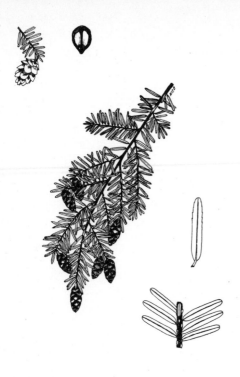

Eastern Hemlock

American Yew

Tamarack

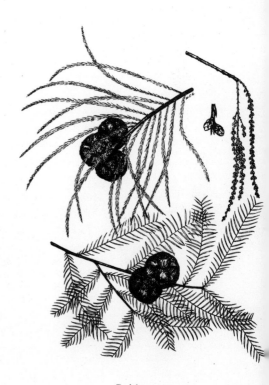

Baldcypress

EVERGREEN TREES OR SHRUBS WITH SOLITARY NEEDLE-LIKE LEAVES,
Continued

EASTERN HEMLOCK *Tsuga canadensis* (L.) Carr.　　　　　Pine Family

FIELD MARKS: A large tree often 80 feet or more tall; growing in cool, moist places and often along the banks of streams. *Leaves* flattened, rounded or notched at tip, dark green above but with 2 whitish bands beneath, ⅓ to about ⅔ inch long, attached to short woody stalks which persist and roughen the branchlets, arranged feather like on the branchlets. *Cones* egg-shaped, drooping, pale brown, ½ to ¾ inch long; the cone scales with smooth rounded edges.

RANGE: Nova Scotia west to eastern Minnesota; south to Maryland, Illinois, and in the Appalachians to northern Georgia and Alabama.

Bark formerly much used in tanneries. Excellent ornamental tree.

AMERICAN YEW *Taxus canadensis* Marsh　　　　　Yew Family

FIELD MARKS. A sprawling evergreen shrub 1 to 3 feet high; growing in cool, moist, usually coniferous woods. *Leaves* narrow, flattened, rigid, abruptly pointed, lustrous dark green above, paler and yellowish green beneath, ⅜ to about 1 inch long; with short stalks running slightly down the branchlets. *Fruits* waxy-looking, orange red, fleshy, about ½ inch across, partly enclosing a large bony seed.

RANGE. Newfoundland to Manitoba; south to western Virginia, Kentucky, and Iowa.

Also called Ground-hemlock.

NONEVERGREEN CONE-BEARING TREES

TAMARACK *Larix laricina* (Du Roi) K. Koch.　　　　　Pine Family

FIELD MARKS: A leaf-losing tree usually 30 to 60 feet tall but sometimes much taller; widespread in the North but growing southward only in cold swamps and bogs. *Leaves* needle-like, very slender, soft, flexible, bluish-green, in dense brush-like clusters or densely crowded along the vigorous shoots, ¾ to 1¼ inches long. *Cones* egg-shaped, rosy-red when young but light brown when mature, ½ to ¾ inch long, usually remaining on branchlets the first winter.

RANGE: Labrador west to Alaska; south to western Maryland, West Virginia and the Great Lakes region.

Leaves become bright yellow before being shed in the fall.

BALDCYPRESS *Taxodium distichum* (L.) Rich.　　　　　Baldcypress Family

FIELD MARKS: A leaf-losing tree sometimes 100 feet or more tall; growing in swamps of the South and Mississippi Valley; producing cone-shaped woody growths called "knees" from the submerged roots. *Leaves* narrow, flattened, yellowish-green, ½ to ¾ inch long, arranged in feather-like sprays on slender branchlets which are shed completely in the fall. *Cones* ball-shaped, ¾ to 1 inch across, with several shield-shaped scales breaking up in the fall.

RANGE: Coastal plain from southern Delaware south to Florida; west to Texas; north in Mississippi Valley to southern Indiana and Illinois.

Valuable timber tree.

PONDCYPRESS (*Taxodium distichum* var. *nutans*)　　　　　Baldcypress Family

This, sometimes considered to be a distinct species, is a smaller tree of coastal plain ponds with short awl-like leaves closely pressed against the branchlets.

EVERGREEN TREES AND SHRUBS WITH SMALL SCALE-LIKE LEAVES

NORTHERN WHITE CEDAR *Thuja occidentalis* L.   True Cypress Family

FIELD MARKS: A narrowly pyramid-shaped evergreen tree 25 to 50 feet tall; growing in northern swamps, along streams, or southward on limestone outcrops. *Leaves* small, scale-like, bright yellowish-green, overlapping and closely pressed against the branchlets which form flattened and fan-like sprays. *Cones* oblong-egg-shaped, ⅓ to ½ inch long, erect, with from 6 to 12 overlapping thin scales.

RANGE: Labrador west to Manitoba; south to Massachusetts, New York, northern Illinois, Minnesota, and in the Appalachian region to western North Carolina and eastern Tennessee.

Also called Arborvitae and often grown as an ornamental tree.

ATLANTIC WHITE CEDAR *Chamaecyparis thyoides* (L.) B.S.P. True Cypress Family

FIELD MARKS: An evergreen tree often 30 to 50 but sometimes 100 feet tall; growing in fresh water swamps and bogs in the Atlantic and Gulf coastal plains. *Leaves* very small, scale-like, bluish-green, overlapping and closely pressed against the slightly flattened branchlets. *Cones* roundish, about ¼ inch across, bluish-purple becoming brown when mature, with about 6 shield-shaped scales.

RANGE: Southern Maine south to northern Florida; west to southern Mississippi.

EVERGREEN TREES AND SHRUBS WITH SMALL SCALE-LIKE OR AWL-LIKE LEAVES

EASTERN REDCEDAR *Juniperus virginiana* L.   True Cypress Family

FIELD MARKS: An evergreen tree often 40 or more feet tall with a broad to narrow pyramid-shaped crown; growing on poor, dry, sandy or rocky soils. *Leaves* dark green; those on the vigorous shoots awl-shaped, prickly, often in 3's, ¼ to ½ inch long; elsewhere they are very small, scale-like and closely pressed against the 4-sided branchlets. *Cones* round, fleshy and berry-like, blue but coated with a whitish bloom, about ¼ inch across.

RANGE: Nova Scotia west to southern Ontario and southwestern North Dakota; south to northern Florida and central Texas.

COMMON JUNIPER *Juniperus communis* L.   True Cypress Family

FIELD MARKS. An evergreen shrub or small tree; growing in exposed rocky or sandy places. *Leaves* awl-like, sharply-pointed, arranged in 3's, grooved and whitened above, ¼ to ¾ inch long. *Fruits* berry-like, roundish to egg-shaped, aromatic, about ¼ inch in diameter, bluish black and whitened with a bloom. The typical variety has an erect or columnar form. The following two varieties in our range are low, spreading, or mat-forming shrubs: var. *saxatilis* Pallas (Mountain Juniper) has relatively short, broad, curved leaves up to ⅛ inch long and is northern in distribution; var. *depressa* Pursh (Oldfield or Prostrate Juniper) has almost straight leaves ⅜ to ¾ inch long and is the most common and widespread variety.

RANGE. Newfoundland to Alberta; south to eastern Virginia, the region of the Great Lakes, and in the mountains to South Carolina and Georgia.

Sometimes used in ornamental planting. The fruits are used medicinally and are eaten by a number of species of wild birds.

Northern White Cedar

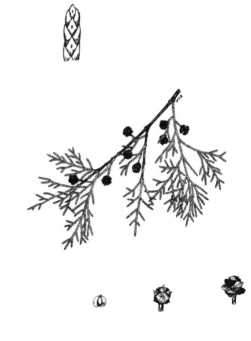

Atlantic White Cedar

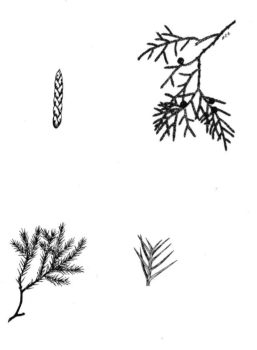

Eastern Redcedar

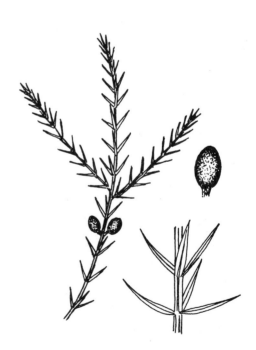

Common Juniper

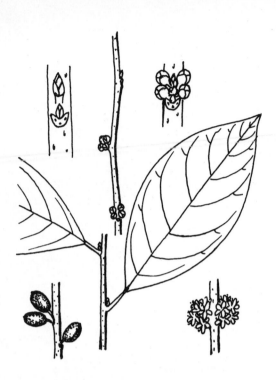

Common Spicebush

Highbush Blueberry

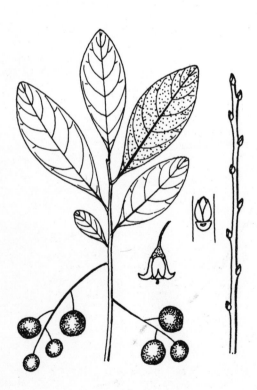

Dangleberry

Swamp Azalea

COMMON SPICEBUSH   *Lindera benzoin* (L.) Blume   Laurel Family

FIELD MARKS. A leaf-losing, aromatic shrub 3 to 15 feet high; growing in moist woods and along streams. *Branchlets* slender, smooth, brittle, greenish brown to olive brown, spicy-fragrant when broken. *Leaves* alternate, elliptic or broadest above the middle, pointed at both ends, untoothed on margin, smooth on both sides or sparingly downy beneath, bright green above, paler beneath, spicy-fragrant when crushed, 2 to 6 inches long. *Flowers* small, honey-yellow, fragrant, clustered at the nodes; blooming in March or April, before the leaves appear. *Fruits* oval-shaped, bright red, 1-seeded, about ⅜ inch long, very spicy-aromatic when crushed; ripening July to September.

RANGE. Southeastern Maine to southern Ontario, southern Michigan, Iowa, and southeastern Kansas; south to Florida and Texas.

Also called Benjamin-bush and Wild-allspice. The leaves have been used to make a tea, and the dried powdered fruits are used as a substitute for allspice. The fruits are eaten by many wild birds, and the twigs are often eaten by deer and rabbits.

HIGHBUSH BLUEBERRY   *Vaccinium corymbosum* L.   Heath Family

FIELD MARKS. A leaf-losing shrub 3 to about 10 feet high; growing in low wet grounds, bogs, swamps, and moist rocky woods. *Branchlets* yellowish green to reddish, warty-dotted, often hairy in lines. *Leaves* short-stalked, elliptic to egg-shaped or broadly lance-shaped, pointed to rounded at base, pointed at tip, untoothed or sometimes with very fine or bristly teeth on margin, paler green and sometimes whitened or slightly downy beneath, 1 to about 3 inches long. *Flowers* white, greenish white, or pinkish, cylindrical urn-shaped, clustered; blooming late February to June, before the leaves or when the leaves are partly grown. *Fruits* blue or bluish black, whitened with a bloom, ¼ to nearly ½ inch in diameter, sweet and juicy; ripening June to August.

RANGE. Nova Scotia to southern Quebec and Wisconsin; south to Florida and Louisiana.

The parent of most cultivated varieties of blueberries. Most common southward in coastal plain but also present in the mountains.

DANGLEBERRY   *Gaylussacia frondosa* (L.) T. & G.   Heath Family

FIELD MARKS. A leaf-losing shrub 2 to 4 feet high; growing in rocky or sandy woods and bogs. *Branchlets* slender, smooth, often whitened with a bloom. *Leaves* elliptic to oval or broadest above the middle, pointed at base, bluntly pointed to roundish at tip, margin untoothed, pale green and smooth above, paler or whitened and resin-dotted beneath, 1 to 2½ inches long. *Flowers* greenish pink, bell-shaped, in rather long drooping clusters; blooming March to June. *Fruits* blue, whitened with a bloom, about ⅜ inch in diameter, sweet and juicy; ripening June to August.

RANGE. Massachusetts to southeastern New York and Ohio, south to Florida and Louisiana.

Also called Tangleberry, Blue-tangle, and Blue Huckleberry.

SWAMP AZALEA   *Rhododendron viscosum* (L.) Torr.   Heath Family

FIELD MARKS. A leaf-losing shrub 3 to 10 feet high; growing in swamps, bogs, along streams, and occasionally on mountain summits. *Branchlets* with scattered, stiff, brownish hairs. *Leaves* narrowly elliptic or broadest above the middle, wedge-shaped at base, blunt or short-pointed at tip, hairy-fringed on margin, dark green and smooth above, pale or slightly whitened and with stiff brownish hairs along midrib beneath, ¾ to 2½ inches long. *Flowers* white to pale pink, tube somewhat longer than the lobes and very sticky-glandular, very fragrant, about 1¼ inches across, 4 to 9 in a cluster; blooming May to July after the leaves are grown. *Fruits* narrowly egg-shaped, glandular-bristly capsules ½ to ¾ inch long.

RANGE. Southwestern Maine to northeastern Ohio; south to Georgia and Tennessee.

Also called the Clammy Azalea and White- or Clammy-honeysuckle.

27

WIDELY DISTRIBUTED IN WET PLACES, Continued
Leaves Alternate—Simple—Entire

PINXTER-FLOWER *Rhododendron nudiflorum* (L.) Torr.   Heath Family

FIELD MARKS. A leaf-losing shrub 2 to 6 (rarely 10) feet high, the stems often unbranched below but with more or less whorled branches above; growing in moist woods, clearings, and swamps. *Branchlets* smooth or with scattered spreading hairs. *Leaves* elliptic or oblong and often broadest above the middle, pointed at tip and wedge-shaped at base, margin fringed with short hairs, dull green and smooth above, paler and with stiff hairs along the midrib beneath, 2 to 4 inches long. *Flowers* pink to almost white, delicately or faintly fragrant, the tube hairy but seldom with gland-tipped hairs on the outside, about 1½ inches across; blooming March to May, before the leaves appear. *Fruits* narrowly egg-shaped, hairy, ½ to ¾ inch long.
RANGE. Massachusetts to New York and southern Illinois; south to central South Carolina and northern Georgia.
Also called Pink or Purple Azalea and Purple-honeysuckle.

LEATHERLEAF *Chamaedaphne calyculata* var. *angustifolia* (Ait.) Rehd.   Heath Family

FIELD MARKS. A much-branched, more or less evergreen shrub 1 to about 3 feet high, with spreading or horizontal branches; growing in peaty soils or in bogs. *Leaves* alternate, narrowly elliptic or broadest above the middle, pointed at base, bluntly pointed to roundish at tip, practically untoothed or with some minute teeth on the slightly rolled margin, dull green dotted with silvery scales above, brownish with minute rusty scales beneath, leathery in texture, ½ to 1½ inches long, often turning reddish in winter. *Flowers* white, bell-shaped, about ¼ inch long, in long and one-sided end clusters, each flower subtended by a leafy bract; blooming March to July. *Fruits* roundish, somewhat flattened, 5-celled capsules about ⅛ inch in diameter.
RANGE. Newfoundland to Alaska; south to the coastal plain and mountains of North Carolina, the region of the Great Lakes, northern Iowa, Alberta, and British Columbia.

Leaves Alternate—Simple—Toothed

AMERICAN ELM *Ulmus americana* L.   Elm Family

FIELD MARKS: A large tree 75 to 100 feet or more tall often with a beautiful rounded or vase-shaped crown; usually growing in wet bottomlands, swamps, or along streams. *Branchlets* reddish-brown, usually smooth. *Leaves* 3 to 5 inches long, oval-shaped, doubly saw-toothed on margin, lop-sided at base, dark green and sometimes slightly rough above, paler and softly downy beneath. *Fruits* oval-shaped, flattened and with a raised seed cavity in center, fringed on margin, deeply notched at tip, about ½ inch long, long-stalked; maturing in early spring before the leaves appear.
RANGE: Newfoundland west to southeastern Saskatchewan; south to Florida and Texas.
Widely planted as a street and shade tree.

AMERICAN HORNBEAM *Carpinus caroliniana* Walt.   Birch Family

FIELD MARKS: A large shrub or small tree to about 30 feet tall; growing in wet soils and frequently along streams. *Trunk* is noticably fluted and looks as if the smooth bluish-gray and often mottled bark fits it too tightly. *Leaves* narrowly oval or egg-shaped, long-pointed at tip, doubly saw-toothed on margin, thin but tough in texture, dark green above, paler beneath, 2 to 4 inches long. *Fruits* small egg-shaped nutlets, each one at the base of a three-lobed leaf-like bract; these arranged in pairs in loose drooping clusters and maturing in late summer or fall.
RANGE: Nova Scotia west to Minnesota; south to Florida and Texas.
Also called Blue Beech, Water Beech, and Ironwood.

28

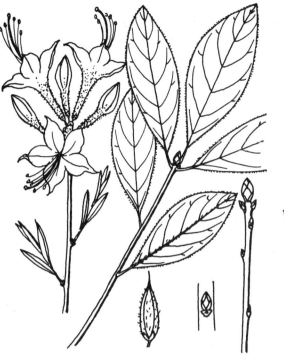

Pinxter-flower

Leatherleaf

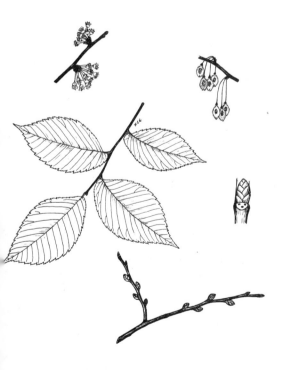

American Elm

American Hornbeam

Eastern Cottonwood

Black Willow

Silky Willow

Common Alder

EASTERN COTTONWOOD *Populus deltoides* Bartr. Willow Family

FIELD MARKS: A large tree sometimes 50 to 100 feet or more tall; growing in wet bottomlands, along streams, and about the shores of lakes. *Branchlets* fairly stout, yellowish-brown, with large and sharp-pointed shiny brown buds having a fragrant sticky resin. Leaves triangular egg-shaped and often flat at base, dark shiny green above, paler and smooth beneath, marginal teeth rather large and somewhat hooked, 3 to 5 inches broad; leaf stalks flattened. *Fruits* small, egg-shaped capsules containing seeds with cottony tufts of hairs, arranged in drooping clusters and maturing in spring.

RANGE: New Hampshire and southern Quebec west to southern Saskatchewan; south to northern Florida and eastern Texas.

BLACK WILLOW *Salix nigra* Marsh. Willow Family

FIELD MARKS: Largest American tree willow sometimes 50 to 80 feet or more tall but in many places merely a large shrub; growing in wet bottomlands and along streams. *Trunks* commonly in clumps. *Branchlets* reddish-brown, smooth, brittle at base. *Leaves* narrowly lance-shaped, finely saw-toothed on margin, bright green and smooth on both surfaces but slightly paler beneath, 3 to 6 inches long; leaf stalks short and often with stipules at base. *Fruits* narrowly vase-shaped capsules containing numerous tiny seeds with tufts of silky hairs, maturing in spring.

RANGE: New Brunswick west to Ontario and South Dakota; south to Georgia, Mississippi, Texas and Oklahoma.

SILKY WILLOW *Salix sericea* Marsh. Willow Family

FIELD MARKS. A shrub 4 to 12 feet high; common and widely distributed along stream banks and other wet places. *Branchlets* brittle at base, purplish brown, smooth or minutely silky. *Leaves* lance-shaped, long-pointed at tip, pointed to rounded at base, margin finely and sharply toothed, smooth above, pale and with silvery-silky hairs beneath, 2 to 4 inches long; stipules small and soon shed.

RANGE. Nova Scotia to Wisconsin; south to Georgia, Tennessee, and Missouri.

COMMON ALDER *Alnus serrulata* (Ait.) Willd. Birch Family

FIELD MARKS. A thicket-forming shrub 5 to 15 feet high; growing along streams and in swampy places. *Bark* with scattered, small, dotlike lenticels. *Leaves* oval or broadest above the middle, broadly pointed to rounded at tip, pointed at base, margin finely toothed with simple teeth, smooth above, paler green and smooth or somewhat rusty-downy beneath, 1 to 6 inches long. *Flowers* blooming late February to April, the smaller catkins at branch tips and erect. *Buds* 2-scaled and noticeably stalked.

RANGE. Nova Scotia and Maine to the region of the Great Lakes, Missouri, and Oklahoma; south to northern Florida and Louisiana.

Also called Smooth Alder and Tag Alder.

RED CHOKEBERRY *Aronia arbutifolia* (L.) Ell.   Rose Family

    FIELD MARKS. A shrub 3 to 8 feet high; growing in wet or boggy places. *Branchlets* more or less woolly. *Leaves* elliptic or broadest above the middle, wedge-shaped to broadly pointed at base, pointed at tip, finely toothed on margin, smooth above, grayish-woolly beneath, 1½ to 4 inches long. *Flowers* white or purplish-tinged; blooming March to June. *Fruits* red, about ¼ inch in diameter; ripening August to November and persisting.
    RANGE. Nova Scotia to Ontario, Michigan, and Missouri; south to Florida and Texas.

WINTERBERRY *Ilex verticillata* (L.) Gray   Holly Family

    FIELD MARKS. A leaf-losing shrub 3 to 15 feet high; growing along streams and in low wet woods and swamps. *Leaves* oval to lance-shaped or broadest above the middle, pointed at both ends, sharply and rather coarsely toothed on margin, sometimes slightly leathery in texture, dull green above, slightly paler and sometimes slightly downy beneath, 1½ to 3 inches long; remaining green until frost, then turning black. *Flowers* bearing the stamens and those bearing the pistils both short-stalked; blooming April to June. *Fruits* bright red (rarely yellow), short-stalked, about ¼ inch in diameter; ripening September and October and persisting after the leaves fall.
    RANGE. Newfoundland to Minnesota; south to Georgia, southeastern Louisiana, and Missouri.
    Also called Black-alder.

HARDHACK *Spiraea tomentosa* L.   Rose Family

    FIELD MARKS. A simple or sparingly branched shrub 1 to (rarely) 4 feet high; growing in wet meadows and bogs. *Stems* angular, purplish brown, at first densely coated with tawny or rusty wool. *Leaves* numerous, egg-shaped to elliptic, pointed at base, pointed to blunt at tip, sharply toothed on margin, bright green and smooth above, densely tawny- to rusty-woolly beneath, 1 to 3 inches long. *Flowers* pink or rose-colored (rarely white), in a dense spirelike end cluster 4 to 7 inches long; blooming June to September.
    RANGE. Nova Scotia to Manitoba; south to Virginia, northern Georgia, Tennessee, and Arkansas.
    Also known as Steeplebush.

Leaves Alternate—Simple—Lobed

COMMON NINEBARK *Physocarpus opulifolius* (L.) Maxim.   Rose Family

    FIELD MARKS. A leaf-losing shrub 3 to 10 feet high, with arching branches and bark peeling off in thin papery layers; growing on rocky slopes, cliffs, and along streams. *Branchlets* with prominent ridges below the leaves or leaf scars, smooth to densely hairy with starry-branched hairs. *Leaves* alternate, roundish to egg-shaped, heart-shaped to roundish or broadly pointed at base, pointed to roundish at tip, commonly more or less 3-lobed and double-toothed on margin, smooth or nearly so above, smooth to downy or coated with starry-branched hairs beneath, ¾ to about 3 inches long. *Flowers* small, white or pinkish, 5-petalled, in often dense umbrella-shaped end clusters; blooming May to July. *Fruits* small, papery, red or purplish, smooth or hairy, inflated pods, 3 to 5 grouped on each stalk in the cluster; maturing July to September and persisting.
    RANGE. Quebec and northern Ontario to Minnesota; south to Georgia, Tennessee, and Arkansas.
    The hairy southern forms have been described as distinct species by some botanists but are not considered valid by others.

32

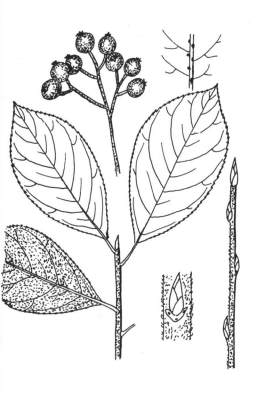

Red Chokeberry

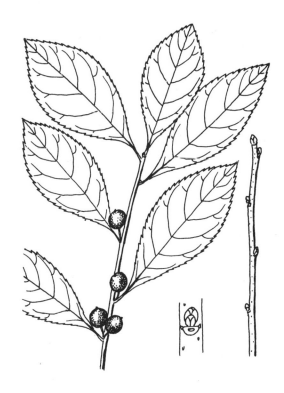

Winterberry

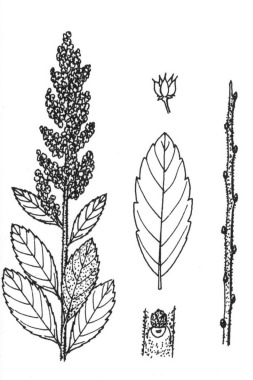

Hardhack

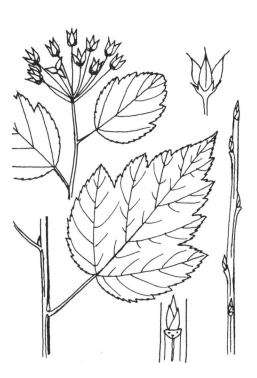

Common Ninebark

Swamp White Oak

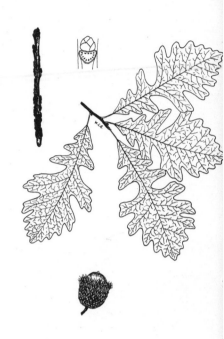

Bur Oak

Pin Oak

American Sycamore

SWAMP WHITE OAK *Quercus bicolor* Willd. Beech Family

FIELD MARKS: A tree 60 to 80 feet or more tall; growing in wet bottomlands and along streams. *Bark* dark brown; peeling off the branches in ragged papery curls and exposing the paler inner bark. *Leaves* 4 to 6 inches long, broadest above the middle, shallowly lobed or with large wavy teeth on margin, shiny dark green above, pale and downy beneath. *Fruit* a light brown egg-shaped acorn about 1 inch long, seated in a deeply bowl-shaped cup, usually paired on a stalk 1 to 3 inches in length; maturing in 1 year; kernel sweetish.

RANGE: Quebec and southern Maine west to Minnesota; south to North Carolina, northern Georgia and Alabama, Tennessee and Oklahoma.

BUR OAK *Quercus macrocarpa* Michx. Beech Family

FIELD MARKS: A large tree 60 to 80 feet or more tall; usually growing in moist bottomlands and along streams. *Branchlets* commonly with corky wings. *Bark* grayish-brown, deeply furrowed and ridged. *Leaves* 6 to 10 inches long, broadest above the middle, with 5 to 9 irregularly rounded lobes and nearly divided about the middle by opposing deep sinuses, shiny dark green above, paler and downy beneath. *Fruit* a light brown, downy, broadly egg-shaped acorn 1 to 2 inches long, half enclosed in a deeply bowl-shaped cup with a fringed rim; maturing in 1 year; kernel sweetish.

RANGE: Nova Scotia west to Manitoba; south to Pennsylvania, Tennessee and Texas.

PIN OAK *Quercus palustris* Muenchh. Beech Family

FIELD MARKS: A tree 40 to 60 feet or more tall; growing in wet bottomlands and along streams. *Bark* rather smooth, grayish-brown, becoming scaly-ridged on older trunks. *Leaves* 3 to 5 inches long with 5 or 7 long, narrow, bristle-tipped and sparingly bristle-toothed lobes, the sinuses between them extending almost to the midrib, smooth, shiny dark green above, paler beneath. *Fruit* a roundish light brown acorn with fine darker stripes, about ½ inch long, its base enclosed in a shallow saucer-like cup; maturing in 2 years; kernel bitter.

RANGE: Massachusetts west to southern Michigan and eastern Kansas; south to North Carolina, Tennessee and eastern Oklahoma.

Widely planted as a shade and street tree.

AMERICAN SYCAMORE *Platanus occidentalis* L. Planetree Family

FIELD MARKS: A large tree 70 to 100 feet or more tall; growing in moist bottomlands and along streams. *Bark* of young trunks and branches of older trees is shed in thin plates of irregular size and shape, exposing the whitish inner bark. *Leaves* maple-like in appearance with 3 to 5 coarsely wavy-toothed lobes, bright green and smooth above, paler and often with crumbly wool beneath; leaf stalk hollow at the base and covering a bud. *Fruits* in usually solitary ball-like heads about 1 inch across and dangling on a slender stalk; remaining on tree all winter and breaking up in early spring.

RANGE: Maine and southern Ontario west to eastern Nebraska; south to northern Florida and Texas.

Also called Buttonwood.

SWAMP ROSE *Rosa palustris* Marsh.   Rose Family

FIELD MARKS. An erect shrub 2½ to 6 feet high, the stems armed with broad-based and commonly hooked prickles; growing in swamps and other wet places. *Leaves* with 5 to 9 (usually 7) leaflets which are oval or elliptic, usually pointed at both ends, sharply toothed on margin, smooth above, paler and smooth or slightly downy beneath, ¾ to 2 inches long; the stipules often broadened upward or with slightly rolled margins. *Flowers* solitary or few in a cluster, pink, 2 to 2½ inches broad; blooming May to August. *Fruits* roundish, red, about ½ inch in diameter, smooth to rather densely glandular-bristly.
RANGE. Newfoundland and Nova Scotia to Ontario and Minnesota; south to Florida, Tennessee, and Arkansas.

POISON SUMAC *Rhus vernix* L.   Cashew Family

CAUTION: All parts of this plant contain a dangerous skin irritant.

FIELD MARKS. A shrub or small tree 4 to about 15 feet high; growing in swamps, bogs, and other wet places. *Branchlets* moderately stout, smooth, the end bud present. *Leaves* alternate, compound, 6 to 12 inches long; the 7 to 13 leaflets short-stalked, elliptic or egg-shaped, broadly pointed at base, pointed at tip, margin untoothed, rather lustrous above, paler beneath, smooth, 2 to 4 inches long; leafstalks usually reddish. *Flowers* small, greenish, in axillary clusters; blooming May to July. *Fruits* roundish, smooth, waxy white, about 3/16 inch in diameter, in rather loose and drooping clusters; ripening August or September and persisting.
RANGE. Southwestern Maine to Ontario and Minnesota, south to Florida and Texas.

Leaves Opposite—Simple—Lobed

SILVER MAPLE *Acer saccharinum* L.   Maple Family
FIELD MARKS: A large tree 60 to 80 feet or more tall; growing in moist bottomlands and along streams. *Branchlets* reddish-brown, giving off a fetid odor when broken. *Leaves* 4 to 6 inches broad, deeply 5-lobed and coarsely toothed, sides of the terminal lobe sloping inward, bright green above, silvery-white beneath. *Flowers* greenish-yellow to reddish, in crowded clusters; blooming February to April before the leaves appear. *Fruits* in pairs, their wide-spreading wings 1½ to 2½ inches long; maturing April to June and promptly shed.
RANGE: New Brunswick west to Minnesota; south to Georgia, Mississippi and Oklahoma.
Frequently planted as a shade tree.

Leaves Opposite—Compound

ASHLEAF MAPLE *Acer negundo* L.   Maple Family
FIELD MARKS: A tree 30 to rarely 75 feet tall; growing in wet bottomlands, swamps, and along streams. *Leaves* 5 to 10 inches long; divided into 3 to 7 usually egg-shaped leaflets which are coarsely toothed or slightly lobed; leaflets 2 to 4 inches long, light green and smooth above, paler and sometimes downy beneath. *Flowers* yellowish-green, stamen-bearing ones on thread-like stalks of about the same length; pistil-bearing ones arranged along a common drooping stalk; borne on separate trees; blooming March to May. *Fruits* in pairs, wings 1 to 1½ inches long and forming a wide to narrow V; in drooping clusters; maturing May to October and often persisting into winter.
RANGE: Maine west to Manitoba; south to Florida and California.

36

Swamp Rose

Poison Sumac

Silver Maple

Ashleaf Maple

Silky Dogwood

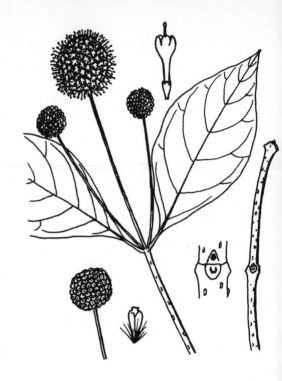

Buttonbush

Sheep-laurel

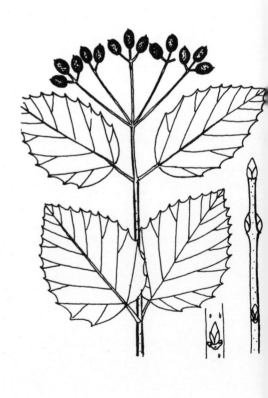

Arrowwood

SILKY DOGWOOD *Cornus amonum* Mill.   Dogwood Family

FIELD MARKS. A shrub 4 to about 10 feet high; growing in wet places and along streams. *Branchlets* purplish red, more or less covered with minute closely pressed hairs; pith large and brownish. *Leaves* egg-shaped to broadly elliptic, rounded at base, pointed at tip, veins 3 to 5 pairs, smooth or nearly so above, pale and usually with some small reddish hairs beneath, 2 to 4 inches long. *Flowers* creamy white, in flat-topped to slightly convex clusters; blooming May to July. *Fruits* roundish, dull blue or partly white, about ¼ inch in diameter; ripening August to October.
RANGE. Southern Maine to Illinois, south to Georgia and Alabama.
Also called Kinnikinnik.

BUTTONBUSH *Cephalanthus occidentalis* L.   Madder Family

FIELD MARKS. A leaf-losing shrub 3 to 10 or rarely 20 feet high; growing in swamps, shallow ponds, and along streams. *Leaves* opposite or in 3's, elliptic to egg-shaped or lance-shaped, pointed at both ends, untoothed on margin, often lustrous above, paler and sometimes downy beneath, 3 to 6 inches long. *Flowers* small, white, tubular, 5-lobed, fragrant, clustered in long-stalked ball-shaped heads 1 to 1½ inches across; blooming May to August. *Fruits* small, top-shaped, 2-seeded capsules in tight ball-shaped heads.
RANGE. Nova Scotia to southern Ontario, Minnesota, and California; south to Florida, Texas, and Mexico.
Also called Honeyballs. Often cultivated as an ornamental shrub.

SHEEP-LAUREL *Kalmia angustifolia* L.   Heath Family

FIELD MARKS. An evergreen shrub 1 to about 3 feet high; growing in bogs and rocky or sandy woods. *Leaves* opposite or in 3's, narrowly elliptic to oblong, pointed at both ends, thin but leathery in texture, smooth above, paler green or slightly whitened and smooth beneath (or grayish-downy beneath in var. *caroliniana* [Small] Fern.), 1 to 2½ inches long. *Flowers* deep pink to rose purple (rarely white), about ⅜ inch across, in clusters on branchlets of the previous year at base of the new growth; blooming April to August. *Fruits* about ⅛ inch in diameter.
RANGE. Newfoundland and Labrador to Manitoba, south to Pennsylvania and Michigan; var. *caroliniana* from Virginia and Tennessee south to Georgia.

Leaves Opposite—Simple—Toothed

ARROWWOOD *Viburnum dentatum* L.   Honeysuckle Family

FIELD MARKS. A bushy leaf-losing shrub 3 to about 10 (rarely 15) feet high; growing along streams or on shores of lakes, and in low wet woods and swamps. *Branchlets* more or less ridged or angled, smooth or sometimes roughish-hairy. *Leaves* with leaf-stalks usually more than ¼ inch long, egg-shaped to roundish, rounded or slightly heart-shaped at base, pointed to blunt at tip, prominent lateral veins ending in the large and sharp-pointed marginal teeth, smooth or nearly so on the upper surface, paler and more or less downy beneath (or smooth except for occasional tufts of down in the axils of the veins in the variety *lucidulum* Ait.), 1½ to about 4 inches long. *Flowers* all alike; blooming late March to July. *Fruits* roundish or egg-shaped, bluish black, ¼ to ⅜ inch long; ripening July to October.
RANGE. New Brunswick to southern Ontario; south to Florida and Texas.
A variable shrub often divided into several species by some botanists.

MOUNTAIN-HOLLY *Nemopanthus mucronata* (L.) Trel.   Holly Family

FIELD MARKS. An erect leaf-losing shrub 3 to 12 feet high; growing in cool, moist, rocky woods, lakeshores, and bogs. *Leaves* alternate, often clustered on short spurs, elliptic, pointed to roundish at base, blunt but with an abrupt little point at tip, (rarely) with a few teeth on margin, thin in texture, smooth, slightly paler beneath, ¾ to 2 inches long; leafstalks smooth and very slender. *Flowers* small, greenish white, on long and slender stalks; blooming about May. *Fruits* berry-like, 3- to 5-seeded, roundish, dull red, about ¼ inch in diameter, on long and slender stalks; ripening July to September.

RANGE. Newfoundland to Minnesota; south to West Virginia, Indiana, and northern Illinois.

LABRADOR-TEA *Ledum groenlandicum* Oeder   Heath Family

FIELD MARKS. An evergreen shrub 1 to (rarely) 3 feet high; growing in peaty soils and cold bogs. *Branchlets* rusty-woolly when young. *Leaves* alternate, short-stalked, elliptic to narrowly oblong, roundish at base, bluntly pointed at tip, margin untoothed and strongly rolled inward beneath, leathery, smooth and bright green above, densely rusty-wooly beneath, ½ to 2 inches long. *Flowers* white, 5-petalled, about ⅜ inch across, in rather dense end clusters; blooming May or June. *Fruits* narrowly oblong capsules about ¼ inch long, opening upward from base into 5 parts.

RANGE. Greenland and Labrador to Alaska; south to northern parts of New Jersey, Pennsylvania, and Ohio, Michigan, Alberta, and Washington.

BOG ROSEMARY *Andromeda glaucophylla* Link   Heath Family

FIELD MARKS. A spreading evergreen shrub 4 inches to 2 feet high, growing in bogs and shallow pools. *Branchlets* whitened. *Leaves* alternate, very short-stalked, narrowly lance-shaped or narrowly oblong, pointed at base, short-pointed at tip, margin strongly rolled, thick and leathery in texture, dark bluish green and lustrous above, very white and minutely downy beneath, ¾ to about 2 inches long. *Flowers* white or pinkish, globe-shaped, about ¼ inch long, in end clusters; blooming May to July or later. *Fruits* turban-shaped, 5-parted capsules about 3/16 inch in diameter.

RANGE. Southwestern Greenland and Labrador to eastern Manitoba; south to northern New Jersey, West Virginia, Indiana, Wisconsin, and Minnesota.

RHODORA *Rhododendron canadense* (L.) Torr.   Heath Family

FIELD MARKS. A leaf-losing shrub 1 to 3 feet high; growing in cold bogs and moist rocky barrens. *Branchlets* smooth, often whitened with a bloom. *Leaves* elliptic or oblong, pointed at both ends, margin slightly rolled and hairy-fringed, dull green above, pale or whitened beneath and with some rusty hairs along the midrib, ¾ to 2 inches long. *Flowers* rose purple, 2-lipped, with a short tube, 5 to 8 in a cluster; blooming April or May. *Fruits* oblong egg-shaped, uneven at base, downy, ½ to ⅝ inch long.

RANGE. Labrador and Newfoundland to south-central Quebec; south to northern New Jersey, northeastern Pennsylvania, and central New York.

40

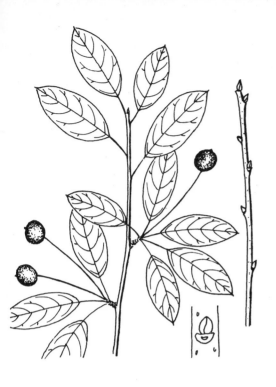

Mountain-holly

Labrador-tea

Bog Rosemary

Rhodora

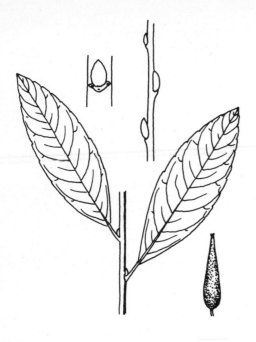

Pussy Willow

Autumn Willow

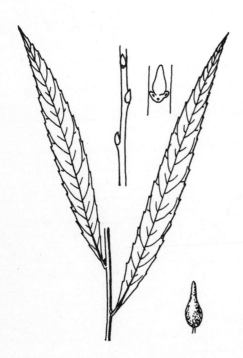

Sandbar Willow

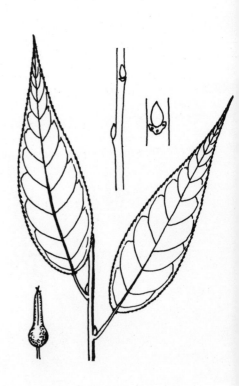

Shining Willow

PUSSY WILLOW   *Salix discolor* Muhl.   Willow Family

FIELD MARKS. A large shrub usually 6 to 12 feet high, or occasionally a small tree; growing in swamps and other wet places. *Branchlets* dark purplish red, smooth or softly hairy. *Leaves* elliptic to lance-shaped, pointed at both ends, occasionally untoothed but usually with irregular and somewhat wavy teeth mostly above the middle, bright green and with a wrinkled-veiny appearance above, whitened and sometimes with rusty hairs beneath, 2 to 4 inches long. Large stipules are often present on vigorous shoots.

RANGE. Nova Scotia to Manitoba; south to Delaware, Maryland, West Virginia, Indiana, northeastern Missouri, and Nebraska.

The large furry catkins appear before the leaves and are a familiar harbinger of spring.

AUTUMN WILLOW   *Salix serissima* (Bailey) Fern.   Willow Family

FIELD MARKS. A shrub 3 to 12 feet high; growing in swamps or bogs, usually in marl or limestone regions. *Branchlets* smooth, lustrous, yellow brown to olive brown. *Leaves* narrowly elliptic or lance-shaped, pointed at tip, rounded to broadly pointed at base, finely and sharply toothed on margin, firm, lustrous above, smooth and pale or whitened beneath, 2 to 4 inches long; slender leafstalks usually have a pair of glands at the summit. *Flowers* blooming in June or July. *Fruits* maturing August or September.

RANGE. Newfoundland to Alberta; south to northern New Jersey, Pennsylvania, the region of the Great Lakes, North Dakota, and Colorado.

SANDBAR WILLOW   *Salix interior* Rowlee   Willow Family

FIELD MARKS. A shrub 3 to 15 feet high; forming thickets on sand or gravel deposits along streams and places subject to frequent flooding. *Branchlets* reddish brown, smooth or nearly so. *Leaves narrowly* lance-shaped, pointed at both ends, margin with shallow and widely spaced teeth, green and smooth on both surfaces or sometimes silvery-silky, 2 to 5 inches long; leafstalks very short; stipules very small if present.

RANGE. New Brunswick to Quebec and Alaska; south to Maryland, Kentucky, Louisiana, and New Mexico.

SHINING WILLOW   *Salix lucida* Muhl.   Willow Family

FIELD MARKS. A shrub 4 to 10 feet high, or occasionally a small tree; growing in swampy places and along the banks of streams. *Branchlets* lustrous, smooth (or hairy in var. *intonsa* Fern.). *Leaves* broadly lance-shaped, long-pointed at tip, broadly pointed to rounded at base, finely and sharply toothed on margin, dark green and very lustrous above, slightly paler green and smooth (or hairy in var. *intonsa*) beneath, 2½ to 5 inches long. The leafstalks usually have large stipules at the base.

RANGE. Labrador to Manitoba; south to Delaware, Maryland, the region of the Great Lakes, and South Dakota.

43

SPECKLED ALDER   *Alnus rugosa* (Du Rois) Spreng.   Birch Family

FIELD MARKS. A shrub very much like the preceding. *Bark* with numerous whitish, horizontally elongated lenticels. *Leaves* oval or broadest above the middle, short-pointed at tip, rounded to slightly heart-shaped at base, margin double-toothed, smooth above, paler or more often whitened and sometimes pale- to rusty-downy beneath, 2 to 5 inches long. *Flowers* blooming March or April, the smaller catkins drooping and not at branch tips. *Buds* 2-scaled and noticeably stalked.

RANGE. Labrador to Saskatchewan; south to Maine, Maryland, West Virginia, the region of the Great Lakes, and northeastern Iowa.

Also called Hoary Alder.

ALDERLEAF BUCKTHORN   *Rhamnus alnifolia* L'Her.   Buckthorn Family

FIELD MARKS. A leaf-losing shrub 1½ to about 3 feet high; growing in cold swamps and bogs. *Branchlets* reddish brown, smooth or nearly so. *Leaves* alternate, oval or elliptic, broadly pointed at base, pointed at tip, finely and bluntly toothed on margin, lustrous and with sunken veins above, paler and usually downy on the veins beneath, 2 to 4½ inches long. *Flowers* small, greenish yellow, fragrant, 1 to 3 in leaf axils; blooming May or June. *Fruits* roundish or slightly egg-shaped, black, 1- to 3-seeded, about ¼ inch in diameter; ripening July or August.

RANGE. Newfoundland to British Columbia; south to northern New Jersey, West Virginia, the region of the Great Lakes, Nebraska, Wyoming, and California.

OBLONG-FRUITED JUNEBERRY   *Amelanchier bartramiana* (Tausch) Roemer   Rose Family

FIELD MARKS. A shrub 1½ to about 8 feet high, usually with several stems in a clump; growing in cold, wet, rocky woods or swamps and bogs. *Leaves* elliptic or narrowly so, more or less pointed at both ends, finely and sharply toothed on margin to below the middle, thin in texture, smooth on both surfaces, bright green above, paler and often somewhat whitened beneath, 1 to 2½ inches long; leafstalks short. *Flowers* 1 to 3 clustered together in the axils of the leaves; blooming May to August. *Fruits* oval or pear-shaped, about ½ inch long, dark purplish with a whitish bloom, sweet and juicy; ripening July to September.

RANGE. Labrador to western Ontario; south to northeastern Pennsylvania, West Virginia, northern Michigan, northern Wisconsin, and Minnesota.

BALSAM POPLAR   *Populus balsamifera* L.   Willow Family

FIELD MARKS: A tree usually 60 to 80 feet tall; growing along streams and the borders of swamps. *Branchlets* moderately stout, reddish-brown and shiny, with brown buds full of sticky and very fragrant resin. *Leaves* egg-shaped, smooth, dark green and shiny above, paler beneath, margin finely toothed, 3 to 6 inches long and 2 to 4 inches broad; or leaves broader and heart-shaped and hairy beneath in the variety *subcordata*; leaf stalks slender and not flattened, hairy in the variety *subcordata*. *Fruits* egg-shaped capsules containing small hairy-tufted seeds; maturing in spring.

RANGE: Newfoundland to Alaska; south to northern New England, New York, Illinois, North Dakota and Colorado.

Also called Balm-of-Gilead. Widely planted in the Northeast as an ornamental tree.

44

Speckled Alder

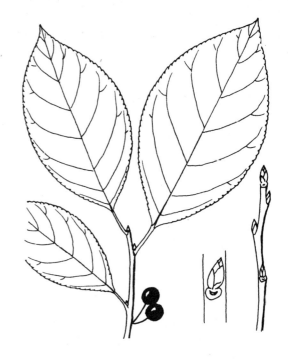

Alderleaf Buckthorn

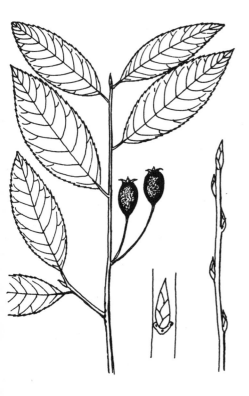

Oblong-fruited Juneberry

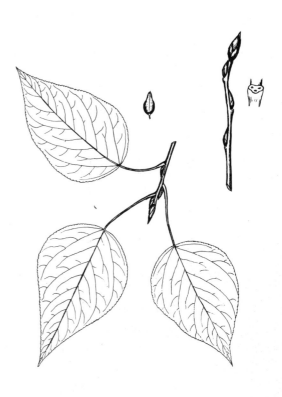

Balsam Poplar

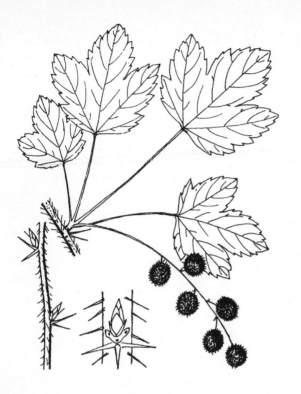

Swamp Black Current

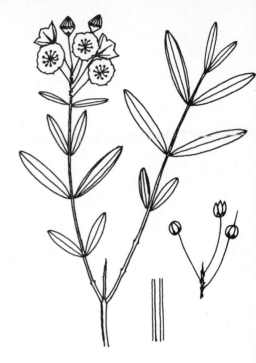

Pale-laurel

Shrubby Cinquefoil

Black Ash

SWAMP BLACK CURRANT *Ribes lacustre* (Pers.) Poir. Saxifrage Family

FIELD MARKS. An erect shrub 1 to 3 feet high, with prickly and bristly stems; growing in cool, moist woods and swamps. *Branchlets* with 1 to 3 long nodal spines and prickly bristles between. *Leaves* roundish, heart-shaped at base, deeply 3- to 5-lobed and toothed on margin, smooth or nearly so on both surfaces, 1 to 3 inches wide. *Flowers* greenish or purplish, several in a drooping cluster; blooming May to July. *Fruits* glandular-bristly, purplish black, about 5/16 inch in diameter, unpleasant to the taste; ripening July to September.

RANGE. Newfoundland to Alaska; south to western Massachusetts, New York, southwestern Pennsylvania, the region of the Great Lakes, Colorado, Utah, and California.

Leaves Opposite—Simple—Entire

PALE-LAUREL *Kalmia polifolia* Wang. Heath Family

FIELD MARKS. A straggling evergreen shrub 6 inches to 2 feet high; growing in cold northern bogs. *Branchlets* strongly 2-edged. *Leaves* opposite or in 3's, stalkless or nearly so, very narrowly elliptic, narrowed at base, blunt or short-pointed at tip, margin rolled, smooth, lustrous above, strongly whitened beneath, ½ to 1¼ inches long. *Flowers* rose purple, about ½ inch across, in end clusters; blooming May to July. *Fruits* about ⅛ inch in diameter.

RANGE. Newfoundland and Labrador to Alaska; south to New Jersey, northern Pennsylvania, Michigan, Minnesota, and Oregon.

Also called Swamp- or Bog-laurel.

Leaves Opposite—Compound

SHRUBBY CINQUEFOIL *Potentilla fruticosa* L. Rose Family

FIELD MARKS. A leaf-losing shrub 1 to 3 feet high, with erect or ascending branches and shreddy bark; growing in cold, moist, rocky places or in northern bogs. *Leaves* alternate, compound, with prominent pointed stipules at the bases of the leafstalks; leaflets usually 5 (rarely 3 or 7), stalkless, lance-shaped, pointed at both ends, margin untoothed but often slightly rolled, silvery-silky on both surfaces, ½ to about 1 inch long. *Flowers* bright yellow, 5-petalled, about ¾ inch across; blooming June to September. *Fruits* greenish becoming brown, small, dry, densely hairy, borne in heads.

RANGE. Newfoundland and southern Labrador to Alaska; south to northern New Jersey, northeastern Pennsylvania, the region of the Great Lakes, northern Iowa, South Dakota, New Mexico, and California.

Found in the northern portions of Europe and Asia, as well as North America, and cultivated in many varieties as an ornamental shrub.

BLACK ASH *Fraxinus nigra* Marsh. Olive Family

FIELD MARKS: A tree 40 to 60 feet or more tall; growing in wet bottomlands and swamps. *Branchlets* grayish, with dark blackish-brown buds and roundish leaf scars. *Leaves* 10 to 16 inches long; usually divided into 9 oblong lance-shaped, stalkless leaflets 3 to 5 inches long, finely saw-toothed on margin, dark green above, paler beneath, smooth or nearly so. *Flowers* in loose clusters and appearing before the leaves. *Fruits* paddle-shaped, 1 to 1½ inches long, the sides of the rather broad and flat wing extending for more than half way down the seed cavity.

RANGE: Newfoundland west to Manitoba; south to northern Virginia, Illinois and Iowa.

Also called Hoop Ash and Basket Ash.

MOUNTAIN FLY HONEYSUCKLE *Lonicera villosa* (Michx.) R. & S.

Honeysuckle Family

FIELD MARKS. A leaf-losing shrub 1 to about 3 feet high, with ascending branches and shredding bark; growing in cold, moist, rocky woods or bogs. *Branchlets* may be hairy or smooth. *Leaves* short-stalked, elliptic to narrowly oblong, mostly roundish at both ends, margin untoothed but often hairy-fringed, usually hairy but sometimes quite smooth, veiny in appearance, pale or somewhat whitened beneath, ¾ to 1½ inches long. *Flowers* pale yellow, bell-shaped, 5-lobed, paired on axillary stalks less than ¼ inch long; blooming May or June. *Fruits* blue or bluish black, oval, 2-eyed berries about ¼ inch in diameter; ripening June to August.

RANGE. Newfoundland and southern Labrador to Manitoba; south to New England, northern Pennsylvania, Michigan, and Minnesota.

Also known as Blue Honeysuckle. The fruits are edible.

SWAMP FLY HONEYSUCKLE *Lonicera oblongifolia* (Goldie) Hook. Honeysuckle

Family

FIELD MARKS. A bushy leaf-losing shrub 2 to 5 feet high; growing in cold swamps and bogs. *Branchlets* stiff, ascending, smooth. *Leaves* short-stalked, oblong or elliptic, pointed at base, pointed or blunt at tip, untoothed on margin, paler beneath and smooth or nearly so on both surfaces, ¾ to 3 inches long. *Flowers* creamy white often tinged with purple, 2-lipped, paired on long axillary stalks; blooming May to July. *Fruits* red or purplish, egg-shaped berries about ¼ inch long, often somewhat united; ripening July to September.

RANGE. Southeastern Quebec to Manitoba; south to Maine, northwestern Pennsylvania, northern Ohio, Michigan, Wisconsin, and Minnesota.

RED-OSIER DOGWOOD *Cornus stolonifera* Michx. Dogwood Family

FIELD MARKS. A shrub 3 to 9 feet high, often with stems partly prostrate and rooting; growing in wet or swampy places. *Branchlets* purplish red to blood-red, with a large white pith. *Leaves* elliptic to egg-shaped, roundish or broadly pointed at base, pointed at tip, veins 4 to 6 pairs, smooth or minutely hairy on both surfaces, whitened beneath, 2 to 4 inches long. Flowers whitish, in flat-topped clusters; blooming May to July. *Fruits* roundish, white, about ¼ inch in diameter; ripening July to September.

RANGE. Newfoundland to Yukon; south to western Maryland, West Virginia, the region of the Great Lakes, Iowa, New Mexico, and California.

Leaves Opposite—Simple—Lobed

HIGHBUSH-CRANBERRY *Viburnum trilobum* Marsh. Honeysuckle Family

FIELD MARKS. A leaf-losing shrub 3 to about 12 feet high; growing in cool moist woods and cold swamps. *Leaves* broadly egg-shaped, with 3 broad and rather long-pointed lobes, rounded to very broadly pointed at base, margin with coarse and rather wavy teeth, sometimes sparingly hairy above, slightly paler and often hairy along the veins beneath, 2 to 4 inches long; leaf stalks grooved, ½ to 1½ inches long, often with small stalked glands at the summit. *Flowers* of 2 kinds, the marginal ones showy, ½ inch or so across, but sterile; blooming May to July. *Fruits* roundish or slightly oval-shaped, bright red, juicy, translucent, about ⅜ inch in diameter; ripening September or October.

RANGE. Newfoundland to British Columbia; south to New England, West Virginia, the region of the Great Lakes, northeast Iowa, South Dakota, and Washington.

The acid fruits are cooked and used like cranberries.

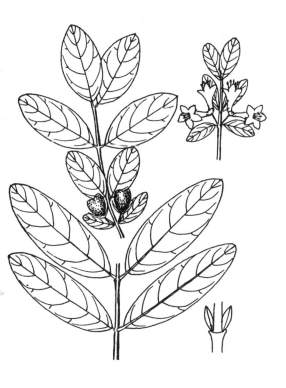

Mountain Fly Honeysuckle   Swamp Fly Honeysuckle

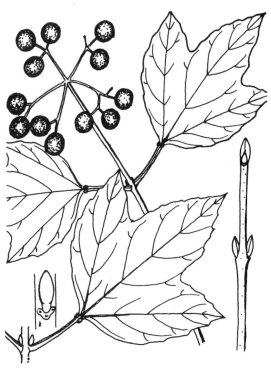

Red-Osier Dogwood   Highbush-cranberry

Redbay

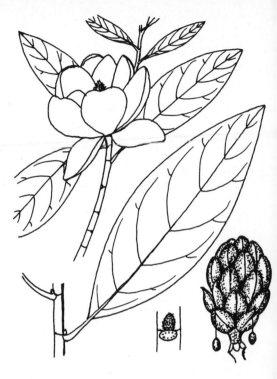

Sweetbay Magnolia

Swamp Cyrilla

Fetterbush

SOUTHERN WOODY PLANTS OF WET PLACES
Leaves Alternate—Simple—Entire

REDBAY *Persea borbonia* (L.) Spreng.   Laurel Family

FIELD MARKS: A small evergreen tree 30 to about 50 feet tall with a spicy-aromatic odor similar to that of the Sassafras; growing in swamps of the South Atlantic and Gulf coastal plains. *Branchlets* smooth or rusty-hairy. *Leaves* 3 to 6 inches long, elliptical to lance-shaped, pointed at both ends, untoothed on margin, bright green and smooth above, smooth and whitened to rusty-hairy beneath. *Flowers* small, yellowish-green; blooming May or June. *Fruits* dark blue, egg-shaped, berry-like drupes about ½ inch long, solitary or in small clusters on stalks ½ to 2 inches long; ripening September or October.

RANGE: Southern Delaware south to Florida; west to southern Texas and Arkansas.
Leaves are sometimes used as a substitute for the official bay leaves.

SWEETBAY MAGNOLIA *Magnolia virginiana* L.   Magnolia Family

FIELD MARKS. A large shrub to medium-sized tree, leaf-losing or evergreen southward; growing in swampy places and along streams. *Branchlets* green, ringed at the nodes with stipule scars, spicy-fragrant when bruised. *Leaves* alternate, oval to narrowly elliptic, usually pointed at both ends, untoothed on margin, lustrous above, whitened beneath, 3 to 5 inches long, spicy-aromatic when crushed. *Flowers* cup-shaped, creamy white, 2 to 3 inches across, very fragrant; blooming April to June. *Fruits* borne in conelike clusters; the individual fruits podlike, splitting down the outside and releasing the scarlet-coated seeds on silklike threads; ripening July to October.

RANGE. Chiefly coastal plain; southeastern Massachusetts and southern Pennsylvania south to Florida, west to Texas, north in Mississippi Valley to eastern Tennessee and southern Arkansas.

SWAMP CYRILLA *Cyrilla racemiflora* L.   Cyrilla Family

FIELD MARKS. A shrub or small tree to 15 (rarely 30) feet high; forming thickets on borders of swamps and ponds. *Leaves* alternate, narrowly elliptic or broadest above the middle, wedge-shaped at base, rounded or blunt-pointed at tip, untoothed on margin, thin but somewhat leathery, lustrous above, paler beneath, smooth, 2 to 4 inches long; leafstalks short. *Flowers* small, white; in long, narrow, drooping end clusters; blooming late April to July. *Fruits* small, yellowish-brown, 4-seeded capsules about ⅛ inch long; maturing August or September and persisting.

RANGE. Coastal plain; Virginia south to Florida, west to Texas.
Also called White-titi. Flowers are important source of honey. Leaves usually turn red in the fall but persist most of the winter.

FETTERBUSH *Lyonia lucida* (Lam.) K. Koch   Heath Family

FIELD MARKS. An evergreen shrub 3 to about 6 feet high, with arching or drooping and sharply 3-angled branches; growing in moist pinelands, swamps, and peaty thickets. *Leaves* alternate, elliptic to oval or sometimes broadest above the middle, pointed or broadly pointed at base, abruptly pointed at tip, stiff and leathery in texture, with a prominent vein paralleling the untoothed and narrowly rolled margin, dark green and lustrous above, paler and dull and glandular-dotted beneath, 1 to 3 inches long. *Flowers* white to deep rose pink, oblong bell-shaped, about ⅜ inch long, the 5 calyx lobes narrow and spreading, 3 to 10 in clusters in the leaf axils; blooming March to May. *Fruits* roundish, 5-parted capsules about 3/16 inch in diameter.

RANGE. Coastal plain, Southeastern Virginia south to Florida, west to Louisiana.
Also called Tetterbush and Hoorah-bush (Okefenokee region).

51

WATER TUPELO *Nyssa aquatica* L.   Tupelo Family

FIELD MARKS: A tree 40 to 100 feet or more tall, usually with a conspicuously swollen base; growing in southern and Mississippi Valley swamps. *Leaves* 5 to 10 inches long, oval-shaped, broadly pointed to rounded at base, pointed at tip, margin untoothed or with an occasional large tooth, shiny dark green above, paler and somewhat downy beneath. *Flowers* small, greenish, the stamen-bearing ones in dense clusters; blooming April or May. *Fruits* oblong egg-shaped, dark blue or purple, about 1 inch long, solitary on long stalks; ripening September or October.

RANGE: Southeastern Virginia south to northern Florida; west to southeastern Texas; north in Mississippi Valley to southern Illinois.

ZENOBIA *Zenobia pulverulenta* (Bartr.) Pollard   Heath Family

FIELD MARKS. A leaf-losing shrub 3 to about 10 feet high; growing in damp sandy or peaty pinelands. *Branchlets* reddish to brown, often more or less whitened with a bloom. *Leaves* alternate, elliptic to oval, pointed at base, blunt or sometimes pointed at tip, untoothed or with rather obscure wavy teeth or margin, leathery in texture, smooth on both surfaces, often whitened with a bloom but sometimes green on both surfaces, ¾ to 2½ inches long. *Flowers* white, broadly bell-shaped, about ¼ inch long, in clusters along growth of the preceding year; blooming May or June. *Fruits* roundish, 5-parted capsules nearly ¼ inch in diameter.

RANGE. Coastal plain; southeastern Virginia south to Georgia.

DAHOON HOLLY *Ilex cassine* L.   Holly Family

FIELD MARKS. An evergreen shrub or small tree 5 to 25 feet high; growing about the borders of swamps and cypress ponds. *Leaves* elliptic or oblong egg-shaped, pointed at base, pointed or blunt at tip, margin untoothed or with a few spiny teeth above the middle, thickish and leathery in texture, dark green and smooth above, usually with minute pale hairs along midrib beneath, 1½ to 3 inches long. *Flowers* blooming in May or June. *Fruits* red (rarely yellow), short-stalked, about ¼ inch in diameter; ripening October or November and persisting.

RANGE. Coastal plain; North Carolina south to Florida, west to Louisiana.

WAX MYRTLE *Myrica cerifera* L.   Bayberry Family

FIELD MARKS. An aromatic evergreen shrub or small tree which grows in wet sandy pinelands and bogs. *Branchlets* smooth or sparsely hairy, resin-dotted, pleasantly fragrant when broken. *Leaves* alternate, narrow, broadest toward the pointed tip and gradually tapered to the pointed base, untoothed or more often sharply toothed on the margin, resin-dotted on both surfaces, 2 to 4 inches long, pleasantly fragrant when crushed. *Fruits* are bony nutlets coated with whitish wax, about ⅛ inch in diameter.

RANGE. Coastal plain; southern New Jersey south to Florida, west to Texas, and northward to Arkansas and Oklahoma.

Wax of the fruits used to make bayberry candles. Fruits eaten by many birds, including the bobwhite quail and wild turkey. Makes a rather attractive ornamental shrub for wet places.

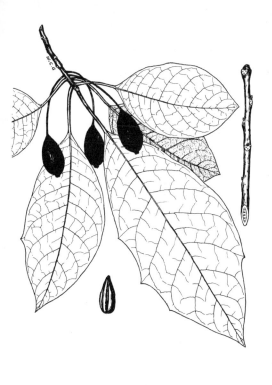

Water Tupelo

Zenobia

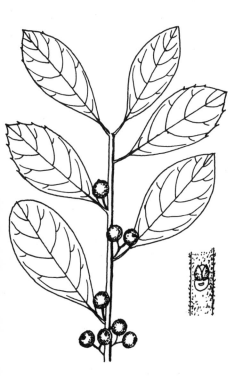

Dahoon Holly

Wax Myrtle

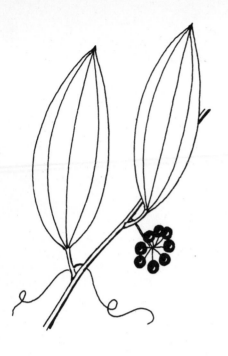

Laurel-leaf Greenbrier

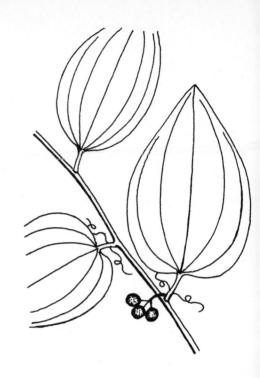

Red-berried Greenbrier

Buckthorn Bumelia

Supplejack

LAUREL-LEAF GREENBRIER *Smilax laurifolia* L.   Lily Family

FIELD MARKS. A high-climbing evergreen vine of low grounds and swamps; the round stems chiefly prickly toward the base and sometimes on the more vigorous shoots. *Leaves* thickish and leathery, pointed at both ends, dark green and lustrous above, paler and sometimes slightly whitened beneath, 3-veined, 2½ to 5 inches long. *Fruits* black, about ¼ inch in diameter.

RANGE. Coastal plain and piedmont; New Jersey south to Florida, west to Arkansas and Texas.

Unique among our greenbriers in having fruits which do not ripen until the second year; thus both ripe fruits and smaller green ones are commonly present. Also known as the Bamboo-vine or Blaspheme-vine.

RED-BERRIED GREENBRIER *Smilax walteri* Pursh   Lily Family

FIELD MARKS. A slender-stemmed, leaf-losing vine with angled branchlets; usually scrambling over bushes about the borders of swamps and in low wet pinelands. The stems usually have scattered and slender prickles only toward the base. *Leaves* rather thin, egg-shaped to broadly egg-shaped, green on both surfaces, 5- to 7-veined, 2 to 4 inches long. *Fruits* bright coral red, about ¼ inch in diameter, persistent throughout the winter.

RANGE. Chiefly coastal plain; New Jersey south to Florida, west to Louisiana.

Easily recognized by its bright-red berries. Also known as the Coral Greenbrier.

BUCKTHORN BUMELIA *Bumelia lycioides* (L.) Pers.   Sapodilla Family

FIELD MARKS. A leaf-losing shrub or small tree 5 to 20 feet or more high; growing in swampy woods or on stream banks, bluffs, and dunes. *Leaves* narrowly elliptic or broadest above the middle, wedge-shaped at base, short-pointed to rounded at tip, untoothed on margin, smooth or nearly so on both surfaces, 2 to 6 inches long. *Flowers* blooming June to August. *Fruits* black, oblong, about ½ inch long; ripening September or October.

RANGE. Southeastern Virginia south to Florida, west to Texas; north in Mississippi Valley to southern Indiana, Illinois, and southeastern Missouri.

Also called Southern-buckthorn and False-buckthorn.

SUPPLEJACK *Berchemia scandens* (Hill) K. Koch   Buckthorn Family

FIELD MARKS. A high-climbing, leaf-losing vine; growing in swamps, sandy woods, or along streams. *Leaves* alternate, elliptic or lance-shaped, roundish to broadly pointed at base, pointed at tip, slightly paler beneath, smooth, with 9 to 12 pairs of prominent straight veins, 1½ to 3 inches long. *Flowers* small, greenish white, in end clusters; blooming April to June. *Fruits* oval-shaped, bluish black, 1-seeded, about ¼ inch long; maturing August to October.

RANGE. Chiefly coastal plain; Virginia south to Florida, west to Texas; north in Mississippi Valley to Kentucky and Missouri.

SWAMP COTTONWOOD *Populus heterophylla* L. Willow Family

FIELD MARKS: A tree often 70 to 90 feet tall; growing in swamps of the coastal plains and Mississippi Valley. *Branchlets* grayish-brown with prominent orange-colored pith. *Leaves* egg-shaped, rounded or blunt at tip, often heart-shaped at base, margin with fine and rounded teeth, dark green and smooth above, paler and woolly beneath when young, 4 to 8 inches long; leaf stalks not flattened. *Fruits* are small capsules containing small seeds with cottony hairs, arranged in catkins and maturing in spring.

RANGE: Connecticut and southeastern New York south to Georgia; northwestern Florida west to Louisiana; north in Mississippi Valley to southern Indiana and Illinois.

RED BIRCH *Betula nigra* L. Birch Family

FIELD MARKS: A tree usually 30 to 50 feet tall; growing in wet bottomlands, swamps, and along streams. *Bark* cinnamon-colored or reddish-brown, peeling in thin papery layers. *Leaves* often paired on short spurs but not opposite, egg-shaped, broadly pointed at base, sharply pointed at tip, margin doubly saw-toothed, dark green above, paler and usually downy beneath. *Fruit* a small 2-winged seed-like nutlet produced in oblong, many-scaled conelike structures 1 to 1½ inches long; maturing in late spring and soon breaking up.

RANGE: Massachusetts west to Minnesota; south to northern Florida and eastern Texas. Also called River Birch.

SWAMP CHESTNUT OAK *Quercus michauxii* Nutt. Birch Family

FIELD MARKS: A tree 60 to 80 feet or more tall; growing in wet bottomlands and swamps. *Bark* ashy-gray, irregularly furrowed and scaly. *Leaves* 5 to 8 inches long, broadest above the middle, margin with coarse and rounded teeth, dark green and shiny above, much paler and coated with white down beneath. *Fruit* a shiny brown, oblong egg-shaped acorn 1 to 1½ inches long, seated in a deeply bowl-shaped cup; maturing in 1 year; kernel sweetish.

RANGE: New Jersey south to central Florida; west to eastern Texas; north in Mississippi Valley to central Illinois and southeastern Ohio.

Also called Cow Oak or Basket Oak.

PLANERTREE *Planera aquatica* Gmel. Elm Family

FIELD MARKS: A small tree 20 to 40 feet tall; growing in swamps and in bottomlands subject to frequent and prolonged flooding. *Leaves* egg-shaped, pointed at tip, unevenly rounded at base, saw-toothed on margin, dull dark green above, paler beneath, roughish on both surfaces. *Flowers* small, greenish; blooming in March or April. *Fruit* a nutlet covered on the outside with numerous, irregular, fleshy projections; maturing April or May.

RANGE: Coastal plain from southeastern North Carolina south to northern Florida; west to Texas; north in Mississippi Valley to southern Illinois.

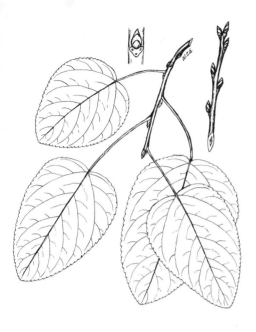

Swamp Cottonwood

Red Birch

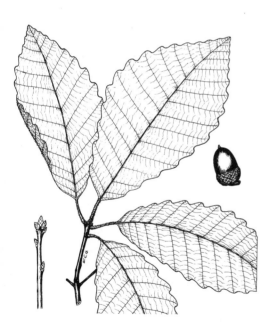

Swamp Chestnut Oak

Planertree

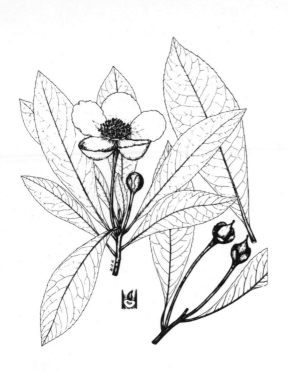

Loblolly Bay

American Snowbell

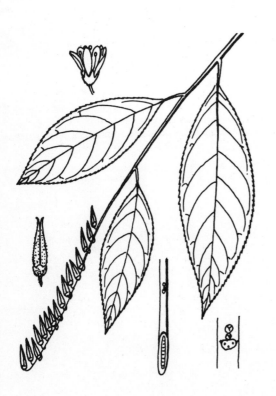

Virginia Willow

Swamp Leucothoë

LOBLOLLY BAY *Gordonia lasianthus* (L.) Ellis   Tea Family

FIELD MARKS: An evergreen tree occasionally 60 to 70 feet tall; growing in bogs and the borders of swamps in the southeastern coastal plains. *Leaves* thick and leathery in texture, narrowly elliptic, pointed at both ends, margin shallowly saw-toothed above the middle, dark green and shiny above, paler beneath, 4 to 6 inches long. *Flowers* 2 to 2½ inches across with 5 white petals and numerous golden stamens, fragrant, long-stalked; blooming July to September. *Fruits* are egg-shaped woody pods about ¾ inch long, containing small blackish winged seeds; maturing in September or October.

RANGE: Southeastern Virginia south to central Florida; west to southern Mississippi.

AMERICAN SNOWBELL *Styrax americana* Lam.   Storax Family

FIELD MARKS. A leaf-losing shrub 3 to about 12 feet high; growing along streams and in swampy places. *Leaves* alternate, elliptic or sometimes broadest above the middle, pointed at both ends, margin untoothed or with rather widely spaced and low teeth, bright green and smooth above, paler and smooth or with scattered starry-branched hairs beneath (scaly and more densely hairy beneath in the variety *pulverulenta* [Michx.] Perkins), ¾ to 3 inches long. *Flowers* white, about ½ inch long, with 5 long and often recurved lobes, solitary or in leafy-bracted clusters of 5 to 20 in leaf axils or at ends of branchlets; blooming April to June. *Fruits* roundish, dry, 1-seeded, about ¼ inch in diameter.

RANGE. Southern Virginia to Ohio Valley region, Missouri, and Arkansas; south to Florida and Texas. Var. *pulverulenta* chiefly on Coastal Plain from Virginia and Arkansas southward.

Also called Mock-orange.

VIRGINIA WILLOW *Itea virginica* L.   Saxifrage Family

FIELD MARKS. A leaf-losing shrub 3 to 8 feet high with slender and wandlike branches; growing in swamps and along streams. *Branchlets* slender, green or reddish-tinged, often minutely downy, the white pith showing interruptions when cut lengthwise. *Leaves* alternate, elliptic or sometimes broadest above the middle, pointed at both ends, finely and sharply toothed on margin, smooth on both surfaces or sparingly hairy beneath, 2 to 4 inches long. *Flowers* rather small, 5-petalled, white, in narrow upright end clusters 3 to 5 inches long; blooming April to June. *Fruits* narrowly cone-shaped, 2-grooved, downy capsules about ¼ inch long; containing numerous small flattened seeds.

RANGE. New Jersey and southeastern Pennsylvania south to Florida; southern illinois, Kentucky, and Missouri south to Louisiana and Texas.

Also called Sweet-spires and Tassel-white.

SWAMP LEUCOTHOË *Leucothoë racemosa* (L.) Gray   Heath Family

FIELD MARKS. A leaf-losing shrub 5 to about 12 feet high, with ascending and spreading branches; growing in swampy thickets, along streams, and about shallow ponds. *Leaves* alternate, lance-shaped or elliptic, pointed at both ends, finely and sharply toothed on margin, bright green and smooth above, paler and usually somewhat downy on the veins beneath, 1 to 3 inches long. *Flowers* white or pale pink, narrowly bell-shaped, fragrant; many standing erect in long, narrow, stiffly spreading clusters; blooming April to June. *Fruits* roundish, somewhat flattened, 5-parted capsules about 3/16 inch in diameter.

RANGE. Massachusetts, southeastern New York, and southeastern Pennsylvania; south to Florida, west to Louisiana.

SWEET-PEPPERBUSH *Clethra alnifolia* L.   White-alder Family

FIELD MARKS. A leaf-losing shrub 3 to 10 feet high, the older stems with dark gray or blackish and flaky bark; growing in wet or swampy, and usually sandy, woods and thickets. *Branchlets* slender, grayish brown, minutely downy. *Leaves* alternate, broadest above the middle, wedge-shaped at base, bluntly pointed or abruptly sharp-pointed at tip, sharply and doubly toothed on margin to somewhat below the middle, green and smooth or nearly so on both surfaces, 1½ to 3 inches long. *Flowers* white or (rarely) pinkish, 5-petalled, fragrant, in narrow end clusters from 2 to 6 inches in length; blooming June to September. *Fruits* roundish capsules about ⅛ inch in diameter, on ascending stalks; maturing September or October.

RANGE. Chiefly coastal plain; southern Maine and New Hampshire, south to Florida, west to eastern Texas.

Leaves Opposite—Simple—Entire or Toothed

SWAMP-PRIVET *Foresteria acuminata* (Michx.) Poir.   Olive Family

FIELD MARKS. A leaf-losing shrub or small tree 4 to (rarely) 25 feet high; growing in river swamps, borders of ponds, and along streams. *Leaves* opposite, slender-stalked, oblong egg-shaped or broadly lance-shaped, tapering to a point at both ends, margin usually finely toothed above the middle, thin in texture, light green and smooth on both surfaces, 1¼ to about 4 inches long. *Flowers* very small, greenish or yellowish, in dense clusters; blooming March to May. *Fruits* dark purple, narrowly ellipsoid and pointed at both ends, 1-seeded, with a rather thin flesh, about ½ inch long; ripening May to July.

RANGE. South Carolina to southern Indiana, Illinois and Missouri, and southeastern Kansas; south to Florida and Texas.

CLIMBING-HYDRANGEA *Decumaria barbara* L.   Saxifrage Family

FIELD MARKS. A semi-evergreen vine climbing trunks of trees by means of aerial root-lets on its stems; growing in rich, moist woods and swamps. *Leaves* opposite, egg-shaped or elliptic, broadly pointed to roundish at base, usually somewhat pointed at tip, margin usually with low teeth above the middle, bright green and lustrous above, paler and sometimes slightly downy beneath, thickish in texture, 1½ to 4 inches long. *Flowers* small, white, fragrant, in stalked flat-topped clusters at ends of branchlets; blooming April to June. *Fruits* small, urn-shaped, prominently ribbed capsules containing numerous small seeds.

RANGE. Southeastern Virginia to northwestern South Carolina and Tennessee, south to Florida and Texas.

Leaves Opposite—Compound

CROSS-VINE *Bignonia capreolata* L.   Bignonia Family

FIELD MARKS. A high-climbing vine which is evergreen southward; growing in moist woods and swamps. *Branchlets* show cross-shaped pith in cross-section. *Leaves* opposite, divided into 2 leaflets with a branched tendril between them; leaflets stalked, oblong-egg-shaped, heart-shaped at base, pointed at tip, untoothed on margin, smooth, paler beneath, 2 to 5 inches long. *Flowers* trumpet-shaped, orange red outside and yellow within, 5-lobed, 1½ to 2½ inches long, 2 to 5 in axillary clusters; blooming April to June. *Fruits* cylindrical, somewhat flattened, 2-celled capsules 4 to 6 inches long, containing many winged and flattened seeds; maturing July or August.

RANGE. Maryland to southern Ohio and Illinois, and Missouri; south to Florida and Louisiana.

Sweet-pepperbush

Swamp-privet

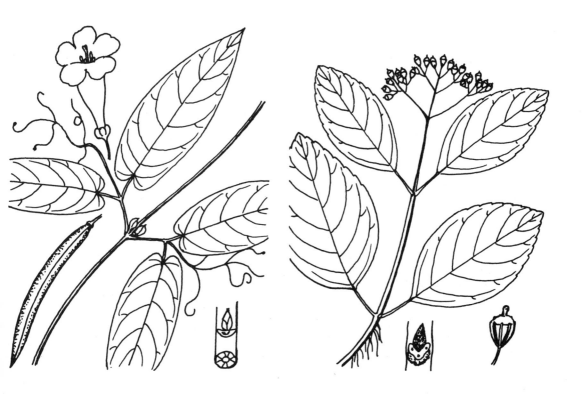

Cross-vine

Climbing-hydrangea

Devilwood

Pinckneya

Stiff Dogwood

Bedstraw St. John's-wort

DEVILWOOD *Osmanthus americanus* (L.) Gray   Olive Family

FIELD MARKS. An evergreen shrub or small tree; growing in woods and borders of coastal swamps. *Leaves* opposite, narrowly elliptic or top-shaped, pointed at base, pointed to rounded at tip, untoothed on margin, leathery, lustrous above, paler beneath, smooth, 2½ to 4½ inches long. *Flowers* small, creamy white, in axillary clusters; blooming April or May. *Fruits* egg-shaped, olive-like, 1-seeded, dark bluish purple, ½ to ¾ inch long; ripening August to October.

RANGE. Coastal plain; Virginia south to Florida, west to Louisiana.

Also called Wild-olive.

PINCKNEYA *Pinckneya pubens* Michx.   Madder Family

FIELD MARKS. A leaf-losing shrub or small tree 5 to rarely 25 feet high; growing in sandy swamps or along streams. *Branchlets* more or less tawny- to rusty-hairy. *Leaves* opposite, elliptic to egg-shaped, pointed to roundish at base, pointed at tip, untoothed on margin, somewhat hairy above, paler and more densely hairy beneath, 5 to 8 inches long. *Flowers* tubular, greenish yellow spotted with red, 5-lobed; with 1 or 2 calyx lobes expanded into a broad pink to whitish, petal-like blade; borne in large and showy end clusters; blooming in May. *Fruits* roundish capsules about ¾ inch in diameter, containing many small seeds with wings.

RANGE. Coastal plain; southeastern South Carolina south to Florida.

Also called Georgia-bark and Fevertree. The bark was used by early settlers for the treatment of malaria.

STIFF DOGWOOD *Cornus stricta* Lam.   Dogwood Family

FIELD MARKS. A shrub or small tree 5 to 15 feet high; growing in wet woods, swamps, and along streams. *Branchlets* slender, smooth, reddish or partly green and becoming gray, with a white pith. *Leaves* elliptic to egg-shaped or broadly lance-shaped, usually pointed at base, pointed at tip, smooth or nearly so on both surfaces, dark dull green above, slightly paler beneath, with 4 or 5 pairs of veins, 2 to 5 inches long. *Flowers* creamy white, in a flat-topped cluster; blooming April to June. *Fruits* pale blue, roundish, about ¼ inch in diameter; ripening July to September.

RANGE. Eastern Virginia to southern Indiana and southeastern Missouri; south to Florida and eastern Texas.

BEDSTRAW ST. JOHN'S-WORT *Hypericum galioides* Lam.   St. John's-wort Family

FIELD MARKS. An evergreen shrub 1 to about 4 feet high; growing in low wet pinelands and swamps. *Branchlets* slender, nearly round. *Leaves* stalkless, flat, narrow but usually slightly broadened upward, pointed at tip, tapering to base, thickish and firm in texture, dark green above, slightly paler beneath, smooth on both surfaces, ½ to about 2 inches long. *Flowers* bright yellow, about ½ inch across, 5-petalled, the sepals narrow and similar to the leaves, in rather narrow and elongate end clusters; blooming June to August. *Fruits* conical egg-shaped, pointed capsules about ¼ inch long.

RANGE. Coastal plain; North Carolina south to Florida, west to Louisiana.

DWARF HUCKLEBERRY *Gaylussacia dumosa* (Andr.) T. & G.   Heath Family

FIELD MARKS. A leaf-losing shrub 6 inches to 2 feet high, with creeping underground stems; growing in dry sandy woods. *Branchlets* slender, zigzag, more or less downy. *Leaves* broadest above the middle, wedge-shaped at base, abruptly short-pointed at tip, margin untoothed, thickish, bright green on both sides, lustrous above, somewhat glandular-hairy and resin-dotted beneath, 1 to 2½ inches long. *Flowers* whitish to greenish pink or reddish, bell-shaped, in leafy-bracted clusters; blooming March to June. *Fruits* black, sometimes glandular-hairy, ¼ to ⅜ inch in diameter; ripening June to August.

RANGE. Newfoundland and New Brunswick to eastern Pennsylvania and Tennessee, south to Florida and Louisiana.

BLACK HUCKLEBERRY *Gaylussacia baccata* (Wang.) K. Koch   Heath Family

FIELD MARKS. A leaf-losing shrub 1½ to 3 feet high, with erect branches and with young growth copiously dotted with sticky resin globules; growing in dry sandy or rocky woods and sometimes in bogs. *Leaves* elliptic to oval or oblong lance-shaped (rarely broadest above the middle) pointed at base, pointed to blunt at tip, margin untoothed, yellowish green above and scarcely paler beneath, resin-dotted on both surfaces but more densely so beneath, 1 to 2½ inches long. *Flowers* greenish tinged with pink or red, egg-shaped, in short clusters; blooming April to June. *Fruits usually* lustrous black, about ¼ inch in diameter, sweet; ripening July and August.

RANGE. Newfoundland to Saskatchewan, south to Georgia and Louisiana.

DEERBERRY *Vaccinium stamineum* L.   Heath Family

FIELD MARKS. A leaf-losing shrub 2 to 10 feet high; growing in dry rocky or sandy woods and thickets. *Branchlets* reddish purple, often downy or with a whitish bloom. *Leaves* elliptic or egg-shaped, pointed to rounded at base, usually pointed at tip, untoothed on margin, thin, smooth above, smooth or downy and often whitened beneath, 1 to 3½ inches long. *Flowers* greenish white or purple-tinged, open bell-shaped, in leafy-bracted clusters; blooming April to June. *Fruits* greenish or pale purplish, often whitened with a bloom, 5/16 to ½ inch in diameter, rather sour but edible when cooked; ripening July to October.

RANGE. Massachusetts to southern Ontario and Kansas; south to Florida and Louisiana.

Also called Squaw-huckleberry.

LATE LOW BLUEBERRY *Vaccinium vacillans* Torr.   Heath Family

FIELD MARKS. A spreading leaf-losing shrub 8 inches to about 2 feet high; growing in dry sandy or rocky woods and clearings. *Branchlets* yellowish green, warty-dotted, somewhat angled. *Leaves* short-stalked, oval to egg-shaped or broadest above the middle, usually broadly pointed at both ends, untoothed or sometimes finely toothed on margin, smooth on both surfaces, paler and sometimes slightly whitened beneath, ½ to 2 inches long. *Flowers* greenish white or pink-tinged, cylindrical urn-shaped, clustered; blooming March to June, when leaves are partly grown. *Fruits* dark blue, usually with a whitish bloom, ¼ to ⅜ inch in diameter, sweet and juicy; ripening June to September.

RANGE. Western Nova Scotia to southern Ontario, Michigan, and northeastern Iowa; south to Georgia, Alabama, and eastern Kansas.

64

Dwarf Huckleberry

Black Huckleberry

Deerberry

Late Low Blueberry

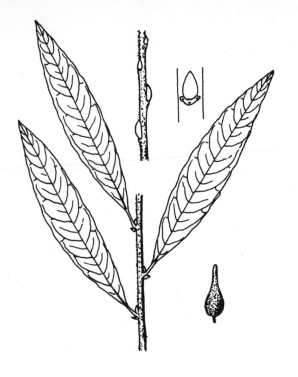

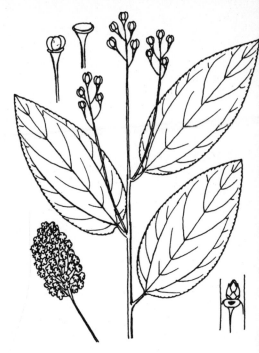

Prairie Willow

New Jersey-tea

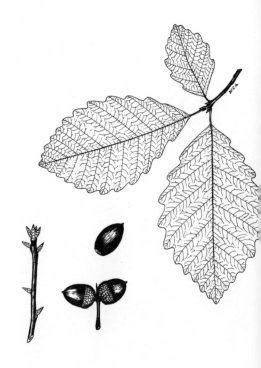

American Hophornbeam

Chestnut Oak

PRAIRIE WILLOW *Salix humilis* Marsh.   Willow Family

FIELD MARKS. A shrub 2 to 10 feet high which is often common on dry and barren soils. *Branchlets* wandlike, erect, usually coated with a dirty-grayish down. *Leaves* narrowly elliptic, often broadest above the middle, pointed at both ends, margin slightly rolled, wavy, usually untoothed but sometimes sparingly toothed, bright green to dull grayish green and wrinkled-veiny above, pale and usually grayish-woolly beneath, 2 to 5 inches long. The leafstalks are stout and often have stipules at the base.

RANGE. Newfoundland and Labrador to Ontario and Minnesota; south to Florida and eastern Texas.

Leaves Alternate—Simple—Toothed

NEW JERSEY-TEA *Ceanothus americanus* L.   Buckthorn Family

FIELD MARKS. A leaf-losing shrub 1 to 3 feet high; growing on dry, rocky, wooded slopes and in clearings. *Leaves* alternate, egg-shaped, rounded or somewhat heart-shaped at base, pointed at tip, finely toothed on margin, more or less hairy above, paler and downy beneath, 1 to 3 inches long, with 3 prominent veins from near summit of the short leafstalks. *Flowers* small, white, in dense, cylindrical, long-stalked clusters; blooming May to August. *Fruits* small, 3-lobed capsules containing 3 pale-brown seeds; maturing August to October; the silvery-lined, cup-shaped bases persisting into the winter.

RANGE. Maine to southern Quebec and Manitoba; south to Florida and Texas.

The leaves were used as a substitute for tea during the American Revolution; and the large red roots yield a dye.

AMERICAN HOPHORNBEAM *Ostrya virginiana* (Mill.) K. Koch   Birch Family

FIELD MARKS: A tree 20 to rarely 60 feet tall; usually growing on dry and often rocky slopes. *Bark* grayish-brown, broken into small rectangular scales which are loose at the ends and give the trunk a shreddy appearance. *Leaves* oblong egg-shaped, pointed at tip, rounded or somewhat heart-shaped at base, margin doubly saw-toothed, thin but tough in texture, dull yellowish-green above, paler and often somewhat hairy beneath, 3 to 5 inches long. *Fruit* a small flattened nutlet enclosed in the base of a papery and bag-like bract, arranged in drooping hop-like clusters; maturing August to October.

RANGE: Nova Scotia west to Minnesota; south to Florida and Texas.

Also called Ironwood.

CHESTNUT OAK *Quercus prinus* L.   Beech Family

FIELD MARKS: A tree usually 50 to 70 feet tall; growing on dry and rocky slopes and ridges. *Bark* blackish, deeply furrowed with blocky, irregular V-shaped ridges. *Leaves* 4 to 8 inches long, elliptic or broadest above the middle, margin with large and rounded teeth, shiny dark yellowish-green above, paler beneath and smooth or nearly so. *Fruit* a shiny chestnut-brown, oblong egg-shaped acorn 1 to 1½ inches long, seated in a deeply bowl-shaped cup; maturing in 1 year; kernel sweetish.

RANGE: Southern Maine and Ontario south to northern Georgia and northeastern Mississippi.

Also called Rock Oak.

COMMON CHINQUAPIN *Castanea pumila* (L.) Mill.   Beech Family

FIELD MARKS. A shrub or small tree to about 30 feet high; growing in dry woods and thickets. *Leaves* narrowly elliptic, pointed at both ends or occasionally rounded at base, coarsely and sharply toothed on margin, smooth above, paler and whitish-downy beneath, 3 to 5 inches long. *Fruits* shiny brown, silky-hairy nuts ¼ to ½ inch across; usually solitary in a densely prickly bur.

RANGE. Massachusetts and New Jersey to Tennessee and Arkansas; south to Florida and eastern Texas.

CHINQUAPIN OAK *Quercus muhlenbergii* Engelm.   Beech Family

FIELD MARKS: A tree 50 to 70 feet or more tall; growing on dry slopes but of largest size in rich bottomlands. *Bark* light ashy-gray, rough and flaky. *Leaves* 4 to 7 inches long, broadly lance-shaped, margin coarsely toothed with often slightly incurved blunt to pointed teeth, shiny dark yellowish-green above, paler and usually somewhat downy beneath. *Fruit* an egg-shaped, brown to blackish acorn ½ to ¾ inch long, seated in a bowl-shaped cup; maturing in 1 year; kernel sweetish.

RANGE: Southern Ontario west to Minnesota and Nebraska; south to Delaware, northwestern Florida and Texas.

Also called Yellow Oak.

Leaves Alternate—Simple—Lobed

POST OAK *Quercus stellata* Wang.   Beech Family

FIELD MARKS: A tree 30 to 50 feet tall; usually growing on poor, dry, rocky or sandy soils. *Leaves* 4 to 6 inches long, broadest above the middle, usually 5-lobed, the center lobes larger with squarish ends giving the leaf a cross-shaped appearance, thick and leathery in texture, shiny dark green above, paler and somewhat downy beneath. *Fruit* an egg-shaped brown acorn ½ to ⅔ inch long, seated in a bowl-shaped cup; maturing in 1 year; kernel sweetish.

RANGE: Massachusetts to southern Pennsylvania west to Iowa; south to northern Florida and Texas.

SCARLET OAK *Quercus coccinea* Muenchh.   Beech Family

FIELD MARKS: A tree 60 to 80 feet or more tall; commonly growing on dry and rocky slopes. *Bark* blackish and rough, the inner bark pale red. *Leaves* 3 to 6 inches long, with 5 to 9 long and narrow bristle-tipped and sparingly bristle-toothed lobes, the deep rounded sinuses between them extending more than half way to the midrib, shiny dark green above, paler and smooth beneath. *Fruit* a light reddish-brown, roundish or short oval acorn about ¾ inch long, about half enclosed by the top-shaped, shiny-scaled cup; maturing in 2 years; kernal mildly bitter.

RANGE: Maine west to southern Ontario and Minnesota; south to northern Georgia, Mississippi and Oklahoma.

The leaves turn a bright red or scarlet in fall. Especially common in the southern Appalachian region.

68

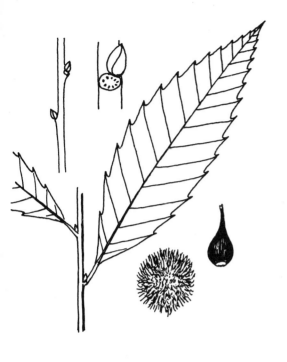

Common Chinquapin

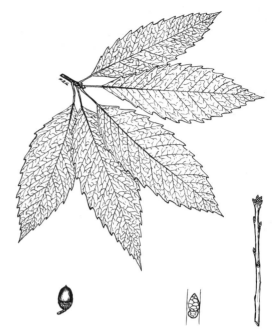

Chinquapin Oak

Post Oak

Scarlet Oak

Black Oak

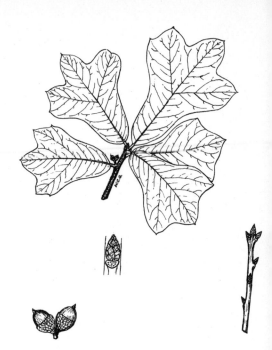

Blackjack Oak

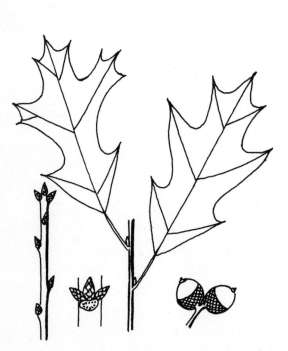

Scrub Oak

Fragrant Sumac

BLACK OAK *Quercus velutina* Lam.   Beech Family

FIELD MARKS: A tree 60 to 80 feet or more tall; growing in dry to fairly moist upland areas. *Bark* black, ridged and furrowed, the inner bark bright yellow. *Leaves* 4 to 8 inches long, with 5 or 7 bristle-tipped and bristle-toothed lobes, the sinuses between them varying from rather shallow to quite deep, shiny dark green above, paler yellowish-green and coated with a powdery yellowish down beneath. *Fruit* an egg-shaped, light brown, often downy acorn ½ to ¾ inch long; seated in a top-shaped, downy-scaled cup with loose-tipped scales toward the rim; maturing in 2 years; kernel yellow and very bitter.

RANGE: Maine west to Minnesota; south to northern Florida and eastern Texas.

BLACKJACK OAK *Quercus marilandica* Muenchh.   Beech Family

FIELD MARKS: A tree 20 to rarely 50 feet tall; growing in poor, dry, sandy or rocky soils. *Leaves* 4 to 7 inches long and almost as broad, much broader above the middle, shallowly 3-lobed toward the tip, narrowed below the middle to a rounded base, thick and leathery in texture, shiny dark green above, paler and coated with pale brownish down beneath. *Fruit* a roundish egg-shaped, yellowish-brown acorn about ¾ inch long, enclosed for about half its length by the bowl of a top-shaped, downy-scaled cup; maturing in 2 years; kernel bitter.

RANGE: Southeastern New York west to southern Michigan and Nebraska; south to central Florida and eastern Texas.

SCRUB OAK *Quercus ilicifolia* Wang.   Beech Family

FIELD MARKS. A leaf-losing shrub or small tree 3 or more feet high; growing on dry and barren uplands and slopes. *Leaves* oblong-oval or often broadest above the middle, with 3 to 7 (usually 5) short, broadly triangular, bristle-tipped, and sparingly bristle-toothed lobes, dark green and lustrous above, whitish-downy beneath, 2 to 4 inches long. *Fruits* egg-shaped acorns about ⅜ inch long which are about half covered by a bowl-shaped cup.

RANGE. Maine to New York and western Pennsylvania; south to Virginia, West Virginia, and western North Carolina.

Also known as the Bear Oak.

Leaves Alternate—Compound

FRAGRANT SUMAC *Rhus aromatica* Ait.   Cashew Family

FIELD MARKS. A leaf-losing, aromatic shrub 2 to 6 feet high; growing on dry rocky banks and hillsides. *Branchlets* pleasantly fragrant when bruised, often with catkin-like flower buds. *Leaves* alternate, rather long-stalked, compound, 4 to 6 inches long; leaflets 3, the end one short-stalked and commonly diamond-shaped, the side ones egg-shaped and almost stalkless, all usually pointed at base, pointed or blunt at tip, coarsely and irregularly toothed on margin, somewhat downy, 1 to 3 inches long. *Flowers* small, yellowish green, in catkin-like clusters; blooming March or April. *Fruits* roundish, red, densely hairy, about 1¼ inch in diameter; maturing July or August.

RANGE. Vermont and southwestern Quebec to Indiana, Kansas, Nebraska, and Oklahoma; south to Florida and Texas.

ST. PETER'S-WORT *Hypericum stans* (Michx.) Adams & Robson.   St. John's-wort
Family

FIELD MARKS. A shrub with a simple or sparingly branched, more or less erect stem 1 to 3 feet high; growing in sandy woods and fields. *Branchlets* prominently 2-edged or 2-winged. *Leaves* oblong-oval, stalkless, rounded to somewhat heart-shaped and often clasping the stem at the base, rounded at tip, thickish and firm in texture, smooth, ½ to 1½ inches long. *Flowers* ¾ to 1¼ inches across, with 4 bright yellow petals, 2 outer sepals which are large and heart-shaped and 2 inner ones very much smaller and narrow, pistil with 3 or 4 styles; blooming July to September. *Fruits* egg-shaped capsules about ⅜ inch long.

RANGE. Southeastern Massachusetts to southeastern Pennsylvania and Kentucky, south to Florida and Texas.

SNOWBERRY *Symphoricarpos albus* (L.) Blake   Honeysuckle Family

FIELD MARKS. A finely branched leaf-losing shrub 1 to about 5 feet high; growing on dry, rocky, wooded slopes and banks. *Branchlets* very slender, smooth or slightly hairy. *Leaves* opposite, short-stalked, oblong-elliptic to roundish, rounded or bluntly pointed at both ends, untoothed or somewhat wavy or margin (sometimes lobed on vigorous shoots), thin in texture, green on both surfaces, smooth above and smooth or slightly downy beneath, ¾ to 2 inches long. *Flowers* pink, about ¼ inch long, corolla 5-lobed, in leaf axils or end clusters; blooming May to July. *Fruits* roundish, white berries ¼ to ½ inch in diameter; ripening August to October.

RANGE. Eastern Quebec to British Columbia; south to Massachusetts, western Virginia, Michigan, Wisconsin, Nebraska, and Colorado.

Often cultivated as an ornamental shrub.

CORALBERRY *Symphoricarpos orbiculatus* Moench.   Honeysuckle Family

FIELD MARKS. A finely branched leaf-losing shrub 2 to about 5 feet high; growing in low woods or dry, rocky, wooded slopes. *Branchlets* very slender, usually finely downy. *Leaves* opposite, short-stalked, egg-shaped to roundish, rounded or bluntly pointed at both ends, untoothed but often wavy on margin, dull green and smooth or nearly so above, paler and finely downy beneath, ½ to 2 inches long. *Flowers* pinkish, about 3/16 inch long, corolla 5-lobed, in short but dense clusters in the leaf axils; blooming July to September. *Fruits* roundish or slightly egg-shaped, purplish- to coral-red berries, about 3/16 inch in diameter; ripening September to November and persisting.

RANGE. Pennsylvania to Ohio, Illinois, Minnesota, South Dakota, and Colorado; south to northern Georgia, Alabama, and Mississippi.

Commonly cultivated as an ornamental and frequently escaping. Also called Indian-currant.

Leaves Opposite—Simple—Toothed

DOWNY ARROWWOOD *Viburnum rafinesquianum* Schultes   Honeysuckle Family

FIELD MARKS. A leaf-losing shrub 2 to 5 feet high, with slender grayish-barked stems; growing on dry wooded slopes and banks. *Branchlets* roundish, smooth or nearly so. *Leaves* stalkless or very short-stalked and with narrow stipules, egg-shaped or oblong egg-shaped, rounded at base, pointed at tip, with prominent lateral veins ending in coarse and sharp marginal teeth, smooth or nearly so above, softly downy beneath, 1½ to 3 inches long. *Flowers* all alike; blooming April to June. *Fruits* oval-shaped, purplish black, about ¼ inch long; ripening July to September.

RANGE. Quebec to Manitoba; south to central North Carolina, northern Georgia, Kentucky, and Missouri.

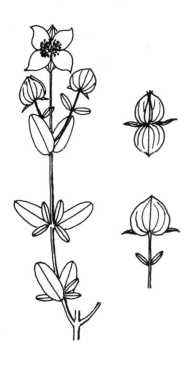

St. Peter's-wort

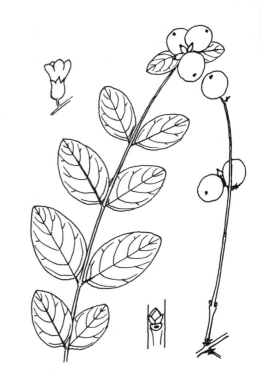

Snowberry

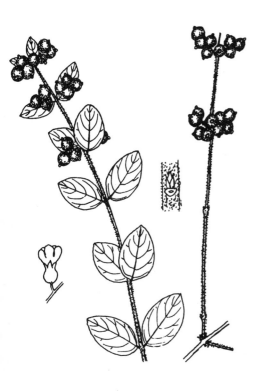

Coralberry

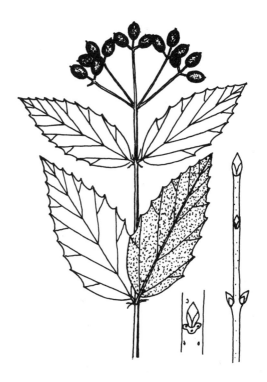

Downy Arrowwood

Bearberry

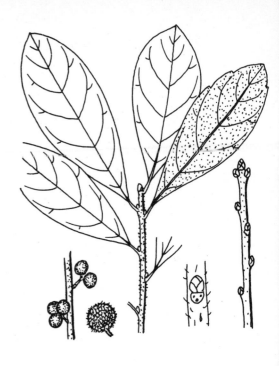

Bayberry

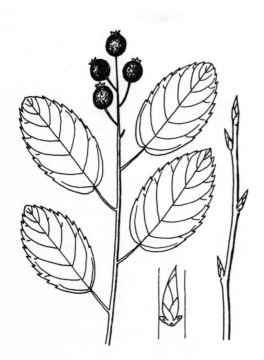

Low Juneberry

Canada Buffaloberry

NORTHERN WOODY PLANTS OF DRY PLACES
Leaves Alternate—Simple

BEARBERRY *Arctostaphylos uva-ursi* (L.) Spreng. Heath Family

FIELD MARKS. A trailing evergreen shrub, the long and flexible branches often rooting at the nodes; growing on tundras and rocky or sandy open areas. *Branchlets* smooth to white-woolly or sticky-downy; later becoming reddish brown to grayish brown, and with papery peeling bark. *Leaves* alternate, short-stalked, usually broadest above the middle, wedge-shaped at base, rounded at tip, untoothed on margin, leathery, smooth or nearly so on both surfaces, lustrous above, paler beneath, ½ to 1¼ inches long. *Flowers* white or pinkish, urn-shaped, almost ¼ inch long, in small end clusters; blooming May to July and rarely October or November. *Fruits* roundish, red, about ¼ inch in diameter, with mealy flesh and 5 to 10 seeds; ripening August or September and persisting.

RANGE. Labrador to Alaska; south to eastern Virginia, the region of the Great Lakes, South Dakota, New Mexico, and California.

Leaves used medicinally, for tanning leather, and for making dyes. Mixed with tobacco by Indians and called Kinnikinnik. Berries eaten by grouse and bears.

BAYBERRY *Myrica pensylvanica* Loisel. Bayberry Family

FIELD MARKS. An aromatic leaf-losing shrub 3 to about 6 feet high; usually growing in dry sandy soils or on sand dunes. *Branchlets* grayish to ashy brown, often slightly hairy and resin-dotted, pleasantly fragrant when broken. *Leaves* alternate, elliptic or slightly broader above the middle, untoothed or sometimes with a few teeth toward the blunt tip, dull green and sometimes a little hairy above, paler and downy and resin-dotted beneath, 1½ to 3½ inches long, pleasantly fragrant when crushed. *Fruits* are bony nutlets which are minutely hairy and coated with whitish wax, about 3/16 inch in diameter.

RANGE. Coastal plain from Newfoundland south to North Carolina, inland near the Great Lakes to northern Ohio.

Wax of the fruits is used to make bayberry candles. The fruits are eaten by many wild birds. Leaves have been used as a substitute for bay leaves in seasoning. Rather attractive as an ornamental shrub and very useful in soil conservation.

LOW JUNEBERRY *Amelanchier humilis* Wieg. Rose Family

FIELD MARKS. A shrub 1 to 3 feet high, with creeping underground stems and colony-forming; growing in dry rocky or sandy places. Leaves oval to oblong, rounded to heart-shaped at base, round or bluntly pointed at tip, margin with rather large teeth to slightly below the middle, smooth or nearly so on both surfaces, 1 to 2 inches long. *Fruits* black but with a whitish bloom, sweet and juicy; ripening July or August.

RANGE. Quebec and Ontario; south to Vermont, West Virginia, the region of the Great Lakes, and South Dakota.

Leaves Opposite—Simple

CANADA BUFFALOBERRY *Shepherdia canadensis* (L.) Nutt. Oleaster Family

FIELD MARKS. A leaf-losing shrub 3 to 5 feet high; growing in sandy or rocky woods and along streams. *Branchlets* slender; densely coated with rusty, branlike scales. *Leaves* opposite, short-stalked, elliptic to egg-shaped, roundish to broadly pointed at base, blunt at tip, margin untoothed, dull green above, coated with silvery starry-branched hairs and rusty scales beneath, ¾ to 1½ inches long. *Flowers* small, yellowish green, bell-shaped, clustered; blooming April or May, before the leaves appear. *Fruits* berry-like, egg-shaped, reddish or yellowish, 1-seeded, about ¼ inch in diameter; ripening June to August.

RANGE. Newfoundland to Alaska; south to Maine, Vermont, the region of the Great Lakes, South Dakota, and New Mexico.

COMMON PERSIMMON *Diospyros virginiana* L.   Ebony Family

FIELD MARKS: A tree 25 to 50 feet or more tall; growing in dry soils and often in old fields. *Bark* blackish, broken into squarish blocks and resembling alligator skin. *Leaves* 3 to 6 inches long, oval to oblong egg-shaped, mostly rounded at base, pointed at tip, untoothed on margin, shiny dark green above, paler and sometimes downy beneath. *Flowers* small, yellowish-green, the stamen-bearing and pistil-bearing ones on separate trees; blooming May or June. *Fruits* roundish, pulpy, orange or purplish-tinged berries 1 to 1½ inches across, with 4 persistent woody calyx lobes at the base; very astringent until ripening about October then sweet and juicy.

RANGE: Connecticut and southeastern New York west to southeastern Iowa; south to Florida and eastern Texas.

STAGGERBUSH *Lyonia mariana* (L.) D. Don   Heath Family

FIELD MARKS. A leaf-losing shrub 8 inches to nearly 4 feet high, with slender upright branches; growing in peaty or sandy open woods. *Leaves* alternate, elliptic or broadest above the middle, pointed at base, sharply to bluntly pointed at tip, untoothed on margin, bright green and smooth above, paler and minutely black-dotted and sometimes downy on the veins beneath, 1 to 3 inches long. *Flowers* white or pale pink, barrel-shaped, about ⅜ inch long, the 5 calyx lobes narrow and spreading, in several whorled clusters on leafless tips of branchlets; blooming April to June. *Fruits* urn-shaped, 5-angled, point capsules about ¼ inch long.

RANGE. Chiefly coastal plain; Southern Rhode Island, southeastern New York, and southeastern Pennsylvania; south to Florida, west to Texas, and north in the Mississippi Valley to Arkansas and eastern Tennessee.

Foliage poisonous to calves and lambs if eaten.

SPARKLEBERRY *Vaccinium arboreum* Marsh.   Heath Family

FIELD MARKS. A leaf-losing, or southward an evergreen, shrub or small tree 4 to 30 feet high; growing in dry sandy or rocky woods. *Leaves* elliptic to oval or broadest above the middle, more or less pointed at both ends, margin sometimes minutely toothed or slightly rolled inward on lower surface, somewhat leathery in texture, lustrous above, paler and sometimes downy beneath, ¾ to 2 inches long. *Flowers* white, bell-shaped, in leafy-bracted clusters; blooming April to June. *Fruits* black, lustrous, about ¼ inch in diameter, rather dry and insipid; ripening September or October.

RANGE. Virginia to southern Indiana and Illinois, Missouri, and Oklahoma; south to Florida and Texas.

Also called Farkleberry and Tree-huckleberry.

DWARF THORN *Crataegus uniflora* Muenchh.   Rose Family

FIELD MARKS. An irregularly branched and sprawling shrub 2 to 5 feet high; growing on sandy soils or rocky banks. *Branches* long, slender, often quite flexible, with thorns ½ to 1 inch long. *Leaves* elliptic or broadest above the middle, wedge-shaped at base, rounded or bluntly pointed at tip, margin bluntly toothed and sometimes obscurely lobed above the middle, thick-textured, dark green and lustrous but sometimes roughish-hairy above and with sunken veins, paler and more or less downy beneath, ½ to 1½ inches long; leafstalks short. *Flowers* usually solitary, blooming April or May. *Fruits* greenish yellow to dull red, 3- to 5-seeded; ripening in October.

RANGE. Southeastern New York and southeastern Pennsylvania south to Florida, west to Texas, and north in Mississippi Valley to southern Missouri.

76

Common Persimmon

Staggerbush

Sparkleberry

Dwarf Thorn

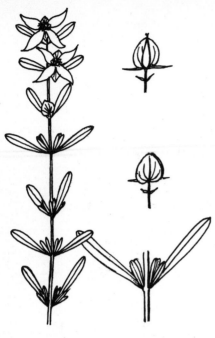

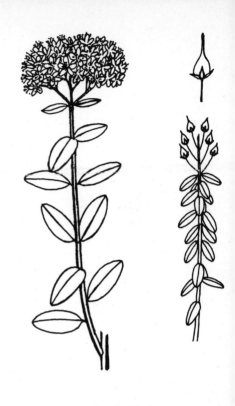

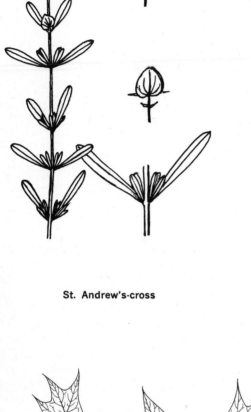

St. Andrew's-cross

Sandmyrtle

Turkey Oak

Poison-oak

SOUTHERN WOODY PLANTS OF DRY PLACES, Continued
Leaves Opposite—Simple—Entire

ST. ANDREW'S-CROSS *Hypericum hypericoides* (L.) Crantz   St. John's-wort
Family

FIELD MARKS. A more or less erect and branching shrub to about 3 feet high; growing in dry sandy or rocky fields and open woods. *Branchlets* flattened and 2-edged. *Leaves* stalkless, ¼ to about 1 inch long and mostly less than ⅛ inch wide, broadest toward the tip, wedge-shaped at base, blunt at tip, smooth. *Flowers* about ½ inch across, with 4 bright-yellow petals, 2 outer sepals which are large and egg-shaped or heart-shaped and 2 inner ones very much smaller and narrow, pistil with 2 styles; blooming May to September. *Fruits* narrowly egg-shaped and somewhat flattened 2-celled capsules about ¼ inch long.
RANGE. Virginia and Tennessee south to Florida and Texas.

SANDMYRTLE *Leiophyllum buxifolium* (Berg.) Ell.   Heath Family

FIELD MARKS. A much-branched evergreen shrub 6 inches to 2½ feet high, with upright branches; growing in sandy pinelands and on rocky places in the mountains. *Leaves* mostly opposite, short-stalked, elliptic to oval, blunt at both ends, untoothed on margin, smooth, leathery, lustrous above, paler and dull beneath, smooth, ⅛ to ⅝ inch long. *Flowers* small, white, 5-petalled, in rather dense end clusters; blooming March to June. *Fruits* egg-shaped, 2- to 5-parted capsules about ⅛ inch long.
RANGE. Coastal plain, New Jersey to South Carolina; upper piedmont and mountains, eastern Kentucky, North and South Carolina.

Leaves Alternate—Simple—Lobed

TURKEY OAK *Quercus laevis* Walt.   Beech Family

FIELD MARKS: A tree rarely more than 20 to 30 feet tall; growing on poor, dry, sandy soils in the southern coastal plains. *Leaves* 5 to 10 inches long with usually 5 long, narrow, often curved, bristle-tipped and bristle-toothed lobes, shiny yellowish-green above, paler beneath, with distinctive pointed bases and short leaf stalks. *Fruit* an egg-shaped brown acorn about 1 inch long, woolly toward the summit, seated in the deep bowls of top-shaped cups; maturing in 2 years; kernel bitter.
RANGE: Southeastern Virginia south to central Florida; west to Louisiana.

Leaves Alternate—Compound

POISON-OAK *Rhus toxicodendron* L.   Cashew Family

CAUTION: All parts of this plant contain a dangerous skin irritant.
FIELD MARKS. A stiffly erect, simple or sparingly branched, leaf-losing shrub 1 to 2½ feet high; growing in dry sandy pine and oak woods and clearings. *Leaves* alternate, long-stalked, compound, 3 to 8 inches long; the 3 leaflets often broadly egg-shaped, pointed at base, blunt at tip, with 3 to 7 often deep lobes, somewhat downy above, more densely so and paler beneath, 2 to 5 inches long; the end leaflet rather long-stalked, the side ones almost stalkless; leafstalks downy. *Flowers* and *fruits* similar to those of Poison-ivy but usually more downy.
RANGE. Chiefly coastal plain; New Jersey and Maryland south to Florida; Tennessee to eastern Oklahoma south to Alabama and Texas.

79

Greenbriers are green-stemmed and often prickly vines which climb by means of paired tendrils on the bases of the leafstalks, these remaining after the leaves fall. The alternate leaves have from 3 to 7 prominent parallel veins and a network of smaller veins. The flowers are small, yellowish green, and borne in stalked umbels in the axils of the leaves. The fruits are small, usually roundish, 1- to 3-seeded berries.

The greenbriers often form impenetrable thickets. The starchy, tuberous roots of some species were used by the Indians as food. Rabbits and deer often eat the stems; the berries are eaten by many birds, including the ruffed grouse, wild turkey, and ring-necked pheasant. In the South, the greenbriers are popularly known as "bamboos."

COMMON GREENBRIER *Smilax rotundifolia* L.   Greenbrier Family

FIELD MARKS. A scrambling or climbing leaf-losing vine with round or sometimes 4-angled stems and branchlets; armed with scattered, stout, broad-based prickles. *Leaves* egg-shaped to broadly egg-shaped or nearly round, often with a heart-shaped base, green and lustrous on both surfaces, 5-veined, 2 to 6 inches long. *Fruits* bluish black, coated with a whitish bloom, about ¼ inch in diameter; the cluster on a stalk hardly as long as the leafstalk.

RANGE. Nova Scotia to Minnesota, south to Florida and Texas.

Widely distributed in moist woods and thickets. The most common species of greenbrier northward as well as southward along the mountains. Also known as Horsebrier and Round-leaf Brier.

BRISTLY GREENBRIER *Smilax hispida* Muhl.   Greenbrier Family

FIELD MARKS. A high-climbing, leaf-losing vine with stems thickly beset with weak bristly or needle-like blackish prickles (at least toward the base). *Leaves* thin, egg-shaped or broadly egg-shaped, lustrous green on both surfaces, 5- to 7-veined, 2 to 5 inches long, the margins roughish with minute bristle-tipped teeth. *Fruits* black, about ¼ inch in diameter, usually with a single shiny reddish-brown seed; the cluster on a stalk usually much longer than the leafstalk.

RANGE. New York to southern Ontario and Minnesota; south to Georgia and Mississippi.

A common greenbrier, especially in low moist thickets and woodlands and along the banks of streams.

GLAUCOUS GREENBRIER *Smilax glauca* Walt.   Greenbrier Family

FIELD MARKS. A leaf-losing, or sometimes partly evergreen, scrambling or high-climbing vine; its round stems whitened with a bloom and usually armed with numerous stout prickles. *Leaves* egg-shaped to broadly egg-shaped, green above but conspicuously whitened and sometimes downy beneath, 3- to 5-veined, 2 to 5 inches long. *Fruits* bluish black, whitened with a bloom, about ¼ inch in diameter; the cluster on a stalk much longer than the leafstalk.

RANGE. Massachusetts to Illinois, south to Florida and Texas.

Also known as Catbrier and Sawbrier. Often common in dry to moist woods, thickets, and clearings, and spreading by underground runners.

CHINABRIER *Smilax bona-nox* L.   Greenbrier Family

FIELD MARKS. A variable species which is sometimes high-climbing or partly evergreen; the 4-angled stems with usually some rigid prickles and starry-branched, scalelike hairs toward the base. *Leaves* more or less thick and leathery, commonly triangular or fiddle-shaped, the margins thickened and usually prickly, lustrous green on both surfaces or sometimes mottled with white, 5- to 7-veined, 2 to 5 inches long. *Fruits* bluish black, whitened with a bloom, about ¼ inch in diameter.

RANGE. Massachusetts to Illinois, south to Florida and Texas.

Also known as Bullbrier and Sawbrier. Often common southward in deciduous woods, old fields, and on sand dunes, but not present in the mountains.

Common Greenbrier

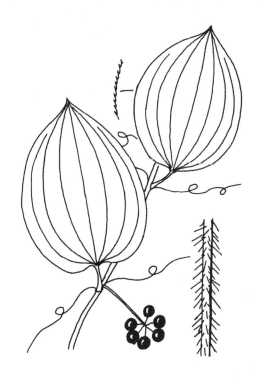

Bristly Greenbrier

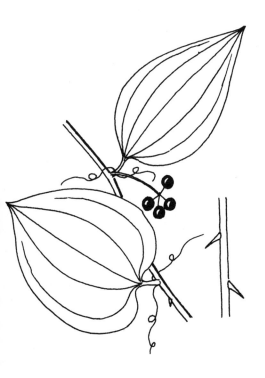

Glaucous Greenbrier

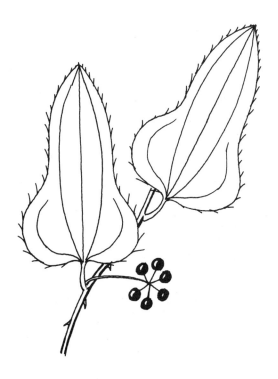

Chinabrier

Mountain-laurel

Leatherwood

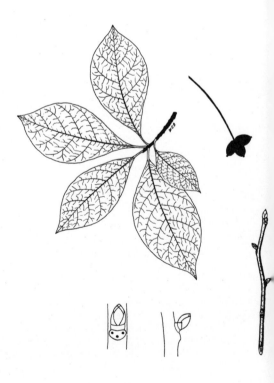

Common Pawpaw

Black Gum

MOUNTAIN-LAUREL *Kalmia latifolia* L.   Heath Family

FIELD MARKS. An evergreen shrub or small tree 3 to (rarely) 35 feet high; growing in rocky or sandy woods. *Leaves* mostly alternate but crowded toward ends of the branchlets, elliptic, pointed at both ends, thick and leathery, smooth, lustrous above, paler yellowish green beneath, 2 to about 4 inches long. *Flowers* deep pink to whitish, about ¾ inch across, in dense end clusters; blooming April to July. *Fruits* about 3/16 inch in diameter.

RANGE. New Brunswick and Maine to Ontario, southern Indiana, and western Kentucky; south to Florida and Louisiana.

Also called Ivy (in southern Appalachians), Calicobush, and Spoonwood. Often cultivated as an ornamental shrub.

LEATHERWOOD *Dirca palustris* L.   Mezereum Family

FIELD MARKS. A leaf-losing shrub 2 to 8 feet high, often with a solitary trunklike stem; growing in rich moist woods. *Branchlets* tough, pliable, enlarged at nodes and at tip, and appearing jointed. *Leaves* alternate, short-stalked, oval to elliptic or broadest above the middle, pointed to roundish at base, blunt or broadly pointed at tip, margin untoothed, smooth or nearly so, 1½ to 3½ inches long. *Flowers* small, pale yellow, 2 to 4 in clusters; blooming April or May, before the leaves appear. *Fruits* berry-like, oval, red, 1-seeded, about ⅜ inch long; ripening May or June.

RANGE. New Brunswick to Ontario and Minnesota, south to Florida and Mississippi.

Bark was used by Indians for bow strings, cordage, and baskets. Taken internally it induces vomiting and purging; externally it may irritate the skin.

COMMON PAWPAW *Asimina triloba* (L.) Dunal.   Custard-apple Family

FIELD MARKS. A shrub or small tree (rarely) to 40 feet high; growing in low woods and along streams. *Branchlets* slender, rusty-hairy to smooth, ill-scented when bruised. *Leaves* broadest toward tip and tapering to a wedge-shaped base, abruptly short-pointed at tip, margin untoothed, thin and veiny in appearance, smooth or nearly so at maturity, paler beneath, 6 to 12 inches long. *Flowers* purplish brown to greenish brown, 1 to 1½ inches across; blooming March to May, before the leaves appear. *Fruits* greenish yellow becoming brown, 2½ to 5 inches long, with elongate and slightly flattened seeds; ripening August to October.

RANGE. New Jersey to Michigan, south to Florida and Texas.

The tropical appearance of the foliage makes this plant a handsome ornamental.

BLACK GUM *Nyssa sylvatica* Marsh.   Tupelo Family

FIELD MARKS: A tree 40 to 80 feet or more tall; growing in swamps, bottomlands, and on rather dry rocky slopes. *Bark* grayish-brown, broken into blocks and often resembling alligator skin. *Leaves* 2 to 5 inches long, usually broadest above the middle, wedge-shaped at base, abruptly pointed at tip, untoothed on margin, shiny dark green above, paler and usually smooth beneath. *Flowers* small, greenish-white, stamen-bearing in dense clusters, pistil-bearing in 2's or 3's at tip of a long stalk; blooming April to June. *Fruits* egg-shaped, bluish-black, about ½ inch long, berry-like in appearance but with a large stone; ripening August to October.

RANGE: Maine west to southern Ontario and Michigan; south to Florida and Texas.

Also called Black Tupelo. Leaves often begin to turn scarlet before the end of summer.

REDBUD *Cercis canadensis* L.   Pea Family

FIELD MARKS. A leaf-losing shrub or small tree to 30 feet high; growing in rocky woods, ravines, or along streams. *Leaves* alternate, heart-shaped, untoothed, smooth or nearly so, 2 to 4 inches wide; leafstalks swollen at summit. *Flowers* somewhat pealike, rose purple or pink; blooming late March to May, before the leaves appear. *Fruits* light brown, flattened pods, 2 to 3 inches long; maturing July or August and persisting.

RANGE. Connecticut to southern Ontario, Wisconsin, and Nebraska; south to Florida and western Texas.

Very popular as an ornamental. Also called Judas-tree.

MALEBERRY *Lyonia ligustrina* (L.) DC.   Heath Family

FIELD MARKS. A leaf-losing shrub 3 to about 12 feet high; growing in moist to dry places, often along streams or in bogs. *Leaves* alternate, commonly elliptic to narrowly egg-shaped but often broadest above the middle, more or less pointed at both ends, usually very finely toothed but sometimes inconspicuously toothed or almost untoothed on margin, smooth above but usually more or less hairy beneath, commonly 1 to 2½ (rarely 4) inches long. *Flowers* white, globe-shaped, about ⅛ inch across, in leafless or leafy-bracted clusters from buds on growth of the previous year; blooming April to July. *Fruits* roundish but somewhat flattened, 5-celled capsules about ⅛ inch in diameter.

RANGE. Central Maine to central New York and Kentucky; south to Florida, Louisiana, and Oklahoma.

Very variable as to leaf size, hairiness of branchlets, etc. Also known as Privet-andromeda, Seedy-buckberry, and Male-huckleberry.

AMERICAN BASSWOOD *Tilia americana* L.   Linden Family

FIELD MARKS: A large tree 60 to 100 feet or more tall; growing in rich bottomlands and often on moist rocky slopes. *Leaves* 4 to 6 inches long, heartshaped but uneven at base, margin saw-toothed, dark green and smooth above, paler and smooth or nearly so beneath; leaf stalks slender and round. *Flowers* 5-petalled, creamy-white, very fragrant, in a loose cluster on a stalk attached to a strap-like leafy bract; blooming June or July. *Fruits* roundish, grayish-downy, woody, about ⅜ inch across; maturing August or September.

RANGE: New Brunswick west to southern Manitoba; south to Delaware, western North Carolina, Tennessee, Missouri and Nebraska.

WHITE BASSWOOD (*Tilia heterophylla* Vent.)   Linden Family

This is similar to the preceding species but its leaves are grayish or whitened and downy or velvety beneath. New York west to southern Illinois, south to northwestern Florida and northern Arkansas. It is the common basswood of the southern Appalachians.

WILD BLACK CHERRY *Prunus serotina* Ehrh.   Rose Family

FIELD MARKS: A tree often 25 to 40 feet tall but in some places as much as 100 feet tall; growing in rich woodlands and often along roadsides and fencerows. *Branchlets* have a strong but not disagreeable bitter almond odor. *Leaves* 2 to 5 inches long, narrowly oval or oblong lance-shaped, rounded or broadly pointed at base, pointed at tip, finely toothed on margin with incurved teeth, dark green above, paler beneath; with similar bitter almond odor when crushed. Flowers white, about ⅓ inch across, in a dense elongate cluster; blooming April to June. *Fruits* roundish, dark purplish-black, ⅓ to ½ inch across, with rather pleasant bitter-sweet taste; ripening July to September.

RANGE: Nova Scotia west to southern Ontario and Minnesota; south to central Florida and eastern Texas.

84

Redbud

Maleberry

American Basswood

Wild Black Cherry

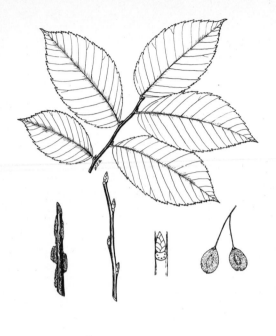

Rock Elm

Slippery Elm

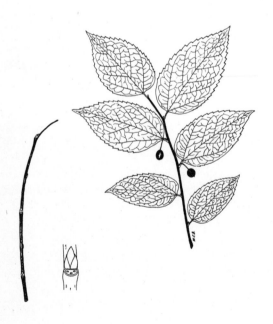

Hackberry

American Chestnut

ROCK ELM *Ulmus thomasii* Sarg.   Elm Family

FIELD MARKS: A tree 60 to 80 feet or more tall; commonly growing on rocky slopes but also in rich bottomlands. *Branchlets* commonly developing corky wings after the first year. *Leaves* 2½ to 4½ inches long, oval or broadest above the middle, margin doubly saw-toothed, pointed at tip, lop-sided at base, dark green and smooth above, paler and downy beneath. *Fruits* oval-shaped, flattened and with indistinct central seed cavity, fringed on margin, notched at tip, long-stalked; maturing in spring, quickly shed.

RANGE: Western Vermont west to southern Ontario and central Minnesota; south to Tennessee and Missouri.

SLIPPERY ELM *Ulmus rubra* Muhl.   Elm Family

FIELD MARKS: A tree often 40 to 60 feet tall; growing in bottomlands and on rich rocky slopes. *Branchlets* rough-hairy, ashy-gray, mucilaginous when chewed. *Leaves* 4 to 7 inches long, oval or broadest above the middle, abruptly pointed at tip, lop-sided at base, margin doubly saw-toothed, dark green and very rough above, paler and roughish beneath. *Fruits* roundish, flattened, smooth on margin, not notched at tip, central seed cavity rusty hairy, about ¾ inch long, very short-stalked; maturing in spring, quickly shed.

RANGE: Maine west through southern Quebec to North Dakota; south to northern Florida and eastern Texas.

The mucilaginous inner bark has been used medicinally.

HACKBERRY *Celtis occidentalis* L.   Elm Family

FIELD MARKS: A shrub or often a tree 25 to 40 feet or more tall; growing in dry and often rocky uplands and on slopes. *Bark* brownish to ashy-gray, commonly with corky wart-like outgrowths. *Leaves* 2 to 4 inches long, egg-shaped, with 3 prominent veins from near the slanted base, sometimes untoothed but more commonly saw-toothed above the middle, dull green and rough above, paler beneath. *Fruits* roundish, orange-brown to purplish, 1-seeded with a thin but very sweet flesh, about ⅓ inch across; ripening in fall and often persisting into winter.

RANGE: New Hampshire and southern Quebec west to southern Manitoba; south to northern Florida and eastern Texas.

AMERICAN CHESTNUT *Castanea dentata* (Marsh.) Borkh.   Beech Family

FIELD MARKS: Formerly a large tree 60 to 100 feet or more tall; now existing as sprout growth from roots of old stumps and snags of blight-killed trees. *Leaves* oblong lance-shaped, pointed at both ends, margin with coarse, sharp, incurved teeth, yellowish green above, paler and smooth beneath, 5 to 8 inches long. *Flowers* creamy-white, in large candle-like clusters; blooming June or July. *Fruits* roundish egg-shaped, flattened, shiny brown nuts ¾ to 1 inch long; 2 or 3 produced in each prickly bur; kernel sweet and edible; ripening September or October.

RANGE: Maine west to southern Ontario; south to Delaware and inland to Georgia and northeastern Mississippi.

AMERICAN BEECH   *Fagus grandifolia* Ehrh.   Beech Family

FIELD MARKS: A tree 60 to 80 feet or more tall; growing in a variety of places but preferring rich, moist soils. *Bark* smooth, bluish-gray and often mottled, frequently disfigured by the carving of initials. *Leaves* oval to oblong egg-shaped, coarsely and sharply toothed on margin, dark green above, paler yellowish-green beneath, smooth, often shiny, 3 to 5 inches long. *Fruit* a small, light brown, 3-sided nut with sweet edible kernel, 2 or 3 produced in each bur which splits into 4 parts at maturity during September or October.

RANGE: Nova Scotia west to Ontario and Wisconsin; south to northern Florida and eastern Texas.

Produces valuable hardwood lumber.

WITCH-HAZEL   *Hamamelis virginiana* L.   Witch-hazel Family

FIELD MARKS. A leaf-losing shrub or small tree 5 to 20 feet high; growing in rich woods, thickets, and clearings. *Branchlets* with stalked, naked buds; both roughish with tawny or rusty hairs. *Leaves* alternate, oval or broadest above the middle, unevenly rounded or heart-shaped at base, pointed or rounded at tip, irregularly wavy-toothed on margin, smooth above, paler and smooth or nearly so beneath, 2½ to 6 inches long (or in the variety *parvifolia* Nutt. with somewhat leathery leaves 1½ to 4 inches long, whitened and rather densely rusty-hairy beneath). *Flowers* bright yellow, with 4 ribbonlike petals; blooming September to November or later, usually after the leaves have fallen. *Fruits* urn-shaped, grayish-downy, woody capsules containing 2 shiny black seeds which are forcibly ejected in October or November.

RANGE. Nova Scotia to southern Ontario, central Michigan, and southeastern Minnesota; south to Florida and Texas.

The plant has astringent properties, and commercial witch-hazel is distilled from the bark. Twigs or bark eaten by deer and rabbits; seeds by ruffed grouse and bobwhite quail.

AMERICAN HAZELNUT   *Corylus americana* Walt.   Birch Family

FIELD MARKS. A shrub 3 to 10 feet high growing in moist to dry thickets, fence rows, roadsides, and borders of woods. *Branchlets* bristly-hairy; *catkins* stalked and often 1 inch long. *Leaves* egg-shaped to roundish, somewhat heart-shaped at base, abruptly pointed at tip, double-toothed on margin, smooth or nearly so above, downy on the veins beneath, 2½ to 6 inches long; leafstalks bristly-hairy. *Fruits* enclosed by a pair of ragged-edged leafy bracts.

RANGE. Maine to Saskatchewan; south to northern Florida, Missouri, and Oklahoma.

BEAKED HAZELNUT   *Corylus cornuta* Marsh.   Birch Family

FIELD MARKS. A shrub quite similar to the American Hazelnut and found in similar situations. *Branchlets* sparingly if at all bristly-hairy; *catkins* stalkless and less than ½ inch long. *Fruits* enclosed by a pair of bracts which are united and form a prolonged, tubelike, bristly-hairy beak.

RANGE. Newfoundland to British Columbia; south principally in the mountains to Georgia, Missouri, and Colorado.

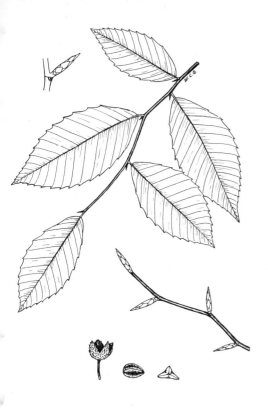

American Beech

Witch-hazel

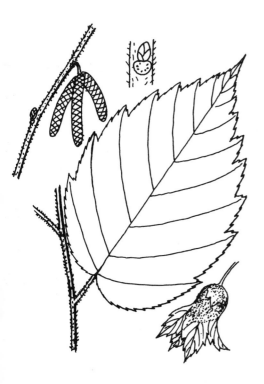

American Hazelnut

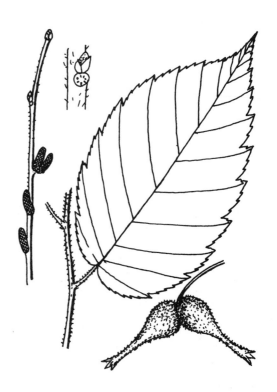

Beaked Hazelnut

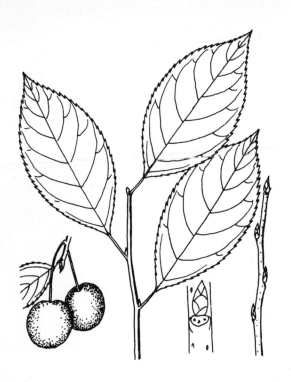

American Plum

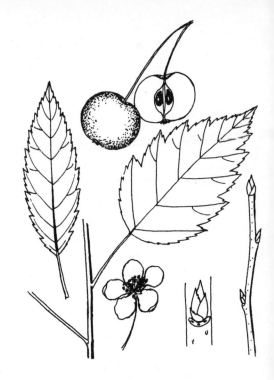

American Crab Apple

Cockspur Thorn

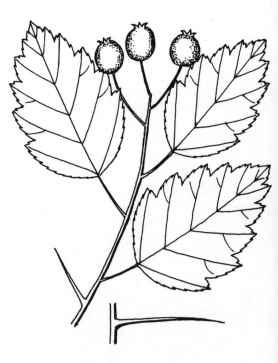

Variable Thorn

WIDELY DISTRIBUTED IN VARIOUS PLACES, Continued
Leaves Alternate—Simple—Toothed or Lobed

AMERICAN PLUM *Prunus americana* Marsh   Rose Family

FIELD MARKS. A leaf-losing shrub or small tree with spine-tipped branches; often forming thickets in woods borders, or along fence rows and streams. *Leaves* oval or broadest above the middle, mostly broadly pointed at base and abruptly pointed at tip, finely and often doubly toothed on margin, smooth or nearly so on both surfaces, 2 to 4 inches long; leafstalks usually without glands. *Flowers* white, ¾ inch across, 2 to 5 in a cluster; blooming April to June. *Fruits* roundish, yellow or red, ¾ to 1 inch in diameter; ripening August to October.

RANGE. Massachusetts to Manitoba; south to Florida, Louisiana, and New Mexico.

AMERICAN CRAB APPLE *Malus coronaria* (L.) Mill.   Rose Family

FIELD MARKS. A bushy shrub or small tree to about 15 or 20 feet; often forming thickets along fence rows, roadsides, and abandoned fields. *Branchlets* smooth, often spurlike and ending in a sharp point. *Leaves* alternate, egg-shaped to oval (or lance-shaped in var. *lancifolia* [Rehd.] Fern.), rounded to pointed at base, pointed at tip, sharply and irregularly toothed on margin, thin-textured, smooth on both surfaces, 2 to 4 inches long. *Flowers* white to pink, 5-petalled, almost 1 inch across, very fragrant, 5 or 6 in clusters; blooming March to May. *Fruits* yellowish green, waxy or greasy, fragrant apples about 1 inch in diameter; ripening October or November.

RANGE. Western New York to Indiana and Missouri, south in the uplands to northern Georgia.

The fruits can be used to make jelly and vinegar.

COCKSPUR THORN *Crataegus crus-galli* L.   Rose Family

FIELD MARKS. A bushy shrub or small tree; growing in old pastures, borders of woods, thickets, etc. *Branches* with many slender, straight or slightly curved thorns 2 to 4 inches long. *Leaves* broadest above the middle, wedge-shaped at base, rounded to pointed at tip, margin sharply and irregularly toothed above the middle, thickish and somewhat leathery in texture, dark green and lustrous above, paler and smooth or nearly so beneath, 2 to 4 inches long. *Flowers* blooming April to June. *Fruits* greenish to dull red, hard, about ⅜ inch in diameter, usually 2-seeded; ripening September or October.

RANGE. Quebec to Ontario and Minnesota; south to Georgia, Kansas, and eastern Texas.

VARIABLE THORN *Crataegus macrosperma* Ashe   Rose Family

FIELD MARKS. A bushy shrub or small tree of stony woods and thickets. *Branches* with many slender thorns 1¼ to 2½ inches long. *Leaves* egg-shaped or broadly egg-shaped, rounded to broadly pointed or flattened at base, pointed at tip, margin with about 5 pairs of broadly triangular and sharply toothed lobes, thin in texture, dark yellowish green above, slightly paler beneath, smooth or nearly so on both surfaces, 1 to 3 inches long. *Flowers* blooming April or May. *Fruits* bright red, about ½ inch in diameter, 3- to 5-seeded; ripening August or September.

RANGE. Southeastern Canada and New England to northern Illinois and Wisconsin; south in the mountains to northern Georgia.

AMERICAN BITTERSWEET *Celastrus scandens* L.   Stafftree Family

FIELD MARKS. A twining, leaf-losing, woody vine climbing to a height of 20 or more feet or scrambling over low vegetation and sometimes trailing on the ground; growing in moist thickets and along the banks of streams. *Leaves* alternate, oval or egg-shaped, rounded to broadly pointed at base, abruptly pointed at tip, finely toothed on margin, thin in texture, dull dark green above, paler beneath, smooth or nearly so on both surfaces, 2 to 4 inches long. *Flowers* yellowish-green, small, many in an elongate end cluster; blooming May or June. *Fruits* ball-shaped, dull orange capsules about ⅜ inch in diameter; splitting when mature in September or October and exposing the bright-scarlet, fleshy-coated seeds.

RANGE. Southern Quebec to southern Manitoba; south to Georgia, Mississippi, Arkansas, and Oklahoma.

Also called Climbing Bittersweet and Waxwort. Often cultivated as an ornamental vine. The fruits are eaten by several species of wild birds.

SERVICEBERRY *Amelanchier arborea* (Michx.f.) Fern.   Rose Family

FIELD MARKS: A small tree 15 to 40 feet tall; growing in both moist bottomlands and on dry rocky slopes. *Bark* grayish or grayish-brown with longitudinal dark streaks or furrows. *Leaves* 2 to 4 inches long, oval or egg-shaped, rounded to heart-shaped at base, finely saw-toothed on margin, bright green and smooth above, paler and smooth or nearly so beneath when mature. Flowers white, showy, in drooping clusters; blooming April or May. *Fruits* dark red or purple, coated with a whitish bloom, ¼ to ½ inch across, varying from sweet and juicy to rather dry and insipid; ripening between May and July.

RANGE: Newfoundland and Nova Scotia west to southern Ontario and Minnesota; south to northern Florida and eastern Texas.

Also called Shadbush, Sarviceberry, and Juneberry.

RED MULBERRY *Morus rubra* L.   Mulberry Family

FIELD MARKS: A tree usually 20 to 40 feet tall; growing in moist bottomlands and on rich moist slopes. *Leaves* 3 to 5 inches long, more or less heart-shaped and sometimes mitten-shaped or 3-lobed, coarsely saw-toothed on margin, dark green and commonly roughish above, paler and often slightly hairy beneath; leaf stalks exude a drop of milky sap when broken. *Fruits* resemble blackberries, oblong in shape, about 1 inch long, dark purple when ripe in May or June, sweet and edible.

RANGE: Massachusetts west to South Dakota; south to Florida and Texas.

Leaves Alternate—Simple—Angled or Lobed

COMMON MOONSEED *Menispermum canadanse* L.   Moonseed Family

FIELD MARKS. A soft-wooded, leaf-losing vine with slender, faintly grooved, twining stems; growing in woods and along streams. *Leaves* alternate, broadly egg-shaped or roundish, untoothed but usually 3- to 7-lobed or angled, dark green and smooth above, paler and often slightly downy beneath, attached to the long leafstalks a little within the margin of the leaf blades, 3 to 8 inches wide. *Flowers* small, greenish white, blooming in June and July. *Fruits* roundish, bluish black with a whitish bloom, about ⅜ inch in diameter; resembling small grapes but with a single flattened and crescent-shaped seed.

RANGE. Western New England and Quebec to Manitoba; south to Georgia, Alabama, Arkansas, and Oklahoma.

Roots have been used medicinally. The fruits are said to be poisonous.

92

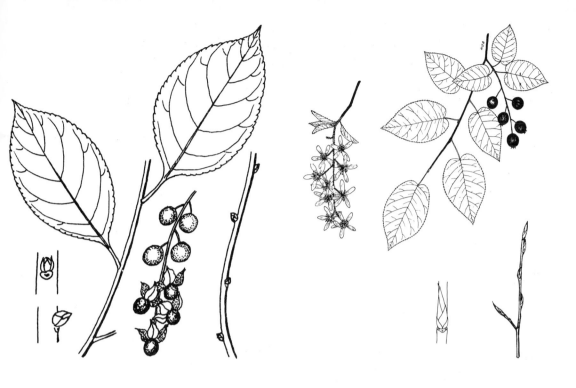

American Bittersweet

Serviceberry

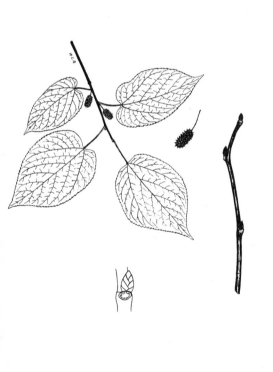

Red Mulberry

Common Moonseed

White Oak

Northern Red Oak

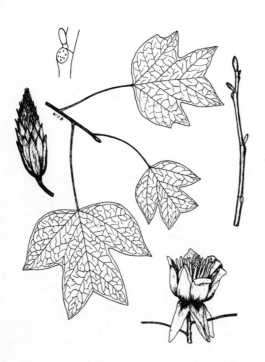

Tuliptree

Sassafras

WIDELY DISTRIBUTED IN VARIOUS PLACES, Continued
Leaves Alternate—Simple—Mostly Lobed

WHITE OAK *Quercus alba* L.   Beech Family

FIELD MARKS: A large tree 80 to 100 feet or more tall; growing in botomlands and slopes with well-drained to dry soils. *Bark* light ashy-gray, broken into blocks or loose scaly plates. *Leaves* 5 to 9 inches long, usually broadest above the middle, with 7 or 9 irregularly rounded lobes and shallow to deep sinuses, bright green above, paler or whitened beneath, smooth. *Fruit* a light brown, oblong acorn about ¾ inch long, seated in a deeply bowl-shaped cup; maturing in 1 year; kernel sweetish.

RANGE: Maine west to Quebec and Minnesota; south to northern Florida and eastern Texas.

Valuable hardwood timber tree.

NORTHERN RED OAK *Quercus rubra* L.   Beech Family

FIELD MARKS: A large tree 60 to 100 feet or more tall; growing in uplands on rich moist to well-drained soils. *Bark* blackish, ridged and furrowed, on upper part of trunk showing flat-topped gray ridges. *Leaves* 5 to 8 inches long with 7 to 11 bristle-tipped and bristle-toothed lobes, the sinuses between them extending no more than half way to the midrib, smooth, dull dark green above, paler beneath. *Fruit* a pale brown egg-shaped acorn ¾ to 1 inch long, most often seated in a shallow saucer-like cup but sometimes in a deeper bowl-shaped one; maturing in 2 years; kernel bitter.

RANGE: Nova Scotia west to Minnesota; south to Georgia, Mississippi and Oklahoma.

Valuable hardwood timber tree.

TULIPTREE *Liriodendron tulipifera* L.   Magnolia Family

FIELD MARKS: A large tree 80 to 100 feet or more tall; growing in moist bottomlands and on rich moist slopes. *Branchlets* spicy aromatic when bruised or broken. *Leaves* 4 to 6 inches long, shaped like a broad keystone with a V-shaped notch at top, usually 4-lobed, shiny dark green above, paler beneath, smooth, long-stalked. *Flowers* cup-shaped, greenish-yellow with orange base, 2 to 3 inches across; blooming between April and June. Fruits in erect cone-like clusters 2 to 3 inches long, winged above the 4-angled seed chamber at base, often persisting into winter.

RANGE: Massachusetts west to southern Michigan; south to northern Florida and Louisiana.

Valuable shade and timber tree. Also called Yellow-poplar.

SASSAFRAS *Sassafras albidum* (Nutt.) Nees   Laurel Family

FIELD MARKS. A leaf-losing, aromatic shrub or tree, sometimes 20 to 40 feet high; growing in borders of woods, old fields, and along fence rows. *Branchlets* yellowish green to reddish, brittle, smooth or finely downy, with a spicy-aromatic odor when broken. *Leaves* alternate, oval or elliptic and often with 1 or 2 lobes, bluntly pointed at tip, pointed at base, smooth or nearly so above but sometimes slightly downy beneath, spicy-aromatic when crushed, 3 to 6 inches long. *Flowers* greenish yellow, clustered; blooming March to May, before the leaves. *Fruits* oval-shaped, dark blue, 1-seeded, borne on club-shaped red stalks; ripening June to October.

RANGE. Southwestern Maine to Michigan and southeastern Iowa, south to Florida and Texas.

The bark of the roots is used to make sassafras tea and is the source of an oil used as a flavoring in candies and medicines and to perfume soaps. The fruits are eaten by many kinds of wild birds, including the bobwhite quail and wild turkey, and the twigs are eaten by deer and rabbits.

FOX GRAPE *Vitis labrusca* L.   Vine Family

FIELD MARKS. A high-climbing vine; growing in rich woods, thickets, or along streams. *Branchlets* more or less rusty-woolly, with a tendril or flower cluster opposite each leaf. *Leaves* heart-shaped, shallowly or sometimes deeply 3-lobed, margin coarsely but shallowly toothed, somewhat leathery, smooth above, felted with tawny or rusty wool beneath, 4 to 8 inches long. *Fruits* purplish black, brownish purple, or (rarely) amber-colored, 3- to 6-seeded, about ½ inch across, usually sweet and somewhat musky.
RANGE. Southern Maine to Michigan, south to Florida and Mississippi.
Parent of Concord, Catawba, Niagra, and other cultivated grapes.

SUMMER GRAPE *Vitis aestivalis* Michx.   Vine Family

FIELD MARKS. A high-climbing vine; growing in woods, thickets, or on stream banks. *Branchlets* usually somewhat downy, no tendril or flower cluster opposite every third leaf. *Leaves* heart-shaped, unlobed or shallowly to deeply 3- to 5-lobed, basal sinus narrowly to broadly U-shaped, smooth above, whitish and with some loose tawny or rusty wool beneath, 3 to 8 inches long. *Fruits* black with a whitish bloom, 2- to 3-seeded, about ⅜ inch across, very tart.
RANGE. Massachusetts to Michigan and Wisconsin, south to Georgia and Texas.

RIVERBANK GRAPE *Vitis riparia* Michx.   Vine Family

FIELD MARKS. A trailing or high-climbing vine; growing along streams and in alluvial bottomlands. *Branchlets* smooth or nearly so, no tendril or flower cluster opposite every third leaf, pith with thin partitions at the nodes. *Leaves* heart-shaped, usually 3-lobed, margin with large and sharply pointed teeth, sinus at base V-shaped but broad and open, bright green and lustrous on both surfaces, sometimes slightly hairy on larger veins beneath, 2½ to 5 inches long. *Fruits* bluish black and with a white bloom, 2- to 4-seeded, about ⅜ inch in diameter, usually sour.
RANGE. New Brunswick to Manitoba; south to Virginia, Tennessee, Missouri, and Texas.

FROST GRAPE *Vitis vulpina* L.   Vine Family

FIELD MARKS. A high-climbing vine; growing in low rich woods or thickets and along streams. *Branchlets* smooth or nearly so, no tendril or flower cluster opposite every third leaf, pith with thick partitions at the nodes. *Leaves* heart-shaped, unlobed or occasionally slightly 3-lobed, margin coarsely and sharply toothed, sinus at base deep and narrowly V-shaped, bright green on both surfaces, lustrous above, sometimes sparingly hairy along the veins beneath, 3 to 5 inches long. *Fruits* lustrous black, 2- to 3-seeded, about ⅜ inch in diameter, often sweet after frost.
RANGE. Southeastern New York and Pennsylvania to Illinois and eastern Kansas; south to Florida and Texas.

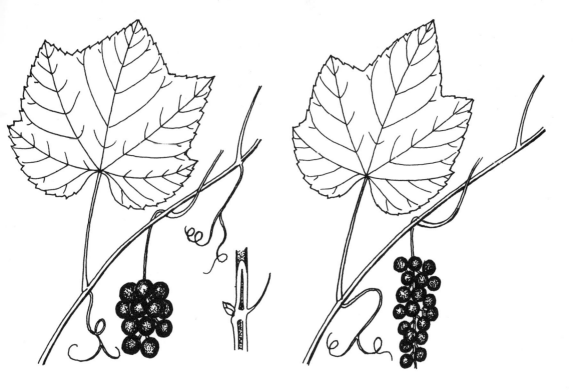

Fox Grape

Summer Grape

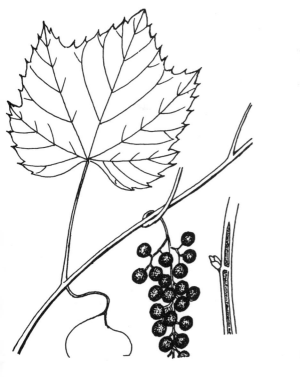

Riverbank Grape

Frost Grape

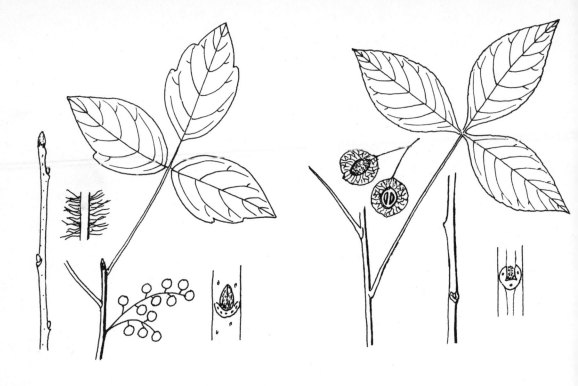

Poison-ivy   Hoptree

Virginia Creeper   Pasture Rose

POISON-IVY *Rhus radicans* L.   Cashew Family

CAUTION: All parts of this plant contain a dangerous skin irritant.

FIELD MARKS. An erect or trailing leaf-losing shrub, or a woody vine climbing by means of aerial rootlets on the stems; growing in wooded areas, thickets, clearings, or along fence rows and roadsides. *Leaves* alternate, long-stalked, compound, 4 to 12 inches long; the 3 leaflets oval or egg-shaped, rounded or broadly pointed at base, pointed at tip, usually with a few coarse teeth on margin, often lustrous above, paler and slightly downy beneath, 1½ to 8 inches long; the end leaflet rather long-stalked, the side ones almost stalkless. *Flowers* small, yellowish green, in axillary clusters; blooming May to July. *Fruits* roundish, waxy white, about 3/16 inch in diameter; maturing August to October and persisting.

RANGE. Nova Scotia to British Columbia; south to Florida, Texas, and Arizona.

HOPTREE *Ptelea trifoliata* L.   Rue Family

FIELD MARKS. A leaf-losing shrub or small tree to 15 feet high, all parts of which are ill-scented when crushed; growing on sandy shores or rocky banks of streams. *Leaves* alternate, long-stalked, compound; the 3 leaflets egg-shaped, pointed at both ends, sometimes obscurely toothed on margin, smooth above, paler and sometimes downy beneath, minutely clear- or black-dotted, 2 to 6 inches long. *Flowers* small, greenish white, clustered; blooming April to July. *Fruits* wafer-like, roundish, thin, papery, with 2 seeds in a central chamber; maturing June to September.

RANGE. Southwestern Quebec to Ontario, south to Florida and Texas.

Also called Wafer-ash and Stinking-ash.

VIRGINIA CREEPER *Parthenocissus quinquefolia* (L.) Planch.   Vine Family

FIELD MARKS. A climbing or sometimes trailing leaf-losing vine; growing in moist woods and thickets. Tendrils opposite some of the leaves are 5- to 12-branched and end in small adhesive disks. *Leaves* alternate, compound, with usually 5 leaflets radiating from the summit of a long leafstalk; leaflets egg-shaped or elliptic, wedge-shaped at base, pointed or abruptly pointed at tip, margin sharply and coarsely toothed to or slightly below the middle, dull above, paler and sometimes downy beneath, 2 to 8 inches long. *Flowers* small, greenish, in branched end clusters; blooming June to August. *Fruits* roundish, dark blue, 2- to 3-seeded berries about ¼ inch in diameter; ripening August to October.

RANGE. Maine and Quebec to Minnesota, south to Florida and Texas.

Often confused with Poison-ivy. Cultivated as an ornamental.

PASTURE ROSE *Rosa carolina* L.   Rose Family

FIELD MARKS. An erect shrub ½ to 2½ feet high, the stems armed with needle-like prickles; growing in dry open woods, thickets, and pastures. *Leaves* with usually 5 leaflets which are elliptic or egg-shaped, pointed to rounded at base, pointed at tip, sharply toothed on margin, usually dull above, paler and sometimes slightly downy beneath, ¾ to 1¼ inches long; the stipules narrow, flat, and untoothed. *Flowers* usually solitary, pink, about 2 inches broad; blooming May to July. *Fruits* roundish, red, about ½ inch in diameter, and with gland-tipped hairs.

RANGE. Nova Scotia to Minnesota and Nebraska, south to Florida and Texas. Also called Low or Carolina Rose.

99

SHRUB YELLOWROOT *Xanthorhiza simplicissima* Marsh.   Buttercup Family

FIELD MARKS. A sparingly-branched, leaf-losing shrub 8 inches to 2 feet high; growing in cool, moist woods and along the banks of streams. *Wood* of both stems and roots is very bright yellow. *Leaves* alternate, more or less clustered toward the summits of the short branchlets, usually divided into 5 leaflets which are deeply cut-toothed and often cleft, thin, bright green and lustrous on both surfaces. *Flowers* small, brownish purple, in drooping clusters; blooming in April or May and occasionally in the fall. *Fruits* small, light yellow, inflated, 1-seeded capsules, 4 to 8 grouped together.

RANGE. Southwestern New York southward, chiefly in the mountains, to Alabama and northwestern Florida.

Roots are used medicinally and to make a yellow dye.

SMOOTH SUMAC *Rhus glabra* L.   Cashew Family

FIELD MARKS. A leaf-losing shrub or small tree 2 to about 15 feet high; growing in old fields, along fence rows, etc. *Branchlets* stout, smooth, whitened with a bloom, exuding milky sap when cut. *Leaves* alternate, compound, 12 to 20 inches long; the 11 to 31 leaflets stalkless, oblong lance-shaped, usually roundish at base, pointed at tip, sharply toothed on margin, smooth, whitened beneath, 2 to 5 inches long. *Flowers* small, yellowish green, in dense erect end clusters; blooming June or July. *Fruits* roundish, red, sticky-hairy, 1-seeded, about ⅛ inch in diameter, in compact end clusters; maturing August or September and persisting.

RANGE. Maine and Quebec to British Columbia, south to Florida and California.

Young fruits of this and other red-fruited sumacs have been used to make a pleasantly acid, lemonade-like drink. The fruits are eaten by many birds, but usually only in an emergency. Twigs and bark are often eaten by rabbits and deer.

STAGHORN SUMAC *Rhus typhina* L.   Cashew Family

This is a shrub or small tree 10 to 20 feet tall, similar to the preceding but with velvety-hairy leaf stalks and branchlets. Nova Scotia west to Minnesota south to northern Georgia and Missouri.

DWARF SUMAC *Rhus copallina* L.   Cashew Family

FIELD MARKS. A leaf-losing shrub or small tree 2 to about 10 feet high; growing in open woods, thickets, fence rows, and old fields. *Branchlets* moderate, smooth or finely downy, exuding a clear sap when cut. *Leaves* alternate, compound, 6 to 12 inches long, with conspicuous wings between the leaflets; the 9 to 21 leaflets stalkless, egg-shaped to lance-shaped, pointed or unevenly rounded at base, pointed at tip, untoothed or nearly so on margin, usually lustrous above, paler and often downy beneath, 1½ to 3 inches long. *Flowers* small, yellowish green, numerous, in large end clusters; blooming July to September. *Fruits* roundish, red, hairy, about ⅛ inch in diameter, in large and often somewhat drooping end clusters; maturing September or October.

RANGE. Southern Maine to New York, Michigan, central Wisconsin, and eastern Kansas; south to Florida and Texas.

Also called Shining Sumac. Rich in tannin used in tanning hides.

BLACK WALNUT *Juglans nigra* L.   Walnut Family

FIELD MARKS: A large tree 50 to 75 feet or more tall; growing in rich soils of slopes and bottomlands. *Branchlets* stout, light brown, with 3-lobed leaf scars notched at top. *Leaves* 12 to 24 inches long with a downy stalk bearing 13 to 23 egg-shaped or lance-shaped leaflets 2 to 4 inches long, dark yellowish green above, paler and usually downy beneath, finely saw-toothed on margin. *Fruit* a roundish, bony-shelled, deeply sculptured nut 1½ to 2 inches across; enclosed by a thick yellowish-green, warty-dotted husk.

RANGE: Massachusetts west to southern Ontario, Wisconsin and southeastern South Dakota; south to northern Florida and eastern Texas.

Valuable hardwood timber tree; produces commercially valuable nuts.

Shrub Yellowroot

Smooth Sumac

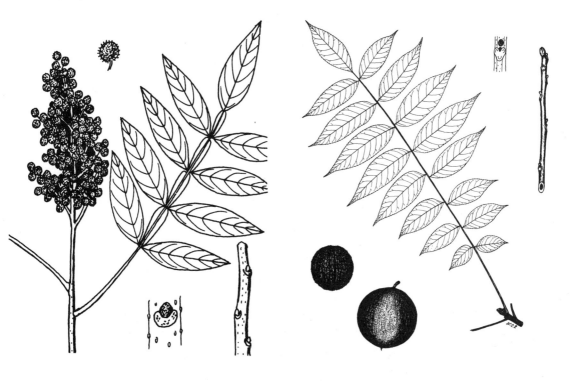

Dwarf Sumac

Black Walnut

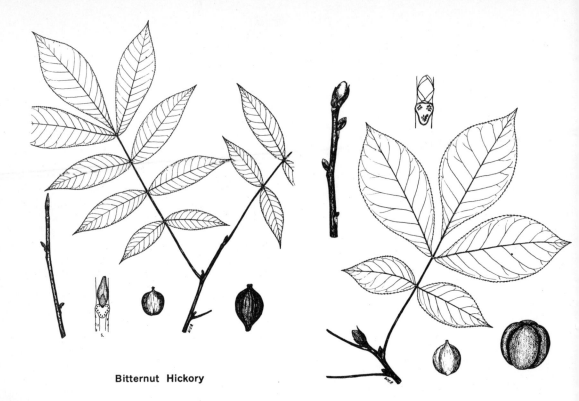

Bitternut Hickory

Shagbark Hickory

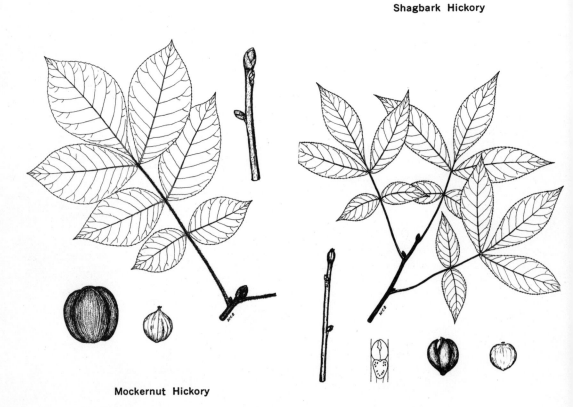

Mockernut Hickory

Pignut Hickory

BITTERNUT HICKORY   *Carya cordiformis* (Wang.) K. Koch   Walnut Family

FIELD MARKS: A tree 50 to 75 feet or more tall; growing along streams, in rich bottomlands, and on rich moist slopes. *Buds* bright sulfur-yellow. Leaves 6 to 10 inches long with from 7 to 11 lance-shaped leaflets, the end one 4 to 6 inches long and slightly larger than the others, bright green above, paler beneath and usually somewhat downy, margins saw-toothed. *Fruit* a roundish nut about ¾ inch across with a thin, pale reddish-brown, rather thin bony shell; husk thin, yellow-dotted, 4-winged above the middle, tardily splitting; kernel very bitter and astringent.

RANGE: Maine west to Quebec and Minnesota; south to northwestern Florida and eastern Texas.

SHAGBARK HICKORY   *Carya ovata* (Mill.) K. Koch   Walnut Family

FIELD MARKS: A tree 50 to 80 feet or more tall; growing in bottomlands and on slopes with a rich soil. *Bark* of the trunks breaks into long and shaggy-looking plates which are loose at one or both ends. *Leaves* 8 to 14 inches long with usually 5 leaflets which are dark yellowish-green and smooth above, paler and often downy beneath, finely saw-toothed on margin; the end one 5 to 7 inches long and larger or about the same size as the pair of leaflets below it. *Fruit* a roundish nut about 1 inch across with a moderately thick, pale brown, bony shell; the husk thick and splitting into 4 sections at maturity; kernel sweet.

RANGE: Maine and Quebec west to Minnesota; south to Georgia and eastern Texas.

MOCKERNUT HICKORY   *Carya tomentosa* Nutt.   Walnut Family

FIELD MARKS: A tree 50 to 75 feet or more tall; growing most often on well-drained to dry soils. *Bark* with shallow furrows, not shaggy. *Leaves* 8 to 12 inches long with usually 7 leaflets which are dark-yellowish green and shiny above, paler and downy beneath, saw-toothed on margin; the end one 4 to 7 inches long and usually a little larger than the pair of leaflets beneath it. *Fruit* a roundish or slightly top-shaped nut 1 to 1¼ inches across with a very think reddish-brown bony shell; the husk thick, splitting nearly to base into 4 parts at maturity; kernel sweet.

RANGE: Massachusetts to southern Michigan and Nebraska; south to northern Florida and eastern Texas.

PIGNUT HICKORY   *Carya glabra* (Mill.) Sweet   Walnut Family

FIELD MARKS: A tree 50 to 60 feet or more tall; growing on moist to dry soils, commonly on slopes and ridges. *Leaves* 6 to 12 inches long with usually 5 leaflets which are a shiny dark green above, paler and smooth beneath, finely saw-toothed on margin; the end one 4 to 7 inches long and usually about the same size as the pair of leaflets beneath it. *Fruit* a roundish or slightly top-shaped nut ¾ to 1 inch across with a thin to moderately thick, pale brown, bony shell; the husk thin, 4-winged near the top, splitting only part way to the base; kernel sweet to slightly bitter.

RANGE: Maine west to Minnesota; south to Florida and Texas.

HERCULES'-CLUB *Aralia spinosa* L.   Ginseng Family

FIELD MARKS. A leaf-losing shrub or small tree 5 to 15 or more feet high; growing in woods, clearings, or along streams. *Branchlets* very stout and armed with prickles. *Leaves* alternate, 2 to 3 feet long, doubly or triply compound; the numerous leaflets egg-shaped, rounded or broadly pointed at base, pointed at tip, sharply toothed on margin, smooth above, paler and sometimes downy beneath, 1½ to 3½ inches long. *Flowers* small, white, in numerous clusters (umbels) and in a large pyramid-shaped end group; blooming June to September. *Fruits* berry-like, egg-shaped, black, about ¼ inch long; ripening August to October.

RANGE. Southern New England and central New York to Michigan and Iowa, south to Florida and Texas.

COMMON INDIGOBUSH *Amorpha fruticosa* L.   Pea Family

FIELD MARKS. A shrub 4 to about 10 feet high; growing in open woods, along streams, or borders of swamps. *Leaves* 6 to 12 inches long; the 11 to 35 oval or elliptic leaflets ½ to 2 inches long, dull green, minutely glandular-dotted, usually with some short grayish hairs (but with long tawny hairs in the variety *croceolanata* [P. W. Wats.] Schneid.), usually rounded at both ends but with an abrupt little point at tip. *Flowers* violet purple, ¼ to ⅜ inch long, usually in several clusters 3 to 6 inches long; blooming April to June. *Fruits* curved, about ⅜ inch long, dotted with large raised glands; maturing June to August.

RANGE. Southern Pennsylvania to southern Michigan, Wisconsin, and Kansas; south to Florida and Texas.

COMMON LOCUST *Robinia pseudoacacia* L.   Pea Family

FIELD MARKS: A tree 40 to 60 feet or more tall. *Branchlets* usually armed with a pair of thorns at the base of each leaf stalk. *Leaves* 8 to 14 inches long, divided into 7 to 19 oval-shaped leaflets from 1 to 2 inches long, untoothed on margin, smooth, bluish-green above, paler beneath. *Flowers* pea-like, white, very fragrant, in showy drooping clusters; blooming May or June. *Fruit* a flattened brown pod 2 to 4 inches long containing from 4 to 8 small, hard, brown seeds.

RANGE: Southern Pennsylvania south in Appalachians to northern Georgia, and Ozark Mountains of Arkansas and Missouri. Widely planted and now naturalized over a much wider area.

HONEY LOCUST *Gleditsia triacanthos* L.   Pea Family

FIELD MARKS: A tree sometimes 50 to 100 feet or more tall. *Trunk* and branches usually armed with clusters of branched thorns. *Leaves* 7 to 10 inches long divided once or often twice into narrowly egg-shaped leaflets ½ to 1½ inches long which are inconspicuously toothed on the margin, smooth, dark green above, paler beneath. *Flowers* rather small, greenish-yellow, not pea-like; blooming April or May. *Fruit* a flattened, strap-shaped, commonly twisted, purplish-brown pod 10 to 18 inches long containing about a dozen dark brown seeds.

RANGE: Western Pennsylvania west to southeastern Minnesota; south to northern Georgia and eastern Texas. Now naturalized over a much larger area.

Hercules'-club

Common Indigobush

Common Locust

Honey Locust

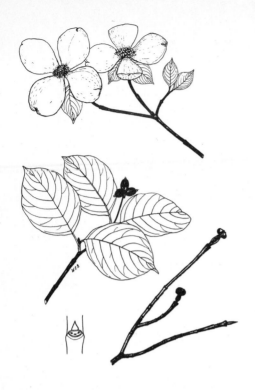

Flowering Dogwood

Gray-stemmed Dogwood

Shrubby St. John's-Wort

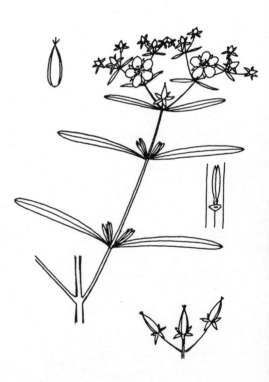

Bushy St. John's-Wort

FLOWERING DOGWOOD *Cornus florida* L. Dogwood Family

FIELD MARKS: A tree 10 to rarely 40 feet tall; growing widely in moist to moderately dry soils. *Branchlets* greenish to purplish-red, often with a button-shaped flower bud at the tip. *Leaves* 3 to 5 inches long, oval, broadly pointed or roundish at base, pointed at tip, bright green above, paler and sometimes slightly hairy beneath. *Flowers* small, greenish-yellow, in a dense head surrounded by 4 large, petal-like, white or sometimes pink bracts which are notched and brown at tip; blooming March to May. *Fruits* egg-shaped, bright red, about ½ inch long; ripening September and October.

RANGE: Southern Maine west to southern Michigan; south to Florida and eastern Texas.

Widely planted as an ornamental tree.

GRAY-STEMMED DOGWOOD *Cornus racemosa* Lam. Dogwood Family

FIELD MARKS. A much-branched, very twiggy, gray-stemmed shrub 3 to 8 feet high; growing in dry to moist thickets, borders of woods, fence rows, etc. *Branchlets* very slender, light brown, and with pale brown or whitish pith. *Leaves* narrowly egg-shaped to lance-shaped, usually pointed at base, long-pointed at tip, with 3 to 5 pairs of veins, smooth or with minute close-pressed hairs on both surfaces, pale or whitened beneath, 1½ to 3 inches long. *Flowers* creamy white, in cone-shaped clusters; blooming June and July. *Fruits* white, roundish, about 3/16 inch in diameter, on bright-red stalks; ripening August or September.

RANGE. Central Maine to southern Ontario and Minnesota; south to Delaware, West Virginia, North Carolina, Kentucky, and Oklahoma.

Also called Panicled Dogwood.

SHRUBBY ST. JOHN'S-WORT *Hypericum spathulatum* (Spach) Steud. St. John's-wort Family

FIELD MARKS. An erect, bushy-branched, leaf-losing shrub 2 to about 4 feet high; usually growing in moist sandy or rocky open woods, fields, and slopes. *Leaves* very short-stalked, narrowly oblong or somewhat broadest toward the tip, pointed at base, blunt at tip, light green above, pale beneath, smooth on both surfaces, ¾ to 3 inches long. *Flowers* bright yellow, about ¾ inch across, 5-petalled, clustered in the axils of the upper leaves; blooming June to September. *Fruits* narrowly egg-shaped, 3-celled capsules about ½ inch long.

RANGE. Southeastern New York to Ontario and Minnesota; south to Georgia, Mississippi, and Arkansas.

One of our most showy species of St. John's-worts; sometimes cultivated and locally escaping as far north as Massachusetts.

BUSHY ST. JOHN'S-WORT *Hypericum densiflorum* Pursh St. John's-wort Family

FIELD MARKS. A much-branched, bushy, leaf-losing shrub 1 to about 6 feet high; growing in swamps, swales, boggy places or sometimes in dry woods. *Leaves* stalkless or almost so, very narrow or narrowly oblong, pointed at base, blunt or somewhat pointed at tip, margin slightly rolled beneath, light green above, slightly paler beneath, smooth on both surfaces, ¾ to 2 inches long. *Flowers* bright yellow, about ⅜ inch across, 5-petalled, in rather crowded, forking, flat-topped end clusters; blooming June to September. *Fruits* narrowly egg-shaped, 3-celled capsules usually less than ¼ inch long.

RANGE. Southeastern New York to southern Pennsylvania and Kentucky; south to Georgia and Alabama.

107

WILD HYDRANGEA   *Hydrangea arborescens* L.   Saxifrage Family

FIELD MARKS. A loosely branched shrub 3 to 6 feet high; growing on shaded banks and along streams. *Branchlets* pale brown, smooth or nearly so. *Leaves* roundish to egg-shaped, elliptic, or broadly lance-shaped, round to heart-shaped or broadly pointed at base, sharply pointed at tip, sharply toothed on margin, smooth or nearly so on both surfaces, dark green above, paler green beneath, 3 to 6 inches long. *Flowers* in flat-topped end clusters, creamy white, usually with several sterile flowers about ⅝ inch across; blooming May to July.

RANGE. New York to Illinois, Missouri, and Oklahoma; south to Florida and Louisiana.

The cultivated Hills-of-snow Hydrangea is a form with only sterile flowers.

SNOWY HYDRANGEA   *Hydrangea arborescens* ssp. *radiata* (Walt.) McClintock
Saxifrage Family

Leaves are snowy white with felted down on the lower surfaces. Grows in rocky woods from western North Carolina and eastern Tennessee to northern Georgia. (Not illustrated)

BLACK HAW   *Viburnum prunifolium* L.   Honeysuckle Family

FIELD MARKS. A leaf-losing shrub or small tree 5 to about 15 feet high; growing chiefly in upland woods or thickets. *Branchlets* slender, rather stiff and spiky. *Leaves* elliptic to oval or egg-shaped, broadly pointed or roundish at base, blunt to broadly pointed at tip, finely and sharply toothed on margin, dull green above, paler beneath, smooth on both surfaces, 1 to 3 inches long; leafstalks grooved but not winged, ⅜ to ⅝ inch long. *Flowers* all alike, the cluster stalkless or nearly so; blooming April or May. *Fruits* oval-shaped, bluish black, sometimes with a slight whitish bloom, about ⅜ inch long, sweet and edible; ripening September or October.

RANGE. Connecticut to southern Michigan, Iowa, and eastern Kansas; south to northern Florida and Texas.

The bark of the roots is used medicinally.

BURNING-BUSH   *Euonymus atropurpureus* Jacq.   Stafftree Family

FIELD MARKS. An erect leaf-losing shrub 6 to about 15 feet high; growing in rich, moist woods, ravines, and stream bottoms. *Branchlets* roundish and 4-lined. *Leaves* oblong egg-shaped to broadly lance-shaped, usually pointed at base and sharply pointed at tip, finely and sharply toothed on margin, thin-textured, dark green and smooth above, paler and usually somewhat downy beneath, 2 to 5 inches long; leafstalks slender, ¼ to ¾ inch long. *Flowers* purplish brown, about ¼ inch across, in clusters of 5 to 15 from the leaf axils; blooming in June. *Fruits* smooth, purplish pink, about ¾ inch across before bursting; ripening September or October.

RANGE. Western New York and southern Ontario to southern Michigan, central Minnesota, and Montana; south to eastern Virginia, northern Georgia and Alabama, Arkansas, and Oklahoma.

Also known as Wahoo.

STRAWBERRY-BUSH   *Euonymus americanus* L.   Stafftree Family

FIELD MARKS. An erect or straggling leaf-losing shrub 2 to 6 feet high; growing in rich woods, ravines, and along stream banks. *Branchlets* 4-sided. *Leaves* egg-shaped to broadly lance-shaped, usually pointed at base and sharply pointed at tip, finely and sharply toothed on margin, bright green and smooth above, slightly paler and smooth or nearly so beneath, 1 to 3½ inches long; almost stalkless. *Flowers* greenish purple, about ¼ inch across, solitary or 2 or 3 in cluster from leaf axils; blooming in May or June. *Fruits* rough-warty, crimson, ½ to ¾ inch across before bursting; ripening September or October.

RANGE. Southeastern New York and Pennsylvania to southern Illinois, Missouri, and Oklahoma; south to Florida and Texas.

Also known as Bursting-heart.

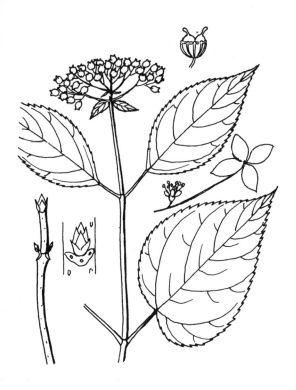

Wild Hydrangea

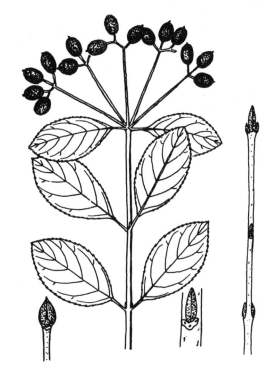

Black Haw

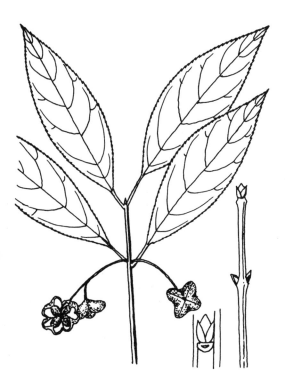

Burning-bush

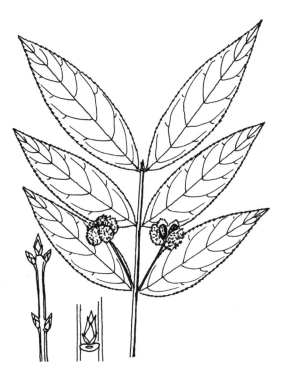

Strawberry-bush

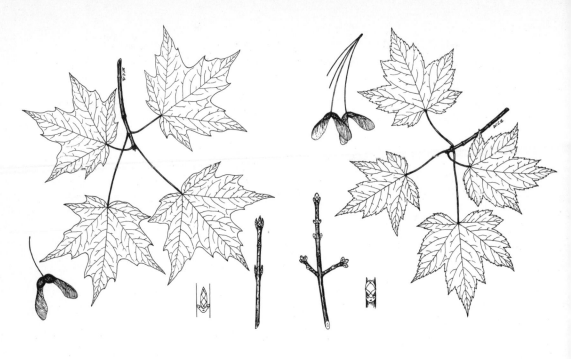

Sugar Maple

Red Maple

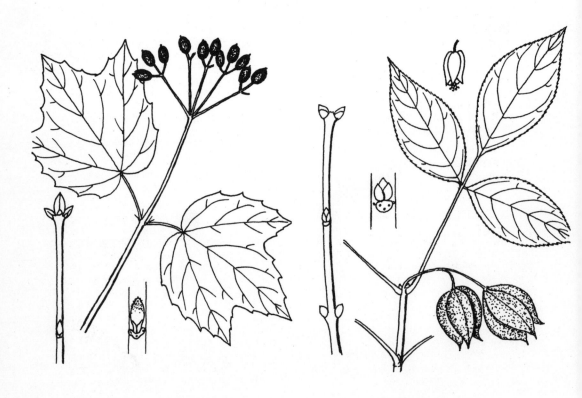

Maple-leaf Viburnum

American Bladdernut

SUGAR MAPLE *Acer saccharum* Marsh.   Maple Family

FIELD MARKS: A large tree 60 to 100 feet or more tall; growing in rich, moist to well-drained, and often rocky soils. *Leaves* 3 to 6 inches broad, usually with 5 pointed and sparingly wavy-toothed lobes separated by broadly U-shaped sinuses, dark green above, paler and often slightly whitened beneath, smooth or nearly so. *Flowers* greenish yellow, clustered, on long and drooping hairy stalks; blooming April to June. *Fruits* paired, the wings about 1 inch long and forming a U; ripening June to September.

RANGE: Newfoundland west to southern Ontario and Minnesota; south to North Carolina, northern Georgia and northern Louisiana.

Valuable hardwood timber tree and chief source of maple syrup and sugar.

RED MAPLE *Acer rubrum* L.   Maple Family

FIELD MARKS: A tree often 40 to 70 feet or more tall; growing in swamps and in well-drained to moderately dry upland areas. *Leaves* 2 to 5 inches broad, 3- to 5-lobed and coarsely toothed, the sides of the terminal lobe parallel or sloping outward, bright green and smooth above, whitened and smooth or white-woolly beneath. *Flowers* blood-red or sometimes yellow, in close clusters; blooming February to April before the leaves appear. *Fruits* paired, the wings about ¾ inch long and forming a V, usually bright red; maturing April to June.

RANGE: Nova Scotia west to Manitoba; south to Florida and eastern Texas.

MAPLE-LEAF VIBURNUM *Viburnum acerifolium* L.   Honeysuckle Family

FIELD MARKS. A leaf-losing shrub 2 to 6 feet high; growing in moist to dry and often rocky woods. *Branchlets* smooth or minutely downy. *Leaves* egg-shaped to roundish, usually with 3 broad and pointed lobes but sometimes almost unlobed or the lobes very short, rounded to heart-shaped at base, coarsely toothed on margin, dull green and smooth or nearly so above, usually more or less downy (rarely nearly smooth) and with minute black dots beneath, 2 to 5 inches long; leafstalks ⅜ to 1 inch long, often with a pair of narrow stipules at base. *Flowers* all alike, sometimes pink-tinged; blooming late April to July. *Fruits* roundish or slightly oval-shaped, bluish black, about ¼ inch long; ripening September or October.

RANGE. Southwestern Quebec to Minnesota south to New England, Georgia, Alabama, and Mississippi.

The pinkish to magenta leaves are very attractive in the fall.

Leaves Opposite—Compound

AMERICAN BLADDERNUT *Staphylea trifolia* L.   Bladdernut Family

FIELD MARKS. A shrub 3 to about 12 feet high; growing in moist thickets, on hillsides, and banks of streams. *Leaves* opposite, compound, long-stalked; the 3 leaflets egg-shaped or elliptic, pointed to roundish at base, abruptly pointed at tip, finely toothed on margin, dark green and smooth above, paler and sometimes downy beneath, end leaflet long-stalked, side ones short-stalked, 2 to 5 inches long. *Flowers* white or creamy white, bell-shaped, about ⅜ inch long, many in elongate and drooping clusters; blooming April to June. *Fruits* 3-sided, inflated, papery, baglike capsules 1 to 3 inches long which contain 3 to 5 light-brown and bony seeds which rattle when capsule is shaken; maturing August to October.

RANGE. Massachusetts to southwestern Quebec, southern Ontario, northern Michigan, and southern Minnesota; south to Georgia, Alabama, southeastern Oklahoma, and southeastern Nebraska.

TRUMPET-CREEPER   *Campsis radicans* (L.) Seem   Bignonia Family

FIELD MARKS. A leaf-losing vine climbing by means of aerial rootlets in 2 short rows at the nodes; growing in moist woods, thickets, or along fence rows. *Leaves* opposite, compound, 8 to 15 inches long; the 9 to 11 leaflets almost stalkless, elliptic to oblong egg-shaped, pointed at both ends, coarsely and sharply toothed on margin, smooth above, slightly paler and often downy on the veins beneath, 1½ to 3 inches long. *Flowers* reddish orange, trumpet-shaped, 5-lobed, 2½ to 3½ inches long, in showy end clusters; blooming June to September. *Fruits* cylindrical, somewhat flattened, 2-ridged capsules 4 to 8 inches long, containing many winged and flattened seeds; maturing September or October.

RANGE. Connecticut and southeastern Pennsylvania to West Virginia, Kentucky, southern Illinois, and Iowa; south to Florida and Texas.

Also called Cow-itch, as the plant causes a severe skin irritation in some people. Often cultivated as an ornamental and sometimes escaping northward.

COMMON ELDER   *Sambucus canadensis* L.   Honeysuckle Family

FIELD MARKS. A leaf-losing shrub 4 to 12 feet high; widely distributed in moist rich soils. *Branchlets* stout, yellowish brown, with warty lenticels, large white pith, and small greenish or brown buds; odor rank when bruised. *Leaves* opposite, compound, 6 to 10 inches long; the 5 to 11 leaflets elliptic or lance-shaped, lower ones often 3-parted, mostly pointed at base and tip, margin sharply toothed, smooth above, paler and sometimes slightly downy beneath, 3 to 6 inches long. *Flowers* small, white, the short corolla tube 5-lobed, in broad flat-topped end clusters; blooming April to August. *Fruits* berry-like, round, purplish black, with 3 to 5 large seeds, about 3/16 inch in diameter; ripening July to October.

RANGE. Nova Scotia to Manitoba; south to Florida and Texas.

Fruits are eaten by birds and used for jelly, pies, and wine.

WHITE ASH   *Fraxinus americana* L.   Olive Family

FIELD MARKS: A large tree 60 to 80 feet or more tall; growing in bottomlands and on rich moist slopes. *Branchlets* have U-shaped leaf scars distinctly notched at the top. *Leaves* 8 to 12 inches long with usually 7 egg-shaped or oblong lance-shaped stalked leaflets 3 to 5 inches long, untoothed or obscurely toothed on margin, dark green and smooth above, pale or whitened and smooth or nearly so beneath. *Fruits* paddle-shaped, 1 to 2 inches long, sides of the flat wing extending less than ⅓ down the seed cavity; maturing August to October.

A variety, the Biltmore Ash, has branchlets, leaf stalks, and lower surfaces of the leaves downy.

RANGE: Newfoundland and Nova Scotia west to Minnesota; south to northern Florida and eastern Texas.

Valuable hardwood timber tree.

RED ASH   *Fraxinus pennsylvanica* Marsh.   Olive Family

FIELD MARKS: A tree 30 to 50 feet or more tall; growing in wet bottomlands and along streams. *Branchlets* have half-round leaf scars which are not notched at the top. *Leaves* 9 to 12 inches long with usually 7 lance-shaped to elliptic stalked leaflets 3 to 5 inches long, margin untoothed or finely saw-toothed above the middle, bright green and smooth above, paler and silky-downy beneath; leaf stalks silky downy. *Fruits* paddle-shaped, 1 to 2 inches long, sides of the flat wing extending more than ⅓ down the seed cavity; maturing August to October.

A variety, the Green Ash, has branchlets, leaf stalks, and lower surfaces of the leaves smooth.

RANGE: Nova Scotia west to Manitoba; south to northern Florida and eastern Texas.

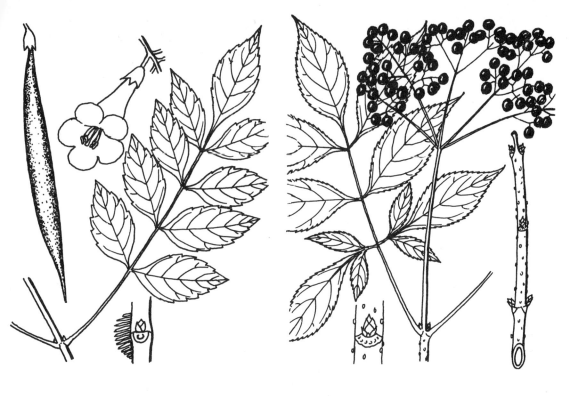

Trumpet-creeper

Common Elder

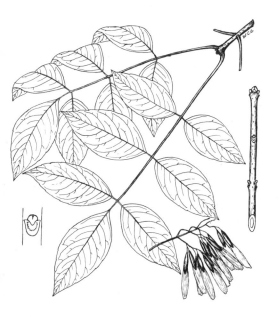

White Ash

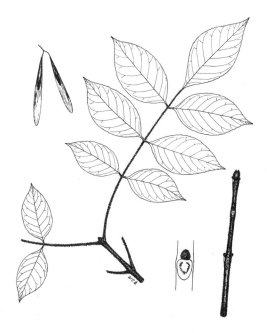

Red Ash

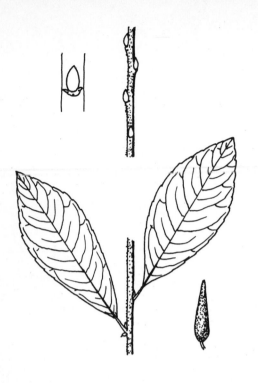

Bebb Willow

Early Low Blueberry

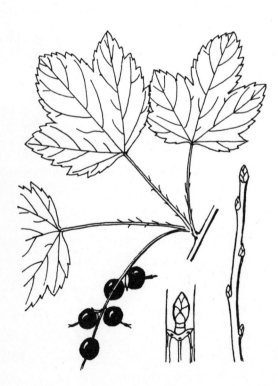

Wild Black Currant

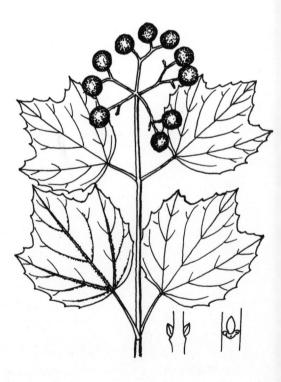

Squashberry

NORTHERN WOODY PLANTS OF VARIOUS HABITATS
Leaves Alternate—Simple—Mostly Toothed

BEBB WILLOW *Salix bebbiana* Sarg.   Willow Family

FIELD MARKS. A large shrub usually 5 to 15 feet high, or occasionally a small tree; growing in either wet or dry places. *Branchlets* gray-downy. *Leaves* rather broad, elliptic or often broadest above the middle, pointed at tip, pointed to rounded at base, wavy-toothed or (more rarely) untoothed on the margin, thick and firm in texture; dull green, minutely downy, and wrinkled-veiny above; densely whitish- or grayish-woolly beneath; 1½ to 3 inches long. The slender, downy leafstalks are often reddish in color, and stipules are small or lacking.

RANGE. Newfoundland and Labrador to Alaska; south to New Jersey, Maryland, the region of the Great Lakes, Nebraska, New Mexico, and California.

Also known as the Beaked Willow.

EARLY LOW BLUEBERRY *Vaccinium angustifolium* Ait.   Heath Family

FIELD MARKS. A spreading leaf-losing shrub 8 inches to about 2 feet high; growing in open rocky woods and clearings. *Branchlets* olive green to yellowish green, somewhat grooved, warty-dotted. *Leaves* short-stalked, narrowly elliptic or lance-shaped, pointed at both ends, finely and sharply toothed on margin, bright green and smooth above, paler green and sometimes whitened or downy beneath, ½ to 1½ inches long. *Flowers* white or pink-tinged, urn-shaped, clustered; blooming April to June. *Fruits* blue, with a heavy whitish bloom, or sometimes lustrous black, about ¼ inch in diameter, sweet and juicy; ripening June to August.

RANGE. Labrador to Saskatchewan; south to western Virginia, West Virginia, Indiana, Minnesota, and northeastern Iowa.

The common commercial wild blueberry of New England.

Leaves Alternate—Lobed

WILD BLACK CURRANT *Ribes americanum* L'Her.   Saxifrage Family

FIELD MARKS. An erect unarmed shrub 1½ to 4 feet high, with spreading branches; growing in rich, moist, often rocky woods. *Branchlets* dotted with small yellow resin-glands. *Leaves* roundish, squarish to somewhat heart-shaped at base, sharply 3- to 5-lobed and double-toothed on margin, smooth or nearly so above, more or less downy and dotted with yellow resin-glands beneath, 1½ to 3 inches wide. *Flowers* rather large, yellow and whitish, several in a drooping cluster; blooming April to June. *Fruits* smooth, black, about 5/16 inch in diameter; ripening July to September.

RANGE. Nova Scotia to Alberta; south to Delaware, West Virginia, the region of the Great Lakes, Missouri, and Oklahoma.

Leaves Opposite—Lobed

SQUASHBERRY *Viburnum edule* (Michx.) Raf.   Honeysuckle Family

FIELD MARKS. A straggling or sprawling leaf-losing shrub 1 to 4 feet high; growing in cool moist woods and ravines. *Leaves* broadly oval or broadest above the middle, usually with 3 broadly pointed short lobes above the middle, rounded to somewhat heart-shaped at base, coarsely and irregularly toothed on margin, smooth above, slightly paler and more or less downy on the veins beneath, 1 to 2½ inches long; leaf-stalks ⅜ to ¾ inch long, often with a pair of small glands near the summit. *Flowers* all alike, the cluster less than 1½ inches broad; blooming May to August. *Fruits* roundish or slightly egg-shaped, light red or orange, about ⅜ inch in diameter; ripening August to October.

RANGE. Labrador to Alaska; south to Maine; northern New York, Michigan, and Minnesota; Colorado and Oregon.

The acid fruits are used for sauce and jelly.

ROSEBAY RHODODENDRON *Rhododendron maximum* L.   Heath Family

FIELD MARKS. An evergreen shrub or small tree commonly 5 to 15 feet (rarely to 40 feet) high; growing along streams and on moist, rocky, wooded slopes and sometimes forming dense thickets. *Leaves* usually broadest above the middle, tapering to a wedge-shaped base, broadly pointed at tip, untoothed on margin, very thick and leathery, lustrous above, paler and dull and sometimes downy beneath, 4 to 8 inches long. *Flowers* white to rose pink, spotted with olive green to orange, open bell-shaped with 5 rounded lobes, about 1½ inches across, in large clusters; blooming June or July. *Fruits* downy, ¾ to 1 inch long.

RANGE. Southwestern Maine to New York, southern Ontario, and Ohio; south in the mountains to northern Georgia and Alabama.

ALTERNATE-LEAF DOGWOOD *Cornus alternifolia* L. f.   Dogwood Family

FIELD MARKS. A shrub or small tree 4 to sometimes 25 feet high, with almost horizontally spreading branches, and larger stems dark green and often streaked with white; growing in moist woods and along streams. *Branchlets* greenish and with a white pith. *Leaves* alternate, very often crowded toward the tips of the branchlets, rather long and slender stalked, oval or broadly egg-shaped, broadly pointed at base, pointed at tip, bright green and smooth above, paler and sometimes slightly downy beneath, 2 to 5 inches long. *Flowers* creamy white, in flat-topped clusters; blooming May or June. *Fruits* bluish black, roundish, ¼ to ⅜ inch in diameter, on bright-red stalks; ripening August or September.

RANGE. Newfoundland to southern Ontario, southeastern Manitoba, and eastern Minnesota; south to Florida, Alabama, and northern Arkansas.

Also called Blue or Pagoda Dogwood.

CUCUMBERTREE *Magnolia acuminata* L.   Magnolia Family

FIELD MARKS: A tree 60 to 90 feet tall; growing on rich moist soils and rocky slopes. *Branchlets* spicy-aromatic when bruised or broken. *Leaves* 5 to 10 inches long, oval or broadly egg-shaped, pointed at tip and broadly pointed at base, untoothed on margin, bright yellowish-green above, paler and often downy beneath. *Flowers* greenish-yellow to yellow, cup-shaped, 2 to 3 inches long; blooming April to June. *Fruits* in knobby, smooth, cone-like clusters 2 to 3 inches long; becoming bright red in late summer when each fruit splits down one side and releases scarlet fleshy-coated seeds on silky threads.

RANGE: Western New York and southern Ontario south to northern Georgia, Mississippi and Arkansas.

SHINGLE OAK *Quercus imbricaria* Michx.   Beech Family

FIELD MARKS: A tree 40 to 60 feet tall; growing in bottomlands and on moist slopes. *Leaves* 4 to 6 inches long, laurel-like, narrowly elliptic or top-shaped, untoothed on margin and with a small bristle at tip, thickish and somewhat leathery in texture, shiny dark green above, paler and downy beneath. *Fruit* a roundish dark brown acorn about ½ inch long, seated in a deeply bowl-shaped cup; maturing in 2 years; kernel bitter.

RANGE: New Jersey and Pennsylvania west to southern Michigan and Nebraska; south to northern Georgia and northern Louisiana.

Rosebay Rhododendron

Alternate-leaf Dogwood

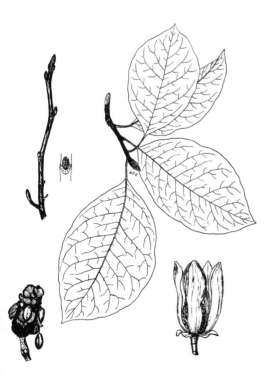

Cucumbertree

Shingle Oak

Large Cranberry

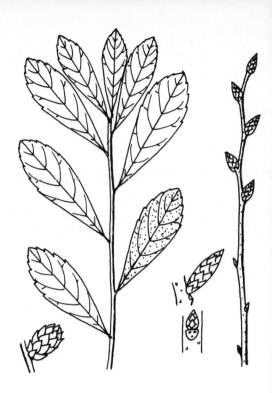

Sweetgale

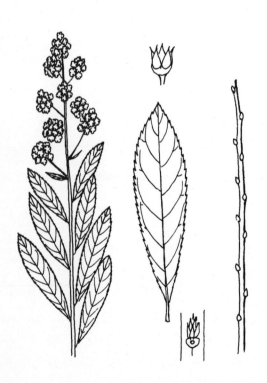

Narrow-leaf Meadowsweet

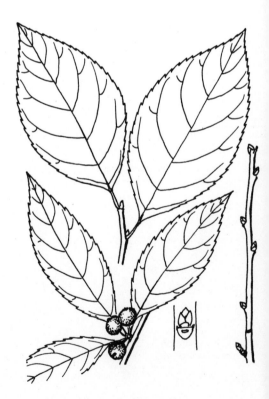

Largeleaf Holly

NORTHERN WOODY PLANTS FOUND SOUTHWARD IN APPALACHIANS,
Continued
Leaves Alternate—Simple—Entire

LARGE CRANBERRY *Vaccinium macrocarpum* Ait. Heath Family

FIELD MARKS. A trailing evergreen shrub with slender stems up to 3 feet long; growing in wet peaty soils and sphagnum bogs. *Leaves* very short-stalked, oblong-elliptic, roundish or blunt at both ends, margin untoothed and sometimes slightly rolled, smooth, leathery in texture, dark green and lustrous above, pale or somewhat whitened beneath, ¼ to ⅝ inch long. *Flowers* pink, with 4 recurved lobes, solitary or 2 to 4 on slender stalks in end clusters; blooming May to August. *Fruits* red, ⅜ to ¾ inch in diameter, sour; ripening August to November.

RANGE. Newfoundland to Minnesota; south to coastal plain and mountains of North Carolina, Tennessee, the region of the Great Lakes, and Arkansas.

The familiar cranberry grown commercially and sold in markets. Also called American Cranberry.

Leaves Alternate—Simple—Toothed

SWEETGALE *Myrica gale* L. Bayberry Family

FIELD MARKS. An aromatic leaf-losing shrub 1 to 4 feet high; growing in cool swamps and the boggy borders of streams and ponds. *Branchlets* often have large pointed flower buds toward the tips, and they are fragrant when broken. *Leaves* alternate, broadest toward the tip and tapering to the base, toothed above the middle, resin-dotted and sometimes with scattered hairs on the lower surface, 1 to 2 inches long, pleasantly fragrant when crushed. *Fruits* small, 2-winged, resin-dotted nutlets borne in conelike clusters.

RANGE. Newfoundland to Alaska; south to northern New Jersey, the region of the Great Lakes, Oregon, and in the Appalachians to western North Carolina.

The leaves have been used in clothes closets to repel moths, as a vermifuge, and as a substitute for tea.

NARROW-LEAF MEADOWSWEET *Spiraea alba* DuRoi Rose Family

FIELD MARKS. An erect shrub 2 to 5 feet high; growing in wet open places, swamp thickets, and along streams. *Branchlets* yellowish brown, more or less angled, often slightly downy. *Leaves* numerous, crowded, narrowly elliptic or broadest above the middle, pointed at both ends, finely and sharply toothed on margin, smooth on both surfaces or slightly downy beneath, 2 to 3 inches long. *Flowers* white, in a narrow and somewhat downy end cluster from 2 to 5 inches in length; blooming June to September.

RANGE. Northwestern Vermont to southwestern Quebec and Saskatchewan; south to Delaware, Ohio, Illinois, Missouri, North Dakota, and in the Appalachian Mountains to North Carolina.

LARGELEAF HOLLY *Ilex ambigua* var. *montana* (T. & G.) Ahles Holly Family

FIELD MARKS. A leaf-losing shrub or small tree 5 to 20 feet high; growing in cool, moist, wooded areas. *Leaves* often clustered on short lateral spurlike branches, elliptic to egg-shaped or lance-shaped, roundish to pointed at base, pointed at tip, sharply toothed on margin, thin in texture, bright green and smooth above, sometimes with scattered soft hairs beneath, 2½ to 5 inches long. *Flowers* blooming April to June. *Fruits* bright red, short-stalked, about ⅜ inch in diameter; ripening August to October but scarcely persisting.

RANGE. Southwestern Massachusetts to western New York; south along the mountains to northern Georgia.

WILD RED CHERRY *Prunus pensylvanica* L. Rose Family

FIELD MARKS: A tree usually less than 30 feet tall; growing in clearings and burned-over areas in cool regions. *Bark* smooth, shiny, reddish-brown, with prominent horizontal lenticels. *Leaves* 3 to 4 inches long, oblong lance-shaped, rounded to broadly pointed at base, taper-pointed at tip, finely saw-toothed on margin, shiny bright green on both surfaces but slightly paler beneath. *Flowers* white, about ½ inch across, on slender stalks in clusters of 4 to 10; blooming April to June. *Fruits* roundish, bright red, about ¼ inch across, with a thin and very sour flesh; ripening July to September.

RANGE: Labrador west to British Columbia; south to Pennsylvania, northern Illinois and North Dakota, and in mountains to North Carolina, Tennessee and Colorado.

Also called Fire Cherry and Pin Cherry.

CHOKE CHERRY *Prunus virginiana* L. Rose Family

FIELD MARKS. A large leaf-losing shrub or small tree; growing along woods borders, fence rows, and wayside thickets. *Branchlets* have a very disagreeable odor when bruised or broken. *Leaves* oval or broadest above the middle, rounded to broadly pointed at base, abruptly pointed at tip, finely and sharply toothed on margin, dull green above, paler beneath, smooth on both surfaces, 2 to 4 inches long; leafstalks with glands at summit. *Flowers* white, about ⅜ inch across, strong-scented, numerous, and in a dense and elongate cluster; blooming April to June. *Fruits* roundish, dark red to purplish black, about ⅜ inch in diameter, very astringent; ripening July to September.

RANGE. Newfoundland to British Columbia; south to Maryland, northern Georgia, eastern Kentucky, Illinois, Kansas, New Mexico and California.

APPALACHIAN CHERRY *Prunus susquehanae* Willd. Rose Family

FIELD MARKS. An erect leaf-losing shrub 2 to about 8 feet high; growing in sandy or rocky woods, thickets, and clearings. *Leaves* elliptic or sometimes broadest above the middle, wedge-shaped at base, blunt or broadly pointed at tip, margin toothed with low and bluntish teeth above the middle, thin but firm in texture, light green above, paler beneath, smooth on both surfaces, 1¼ to 2½ inches long. *Flowers* white, about ⅜ inch across, 2 to 4 in a cluster; blooming May or June. *Fruits* roundish, purplish black, about ⅜ inch in diameter; ripening July to September.

RANGE. Southwestern Maine and Quebec to southeastern Minnesota; south to Long Island, Virginia, central and western North Carolina, Ohio, Illinois, and Minnesota.

BLACK CHOKEBERRY *Aronia melanocarpa* (Michx.) Ell. Rose Family

FIELD MARKS. A shrub 2 to 6 feet high, growing in swamps and moist to fairly dry thickets and woods. *Branchlets* smooth. *Leaves* elliptic or more often broadest above the middle, pointed at base, pointed to blunt at tip, finely and sharply toothed on margin, smooth on both surfaces, paler beneath, 1 to 3 inches long. *Flowers* blooming in June. *Fruits* black, about ¼ inch in diameter; ripening September or October.

RANGE. Newfoundland to northwestern Ontario and Minnesota, south to Pennsylvania and along the mountains to northern Georgia.

Wild Red Cherry

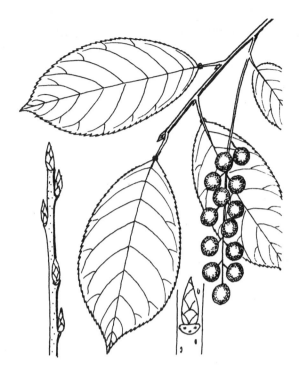

Choke Cherry

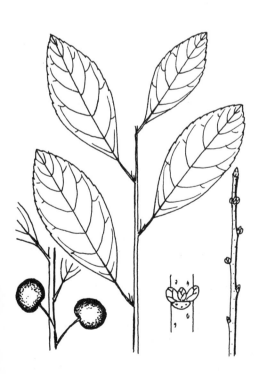

Appalachian Cherry

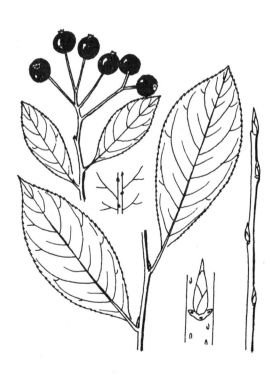

Black Chokeberry

Yellow Birch

Black Birch

Paper Birch

Gray Birch

YELLOW BIRCH *Betula alleghaniensis* Brit.   Birch Family

FIELD MARKS: A tree 60 to 80 feet or more tall; growing in cool, moist, and usually rocky places. *Bark* yellowish to bronze or silvery-gray, peeling in thin film-like curls. *Branchlets* with a faint odor and taste of wintergreen. *Leaves* paired on short spurs but not opposite, egg-shaped to oblong, doubly saw-toothed on margin, dark green above, paler beneath, smooth or nearly so, 3 to 4½ inches long. *Fruit* a small 2-winged, seed-like nutlet; borne in egg-shaped cone-like structures 1 to 1½ inches long that break up in late fall or winter.

RANGE: Newfouland west to southeastern Manitoba; south to Delaware, Pennsylvania, northeastern Iowa, and in Applachians to northern Georgia.

A valuable hardwood timber tree.

BLACK BIRCH *Betula lenta* L.   Birch Family

FIELD MARKS: A tree 50 to 75 feet or more tall; growing in rich moist and often rocky soils. *Bark* shiny reddish-brown and cherry-like; on large trunks becoming black and broken into plates. *Branchlets* have a decided odor and taste of wintergreen. *Leaves* paired on short spurs but not opposite, egg-shaped to oblong, finely saw-toothed on margin, dark green above, paler beneath, smooth or nearly so, 2 to 4 inches long. *Fruit* a small 2-winged, seed-like nutlet; borne in cylindrical cone-like structures 1 to 1½ inches long that break up in late fall or winter.

RANGE: Southern Maine west to southern Ontario; south to Delaware, Ohio, and in the Appalachians to northern Georgia and Alabama.

Also called Sweet Birch. Formerly the chief source of oil of wintergreen.

PAPER BIRCH *Betula papyrifera* Marsh.   Birch Family

FIELD MARKS: A tree 50 to 75 feet or more tall; growing along streams or lake shores and widespread on burned-over areas in the North. *Bark* chalky-white or creamy-white, peeling in thin papery layers; inner bark orange. *Leaves* paired on short spurs but not opposite, egg-shaped, doubly saw-toothed on margin, dark green above, paler beneath, smooth or nearly so, 2 to 3 inches long. *Fruit* a small 2-winged, seed-like nutlet; borne in narrowly cylindrical, long-stalked cone-like structures 1 to 1½ inches long that break up in late fall or winter.

RANGE: Labrador west to Alaska; south to New England, northern Pennsylvania and Illinois, Montana, Washington, and locally in the Appalachians to North Carolina.

Also called Canoe Birch and White Birch.

GRAY BIRCH *Betula populifolia* Marsh.   Birch Family

FIELD MARKS: A small tree seldom 30 feet tall with several trunks often in a clump; growing in abandoned fields and burned-over areas. *Bark* chalky white, not peeling, marked with triangular black patches below the branches. *Leaves* paired on short spurs but not opposite, triangular in outline, long-pointed at tip, doubly saw-toothed on margin, dark green above, paler beneath, 2 to 3 inches long, with long and slender leaf stalks. *Fruit* a small 2-winged, seed-like nutlet; borne in cylindrical, stalked, cone-like structures 1 to 1½ inches long that break up in late fall or winter.

RANGE: Nova Scotia west to southern Ontario; south to Delaware, Pennsylvania, northwestern Indiana, and locally in the Appalachians to North Carolina.

Also called Old-field Birch.

TREMBLING ASPEN *Populus tremuloides* Michx.   Willow Family

FIELD MARKS: A tree usually 20 to 40 feet tall; often pioneering on cut-over or burned-over land in the North. *Bark* of young trees is smooth, greenish, with blackish horizontal patches or blotches beneath the branches. *Branchlets* and buds are reddish-brown and shiny. *Leaves* nearly round or slightly egg-shaped with a finely saw-toothed margin, shiny green above, paler beneath, smooth, 1 to 3 inches across; with slender and flattened leaf stalks. *Fruits* are small bottle-shaped capsules containing tiny seeds with a tuft of silky hairs, borne in catkins and maturing in spring.

RANGE: Newfoundland and Labrador west to Alaska; south to New Jersey, northern Virginia, Kentucky, Iowa, and throughout the western mountains to northern Mexico.

Also called Quaking Aspen.

BIGTOOTH ASPEN *Populus grandidentata* Michx.   Willow Family

FIELD MARKS: A tree quite similar to the Trembling Aspen but preferring richer soils. *Bark* darker than that of the Trembling Aspen. *Branchlets* dull grayish-brown with dull and dusty looking buds. *Leaves* roundish or broadly egg-shaped with large and coarse teeth on margin, dark green above, paler beneath, smooth or nearly so, 2 to 3 inches across, with slender and flattened leaf stalks. *Fruits* similar to those of the Quaking Aspen.

RANGE: Nova Scotia west to Ontario; south to Delaware, Pennsylvania, Illinois and Minnesota; and in the Appalachians to North Carolina and Tennessee.

ROUNDLEAF JUNEBERRY *Amelanchier sanguinea* (Pursh) DC.   Rose Family

FIELD MARKS. A somewhat straggling shrub 3 to 8 feet high, with a solitary stem or a few stems in a clump; growing in dry, upland, rocky woods. *Leaves* roundish to oblong oval, blunt or rounded at tip, often heart-shaped at base, margin coarsely and sharply toothed nearly to the base, 1 to 2½ inches long. *Fruits* purplish black with a whitish bloom, sweet and juicy; ripening July or August.

RANGE. Quebec and Ontario; south to New York, western North Carolina, Michigan, Wisconsin, and Iowa.

Leaves Alternate—Simple—Lobed

SWEETFERN *Comptonia peregrina* (L.) Coult.   Bayberry Family

FIELD MARKS. An aromatic, much-branched, leaf-losing shrub from 1 to about 3 feet high; growing on dry rocky or sandy, and usually sterile, soils. *Branchlets* slender, downy, resin-dotted when young, fragrant when broken, often with clusters of catkins at the tips. *Leaves* alternate, fernlike, and deeply cut into numerous lobes, dark green above, paler and downy beneath, with numerous small resin dots on both surfaces, 1½ to 4 inches long, pleasantly fragrant when crushed. *Fruits* small olive-brown nutlets which are surrounded by pointed bracts and borne in little burrlike heads.

RANGE. Nova Scotia to Manitoba, south to interior North Carolina, and along the mountains to northern Georgia.

The leaves have astringent and tonic properties and were once used in home remedies and as a substitute for tea. Often heavily browsed by deer.

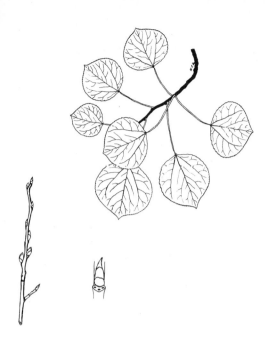

Trembling Aspen

Bigtooth Aspen

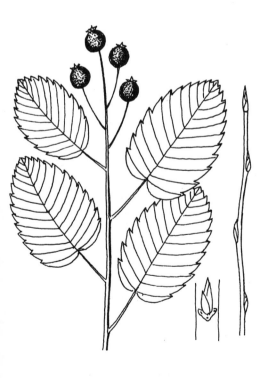

Roundleaf Juneberry

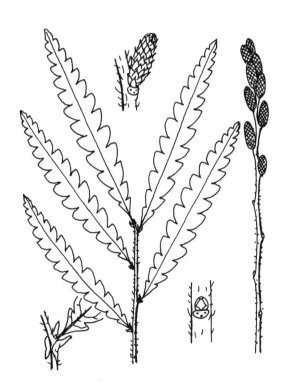

Sweetfern

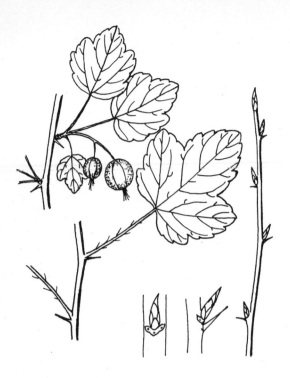

Roundleaf Gooseberry

Prickly Gooseberry

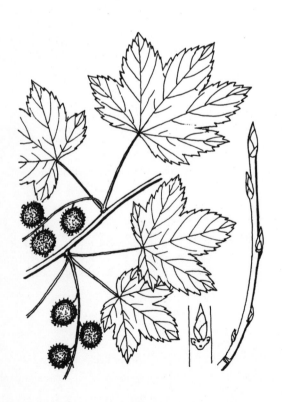

Skunk Currant

Purple-flowering Raspberry

NORTHERN WOODY PLANTS FOUND SOUTHWARD IN APPALACHIANS,
Continued
Leaves Alternate—Simple—Lobed

ROUNDLEAF GOOSEBERRY *Ribes rotundifolium* Michx.   Saxifrage Family

FIELD MARKS. A shrub 2 to 3 feet high; growing in cool rocky mountain woods. *Branchlets* pale brown or grayish, unarmed or with short nodal spines. *Leaves* roundish, often heart-shaped at base, usually with 3 bluntly toothed lobes, smooth or minutely downy above, sometimes sparingly hairy beneath, ¾ to 3 inches wide. *Flowers* greenish purple, solitary or 2 or 3 in a cluster; blooming April to July. *Fruits* smooth, purplish, ¼ to ⅜ inch in diameter, sweet; ripening June to September.
RANGE. Massachusetts to New York and Kentucky; south to western North Carolina and eastern Tennessee.
Also called Mountain Gooseberry.

PRICKLY GOOSEBERRY *Ribes cynosbati* L.   Saxifrage Family

FIELD MARKS. A shrub 1½ to 4 feet high; growing in rocky woods and clearings. *Branchlets* pale brown or grayish, with slender nodal spines and often scattered prickles. *Leaves* roundish, often heart-shaped at base, 3- to 5-lobed and bluntly toothed, soft-hairy on both surfaces or nearly smooth, 1½ to 2½ inches wide. *Flowers* greenish, solitary or 2 or 3 in a cluster; blooming April to June. *Fruits* prickly, reddish purple, ⅓ to ½ inch in diameter, sweet; ripening July to September.
RANGE. New Brunswick to Manitoba; south to Georgia, Alabama, and Missouri.
Also called Pasture Gooseberry and Dogberry.

SKUNK CURRANT *Ribes glandulosum* Grauer   Saxifrage Family

FIELD MARKS. A low, prostrate, sprawling or reclining unarmed shrub, all parts giving off a skunklike odor when crushed; growing in cold, damp, rocky woods. *Leaves* broader than long, deeply 5- to 7-lobed and doubly toothed on margin, heart-shaped at base, smooth above, sometimes slightly downy beneath, 1½ to 3 inches wide. *Flowers* yellowish green or purplish, several in a slender-stalked cluster; blooming May or June. *Fruits* glandular-bristly, coral red, unpleasant to the taste; ripening July to September.
RANGE. Newfoundland to British Columbia; south to New England, New York, northern Ohio, Michigan, Minnesota, and in the Appalachian Mountains to western North Carolina and northwestern South Carolina.

PURPLE-FLOWERING RASPBERRY *Rubus odoratus* L.   Rose Family

FIELD MARKS. A straggling, unarmed shrub 2 to 5 feet high; growing in moist rocky woods and ravines. *Branchlets,* leafstalks, and flower stalks are covered with sticky, reddish, bristly hairs; the bark peels freely off the canes. *Leaves* maple-like, 3- to 5-lobed and sharply toothed on margin, bright green and more or less downy on both surfaces, 4 to 7 inches wide. *Flowers* 1½ to 2 inches across, roselike, rose purple; blooming June to August. *Fruits* dull red, rather insipid, in somewhat flattened dome-shaped clusters ½ to ¾ inch across; ripening July to September.
RANGE. Nova Scotia and southern Ontario to southern Michigan; south to New York, northern Georgia, and Tennessee.

BUTTERNUT *Juglans cinerea* L.   Walnut Family

FIELD MARKS: A tree 30 to 60 feet or more tall; growing on rich moist to well-drained slopes and along streams. *Branchlets* stout, greenish-gray to buffy; the 3-lobed leaf scars with a raised downy pad above them. *Leaves* 15 to 30 inches long with a sticky-hairy stalk; divided into 11 to 17 oblong lance-shaped and stalkless leaflets, 2 to 4 inches long, finely saw-toothed on margin, dark yellowish-green above, paler and downy beneath. *Fruit* an oblong egg-shaped, bony-shelled and deeply sculptured nut 1½ to 2½ inches long; covered with a greenish-brown and sticky-hairy husk.

RANGE: New Brunswick west to southern Ontario and Wisconsin; south to northern Georgia, Mississippi and Arkansas.

Also called White Walnut.

AMERICAN MOUNTAIN-ASH *Sorbus americana* Marsh.   Rose Family

FIELD MARKS. A tall shrub or small tree to 20 or 25 feet; growing in cold swamps or bogs and on rocky ridges at high elevations. *Branchlets* rather stout and with large gummy buds. *Leaves* alternate, compound, 6 to 10 inches long; leaflets 11 to 17, lance-shaped, rounded to pointed at base, long-pointed at tip, sharply toothed on margin, smooth on both surfaces, 2 to 3 inches long. *Flowers* small, white, 5-petalled, many in a broad flat-topped end cluster; blooming May or June. *Fruits* apple-like, bright orange red, shiny, about ¼ inch in diameter; ripening August to October.

RANGE. Newfoundland to Manitoba; south to New Jersey, northern Illinois, and along the mountains to northern Georgia.

The fruits are eaten by the ruffed grouse and many other wild birds; the twigs are browsed by deer.

RED RASPBERRY *Rubus idaeus* var. *strigosus* (Michx.) Maxim.   Rose Family

FIELD MARKS. A shrub with arching, round canes 2 to 6 feet high, sometimes slightly whitened when young and usually bristly but with few or no prickles; growing on rocky slopes and in clearings. *Leaves* with 3 to 5 leaflets which are egg-shaped, rounded to somewhat heart-shaped at base, pointed at tip, double-toothed on margin, whitened and downy beneath, 2 to 3 inches long; leafstalks bristly. *Flowers* white, petals small; blooming May to July. *Fruits* red, in half-round clusters; ripening July to September.

RANGE. Newfoundland to British Columbia; south to western North Carolina, Ohio, Indiana, Nebraska, and Wyoming.

BLACK RASPBERRY *Rubus occidentalis* L.   Rose Family

FIELD MARKS. Different from the preceding in having strongly whitened canes with scattered, hooked prickles and leafstalks with smaller but similar prickles. *Fruits* purplish black, in half-round clusters; ripening June or July.

RANGE. New Brunswick to Minnesota, south to Georgia and Colorado.

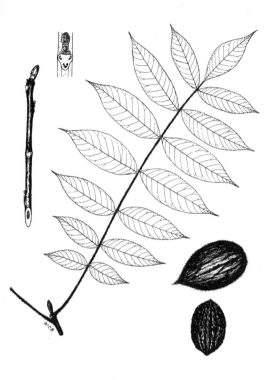

Butternut

American Mountain-ash

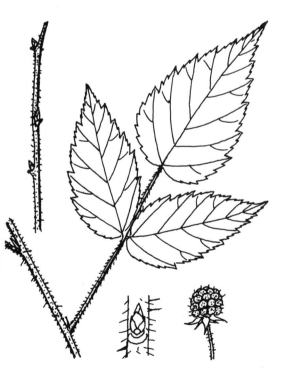

Red Raspberry

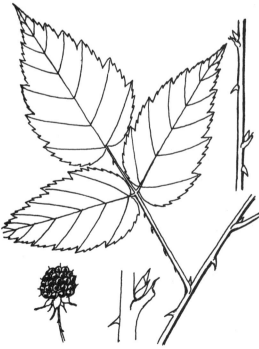

Black Raspberry

Highbush Blackberry

Mountain Blackberry

Swamp Dewberry

Northern Prickly-ash

HIGHBUSH BLACKBERRY *Rubus allegheniensis* Porter   Rose Family

FIELD MARKS. A shrub with erect or arching, often stout, angled, purplish-red canes 3 to 6 feet high; well armed with stout, straight, broad-based prickles; growing in woods borders, clearings, and wayside thickets. *Leaves* with prickly leafstalks and 3 or 5 leaflets which are egg-shaped, rounded to somewhat heart-shaped at base, pointed at tip, sharply and doubly toothed on margin, smooth or nearly so above, densely downy beneath, 2 to 4½ inches long. *Flowers* white, about 1 inch across, clustered; blooming April to June. The younger branchlets and the flower stalks are quite densely covered with gland-tipped hairs. *Fruits* black, in roundish to thimble-shaped clusters; ripening July or August.

RANGE. New Brunswick to Minnesota; south to Maryland, Missouri, and in the Appalachians to nothern Georgia.

MOUNTAIN BLACKBERRY *Rubus canadensis* L.   Rose Family

FIELD MARKS. Similar to Highbush Blackberry but stems unarmed or with only an occasional weak prickle. *Leaves* smooth and green on both surfaces. Young growth and flower stalks smooth.

RANGE. Newfoundland to Ontario and Minnesota, south along the higher Appalachians to northern Georgia.

SWAMP DEWBERRY *Rubus hispidus* L.   Rose Family

FIELD MARKS. A semi-evergreen plant with slender, trailing, bristly-hairy stems; growing in cool moist woods and bogs. *Leaves* usually with 3 leaflets which are elliptic to roundish or broadest above the middle, rounded to pointed at both ends, sharply toothed on margin, dark green and lustrous above, paler and often slightly downy beneath, ¾ to 2 inches long. *Flowers* small, white; blooming June to September. *Fruits* small, purplish to black, few in a cluster; ripening August to October.

RANGE. Nova Scotia to Wisconsin; south to Maryland, the region of the Great Lakes, and in the mountains to northern Georgia.

NORTHERN PRICKLY-ASH *Zanthoxylum americanum* Mill.   Rue Family

FIELD MARKS. A leaf-losing shrub 4 to about 15 feet high; growing in rocky woods or along streams. *Branchlets* with pairs of broad-based nodal prickles, with a lemon-like odor when bruised; buds hairy, rusty-red. *Leaves* alternate, compound, 3 to 10 inches long; the 5 to 11 leaflets almost stalkless, egg-shaped, rounded to broadly pointed at base, pointed at tip, untoothed on margin, smooth or nearly so above, often slightly downy beneath, glandular-dotted, with lemon-like odor when crushed, 1 to 2½ inches long. *Flowers* small, greenish, clustered; blooming in April or May. *Fruits* dry, reddish-brown pods about 3/16 inch long, containing 1 or 2 shiny black seeds; maturing August or September.

RANGE. Quebec and Ontario to South Dakota; south to northern Georgia, Alabama, and northeastern Oklahoma.

Also called Toothache-tree; once used as a remedy for toothache, rheumatism, ulcers, colic, etc.

AMERICAN FLY HONEYSUCKLE   *Lonicera canadensis* Marsh.   Honeysuckle Family

FIELD MARKS. A leaf-losing shrub 2 to 4 feet high; growing in cool, moist woodlands. *Branchlets* smooth, flexible, spreading. *Leaves* egg-shaped, rounded or heart-shaped at base, broadly pointed or blunt at tip, margin untoothed but hairy-fringed, smooth or nearly so on both surfaces, 1 to 3½ inches long. *Flowers* greenish yellow, funnel-shaped, 5-lobed, paired on long axillary stalks; blooming April to June. *Fruits* bright red, egg-shaped, paired but distinct berries about ¼ inch long; ripening July to September.

RANGE. Nova Scotia to Saskatchewan; south to northern New Jersey, northern Georgia, Indiana, and northeastern Iowa.

NORTHERN WITHEROD   *Viburnum cassinoides* L.   Honeysuckle Family

FIELD MARKS. A leaf-losing shrub 3 to 8 feet high; growing in cool, moist, usually rocky woods and swamps. *Branchlets* slender, dull, rather flexible. *Leaves* narrowly egg-shaped to oblong-elliptic, pointed to roundish at base, pointed to blunt at tip, sometimes obscurely toothed on margin, dull above, paler and sometimes rusty-scurfy on midrib beneath, 1½ to 4 inches long. *Flowers* all alike, the cluster on a distinct *stalk;* blooming May or June. *Fruits* roundish or slightly oval, bluish black, whitened with a bloom, about 5/16 inch long; ripening August to October.

RANGE. Newfoundland to Ontario; south to Delaware, Maryland, northern Georgia, and Alabama, and the region of the Great Lakes.

Also called Wild-raisin.

Leaves Opposite—Simple—Toothed

SWEET VIBURNUM   *Viburnum lentago* L.   Honeysuckle Family

FIELD MARKS. A leaf-losing shrub or small tree 5 to 15 (rarely 30) feet high; growing in moist woods, thickets, and borders of swamps. *Branchlets* long, slender, flexible. *Leaves* oval or egg-shaped, rounded to broadly pointed at base, abruptly long-pointed at tip, finely and sharply toothed on margin, smooth, paler beneath, 2 to 4 inches long; leafstalks ½ to 1 inch long, prominently winged. *Flowers* all alike, the cluster stalkless or nearly so; blooming May or June. *Fruits* oval-shaped, bluish black, whitened with a bloom, about ½ inch long; ripening September and October.

RANGE. New England and Quebec to Manitoba; south to New Jersey, West Virginia, Ohio, Missouri, and Colorado.

Also called Nannyberry and Sheepberry. The wood has a rank odor.

HOBBLEBUSH   *Viburnum alnifolium* Marsh.   Honeysuckle Family

FIELD MARKS. A leaf-losing shrub 3 to 10 feet high, the forked branches often bending over and rooting at the tip; growing in cool, moist, rocky woods or along streams. *Branchlets* and large naked end buds densely coated with cinnamon-colored, starry-branched hairs. *Leaves* roundish or heart-shaped, broadly pointed at tip, finely toothed on margin, veiny, becoming smooth or nearly so above but remaining rusty-hairy on the veins beneath, 4 to about 7 inches long. *Flowers* of 2 kinds; the marginal ones about ½ inch across and sterile; blooming April to June. *Fruits* egg-shaped, bright red becoming purplish black, about ⅜ inch long; ripening July to September.

RANGE. New Brunswick to Ontario; south to northern New Jersey, Pennsylvania, Ohio, and Michigan, and in the mountains to northern Georgia.

Also called Witch-hobble.

American Fly Honeysuckle

Northern Witherod

Sweet Viburnum

Hobblebush

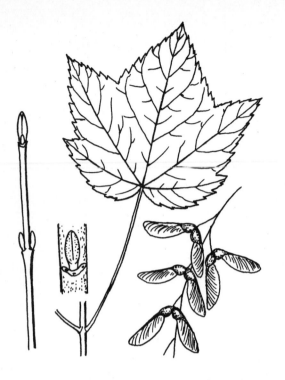

Mountain Maple

Striped Maple

Northern Bush-honeysuckle

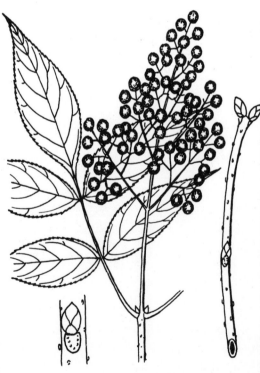

Red-berried Elder

NORTHERN WOODY PLANTS FOUND SOUTHWARD IN APPALACHIANS,
Continued
Leaves Opposite—Simple—Lobed

MOUNTAIN MAPLE *Acer spicatum* Lam. Maple Family

FIELD MARKS. A shrub or small tree 5 to 20 feet high; growing in cool moist, usually rocky woods. *Leaves* usually heart-shaped at base, 3-lobed or sometimes 5-lobed above the middle, the lobes short but broad and pointed, margin coarsely toothed, smooth above, slightly paler and usually downy beneath, 3 to 5 inches broad. *Flowers* greenish yellow, in elongate upright clusters; blooming May or June. *Fruits* with wings slightly spread, about ½ inch long; maturing August or September.

RANGE. Newfoundland to Saskatchewan; south to New York, the region of the Great Lakes, northeastern Iowa, and in the mountains to northern Georgia.

STRIPED MAPLE *Acer pensylvanicum* L. Maple Family

FIELD MARKS. A shrub or small tree to about 30 feet high; growing in cool, moist, rocky woods. *Bark* of the larger stems greenish and with conspicuous whitish streaks. *Leaves* rounded or heart-shaped at base, with 3 rather short but broad and taper-pointed lobes, margin finely toothed, smooth above, paler and smooth or nearly so beneath, 4 to 8 inches broad. *Flowers* greenish yellow, in loose drooping clusters; blooming May or June. *Fruits* with widely spread wings, about ¾ inch long; maturing August to October.

RANGE. Nova Scotia to Manitoba; south to New England, the region of the Great Lakes, and along the mountains to northern Georgia.

Also called Goosefoot Maple and Moosewood.

Leaves Opposite—Simple—Toothed

NORTHERN BUSH-HONEYSUCKLE *Diervilla lonicera* Mill. Honeysuckle Family

FIELD MARKS. A bushy-branched shrub 1 to about 3 feet high; growing in dry, rocky, open woodlands and in wayside thickets. *Branchlets* nearly round with a hairy-lined ridge running down from a line connecting the bases of the leafstalks. *Leaves* obviously stalked, egg-shaped or lance-shaped, rounded or broadly pointed at base, long-pointed at tip, finely and sharply toothed and hairy-fringed on margin, smooth above, paler and sometimes downy on the veins beneath, 1½ to 5 inches long. *Flowers* pale yellow, usually 3 in a cluster; blooming June to August. *Fruits* slender, about ½ inch long.

RANGE. Newfoundland to Manitoba; south to Delaware, western North Carolina, Ohio, and Iowa.

Leaves Opposite—Compound

RED-BERRIED ELDER *Sambucus pubens* Michx. Honeysuckle Family

FIELD MARKS. A leaf-losing shrub 3 to 10 feet high; growing in cool, moist, rocky woods and ravines. *Branchlets* stout, light brown, with warty lenticels, large brownish pith, and egg-shaped purplish-red buds. *Leaves* opposite, compound, 5 to 8 inches long; the 5 to 7 leaflets lance-shaped, pointed to unevenly rounded at base, long-pointed at tip, finely and sharply toothed on margin, smooth above, paler and usually downy beneath, 2 to 5 inches long. *Flowers* small, creamy white, the short corolla tube 5 lobed, in pyramid-shaped end clusters; blooming April to June. *Fruits* berry-like, round, bright red, about 3/16 inch in diameter; ripening June to August.

RANGE. Newfoundland to Alaska; south to New Jersey, Pennsylvania, the region of the Great Lakes, Iowa, and along the mountains to northern Georgia.

135

UMBRELLA MAGNOLIA *Magnolia tripetala* L. Magnolia Family

FIELD MARKS: A small tree 15 to seldom 40 feet tall; growing on rich moist soils and often along streams. *Leaves* 10 to 24 inches long, broadset above the middle, short pointed at tip, gradually tapering to the sharply pointed base, untoothed on margin, bright green and smooth above, paler and downy beneath; clustered at the tips of the stout branchles. *Flowers* creamy-white, 6 to 10 inches across, with a strong and unpleasant odor; blooming in April or May. *Fruits* in an oblong, smooth, cone-like cluster 2½ to 4 inches long; becoming rosy-red in late summer when each fruit splits down one side and releases scarlet flesh-coated seeds on silkey threads.

RANGE: Southwestern Pennsylvania, eastern Virginia, central Kentucky and southwestern Arkansas south to northern Georgia, Alabama and Mississippi.

SWEETLEAF *Symplocos tinctoria* (L.) L'Her. Sweetleaf Family

FIELD MARKS. A leaf-losing or semi-evergreen shrub or small tree 5 to about 30 feet high; growing in moist rocky or sandy woods and along streams. *Leaves* alternate, oblong to narrowly elliptic, pointed at both ends, untoothed or with obscure wavy teeth on margin, thickish and somewhat leathery in texture, dark yellowish green and smooth above, paler and often slightly downy beneath, 2 to 6 inches long. *Flowers* small, creamy white or pale yellow, with very conspicuous stamens, fragrant, in showy clusters along the branchlets; blooming March to May, before the leaves appear. *Fruits* elliptic, orange brown, dry, 1-seeded, about ½ inch long; maturing August or September.

Also called Horse-sugar, both horses and cattle relishing the sweetish-tasting leaves. Sometimes called Yellowwood, as it yields a yellow dye.

RANGE. Delaware, North Carolina, Tennessee, and southern Arkansas; south to northern Florida and eastern Texas.

WATER OAK *Quercus nigra* L. Beech Family

FIELD MARKS: A tree 50 to 80 feet or more tall; growing in wet bottomlands and along streams. *Leaves* very variable, usually 2 to 4 inches long, broadest above the middle and tapered to the pointed base, or more or less diamond-shaped; sometimes shallowly 3-lobed toward the tip, or on vigorous shoots and sprout growth with several side lobes; dull bluish-green above, paler beneath, smooth, often remaining green very late in the fall or even early winter. *Fruit* a roundish, blackish acorn about ½ inch long, seated in a shallow saucer-like cup; maturing in 2 years; kernel bitter.

RANGE: Southern New Jersey, northern Georgia, southeastern Missouri and eastern Oklahoma south to Florida and eastern Texas.

Widely planted in the South as a shade and street tree.

WILLOW OAK *Quercus phellos* L. Beech Family

FIELD MARKS: A tree 60 to 80 feet or more tall; growing in wet bottomlands and along streams. *Leaves* 2 to 5 inches long, narrow and willow-like, untoothed on margin, tipped with a small bristle, bright green above, paler and often somewhat downy beneath. *Fruit* a roundish, yellowish-brown to greenish-brown acorn about ⅜ inch long, seated in a shallow saucer-like cup; maturing in 2 years; kernel bitter.

RANGE: Southeastern New York, northern Georgia, southern Illinois and southeastern Oklahoma south to northern Florida and eastern Texas.

Often planted as a street and shade tree in the South.

Umbrella Magnolia

Sweetleaf

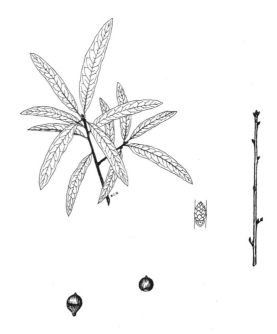

Water Oak

Willow Oak

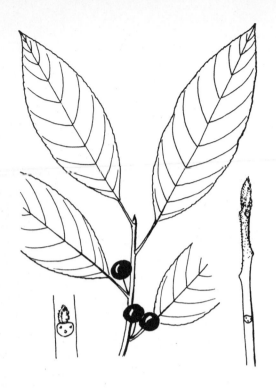

Carolina Buckthorn

Elliott Blueberry

American Holly

Sourwood

CAROLINA BUCKTHORN *Rhamnus caroliniana* Walt.   Buckthorn Family

FIELD MARKS. A leaf-losing shrub or small tree to 30 feet high; growing along streams and on wooded hillsides. *Branchlets* reddish brown to ashy brown; with an elongate, naked, hairy end bud. *Leaves* alternate, elliptic, rounded to broadly pointed at base, pointed at tip, obscurely toothed on margin, lustrous above, paler and sometimes downy beneath, prominently veined, 2 to 6 inches long. *Flowers* small, yellowish green, 3 to 5 clustered in leaf axils; blooming May or June. *Fruits* roundish, black, 2- to 4-seeded, about ⅓ inch in diameter; ripening September or October.

RANGE. Southwestern Virginia, West Virginia, the Ohio Valley, and Nebraska; south to Florida and Texas.

Also called Indian-cherry.

ELLIOTT BLUEBERRY *Vaccinium elliottii* Chapm.   Heath Family

FIELD MARKS. A leaf-losing shrub 3 to about 8 feet high; growing along streams, in sandy woods, and in swamps. *Branchlets* warty-dotted, greenish, often downy. *Leaves* almost stalkless, egg-shaped to elliptic or oval, mostly rounded at base, blunt to pointed at tip, finely toothed or almost untoothed on margin, lustrous green and smooth above, duller and often somewhat downy beneath, ⅜ to about 1 inch long. *Flowers* pink or reddish, narrowly urn-shaped or vase-shaped, clustered; blooming March or April, as the leaves are expanding. *Fruits* black or bluish black, about 5/16 inch in diameter, sweet but rather dry; ripening June or July.

RANGE. Southeastern Virginia south to Florida, west to Louisiana; north in Mississippi Valley to Arkansas.

AMERICAN HOLLY *Ilex opaca* Ait.   Holly Family

FIELD MARKS: An evergreen tree 40 to 60 feet or more tall; growing in moist to well-drained soils. *Leaves* 2 to 4 inches long, stiff and leathery in texture, usually coarsely spine-toothed on margin but sometimes with only a spine at the tip, dark dull yellowish-green above, paler beneath, smooth. *Flowers* small, greenish-white, fragrant, the stamen-bearing and pistil-bearing ones on separate plants; blooming April to June. *Fruits* bright red or orange, rarely yellow, ¼ to ⅜ inch across, ripening September or October and persisting all winter.

RANGE: Southern Massachusetts, southern Pennsylvania and Missouri south to Florida and eastern Texas.

SOURWOOD *Oxydendrum arboreum* (L.) DC.   Heath Family

FIELD MARKS: A tree 20 to 60 feet tall; growing on well-drained, acid, often rocky slopes. *Leaves* 4 to 7 inches long, oblong lance-shaped, broadly pointed at base, pointed at tip, finely saw-toothed on margin, shiny, dark yellowish-green above, paler beneath, smooth or nearly so, with sour taste when chewed. *Flowers* small, bell-shaped, white, arranged along the slender branches of a terminal cluster; blooming June or July. *Fruits* bottle-shaped, 5 angled, woody capsules about ½ inch long; maturing September or October.

RANGE: New Jersey west to southern Illinois; south to northern Florida and eastern Louisiana.

WINGED ELM *Ulmus alata* Michx.   Elm Family

FIELD MARKS: A tree 40 to 50 feet tall; growing on moist to well-drained upland soils and sometimes along streams. *Branchlets* soon developing a pair of rather broad corky wings. *Leaves* 1½ to 3 inches long, elliptical or broadly lance-shaped, doubly saw-toothed on margin, lop-sided at base, dark green and smooth above, paler and downy beneath. *Fruits* oval, flattened, with a hairy raised seed cavity in center, notched at tip, hairy-fringed on margin, long-stalked; maturing in March or April.

RANGE: Virginia west to southern Indiana, Illinois and Missouri; south to central Florida and Texas.

SOUTHERN CRAB APPLE *Malus angustifolia* (Ait.) Michx.   Rose Family

FIELD MARKS: A shrub or small tree similar to the American Crab Apple. *Leaves* elliptic, pointed at base, rounded or blunt at tip, sparingly or bluntly toothed on margin, thick-textured, smooth on both surfaces, 1 to 2½ inches long. *Flowers* similar to those of American Crab Apple. *Fruits* also similar but somewhat more flattened, 1 to 1½ inches in diameter.

RANGE. Chiefly coastal plain; Maryland to northern Florida, west to Louisiana and north in Mississippi Valley to southern Illinois.

Also known as Narrow-leaf Crab apple.

CHICKASAW PLUM *Prunus angustifolia* Marsh.   Rose Family

FIELD MARKS. A leaf-losing shrub or small tree with spiny-tipped branches; often forming thickets along fence rows, abandoned fields, and woods borders. *Leaves* lance-shaped, pointed at base, long-pointed at tip, finely toothed on margin, smooth, 1 to 2½ inches long; leafstalks with glands at summit. *Flowers* white, about ⅓ inch across, 2 to 4 in a cluster; blooming March or April. *Fruits* roundish, red or yellow with a whitish bloom, ¾ to 1 inch in diameter; ripening June or July and often quite sweet.

RANGE. New Jersey to southern Illinois and Nebraska; south to Florida and Texas.

MUSCADINE GRAPE *Vitis rotundifolia* Michx.   Vine Family

FIELD MARKS. A high-climbing vine; growing in woods, thickets, sandhills, and swamps. Differs from all other grapes in having smooth bark dotted with paler lenticels, no woody partitions in the pith at the nodes, and tendrils which are not branched. *Leaves* roundish or broadly egg-shaped, the sinus at the base broadly V-shaped and shallow, margin with large and triangular teeth, lustrous above, yellowish green and sometimes slightly downy on the veins beneath, 2 to 4 inches wide. *Fruits* purplish black to bronze, without a bloom, with very tough skin, sweet with musky flavor, ½ to 1 inch in diameter.

RANGE. Southern Delaware and Virginia to southern Indiana, southeastern Missouri, and Oklahoma; south to Florida and Texas.

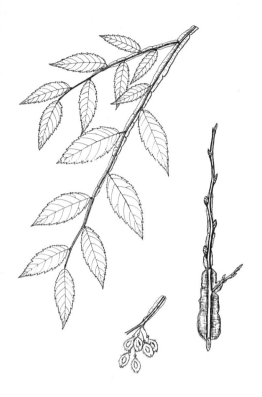

Winged Elm

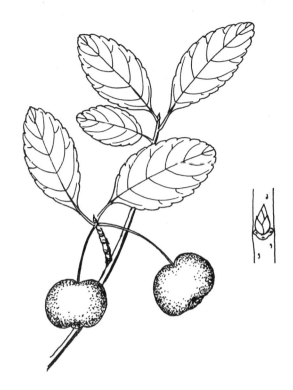

Southern Crab Apple

Chickásaw Plum

Muscadine Grape

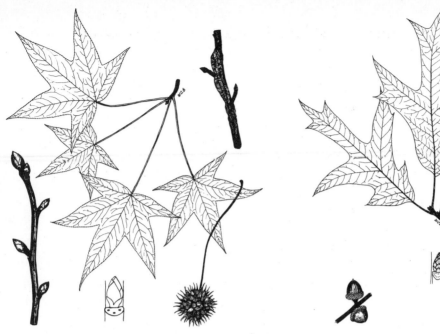

Sweetgum

Southern Red Oak

Bristly Locust

American Wisteria

SWEETGUM *Liquidambar styraciflua* L. Witch-hazel Family

FIELD MARKS: A large tree 80 to 100 feet or more tall; growing in rich moist bottomlands and in swamps. *Branches* developing corky wings. *Leaves* distinctively star-shaped with usually 5 pointed lobes, finely saw-toothed on margin, shiny bright green above, paler beneath, smooth, 4 to 7 inches long, long-stalked, pleasantly fragrant when crushed. *Flowers* small, yellowish-green, stamen-bearing and pistil-bearing ones in seperate head-like clusters on the same tree; blooming April or May. *Fruits* in long-stalked, dangling, spiny ball-shaped heads 1 to 1½ inches across; persisting on the trees all winter.

RANGE: Connecticut west to southern Illinois; south to Florida and eastern Texas.

Valuable hardwood timber tree and often planted as a shade and street tree.

SOUTHERN RED OAK *Quercus falcata* Michx. Beech Family

FIELD MARKS: A large tree 60 to 100 feet or more tall; growing on both dry and wet sites in the Southeast. *Leaves* 5 to 9 inches long, sometimes with 3 short lobes toward the tip; often with 5 to 7 long, narrow, somewhat curved, bristle-tipped and bristle-toothed lobes; shiny dark green above, coated with whitish or tawny down beneath. *Fruit* a roundish, orange-brown acorn about ½ inch long, seated in a shallow saucer-like cup; maturing in 2 years; kernel bitter.

RANGE: New Jersey west to southern Illinois and Iowa; south to northern Florida and eastern Texas.

Also called Spanish Oak. The swamp variety has a scaly bark resembling that of the Wild Black Cherry and is called the Cherrybark Oak.

Leaves Alternate—Compound

BRISTLY LOCUST *Robinia hispida* L. Pea Family

FIELD MARKS. A shrub 2½ to about 10 feet high with stems, branchlets, leafstalks and stalks of the flower clusters densely covered with reddish-brown bristles; growing in open woods and on slopes and ridges. *Leaves* 4 to 8 inches long, with 9 to 15 leaflets which are egg-shaped, rounded at base, prominently bristle-pointed at tip, ¾ to about 2 inches long. *Flowers* large, rose pink, in clusters of 3 to 8; blooming May and June. *Fruits* at first sticky-glandular, later dry and bristly, 1½ to 2½ inches long.

RANGE. Virginia, West Virginia, and Kentucky south to North Carolina; and northern Georgia and Alabama.

Also called Rose-acacia. Often planted as an ornamental and escaping north of its natural range.

AMERICAN WISTERIA *Wisteria frutescens* (L.) Poir. Pea Family

FIELD MARKS. A climbing, leaf-losing vine; growing on the borders of swamps and low woods or along streams. *Leaves* alternate, compound, 4 to 9 inches long; the 9 to 15 leaflets elliptic or egg-shaped, rounded to pointed at base, pointed at tip, untoothed on margin, smooth above, often sparingly hairy beneath, ¾ to 2¼ inches long. *Flowers* showy, lilac purple to white, in dense end clusters 2 to 4½ inches long; blooming April to June. *Fruits* knobby beanlike pods 2 to 4 inches long; maturing June to September.

RANGE. Chiefly coastal plain; eastern Maryland and Virginia south to Florida, west to Alabama.

PEPPERVINE *Ampelopsis arborea* (L.) Koehne   Vine Family

FIELD MARKS. A leaf-losing, somewhat bushy to high-climbing vine; growing in rich moist woods and thickets. Tendrils may be present opposite some of the leaves. *Leaves* alternate, twice or thrice compound, 2 to about 8 inches long; the leaflets more or less egg-shaped, rounded to pointed at base, pointed at tip, sharply and coarsely toothed on margin, smooth on both surfaces or slightly downy along the veins beneath, ½ to 1½ inches long. *Flowers* small, greenish, in loose, long-stalked clusters opposite some of the leaves; blooming June or July. *Fruits* roundish or slightly flattened, dark purple to black, 1- to 3-seeded berries about ¼ inch in diameter, bitter and inedible; ripening August to October.

RANGE. Eastern Maryland, West Virginia, southern Illinois, Missouri, and Oklahoma; south to Florida and Texas.

Leaves Opposite—Compound

RED BUCKEYE *Aesculus pavia* L.   Horsechestnut Family

FIELD MARKS. A shrub or small tree usually 3 to 10 (rarely 30) feet high, spreading by underground runners; growing in hammocks and pinelands near the coast. *Leaves* with 5 (rarely 7) leaflets which are elliptic or broadest above the middle, wedge-shaped at base, pointed at tip, finely toothed on margin, paler yellowish green and smooth to downy beneath, 4 to 6 inches long. *Flowers* bright red, in erect clusters 5 or 6 inches long; blooming April or May. *Fruits* smooth, 1 to 2 inches across; maturing July or August.

RANGE. Coastal plain; Virginia south to Florida, west to Louisiana, north in Mississippi Valley to southern Illinois and Oklahoma.

Leaves Opposite—Simple—Entire

STRAWBERRY-SHRUB *Calycanthus floridus* L.   Calycanthus Family

FIELD MARKS. A leaf-losing, aromatic shrub 3 to 9 feet high; growing in rich woods and along streams. *Branchlets* dark brown, somewhat enlarged and flattened at nodes, spicy-aromatic when bruised. *Leaves* opposite, elliptic or egg-shaped, pointed at tip, pointed to roundish at base, untoothed on margin, often roughish or rather lustrous above, smooth to somewhat downy beneath, 2 to 6 inches long, spicy-aromatic when crushed (or in var. *laevigatus* (Willd.) T. & G. lustrous green and smooth or whitened beneath). *Flowers* greenish brown to dark reddish brown or maroon, 1 to 2 inches across, almost odorless or with a decided strawberry-like fragrance; blooming April to August. *Fruits* urn-shaped capsules 2 to 2½ inches long; containing many large hard-coated seeds.

RANGE. South-central Pennsylvania and southern Ohio south, chiefly in mountains and upper piedmont, to Florida and Mississippi.

Also called Sweetshrub or Carolina-allspice. Commonly cultivated.

YELLOW JESSAMINE *Gelsemium sempervirens* (L.) Ait. f.   Logania Family

FIELD MARKS. A smooth, slender-stemmed, evergreen, twining vine; growing in borders of woods, swamps, and wayside thickets. *Leaves* opposite, lance-shaped or narrowly egg-shaped, broadly pointed to rounded at base, taper-pointed at tip, untoothed on margin, slightly leathery, lustrous above, paler beneath, smooth, 1½ to 3 inches long. *Flowers* bright yellow, trumpet-shaped, 5-lobed, very fragrant, about 1½ inches long, 1 to 3 on short stalks in leaf axils; blooming late February to May. *Fruits* oblong egg-shaped, pale-brown capsules ½ to ¾ inch long; containing flattened, winged seeds.

RANGE. Coastal plain and piedmont; Virginia south to Florida, west to Texas; north in Mississippi Valley to Arkansas.

Also called Carolina- or False-jessamine. Roots used medicinally. Children have been poisoned by sucking nectar from the flowers.

144

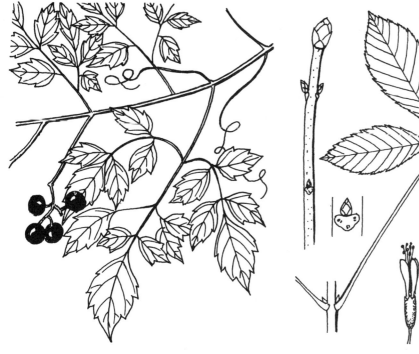

Peppervine

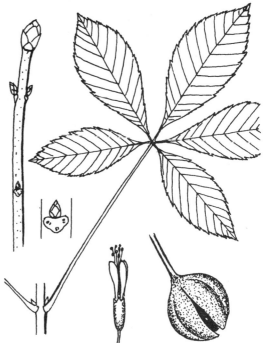

Red Buckeye

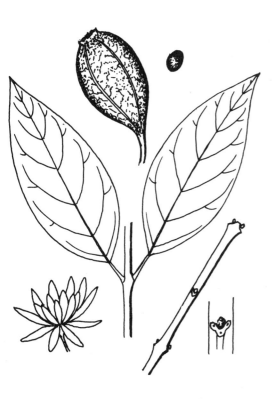

Strawberry-shrub

Yellow Jessamine

Trumpet Honeysuckle

Fringetree

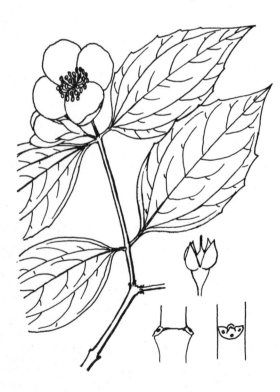

Common Mock-orange

Beautyberry

TRUMPET HONEYSUCKLE *Lonicera sempervirens* L.   Honeysuckle Family

FIELD MARKS. A twining and sometimes high-climbing, leaf-losing or (southward) evergreen shrub; growing in woodlands, thickets, and along fencerows. *Leaves* oval to egg-shaped or narrowly elliptic, short-stalked, pointed to roundish at base, rounded to bluntly pointed at tip, untoothed on margin, somewhat leathery in texture, dark green and smooth above, whitened and smooth or somewhat downy beneath, 1½ to 3½ inches long; the uppermost 1 or 2 pairs united at the base to form an oval-shaped or roundish disk. *Flowers* narrowly trumpet-shaped with 5 nearly equal lobes at summit, bright red outside, yellow within, 1½ to 2 inches long, in several whorls on an end stalk; blooming March to June or later. *Fruits* bright red, egg-shaped, about ¼ inch in diameter; ripening July to October.

RANGE. Southern Maine to New York, Ohio, Iowa, and Nebraska; south to Florida and Texas.

Also called Coral Honeysuckle. Often cultivated and frequently escaping.

FRINGETREE *Chionanthus virginica* L.   Olive Family

FIELD MARKS. A leaf-losing shrub or small tree to 20 or rarely 40 feet high; growing in woods, savannahs, and along streams. *Leaves* opposite, elliptic or broadest above the middle, pointed at both ends, untoothed on margin, thickish, smooth or nearly so and paler beneath, 3 to 8 inches long. *Flowers* white, petals 4 and ribbon-like, fragrant, ¾ to 1 inch long, in rather large and drooping clusters; blooming April or May. *Fruits* oval-shaped, olive-like, 1-seeded, bluish black, usually with a whitish bloom, ⅜ to ¾ inch long; ripening July to September.

RANGE. New Jersey to southern Ohio and Missouri, and southeastern Oklahoma; south to Florida and Texas.

Also called Flowering-ash, Old-man's beard, and Grancy-graybeard.

Leaves Opposite—Simple—Mostly Toothed

COMMON MOCK-ORANGE *Philadelphus inodorus* L.   Saxifrage Family

FIELD MARKS. A shrub 3 to 10 feet high, growing on rocky slopes and along streams. *Branchlets* smooth, with reddish-brown bark that is soon shed in thin papery flakes; the buds concealed by the leaf scars. *Leaves* egg-shaped, sharply pointed at tip, somewhat pointed or rounded at base, margin usually with some widely spaced but sharply pointed teeth, usually smooth on both surfaces but sometimes roughish above or sparingly hairy beneath, 2 to 4 inches long. *Flowers* 1 to 4 at tips of short branchlets, 1½ to 2 inches across, odorless or nearly so, with distinctly separate stigmas; blooming in May or June. *Fruits* usually smooth and with ascending calyx lobes.

RANGE. Virginia and Tennessee south to Florida and Alabama.

BEAUTYBERRY *Callicarpa americana* L.   Vervain Family

FIELD MARKS. A leaf-losing shrub 3 to about 6 feet high; usually growing in moist sandy or rocky woods. *Branchlets* ashy gray, hairy or roughish. *Leaves* opposite, elliptic to oval or egg-shaped, tapering to a point at both ends, sharply toothed on margin, roughish-hairy above, paler and woolly-hairy beneath, 3 to 6 inches long. *Flowers* small, bluish to lavender pink, funnel-shaped, clustered in leaf axils; blooming May to July. *Fruits* berry-like, violet or magenta purple, juicy, about ⅛ inch in diameter, in dense axillary clusters; ripening August to October.

RANGE. Maryland to Tennessee, Arkansas, and Oklahoma; south to Florida and Texas.

Also called French-mulberry. Handsome as an ornamental shrub.

CATAWBA RHODODENDRON   *Rhododendron catawbiense* Michx. Heath Family

FIELD MARKS. A spreading and often thicket-forming evergreen shrub usually 4 to 10 (rarely 20) feet high; growing on rocky slopes, ridges, and mountain tops, usually above 3,000 feet.. *Leaves* elliptic or oblong, rounded at base, blunt or slightly pointed at tip, margin untoothed, very thick and leathery, smooth, dark green and lustrous above, paler or whitened and dull beneath, 3 to 5 inches long. *Flowers* lilac purple to rose purple spotted with olive green, open bell-shaped with 5 rounded lobes, about 2 inches across, in large and showy clusters; blooming April to June. *Fruits* narrowly oblong, rusty-hairy, ¾ to 1 inch long.

RANGE. Southwestern Virginia, southern West Virginia, and southeastern Kentucky; south to northern Georgia and Alabama; locally eastward to north-central North Carolina.

Also called Purple Rhododendron and Mountain Rosebay. Often cultivated and a parent of many cultivated hybrid rhododendrons.

CAROLINA RHODODENDRON   *Rhododendron minus* Michx.   Heath Family

FIELD MARKS. An evergreen shrub 3 to about 8 feet high; growing on exposed or wooded slopes and along streams. *Leaves* elliptic to narrowly elliptic, pointed at both ends, margin untoothed, thick and leathery, dark green and smooth above, pale or whitened and covered with minute dotlike brown scales beneath, 2 to about 4 inches long. *Flowers* white to deep rose pink, often spotted with olive-green or orange, open bell-shaped with 5 rounded lobes, 1 to 1½ inches across, in dense or fairly open clusters; blooming April to July or later. *Fruits* oblong egg-shaped, ⅜ to ¾ inch long, rusty brown.

RANGE. South-central and western North Carolina, eastern Tennessee, and northwestern South Carolina south into Georgia and Alabama.

Also known as Piedmont and Small Rhododendron.

FLAME AZALEA   *Rhododendron calendulaceum* (Michx.) Torr.   Heath Family

FIELD MARKS. A leaf-losing shrub 3 to (rarely) 15 feet high; growing in oak or pine woods and on mountain balds. *Branchlets* downy and with scattered spreading hairs. *Leaves* elliptic or broadest above the middle, pointed at both ends, margin hairy-fringed, bright green and often with scattered hairs above, paler and downy and with stiff hairs along midrib beneath, 1 to 3 inches long. *Flowers* yellow, orange, or scarlet, the tube with gland-tipped hairs, not fragrant, 1½ to 2 inches across, 5 to 9 in a cluster; blooming April to June, as new leaves unfold. *Fruits* narrowly egg-shaped, somewhat downy and with spreading hairs, about ¾ inch long.

RANGE. Southwestern Pennsylvania, southeastern Ohio, and West Virginia; south to northern Georgia and Alabama.

Often cultivated as an ornamental shrub.

DUTCHMAN'S-PIPE   *Aristolochia durior* Hill   Birthwort Family

FIELD MARKS. A twining and high-climbing, leaf-losing, woody vine; growing in rich woods and along streams. *Leaves* alternate, heart-shaped, untoothed on margin, thin in texture, dark green and smooth above, paler and smooth or nearly so beneath, 3 to 8 inches wide. *Flowers* with a yellowish-green, U-shaped and pipelike calyx tube, spreading at summit into a 3-lobed and brownish-purple border; blooming in May and June. *Fruits* cylindrical, 6-ribbed capsules, 2 to 3 inches long, and containing many seeds.

RANGE. Appalachian region; western Pennsylvania and West Virginia south to Georgia and Alabama.

Cultivated and grown on trellises and porches; often listed in nursery catalogs as *Aristolochia sipho*.

148

Catawba Rhododendron

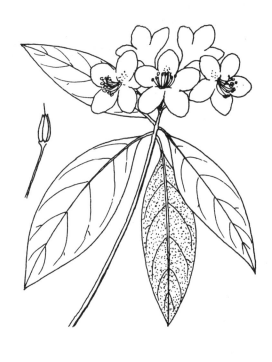

Carolina Rhododendron

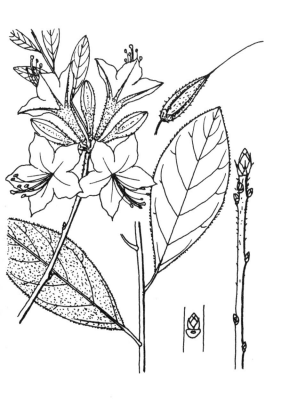

Flame Azalea

Dutchman's-pipe

Fraser Magnolia

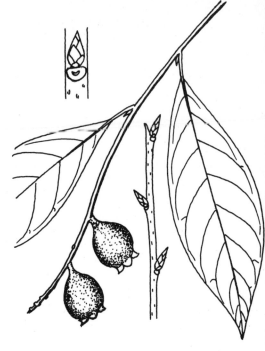

Buffalonut

Buckberry

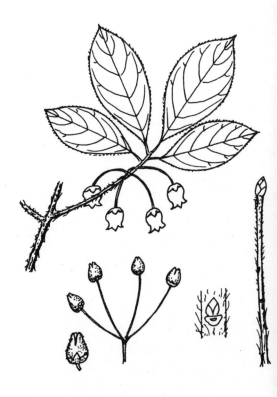

Allegheny Menziesia

FRASER MAGNOLIA *Magnolia fraseri* Walt. Magnolia Family

FIELD MARKS: A tree 30 to 40 feet tall; growing in rich, moist to well-drained soils of the southern Appalachians. *Branchlets* spicy-aromatic when bruised or broken. *Leaves* 8 to 12 inches long, broadest above the middle and contracted to the narrow base which has a pair of ear-like lobes, bright green above, paler beneath, smooth. *Flowers* pale yellow or white, fragrant, 8 to 12 inches across; blooming April or May. *Fruits* in an oblong, smooth, cone-like cluster 2½ to 4 inches long; becoming rosy-red in late summer when each fruit splits down one side and releases scarlet fleshy-coated seeds on silky threads.

RANGE: Western Virginia and eastern Kentucky south to northern Georgia and Alabama.

Also called Mountain Magnolia.

BUFFALONUT *Pyrularia pubera* Michx. Sandalwood Family

FIELD MARKS. An upright, but often straggling, leaf-losing shrub 3 to about 12 feet high; growing on moist, often rocky, wooded slopes. *Leaves* alternate, elliptic or broadest above the middle, pointed at both ends, margin untoothed, soft and very veiny in appearance, smooth or nearly so at maturity, with minute clear dots which are visible when the leaf is held up to light, 2 to about 6 inches long. *Flowers* small, pale green, in short clusters; blooming in April or May. *Fruits* more or less pear-shaped, leathery, yellowish green, about 1 inch long; containing a solitary large oily seed; maturing July to October.

RANGE. Chiefly mountains; Pennsylvania south to Georgia and Alabama.

A root parasite of other shrubs and trees. All parts of the plant, but particularly the seeds, contain a bitterly pungent and poisonous oil. Also known as Oilnut.

BUCKBERRY *Gaylussacia ursina* (M. A. Curtis) T. & G. Heath Family

FIELD MARKS. A leaf-losing shrub 2 to about 4 feet high; growing throughout woodlands of the southern Appalachians. *Branchlets* somewhat downy when young. *Leaves* elliptic or sometimes broadest above the middle, pointed to roundish at base, pointed at tip, margin untoothed but often hairy-fringed, thin in texture, bright green and smooth or nearly so except for some hairs along the midrib beneath, minutely and rather inconspicuously resin-dotted on the lower surface, 1½ to 4 inches long. *Flowers* greenish white to reddish, bell-shaped, about 3/16 inch across, in elongate clusters; blooming May or June. *Fruits* lustrous black, about ⅜ inch in diameter, insipid to rather sweet; ripening July to September.

RANGE. Southwestern North Carolina and eastern Tennessee, south into northwestern South Carolina and northern Georgia.

ALLEGHENY MENZIESIA *Menziesia pilosa* (Michx.) Juss. Heath Family

FIELD MARKS. A rather straggling leaf-losing shrub 2 to 6 feet high, with bark freely shredding; growing in bogs or on thinly wooded slopes and balds in the southern Appalachians. *Branchlets* bristly-hairy and somewhat rusty-chaffy. *Leaves* alternate, often crowded toward tips of branchlets, elliptic to oval or broadest above the middle, pointed at base, abruptly pointed at tip, untoothed but hairy-fringed on margin, roughish-hairy above, pale or whitened and usually rusty-chaffy along the veins beneath, ¾ to 2 inches long. *Flowers* greenish white or greenish yellow often tinged with red, bell-shaped, about ¼ inch long, 3 to 6 in a cluster and nodding on slender stalks; blooming May to July. *Fruits* egg-shaped, bristly-hairy capsules about 3/16 inch long; maturing August to October.

RANGE. Southern Pennsylvania and West Virginia south to eastern Tennessee and northern Georgia.

Also called Minniebush.

MOUNTAIN-CAMELLIA *Stewartia ovata* (Cav.) Weath.   Tea Family

FIELD MARKS. A leaf-losing shrub or small tree similar to the preceding; growing in rich woods, usually along streams, chiefly in the mountains. *Leaves* alternate, oblong-elliptic or egg-shaped, mostly rounded at base, sharply pointed at tip, minutely toothed and hairy-fringed on margin, dark green and smooth above, grayish green and slightly hairy beneath, 2 to 5 inches long. *Flowers* similar to those of the Silky-camellia, but the stamens usually with yellow (rarely purple) anthers and the styles distinct; blooming June to August. *Fruits* egg-shaped, pointed, sharply 5-angled capsules about ⅝ inch long; seeds dull and winged.

RANGE. Virginia and southeastern Kentucky; south to central North Carolina, and northern Georgia and Alabama.

MOUNTAIN SWEET-PEPPERBUSH *Clethra acuminata* Michx.   White-alder Family

FIELD MARKS. A leaf-losing shrub 4 to about 15 feet high, the older stems with reddish-brown or cinnamon-colored bark which comes off in long strips; growing in rich, moist woods and along streams in the southern Appalachians. *Branchlets* slender, pale brown or ashy, more or less downy. *Leaves* alternate, rather long-stalked, oval to oblong-elliptic, pointed or roundish at base, pointed at tip, finely and sharply toothed on margin nearly to base, bright green and smooth above, paler and usually somewhat downy beneath, 2 to 7 inches long. *Flowers* white, 5-petalled, fragrant, in narrow end clusters from 4 to 8 inches in length; blooming July to September. *Fruits* roundish or slightly egg-shaped capsules about 3/16 inch in diameter, on nodding stalks; maturing September or October.

RANGE. Western Pennsylvania, western Virginia, and West Virginia south to northern Georgia.

Also known as Cinnamon Clethra.

MOUNTAIN FETTERBUSH *Pieris floribunda* (Pursh) B. & H.   Heath Family

FIELD MARKS. An evergreen shrub 3 to about 6 feet high; growing on dry to moist slopes or balds in the Appalachian Mountains. *Branchlets* slender, hairy, nearly erect. *Leaves* alternate, narrowly egg-shaped or oblong, pointed at base, sharply pointed at tip, finely toothed and bristly-hairy on margin, leathery in texture, smooth, green above, paler and minutely black-dotted beneath, 1½ to 3 inches long. *Flowers* white, vase-shaped, nodding, about 3/8 inch long, in a group of slender clusters at tips of branches; blooming March to June. *Fruits* egg-shaped, slightly 5-angled capsules about 3/16 inch long.

RANGE. West Virginia south to western North Carolina and eastern Tennessee.

Often cultivated as an ornamental shrub.

SOUTHERN MOUNTAIN-CRANBERRY *Vaccinium erythrocarpum* Michx. Heath
                                                                Family

FIELD MARKS. A leaf-losing shrub 1 to about 6 feet high, with spreading branches; growing in cool moist woods or bogs in the southern Appalachians. *Branchlets* downy. *Leaves* short-stalked, egg-shaped to oblong lance-shaped, rounded to broadly pointed at base, tapering to a sharp point at tip, margin finely toothed with bristle-tipped teeth, green and often slightly downy on both surfaces, 1 to about 3 inches long. *Flowers* pale red with 4 recurved corolla lobes, solitary in the axils of leaves or leaf-like bracts; blooming May to July. *Fruits* dark purplish red, about 3/16 inch in diameter, sweetish to sour or insipid; ripening August and September.

RANGE. Western Virginia and West Virginia south to northern Georgia and eastern Tennessee.

Also called Bearberry.

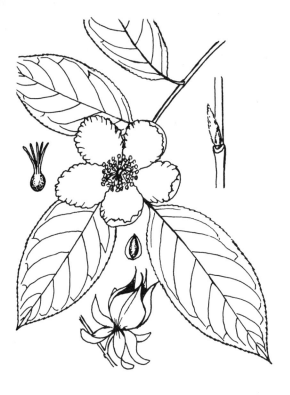

Mountain-camellia

Mountain Sweet-pepperbush

Mountain Fetterbush

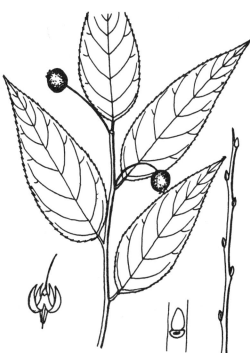

Southern Mountain-cranberry

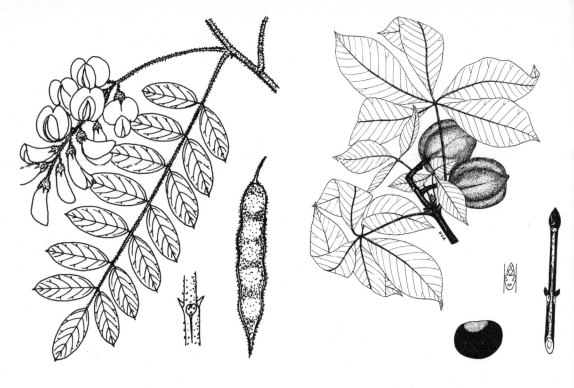

Clammy Locust

Yellow Buckeye

Drooping Leucothoë

Recurved Leucothoë

CLAMMY LOCUST   *Robinia viscosa* Vent.   Pea Family

FIELD MARKS. A shrub or small tree to 20 or more feet high; growing in open woods or on wooded slopes in the southern Appalachians. *Branchlets* have small nodal thorns and are densely covered with sticky stalkless or short-stalked glands. *Leaves* 6 to 12 inches long; the 11 to 25 leaflets elliptic to egg-shaped, broadly pointed to rounded at base, usually rounded but with an abrupt bristle-point at tip, 1 to 2 inches long; leafstalks glandular-sticky. *Flowers* pink or lavender pink, not fragrant, the calyx and stalks of the flower cluster sticky-glandular; blooming May or June. *Fruits* 2 to 3 inches long, at first sticky-glandular, later dry.

RANGE. Western Virginia south to northern Georgia and Alabama. Often found as an escape from cultivation northward.

Leaves Opposite—Compound

YELLOW BUCKEYE   *Aesculus octandra* Marsh.   Horsechestnut Family

FIELD MARKS: A tree 40 to 90 feet or more tall; growing in rich moist soils. *Leaves* with usually 5 leaflets which are elliptical or broadest slightly above the middle, wedge-shaped at base, pointed at tip, finely saw-toothed on margin, dark yellowish-green above, paler and often somewhat downy beneath, 4 to 8 inches long. *Flowers* pale yellow, in pyramid-like, erect clusters 5 to 8 inches long; blooming April to June. *Fruits* smooth, oblong pear-shaped, 2 to 3 inches long, usually containing 2 large shiny brown seeds; maturing August or September.

RANGE: Southwestern Pennsylvania west to southern Illinois; south to northern Georgia and Alabama.

Also called Sweet Buckeye.

Leaves Alternate—Simple—Toothed

DROOPING LEUCOTHOË   *Leucothoë fontanesiana* (Steud.) Sleumer   Heath Family

FIELD MARKS. An evergreen shrub 2 to about 6 feet high, with spreading and arching, reddish branches; growing in moist mountain woodlands. *Leaves* alternate, narrowly egg-shaped to lance-shaped, rounded or broadly pointed at base, long-pointed at tip, finely toothed on margin with bristle-tipped teeth, leathery in texture, dark green and lustrous above, paler and smooth beneath, 2½ to 6 inches long; leafstalks ⅜ to ⅝ inch long. *Flowers* white, bell-shaped, fragrant, about ⅜ inch long; in many-flowered, narrow, drooping clusters arising in the axils of the leaves; blooming April and May. *Fruits* roundish, somewhat flattened, 5-lobed capsules about 3/16 inch in diameter.

RANGE. Western Virginia south to northern Georgia and northern Alabama.

Also called Dog-hobble and Switch-ivy.

RECURVED LEUCOTHOË   *Leucothoë recurva* (Buckley) Gray   Heath Family

FIELD MARKS. A widely branched, straggling, leaf-losing shrub 3 to 10 feet high; growing on dry, often rocky, wooded slopes in the mountains. *Leaves* alternate, egg-shaped or elliptic, pointed at both ends, finely and sharply toothed on the margin, thin in texture, bright green and smooth above, paler and sometimes slightly downy on the veins beneath, 1½ to 4 inches long. *Flowers* white, narrowly bell-shaped, fragrant; many hanging downward in 1-sided, spreading and recurved, narrow end clusters; blooming April to June. *Fruits* roundish, somewhat flattened, deeply 5-lobed capsules about 3/16 inch in diameter.

RANGE. Western Virginia and West Virginia south to northern Georgia and northern Alabama.

Also called Redtwig Leucothoe. The leaves turn bright red in fall.

SOUTHERN APPALACHIAN SPECIALTIES, Continued
Leaves Alternate—Simple—Toothed

CAROLINA SILVERBELL *Halesia carolina* L. Storax Family

FIELD MARKS. A leaf-losing shrub or small tree 5 to 30 feet or more high; growing in rich moist woods and along streams. *Leaves* alternate, elliptic to oblong or egg-shaped, broadly pointed to rounded at base, pointed or long-pointed at tip, finely toothed on margin, bright green and smooth or nearly so above, slightly paler and downy beneath, 2 to 5 inches long. *Flowers* white or pinkish, bell-shaped with 4 lobes, ⅓ to about 1 inch long, 2 to 5 in a cluster; blooming March to May. *Fruits* oblong-oval, dry, 4-winged, 1 to 1¾ inch long.

RANGE. Virginia and West Virginia to southern Ohio, southeastern and western Kentucky, and southern Illinois; south to northwestern Florida, Alabama, and western Tennessee. Also in Arkansas and southeastern Oklahoma.

Also called Snowdrop-tree and Opossumwood.

Leaves Opposite—Simple—Toothed

SOUTHERN BUSH-HONEYSUCKLE *Diervilla sessilifolia* Buckl. Honeysuckle Family

FIELD MARKS. A bushy-branched shrub 1½ to 5 feet high; growing in moist rocky places and bogs in the southern Appalachians. *Branchlets* prominently 4-angled and with hairy lines. *Leaves* stalkless or nearly so, egg-shaped to broadly lance-shaped, rounded to somewhat heart-shaped at base, long-pointed at tip, sharply toothed and hairy-fringed on margin, smooth above, sometimes slightly downy beneath, 2 to 6 inches long. *Flowers* sulfur-yellow, in 3- to 7-flowered clusters; blooming June to August. *Fruits* oblong, ⅝ to ¾ inch long.

RANGE. Western Virginia and eastern Tennessee, south to northwestern Georgia and northern Alabama.

SOUTHERN COASTAL REGION SPECIALTIES

SAW-PALMETTO *Serenoa repens* (Bartr.) Small Palm Family

FIELD MARKS. A dwarf palm with stout, creeping underground stems; growing in hammocks and sandy coastal plain pinelands. *Leaves* fan-shaped, nearly circular, deeply cleft into many radiating divisions, green or yellowish green, 1 to 3 feet broad; leafstalks slender, armed with numerous, small, very sharp spines. *Flowers* small, creamy white, in a large branched cluster; blooming May to July. *Fruits* oval-shaped, black, 1-seeded, ½ to about 1 inch long; ripening October or November.

RANGE. Southeastern South Carolina south to Florida, west to Louisiana. Fruits edible and used medicinally. Important as a honey plant.

CABBAGE PALMETTO *Sabal palmetto* (Walt.) Lodd. Palm Family

FIELD MARKS: A distinctive evergreen tree 15 to 80 feet tall with a cluster of large fan-shaped leaves at summit of trunk; growing on hammocks and in brackish marshes. *Leaves* about 3 feet across, deeply cleft into many radiating, drooping segments with loose thread-like fibers on margin; leaf stalks 5 to 7 feet long, flat on upper surface, rounded beneath, unarmed. *Flowers* small, white, in a large branched and drooping cluster; blooming June or July. *Fruits* roundish, nearly black, about ⅓ inch across; ripening October or November.

RANGE: Southeastern North Carolina south to Florida.

Carolina Silverbell

Southern Bush-honeysuckle

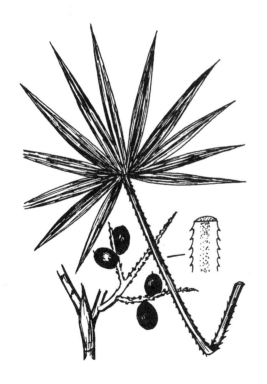

Saw-palmetto

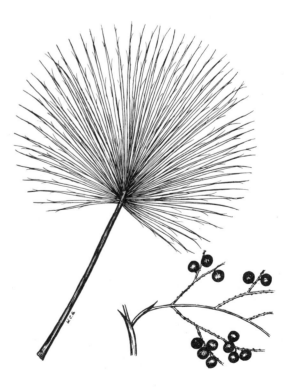

Cabbage Palmetto

Southern Magnolia

Live Oak

Carolina Laurel Cherry

Southern Prickly-ash

SOUTHERN MAGNOLIA *Magnolia grandiflora* L.   Magnolia Family

FIELD MARKS: An evergreen tree 60 to 90 feet or more tall; growing in low wet places and in swamps of the southern coastal plains. *Leaves* 5 to 8 inches long, elliptical, untoothed on margin, thick and leathery in texture, glossy dark green above, usually rusty-woolly beneath. *Flowers* white or creamy-white, lemon-scented, 6 to 8 inches across; blooming April to July. *Fruits* in egg-shaped, rusty-woolly, cone-like clusters 3 to 4 inches long; becoming dull red when mature when each fruit splits down one side to release scarlet fleshy-coated seeds on silky threads.

RANGE: Southeastern North Carolina south to central Florida; west to eastern Texas.

Also called Bull Bay. Widely planted as an ornamental tree in the South.

LIVE OAK *Quercus virginiana* Mill.   Beech Family

FIELD MARKS: An evergreen tree 40 to rarely 80 feet tall with a widespreading crown, or sometimes merely a shrub; growing in the sandy southern coastal plains. *Leaves* 2 to 4 inches long, stiff and leathery in texture, elliptical or broadest toward the tip, margin rolled inward and usually untoothed, shiny dark green above, paler and usually downy beneath. *Fruit* a narrowly oval-shaped, dark brown acorn about ¾ inch long, seated in a deeply bowl-shaped and downy-scaled cup, often paired on a long stalk; maturing in 1 year; kernel sweetish.

RANGE: Southeastern Virginia south to Florida; west to Texas.

CAROLINA LAUREL CHERRY *Prunus caroliniana* (Mill.) Ait.   Rose Family

FIELD MARKS: A small evergreen tree 15 to 40 feet tall; growing in the southern coastal plains. *Leaves* 2 to 4½ inches long, oblong lance-shaped, untoothed or very sparingly toothed on margin, leathery in texture, shiny dark green above, smooth, with a pleasant cherry-like odor when crushed. *Flowers* white, about ¼ inch across, in rather short narrow clusters; blooming March or April. *Fruits* roundish or slightly oblong, dull black, about ½ inch across; ripening September or October and often persisting until late the following spring.

RANGE: Southeastern North Carolina south to central Florida; west to eastern Texas.

Often planted as an ornamental in the South.

Leaves Alternate—Compound

SOUTHERN PRICKLY-ASH *Zanthoxylum clava-herculis* L.   Rue Family

FIELD MARKS. A large shrub or small somewhat evergreen tree; growing in dry sandy woods or on sandhills. *Branchlets* with paired nodal prickles and some scattered ones, on larger stems developing into corky knobs with a stout prickle at tip; lime-like odor when bruised. *Leaves* alternate, compound, 5 to 8 inches long; the 7 to 19 leaflets almost stalkless, often rather sickle-shaped, unevenly rounded or pointed at base, pointed at tip, margin bluntly toothed, somewhat leathery in texture, lustrous above, paler and usually smooth beneath, 1 to 2½ inches long, with limelike odor when crushed. *Flowers* small, greenish, clustered; blooming April to June. *Fruits* dry, reddish-brown pods about 3/16 inch long, containing 1 or 2 shiny black seeds; maturing July to September.

RANGE. Coastal plain; southeastern Virginia south to Florida, west to Texas; north in Mississippi Valley to Arkansas and southeastern Oklahoma.

INKBERRY *Ilex glabra* (L.) Gray   Holly Family

FIELD MARKS. An evergreen shrub 1 to about 4 feet high; growing in low sandy woods and about the borders of swamps or bogs. *Leaves* narrowly elliptic to oval and often broadest above the middle, wedge-shaped at base, broadly pointed at tip, margin with some low and bluntish teeth above the middle, thickish and leathery in texture, dark green and lustrous above, paler and smooth and with minute black dots beneath, ¾ to 2 inches long. *Flowers* blooming May to August. *Fruits* black, about ¼ inch in diameter, on stalks about ⅜ inch long; ripening September to November and persisting.

RANGE. Coastal plain; Nova Scotia south to Florida, west to Louisiana.

Also called Gallberry. An important honey plant in the southeast. The fruits are eaten by many birds, including the bobwhite quail and wild turkey.

YAUPON HOLLY *Ilex vomitoria* Ait.   Holly Family

FIELD MARKS. An evergreen shrub or small tree 4 to about 20 feet high; growing in sandy woods and on dunes. *Branchlets* stiff and spiky. *Leaves* oval to elliptic or egg-shaped, rounded to broadly pointed at the base, bluntly pointed at tip, margin with rounded or bluntish teeth, thickish and leathery in texture, lustrous green above, slightly paler beneath, smooth on both surfaces, ½ to 1½ inches long; the leafstalks very short. *Flowers* blooming March to May. *Fruits* bright red (rarely yellow) short-stalked, about ¼ inch in diameter; ripening in October or November and persisting.

RANGE. Coastal plain; southeastern Virginia south to Florida, west to south central Texas; north in the Mississippi Valley to Arkansas and Oklahoma.

Also called Cassine and Christmas-berry. The leaves have been used as a substitute for tea and were formerly used by the Indians to make their ceremonial "black drink." Cultivated as an ornamental shrub.

MAY HAW *Crataegus astivalis* (Walt.) Torrey & Gray   Rose Family

FIELD MARKS. A rather distinctive shrub or small tree; growing on wet soils, chiefly in coastal regions. *Leaves* broadest above the middle, wedge-shaped at base, rounded to pointed at tip, margin sharply toothed to or below the middle, sometimes 3-lobed, smooth or nearly so on both surfaces or somewhat rusty-hairy beneath, 1 to 2½ inches long; leafstalks short. *Fruits* red, dotted, about ½ inch in diameter, with 3 to 5 bony seeds; ripening in May.

RANGE. North Carolina south to Florida and west to Texas.

SPANISH BAYONET *Yucca aloifolia* L.   Lily Family

FIELD MARKS. A plant with a stem to about 15 feet high, commonly covered with downward-pointing old leaves, and with a dense cluster of spreading ones at the summit or ends of branches; growing in sandy woods and among coastal sand dunes. *Leaves* rigid, dagger-like, sharply pointed at tip, minutely saw-toothed on margin, 1½ to 2½ feet long. *Flowers* 1 to 2 inches long, white or creamy white, in a large and dense end cluster; blooming May or June. *Fruits* 2½ to 4 inches long, drooping, containing plump, marginless seeds.

RANGE. Coastal plain; North Carolina south to Florida, west to Alabama.

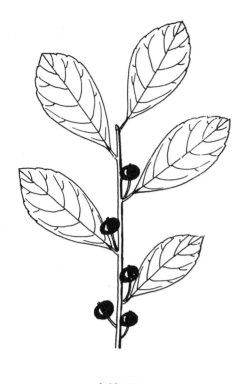

Inkberry

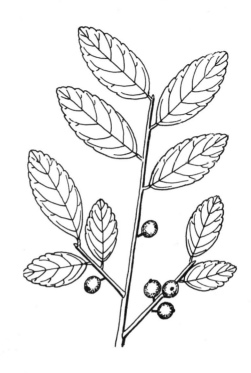

Yaupon Holly

May Haw

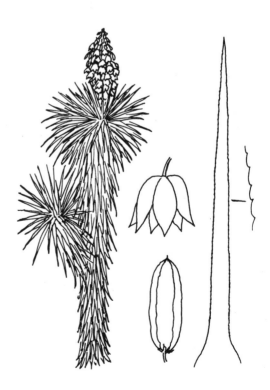

Spanish Bayonet

PART II
Wildflowers

SPRING FLOWERS OF THE WOODLANDS

ROUND-LOBED HEPATICA *(Hepatica americana)*   Buttercup Family

Hepaticas are among the very first wild flowers to bloom in the spring, their blooming season being between March and May. Each flower stands on a silky-hairy stalk a few inches tall. It has no petals but its 5 to 9 sepals are delicate and petal-like; being white, pink, lilac, or even a deep lavender-blue in color. The numerous stamens have whitish or pale anthers; and in the center of the flower there is a little cluster of pistils. Just beneath the petal-like sepals are 3 green bracts which, in this species, have roundish tips. At flowering time the new leaves of the plant have not yet appeared, or are just beginning to put in their appearance. Usually there are some of the leaves of the previous year still present. Although now mostly brown, they are somewhat thick and leathery and they have 3 roundish lobes. The hepatica grows in woodlands, and it makes a good subject for the shady wild flower garden.
  RANGE: N.S. to Man. south to Fla., Ala., and Mo.

VIRGINIA SPRING-BEAUTY *(Claytonia virginica)*   Purslane Family

Spring-beauties have 2 to several flower stems which arise from a deeply buried tuber. In this one the stems are usually 4 to 8 inches tall. Near the middle they have a pair of narrow and rather fleshy leaves from 2 to 4 inches in length. Along the upper part of the stem is a narrow cluster of 5-petalled white or pale pink flowers which have deeper pink veins. They are about a half inch across. The lowermost one opens first, the others open progressively up the stem. This plant is often very common in rich, moist woods and thickets; blooming between March and May. It grows well in a woodland flower garden. RANGE: Que. to Ont. and Minn. south to Ga. and Tex.

CAROLINA SPRING-BEAUTY *(Claytonia caroliniana)*   Purslane Family

This species closely resembles the preceding one but it has narrowly egg-shaped or elliptic leaves from 1½ to 3 inches long, and ¼ to 1 inch broad. It grows in rich, moist, open woods and thickets; it blooms between March and May, or later northward. It is also called the Broad-leaved Spring-beauty.
  RANGE: Nfd. to Sask. south to w. N.C., e. Tenn., Ill., and Minn.

TWINLEAF *(Jeffersonia diphylla)*   Barberry Family

So-called because its leaves are so deeply divided that they seem to have 2 blades, the Twinleaf is very easy to recognize. At flowering time, in April or May, the leaves are only partly developed and 2 halves may be folded together. When fully mature, the leaves are 3 to 6 inches long and from 2 to 4 inches wide. Each flower is on a smooth stalk 6 to 8 inches in length. About an inch across, they have 4 sepals which soon fall, 8 white petals, and 8 stamens. The pistil becomes a many-seeded pod. The Twinleaf grows in rich, moist woods but it is not very common. Its generic name *Jeffersonia* honors our illustrious scientist-president, Thomas Jefferson.
  RANGE: N.Y. and Ont. to Wis. south to Va. and Ala.

BLOODROOT *(Sanguinaria canadensis)*   Poppy Family

In early spring—between March and early May—the bright white flowers of the Bloodroot appear above the fallen leaves in our woodlands. As they open, their 2 sepals fall away; but the 8 to 12 petals spread into a blossom 1½ to 2 inches across. Each flower is accompanied by an enveloping leaf, which has not yet unfolded. Later this 5- to 9-lobed and bluntly toothed leaf may become 6 or more inches in width, persisting until about mid-summer. The Bloodroot gets its name, and another name of Red Puccoon, from the bright orange-red juice of its thick rootstock. It is easily grown in the woodland flower garden. RANGE: Que. to Man. south to Fla. and Tex.

JACK-IN-THE-PULPIT *(Arisaema triphyllum)*   Arum Family

This plant is quite familiar to country boys as the "Indian-turnip". Jack is the club-like spadix which bears tiny flowers toward its base. The spathe forms what looks like an old-fashioned canopied pulpit from which Preacher Jack preaches. The hood portion of the spathe may be green or purple, quite often marked with paler or whitish stripes. Jack-in-the-Pulpits are often quite common in rich, moist woods and thickets. The plants grow from 1 to rarely 3 feet tall, and each of the two leaves are divided into 3 leaflets. Towards fall the spathe withers and discloses a cluster of brilliant red, berry-like fruits. The flowering season is between late March and June.
  RANGE: N.B. to Man. south to n. Fla. and Miss.

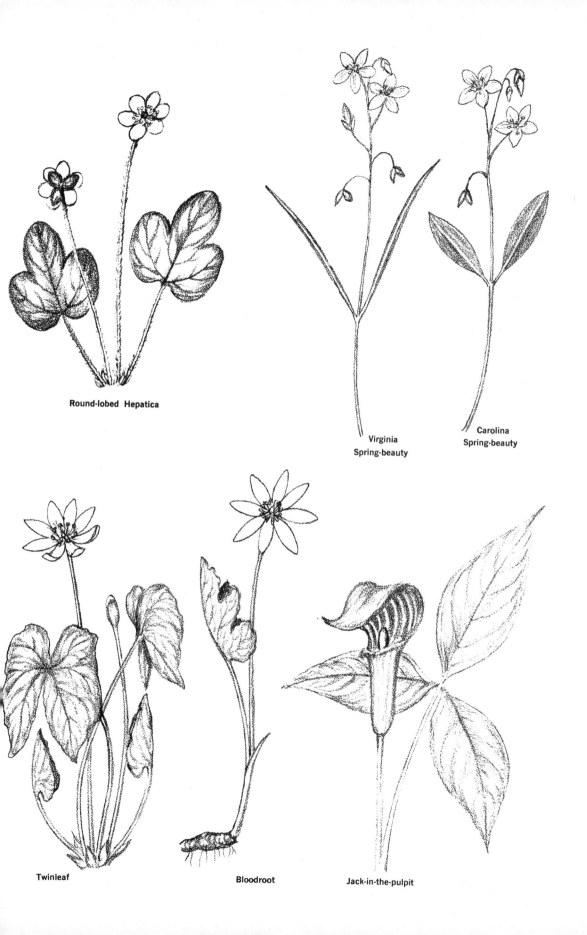

Round-lobed Hepatica

Virginia
Spring-beauty

Carolina
Spring-beauty

Twinleaf

Bloodroot

Jack-in-the-pulpit

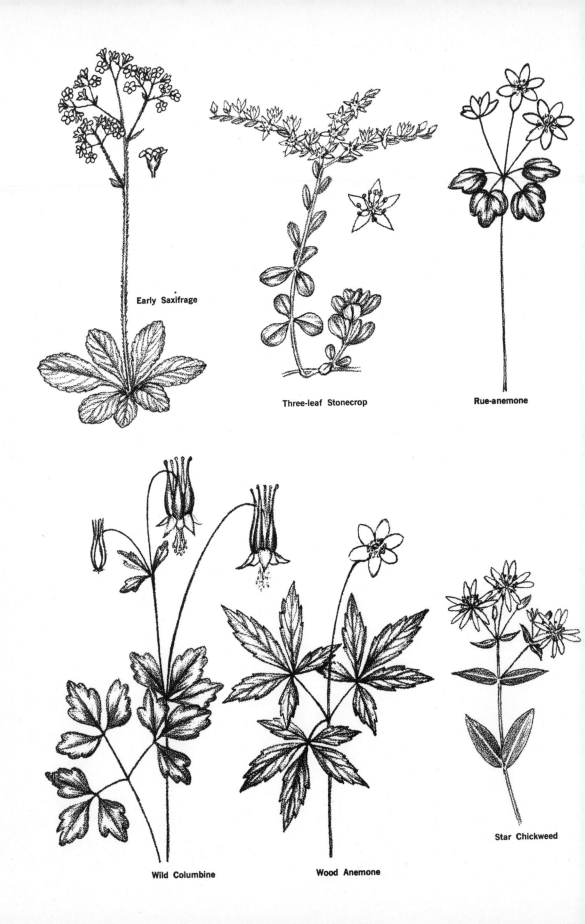

Early Saxifrage

Three-leaf Stonecrop

Rue-anemone

Wild Columbine

Wood Anemone

Star Chickweed

EARLY SAXIFRAGE *(Saxifraga virginiensis)*   Saxifrage Family

When the Early Saxifrage begins to bloom in late March or early April, it has a sticky-hairy flower stalk only 4 to 6 inches high. It continues to bloom for several weeks, often into June, becoming branched and up to a foot high. At the base of the flower stalk it has a rosette of rather fleshy, oval or egg-shaped leaves from 1 to 3 inches long which are often purplish-beneath. Their margins may have low and blunt teeth or be coarsely toothed or scalloped. Similar but smaller leaves subtend the branches of the flower stalk. The flowers are about ¼ inch across and have 5 oblong or top-shaped white petals and 10 stamens with bright yellow anthers. This is our most common and widespread species of saxifrage, growing on wet to dry rock ledges and rocky slopes.
    RANGE: N.B. to Ont. and Minn. south to Ga., Tenn., and Mo.

THREE-LEAF STONECROP *(Sedum ternatum)*   Orpine Family

The Three-leaf Stonecrop is a small, succulent plant with a creeping stem and ascending flowering branches from 3 to 6 inches high. Its lower leaves are top-shaped and arranged in whorls of 3's, but those on the upper portion of the stem are scattered singly. Its flowers are almost ½ inch across, starry in appearance, with 5 narrow white petals and twice as many stamens which have dark-colored anthers. They suggest another common name of Pepper-and-salt. This plant is usually common on moist cliffs and rocky, wooded slopes; blooming between April and June. RANGE: N.Y. to Mich. south to Ga. and Tenn.

RUE-ANEMONE *(Anemonella thalictroides)*   Buttercup Family

The Rue-anemone is a delicate little plant with a very slender stem 4 to 8 inches high. At the summit it bears a whorl of thin, pale green, 3-lobed, leaf-like bracts together with several slender-stalked flowers. The flowers are about ¾ of an inch across and have from 5 to 10 white or pale-pink, petal-like sepals. A bit later the basal leaves develop. They are ternately compound and the leaflets very much resemble the bracts of the flower stalk, but they are not present when the plant blooms in April or May. It grows in rich and rather open woodlands.
    RANGE: Me. to Minn. south to Fla., Miss., Ark., and Okla.

WILD COLUMBINE *(Aquilegia canadensis)*   Buttercup Family

The Wild Columbine grows in rocky woodlands and on shaded rocks and cliffs, blooming between April and June. It is a smooth plant from 1 to about 2 feet tall. The flowers, like red and yellow bells, nod from the tips of the long and slender stem or its branches. Each one is about 1½ inches long, with 5 petal-like sepals and 5 true petals which are prolonged backward as hollow spurs. Nectar is secreted in the ball-like tips of these spurs. The numerous stamens protrude beyond the mouth of the flower. The ovaries of its 5 pistils mature into slender, dry, pod-like fruits which contain many shiny, black seeds. Its leaves are compound, divided into 3s, and the leaflets are more or less 3-lobed and bluntly toothed. It blooms between April and July, and it is quite easy to grow in the wild flower garden.
    RANGE: Que. and Ont. to Wis. south to Fla. and Tex.

WOOD ANEMONE *(Anemone quinquefolia)*   Buttercup Family

The Wood Anemone, or Windflower, has a stem from 4 to 9 inches tall. At its summit is a whorl of 3 leaves, each of which is divided into from 3 to 5 narrow and sharply toothed segments, and a solitary flower. The basal leaves are similar to the ones on the flower stem but they are either not present or just starting to grow at flowering time. The flower is about an inch across and it has from 5 to 7 white, petal-like sepals. It grows in open woods, thickets, and clearings; blooming between April and June.
    RANGE: Que. to Man. south to S.C., Tenn., and Iowa.

STAR CHICKWEED *(Stellaria pubera)*   Pink Family

The half-inch, bright white, starry flowers of this plant are often seen on rocky, wooded slopes in the early spring. They have 5 petals which are so deeply notched that there appears to be 10, and there are 10 stamens. The weak stems are 4 to 12 inches tall and have 2 finely hairy lines. On them are pairs of elliptic or oblong leaves from ½ to 2 inches long which are pointed at both ends. Blooming between March and May. It is also known as the Great Chickweed.
    RANGE: N.J. to Ill. south to n. Fla. and Ala.

WILD GINGER *(Asarum canadense)*   Birthwort Family

The Wild Ginger is a low hairy plant, with a pair of very veiny leaves at the tip of its creeping underground stem. A solitary flower is produced between the bases of the leaf-stalks and is often hidden among the fallen leaves. It is shaped like a little bell and there are 3 spreading or recurved, pointed, brownish-purple lobes at the summit. In the variety *acuminatum* the lobes have tail-like tips up to 1½ inches long. Often common on rich and usually rocky wooded slopes, it blooms in April or May. The rootstocks have a ginger-like odor.

RANGE: Que. to Man. south to nw. S.C., Mo. and Kan.

YELLOW ADDER'S-TONGUE *(Erythronium americanum)*   Lily Family

Other names given to this little lily family member are Fawn-lily, Trout-lily, and Dog's-tooth Violet. The plant has a pair of elliptic leaves 4 to 6 inches long which are pale green and mottled with purplish-brown. Between them rises a flower stalk which bears a nodding, open bell-shaped, yellow flower about 1½ inches across. Its 6 perianth parts are often tinged with purplish on the back, and usually curve gracefully backward. It grows in rich woods and bottomlands and blooms between March and May. It requires several years for the plants to attain the flowering stage. Younger plants have just 'one leaf which arises from a deeply buried corm.

RANGE: Ont. to Minn. south to Ga., Ala., Ark. and Tex.

PERFOLIATE BELLWORT *(Uvularia perfoliata)*   Lily Family

This plant has a slender forking stem 8 to 20 inches tall; and smooth, pale green leaves which are coated with a thin whitish bloom. The bases of the leaves completely surround the stem, which appears to grow through them. It usually has a solitary pale yellow flower about an inch long, which is shaped like a narrow bell. On the inner surface of the 6 perianth parts there are small grain-like hairs. It grows in moist open woods and blooms in April or May.

RANGE: Mass. to Ont. south to Fla. and La.

LARGE-FLOWERED BELLWORT *(Uvularia grandiflora)*   Lily Family

This species looks very much like a larger edition of the preceding one, but it has a stouter stem 1 to 2 feet tall and its leaves are finely downy beneath and brighter green above. Its flowers are about 1½ inches long, deeper lemon-yellow in color, and the 6 perianth parts are smooth within. It also grows in rich woods, southward only in the mountains, and blooms in April and May.

RANGE: Que. to N.D. south to n.Ga., Miss., Ark. and Okla.

SESSILE-LEAF BELLWORT *(Uvularia sessilifolia)*   Lily Family

The leave of this species are stalkless but their bases do not surround the stem. It has a slender, smooth, forking stem 8 to 16 inches tall. The leaves are pale or somewhat whitened on the lower surface. The 6 perianth parts of the inch-long, pale yellow flowers are smooth within. It likewise grows in rich woods and blooms in April or May. It is also known as Wild-oats.

RANGE: N.B. to N.D. south to n. Fla., Ala. and Mo.

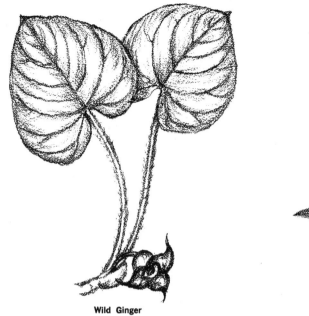

Wild Ginger

Yellow Adder's-tongue

Large-flowered Bellwort

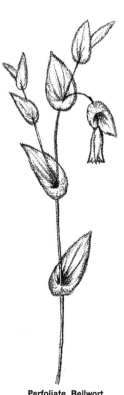

Perfoliate Bellwort

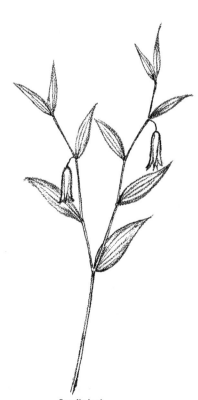

**Sessile-leaf
Bellwort**

Great Solomon's-seal   **Hairy Solomon's-seal**   **Clasping-leaf Twisted-stalk**   **Hairy Disporum**

Sessile-leaf Twisted-stalk

GREAT SOLOMON'S-SEAL *(Polygonatum canaliculatum)* Lily Family

Largest of the Solomon's-seals, this species has a stout, arching stem from 2 to nearly 6 feet tall. Along it are a number of broad, more or less corrugated leaves from 3 to 6 inches long; which have clasping bases. From the leaf axils arise drooping clusters of from 2 to 8 greenish-white flowers a half inch or more long, which are shaped like cylindrical bells. Later these flowers develop into ball-shaped, bluish-black berries. The Great Solomon's-seal grows in rich, moist, woods and swampy thickets; and also along the banks of streams. It blooms in May and June. Solomon's-seals get their name from the seal-like scars which the upright leafy branches leave on the underground, creeping rootstocks. RANGE: N.H. to Man. south to S.C., Mo., and Okla.

HAIRY SOLOMON'S-SEAL *(Polygonatum pubescens)* Lily Family

This is a much smaller plant with an arching stem from about 1 to 3 feet tall, which grows in woods and thickets. On its slender stem are a number of leaves 2 to about 4 inches long, which are pale and somewhat downy beneath. In their axils hang half-inch, narrowly bell-shaped, greenish-white flowers, which are sometimes solitary but usually in pairs. It blooms in May or June, and the flowers are followed by round, bluish-black berries. RANGE: Que. to Man. south to S.C., Ky., and Iowa.

SMOOTH SOLOMON'S-SEAL *(Polygonatum biflorum)* Lily Family

Like the preceding species, the Smooth Solomon's-seal usually has its flowers in pairs. The most obvious difference between the two species is in their leaves, those of the Smooth Solomon's-seal being smooth on both surfaces. It is often common in dry to moist, often rocky woods and thickets; blooming in May or June.
RANGE: Ont., Mich., and Neb. south to Fla. and Tex. (Not illustrated)

SESSILE-LEAF TWISTED-STALK *(Streptopus roseus)* Lily Family

Twisted-stalks get their name from the fact that the stalks of their flowers are abruptly bent or twisted near the middle. Instead of arising from the leaf axils, the slender stalks which bear the open bell-shaped flowers arise to the side or more nearly opposite the leaves. In general appearance, the plants resemble the Solomon's-seals but they have somewhat more zig-zag and often forked stems. This species has a stem from 1 to 2 feet tall. The leaves are deeply corrugated and seated directly on the stem but their bases are not clasping. Between April and July it has pink or rose-purple flowers, which are followed by red berries. It grows in cool, moist woods and the borders of swamps. Another name for it is Rose Mandarin. RANGE: Lab. to Man. south to n. Ga., Tenn. and Minn.

CLASPING-LEAF TWISTED-STALK *(Streptopus amplexifolius)* Lily Family

From the preceding species, this one can be distinguished by its clasping leaf bases. It has a stem from 1½ to 3 feet tall. The flowers are greenish-white (sometimes dark purple) and the fruits are red berries. It grows in cool, moist woods and thickets; blooming between May and July. It is also known as the White Mandarin.
RANGE: Lab. to Alaska south to N.C., the Great Lakes region, and N. Mex.

HAIRY DISPORUM *(Disporum lanuginosum)* Lily Family

Disporums are plants similar to the twisted stalks but they have 1 or 2 open bell-shaped flowers at the tips of the stems or their branches. This one has a stem 1 to 2 feet tall which is sparingly branched above. Its leaves are stalkless, pointed at the tip, and rounded to slightly heart-shaped at the base. Their lower surfaces, as well as the younger parts of the stems, are minutely woolly-hairy. The 6 perianth parts of the flowers are about ¾ inch long and greenish-white in color. Smooth red berries follow the flowers which bloom in May or June. This plant grows in rather moist, rich woods. It is also known as the Yellow Mandarin. RANGE: N.Y. to Ont. south to Ga., Ala., and Tenn.

171

YELLOW CLINTONIA *(Clintonia borealis)* Lily Family

This plant usually has 3 oval-shaped, somewhat leathery, lustrous leaves with hairy-fringed margins. They are from 5 to about 10 inches long. The greenish-yellow, bell-shaped flowers are borne in a cluster (umbel) of 3 to 8 at the top of a naked stalk 6 to 8 inches tall. Both leaves and flower stalk arise directly from an underground rootstock. The plants bloom in May or June, the flowers being followed by oval-shaped blue berries. The Yellow Clintonia is a plant of cool, moist woods and thickets.
RANGE: Lab. to Man. south to N. Eng., n. Ga., and the Great Lakes region.

WHITE CLINTONIA *(Clintonia umbellata)* Lily Family

The White Clintonia has a whorl of 3 or 4 leaves very much like those of the preceding species. It differs in having smaller and more numerous (up to 30) white flowers which are minutely speckled with purple and green. The fruits which follow the flowers are ball-shaped black berries. This species is usually more common in rich woods southward. It blooms between May and early July.
RANGE: N. Y. to Ohio south in the mts. to n. Ga. and Tenn.

INDIAN CUCUMBER-ROOT *(Medeola virginica)* Lily Family

A distinctive plant with a slender stem usually 1 to 2 feet tall, with a whorl of 5 to 9 leaves near the middle and another whorl of 3 smaller ones near the top. From the axils of the latter leaves arise the slender stalks bearing the nodding, greenish-yellow flowers. Both sepals and petals, as well as the 3 slender stigmas of the pistil, curve backward. The plant blooms in May or June. Later the flowers produce dark purple berries. In the ground, at the base of the stem, is a whitish tuber which has a taste very much like that of a cucumber—hence the common name. It grows in rich, moist woodlands.
RANGE: Que. to Ont. and Minn. south to n. Fla. and La.

WHITE COLIC-ROOT *(Aletris farinosa)* Lily Family

Close to the ground this plant has a star-like cluster of flat, rather thin, yellowish-green, and grass-like leaves. Sometime between May and July or August, it sends up an almost naked stalk usually 1 to about 3 feet tall. Along the upper part of it are scattered white flowers which are shaped like narrow urns, and have a peculiar mealy surface. The plant grows in moist to dry open woods on sandy or peaty soils. It is abundant in the coastal plain pinelands of the Southeast and is also often common in the mountains. Other names for it are White Star-grass and Mealy Starwort.
RANGE: Me. to Ont. and Wis. south to Fla. and Tex.

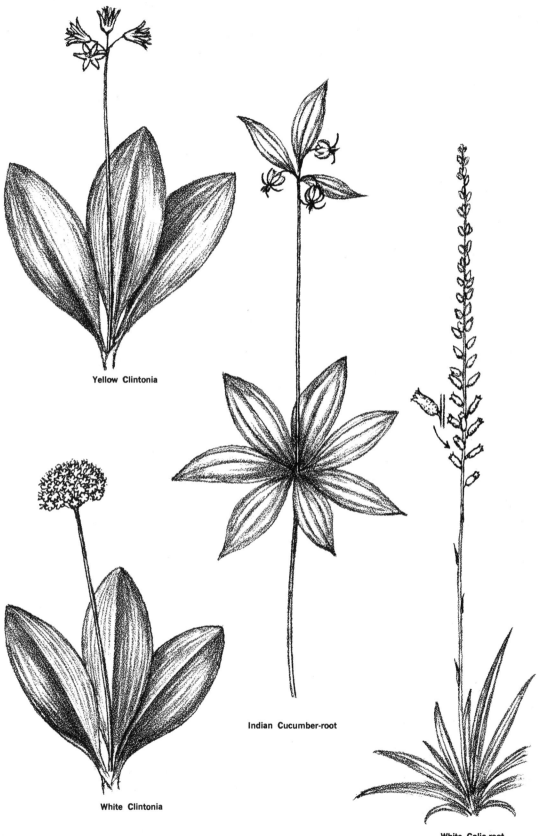

Yellow Clintonia

Indian Cucumber-root

White Clintonia

White Colic-root

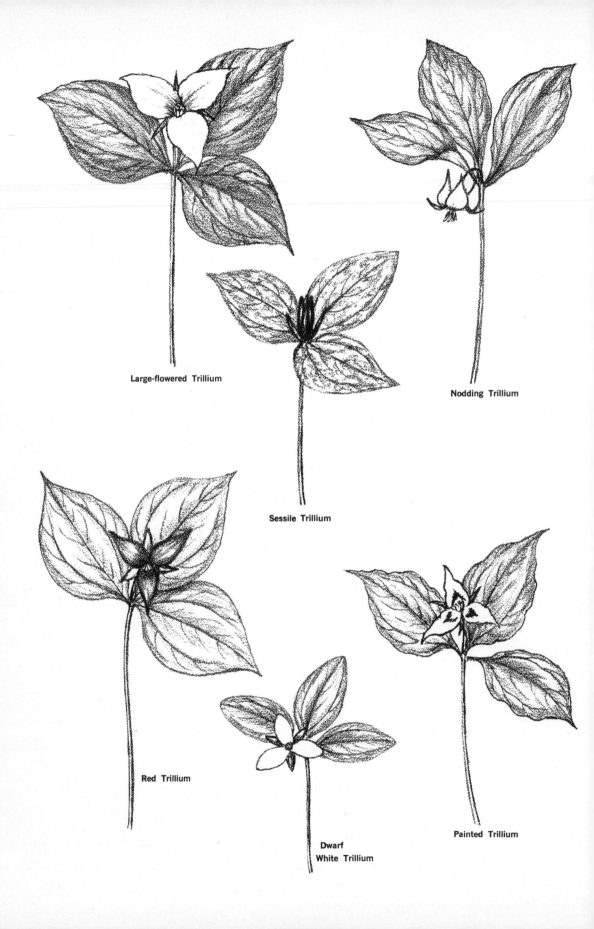

Large-flowered Trillium

Nodding Trillium

Sessile Trillium

Red Trillium

Dwarf
White Trillium

Painted Trillium

LARGE-FLOWERED TRILLIUM *(Trillium grandiflorum)*   Lily Family

This is one of the most common trilliums, being widespread in rich moist woods and thickets. It has a stout stem 8 to 18 inches tall with 3 large, broadly oval or egg-shaped, nearly stalkless leaves. The flower is 2 to 3½ inches across and stands on an erect or slightly leaning stalk. The 3 broad petals overlap at the base forming a sort of tube. They are white when the flower first opens but turn pink with age. It blooms in April or May.

RANGE: Me. and s. Que. west to Minn. south to n. Ga. and Ark.

SESSILE TRILLIUM *(Trillium sessile)*   Lily Family

Often called the Toadshade Trillium, this species has 3 stalkless, oval or egg-shaped leaves which are strikingly mottled in two or three shades of green. The plant grows from 4 to about 12 inches tall. The stalkless flower has 3 narrow and more or less erect petals from ¾ to 1½ inches long, which vary from maroon or purplish-brown to greenish-yellow. The flowers have a strong odor which is not altogether unpleasant. It grows in rich moist woods and stream bottoms, blooming in April or May.

RANGE: w. N.Y. to Ill. and Mo. south to w. Ga., Miss. and Ark.

NODDING TRILLIUM *(Trillium cernuum)*   Lily Family

Like the flowers of the preceding species, those of this trillium have petals which overlap at the base forming a sort of short tube. A distinctive feature is its purplish anthers and the fact that the flower nods on a slender stalk and hangs below the leaves. The petals are white, creamy-white, or pale pink. It grows in rich moist woods and swamps, blooming between April and June.

RANGE: Nfd. to Que. and Wis. south to n. Ga., Tenn. and Iowa.

RED TRILLIUM *(Trillium erectum)*   Lily Family

This is one of the commonest and most variable of our trilliums. The flowers are not always red for the petals, varying greatly in width, range from deep purplish red or maroon to pink, greenish-yellow, and even white. The flower stalks may be erect or they may be inclined or even bent downward. The petals, however, do not overlap but spread from the base. Such names as Ill-scented Wake-robin, Stinking-Beth and Stinking-Benjamin attest to the fact that the flowers are ill-scented. Often they are but this is not always true. The plants are commonly 8 to 16 inches tall and have rather broadly oval or somewhat diamond-shaped, stalkless or nearly stalkless leaves. It grows in rich moist woods and thickets, blooming between April and June.

RANGE: N.S. to Ont. south to Del., n. Ga. and n. Ala.

DWARF WHITE TRILLIUM *(Trillium nivale)*   Lily Family

Often called the Snow Trillium, this is a small species with a stem 2 to 5 inches tall; with oval, egg-shaped or roundish, stalked leaves from 1 to 2 inches long. The stalked flower, little more than an inch across, has oval-shaped white petals. It grows in rich woods and along streams; blooming between March and early May.

RANGE: w. Pa. to Minn. south to Ky. and Mo.

PAINTED TRILLIUM *(Trillium undulatum)*   Lily Family

This trillium is readily recognized by the V-shaped purplish-pink marks toward the bases of its white, wavy-margined, recurved petals. It is a slender-stemmed plant 5 to about 20 inches tall. The broadly egg-shaped leaves are definitely stalked and are taper-pointed at the tip. It grows in cool wet woods and swamps, blooming between April and June.

RANGE: N.S. to Man. south to N.J., n.Ga., e. Tenn. and Wis.

175

CUT-LEAF TOOTHWORT *(Dentaria laciniata)*   Mustard Family

On a smooth or somewhat hairy stem 8 to 15 inches tall, this toothwort has a whorl of 3 leaves; each of them being divided into 3 narrow and sharply toothed or lobed segments. The basal leaves are similar but they are seldom present at flowering time, between March and May. The flowers are about ½ inch across and have 4 white or lavender tinged petals. Several of them occur along a stalk which stands above the leaves. Beneath the ground the plant has a jointed rootstock which readily separates into inch-long tubers shaped like sweet-potatoes. Being slightly peppery, they afford a quite pleasant nibble. It is often common in rich, moist woods and on rocky slopes. Another name for it is Pepperroot.
RANGE: Vt. and Que. to Minn. and Neb. south to Fla. La., and Kan.

TWO-LEAF TOOTHWORT *(Dentaria diphylla)*   Mustard Family

Another name for this plant is Crinkleroot; a name suggested by its long, continuous, crinkled rootstock. It has a smooth stem from 6 to 12 inches tall on which is a pair of leaves, both of them divided into 3 broadly egg-shaped and bluntly toothed leaflets. The basal leaves are similar but they are long-stalked. Along the stem, and above the 2 leaves, is a loose cluster of white flowers with 4 white petals. This toothwort is usually quite common in rich, moist, rocky woods and thickets; blooming between April and June.
RANGE: N.S. and Ont. south to S.C., Ky., and Mich.

EARLY BUTTERCUP *(Ranunculus fascicularis)*   Buttercup Family

Usually the first buttercup to bloom in the spring, the Early Buttercup may flower between late March and May. It grows on wooded hillsides, usually where the soil is quite thin. The plant may be only a few inches tall when the first flowers appear but it later becomes from 6 to 10 inches in height. It is covered with close-pressed, fine, and silky hairs. The bright yellow flowers are almost an inch across, and the leaves have from 3 to 5 cut or lobed divisions. The specific name, *fascicularis,* refers to the cluster (fascicle) of thick, fibrous roots.
RANGE: N.H. to Ont. and Minn. south to Ga. and Tex.

DUTCHMAN'S-BREECHES *(Dicentra cucullaria)*   Fumitory Family

This well-known wild flower gets its name from the resemblance of its flowers to a Dutchman's baggy breeches, hanging upside down along the nodding stalks which are 5 to 10 inches long. They are about ¾ inch long, white or faintly pinkish, and their 2 broad spurs are spread like the letter V. The leaves are all at the base and are ternately divided and cut into numerous narrow segments which are pale beneath. Both the flower stalks and the leaves arise from a knobby-scaled bulb. The Dutchman's-breeches grows in rich woods and on rocky slopes; blooming during April or May.
RANGE: N.S. to S.D. south to Ga., Ala., and Kan.

SQUIRREL-CORN *(Dicentra canadensis)*   Fumitory Family

Leaves of the Squirrel-corn are just like those of the Dutchman's-breeches, but the flowers afford a fine point of distinction. Those of the Squirrel-corn have 2 short and rounded spurs which point upward. They are a little more than ½ inch long, white or pale pinkish, rather heart-shaped, and arranged along an arching stalk 6 to 8 inches high. The plant gets its name from the yellow tubers which occur on its rootstocks. It grows in rich woods and on rocky slopes, blooming in April or May.
RANGE: Que. to Minn. south to Va., N.C., n. Ga., and Mo.

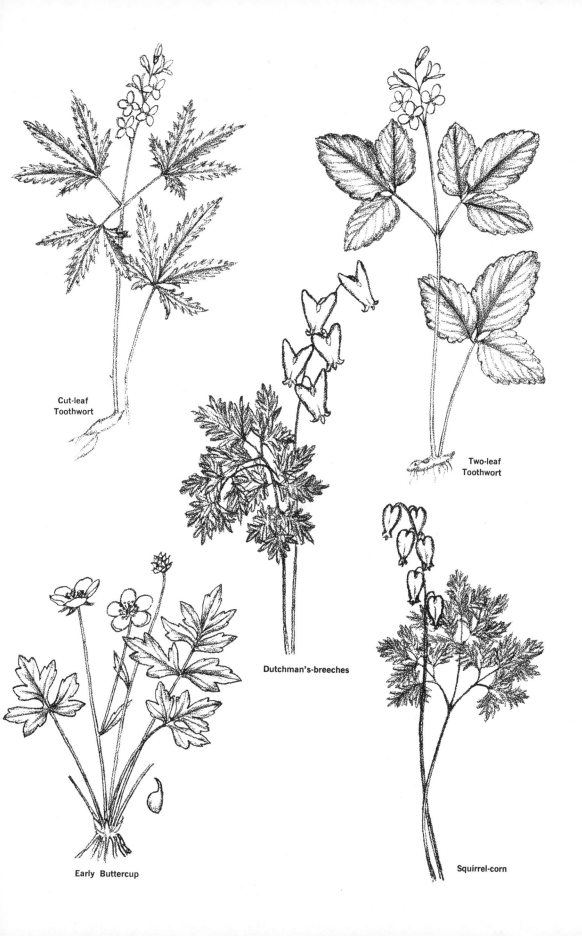

Cut-leaf
Toothwort

Two-leaf
Toothwort

Dutchman's-breeches

Early Buttercup

Squirrel-corn

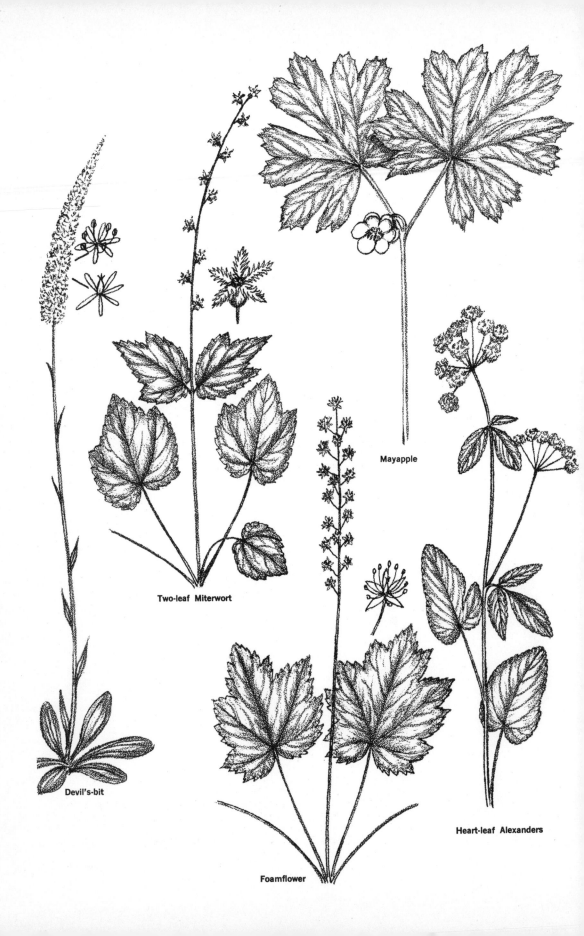

Mayapple

Two-leaf Miterwort

Devil's-bit

Heart-leaf Alexanders

Foamflower

DEVIL'S-BIT *(Chamaelirium luteum)*   Lily Family

Another and much more attractive name for this plant is Fairy-wand. Most of the leaves are in a rosette at the base of its slender 2 to 3 foot flower stalk. Along the stalk are just a few smaller and narrower leaves; and toward the summit there is a long, slender cluster of small white flowers. The flowers on a given plant have either stamens or pistils, but not both. It grows in rich moist woods and thickets; blooming between April and June. A good subject for a woodland wild flower garden.
RANGE: Mass. to Ont. south to Fla., Miss. and Ark.

TWO-LEAF MITERWORT *(Mitella diphylla)*   Saxifrage Family

The Two-leaf Miterwort has a flower stalk 10 to 18 inches tall with a pair of quite stalkless, heart-shaped, 3-lobed, and toothed leaves about the middle. Above them is a slender cluster of small, short-stalked, starry flowers in which the 5 white petals are delicately fringed. The 10 stamens are short and in the mouth of the cup-like calyx. The basal leaves are broadly egg-shaped, heart-shaped at the base, 3- to 5-lobed, and sharply toothed. The entire plant is minutely hairy. It grows in rich and often rocky woodlands, blooming in April or May. Another name is Bishop's-cap.
RANGE: N.H., Que., and Minn. south to w. S.C., Tenn., Miss., and Mo.

FOAMFLOWER *(Tiarella cordifolia)*   Saxifrage Family

The Foamflower, or False Miterwort, is a low plant which spreads by means of slender runners and forms little colonies. It usually has a leafless flower stalk 6 to 12 inches tall, with a narrow cluster of small white flowers along the upper portion. Occasionally the flower stalks do have a pair of small leaves, in which case one will have to look closer at the flowers to distinguish it from the true miterwort. The flowers have 5 small petals which taper into stalked bases, and 10 very conspicuous long stamens. The leaves are roundish to egg-shaped, heart-shaped at the base, and have from 3 to 7 rather shallow but sharply toothed lobes. They are 2 to 4 inches broad and have long stalks. The entire plant is more or less hairy. It grows in cool, moist, rich and often rocky woodlands; blooming between April and June.
RANGE: N.B. to Ont. and Mich. south to N.Eng., w. N.C. and e. Tenn.

MAYAPPLE *(Podophyllum peltatum)*   Barberry Family

The Mayapple is readily recognizable by the pair of large, stalked, umbrella-like leaves on its foot-high stem. They are attached to their stalks near the middle; and deeply divided into from 5 to 7 lobes, each of which is 2-cleft at the end and coarsely toothed. In the fork of the two leafstalks hangs a solitary flower an inch or more across. The 6 sepals are shed as the flower opens but the 6 to 9 large, waxy-white petals remain; and there are from 12 to 18 stamens with bright yellow anthers, and a solitary pistil. The latter develops into a large berry, about the size and color of a small lemon, which is edible and enjoyed by some. Non-flowering plants have but a single umbrella-like leaf at the top of their stem. Mayapples commonly grow in colonies in rich open woods, thickets, and clearings; blooming between April and June. Their rootstocks contain a poisonous substance but they are used medicinally. Another name often given it is Mandrake, but this name properly belongs to an Old World plant of no relationship to the Mayapple. RANGE: Que., Ont., and Minn. south to Fla. and Tex.

HEART-LEAF ALEXANDERS *(Zizia aptera)*   Parsley Family

This is an erect and usually smooth plant from 1 to 2 feet tall. At the base it has long-stalked leaves which are egg-shaped to roundish, heart-shaped at the base, bluntly toothed on the margin and sometimes lobed, and 2 to 3 inches long. Those upward along the stem are short-stalked and divided into 3 leaflets. The small yellow flowers are in several umbels, the central flower in each umbel being stalkless. It grows in wooded bottomlands and meadows, blooming between April and June. The plant closely resembles the Meadow-parsnip.
RANGE: R.I. to Minn. and B.C. south to n. Fla., Miss., Mo., Col., Utah, and Ore.

YELLOW PIMPERNEL *(Taenidia integerrima)*   Parsley Family

The Yellow Pimpernel is an erect, smooth, slender stemmed plant 1 to 3 feet tall, which is more or less whitened with a bloom. Its leaves are ternately divided into oval, egg-shaped, or lance-shaped leaflets ½ to an inch long which have untoothed margins. The small yellow flowers are in several long-stalked umbels, blooming April to June. It is a plant of dry rocky or sandy woods and thickets; southward only in the piedmont and mountains.

RANGE: Que. to Minn. south to Ga. and Tex.

FALSE LILY-OF-THE-VALLEY *(Maianthemum canadense)*   Lily Family

The small white flowers of this plant are unique among members of the Lily Family in that they have a 4-parted perianth and 4 stamens. The plant has an erect stem usually from 3 to 6 inches tall, bearing 2 or 3 smooth leaves which have heart-shaped bases. It has rootstocks which creep extensively and it usually occurs in colonies; in which there are many single, stalked, heart-shaped leaves. The flowers are borne in simple little end clusters above the leaves, sometime between May and July. They are followed by small, round, pale greenish and spotted berries which eventually become a dull red. Other names for the plant are Two-leaf Solomon's-seal and Canada Mayflower. It is often common in damp mossy woods and bogs and not infrequently on the decaying trunks of fallen trees.

RANGE: Lab. to B.C. south to Del., n. Ga., Tenn. and Iowa.

MEADOW-PARSNIP *(Thaspium trifoliatum)*   Parsley Family

One variety of this plant has greenish or purplish flowers and is called the Purple Mea-dow-parsnip or Purple Alexanders. More common and widespread is the variety which has yellow flowers. Both are smooth erect plants 1 to 2½ feet tall. The long-stalked basal leaves may be undivided, or divided into 3 egg-shaped to lance-shaped, toothed leaflets 1 to 2 inches long. All of the flowers in the umbels are stalked. It grows in open woods and thickets, blooming between April and June. It closely resembles the Heart-leaf Alex-anders. RANGE: N.Y. to Minn. south to Fla. and La.

FALSE SPIKENARD *(Smilacina racemosa)*   Lily Family

The False Spikenard, or False Solomon's-seal, has an arching, slightly zig-zag stem from 2 to 3 feet tall which arises from a rootstock. Scattered along it are a number of conspic-uously veined and almost stalkless leaves. It small white or creamy-white flowers are disposed in a plumy-branched end cluster sometime between April and July. They are followed by round berries which at first are yellowish-white and speckled. Later they be-come translucent and ruby-red. The plant is often common on rocky wooded slopes. It grows well in a woodland flower garden.

RANGE: Que. to B.C. south to Ga. and Ariz.

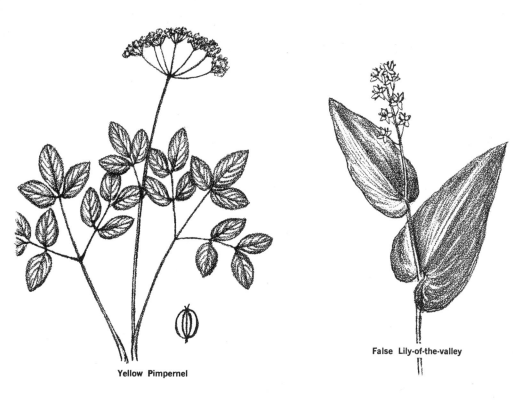

Yellow Pimpernel

False Lily-of-the-valley

Meadow-parsnip

False Spikenard

Crested Dwarf Iris

Dwarf Iris

Fire-pink

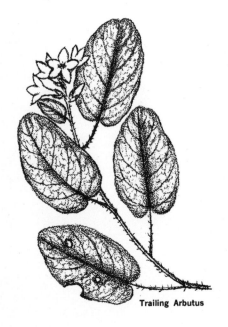

Trailing Arbutus

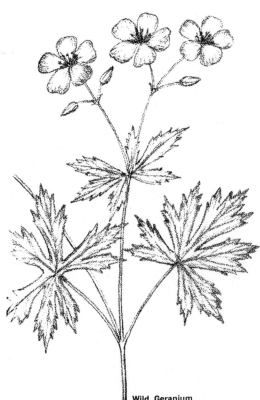

Wild Geranium

FIRE-PINK *(Silene virginica)*   Pink Family

This is one of our most conspicuous wild flowers. The flowers are an inch or more across and have 5 spreading petals of the most brilliant red, each one being 2-pronged at the tip. The sepals are greenish but tinged with red and united into a sticky tube with a 5-toothed rim. The plant has an ascending, sticky-hairy stem becoming a foot to 2 feet tall and branching above. Along it are widely spaced pairs of narrow leaves, the lower ones being 3 to 5 inches long. The Fire-pink is common in open woods and on rocky slopes. In the South it begins to bloom in late March and it may continue to bloom until June or later.

RANGE: N.Y. to Ont. and Minn. south to Ga., Ala., and Ark.

CRESTED DWARF IRIS *(Iris cristata)*   Iris Family

This is a little iris with flower stalks 3 to 6 inches tall. The flowers range from pale to a deep lavender-blue and each of the 3 sepals has a white patch and a 3-ridged, fringed, orange and white crest. The leaves tend to be curved and are ½ to about ¾ of an inch wide. It grows on rich rocky wooded slopes or bluffs, and in ravines; blooming in April or May.

RANGE: Md. to Ind. and Mo. south to n. Ga and Miss.

DWARF IRIS *(Iris verna)*   Iris Family

This is another dwarf species with flower stalks from 1 to 3 inches tall. Its flowers range from a deep to a rather pale violet-blue. The 3 sepals are but little larger than the 3 petals and have a smooth orange-yellow spot at the base. Its leaves are rather stiff, straight-sided, and about ¼ of an inch wide; greatly elongating after the flower fades. It grows in sandy or rocky woods, blooming between March and May. Sometimes it is called the Violet Iris.

RANGE: Md. to s. Pa. south to Fla. and Ala.

TRAILING ARBUTUS *(Epigaea repens)*   Heath Family

Trailing Arbutus is a prostrate or trailing plant with branches 6 to 15 inches long; and evergreen, veiny, oval to roundish leaves 1 to 3 inches long, which are heart-shaped at the base. Its fragrant whitish or pink flowers are about ⅝ inch long, and are in small axillary or end clusters; blooming between late February and May. Also known as the Mayflower and Ground-laurel, it grows in sandy or rocky woods and banks.

RANGE: Lab to Sask. south to Fla. and Miss.

WILD GERANIUM *(Geranium maculatum)*   Geranium Family

On a hairy stem usually 1 to 2 feet tall, the Wild Geranium has a pair of deeply 5-parted and sharply toothed leaves 3 to 6 inches wide. Other ones at the base are similar but long-stalked. Between April and June it has lavender-purple flowers an inch or more across. This is one of our most common woodland wild flowers and it sometimes is found in open areas. It is also known as the Spotted Cranesbill. The slender capsules have a fancied resemblance to a crane's bill.

RANGE: Me. to Man. south to Ga., Tenn., Mo., and Kan.

183

YELLOW LADY'S-SLIPPER *(Cypripedium calceolus* var. *pubescens)* **Orchid Family**

From 1 to 3 flowers are borne on a leafy stem from 8 inches to about 2 feet tall. Often there are several stems in a clump. The prominently veined leaves are hairy and from 3 to 6 inches in length. The flowers have a bright yellow pouch-like lip from ¾ to 2 inches long; and 3 sepals and 2 spirally twisted side petals which are yellowish-green to purplish-brown and often streaked with purple. They are more or less fragrant. Hairs of the plant may cause a dermatitis in sensitive persons. It grows in dry to wet woods and swamps, blooming between April and June.
RANGE: Nfd. and N.S. to B.C. south to N.C., n.Ga., n.La., Tex., Ariz. and Wash.

STEMLESS LADY'S-SLIPPER *(Cypripedium acaule)* **Orchid Family**

This species is also called the Pink Lady's-slipper and Moccasin-flower and, like other lady's-slippers, it is also known as the Whip-poor-will's-shoe. It is distinctive as the flower stands on a naked stalk 6 to 15 inches tall, at the base of which is a pair of large elliptic leaves. The pouch-like lip is about 2 inches long and pink with deeper colored veins (rarely white). The sepals and 2 side petals are greenish yellow and tinged with purplish. It grows in dry to moist woods and in bogs, blooming between April and July.
RANGE: Nfd. to Alb. south to Ga., Ala., Tenn. and Mo.

FRINGED MILKWORT *(Polygala paucifolia)* **Milkwort Family**

Also known as the Flowering Wintergreen, Gay-wings, and Bird-on-the-wing, this milkwort has very showy, rose-purple flowers about ¾ of an inch long, with a beautifully fringed crest. The plant has slender creeping rootstocks which, in the spring, send up stems 3 to 6 inches high; bearing from 1 to 4 of the pretty flowers and a few small, egg-shaped leaves, with smaller scale-like leaves down along the stem. It grows in rich woods and on rocky slopes, blooming between April and July.
RANGE: N.B. to Man. south to Va., n. Ga., Ill., and Minn.

SHOWY ORCHIS *(Orchis spectabilis)* **Orchid Family**

On a stem from 5 to 9 inches tall, the Showy Orchis displays several, leafy-bracted, attractive flowers. Each one is about an inch long, and from the base of the flat white lip hangs a spur. The other petals and the sepals are joined together to form a lilac or magenta, erect hood. There are 2 smooth, lustrous leaves, from 4 to 8 inches long, at the base of the upright flower stalk. It is found in rich, moist and usually rocky woodlands and it blooms between April and June.
RANGE: N.B. to Ont. south to N.Eng., n. Ga., Tenn., Mo. and Kan.

SHOOTING-STAR *(Dodecatheon meadia)* **Primrose Family**

The Shooting-star or American Cowslip is a smooth plant with a basal cluster of narrowly elliptic or top-shaped leaves 3 to 10 inches long, their bases often marked with red. The distinctive flowers are about an inch long and have 5 lilac, pink or white petals which point backward; the stamens forming a beak-like cone in the center of the flower. From a few to sometimes a hundred or more of the flowers are arranged in an umbel, and nod from the summit of a naked flower stalk 8 inches to 2 feet tall. It grows in rich moist woods, meadows, prairies and cliffs; blooming between late March and June.
RANGE: D.C. to w. Pa., Wis. and Alb. south to n. Ga., La. and Tex.

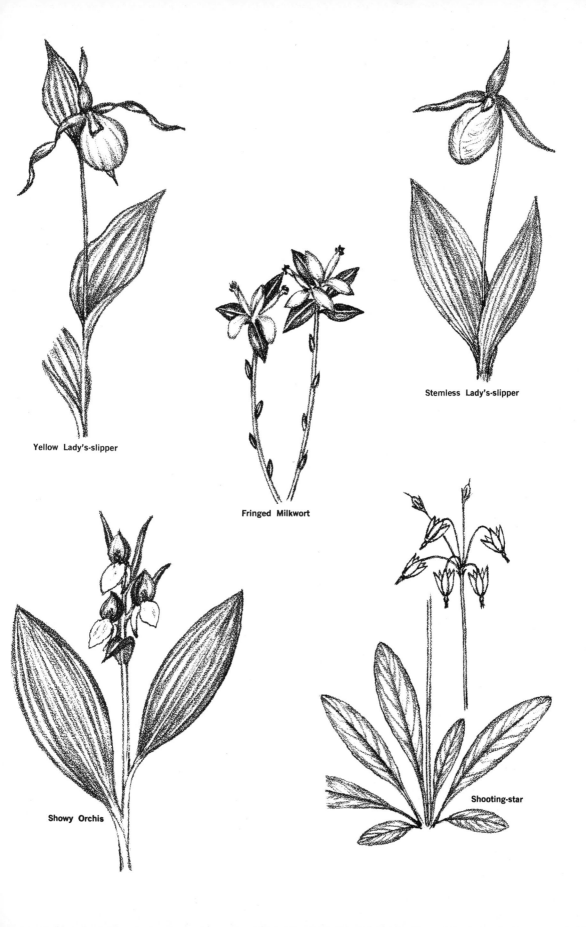

Yellow Lady's-slipper

Fringed Milkwort

Stemless Lady's-slipper

Showy Orchis

Shooting-star

Virginia Bluebell

Greek-valerian

Wild Blue Phlox

Moss-pink

Erect Silky Leather-flower

VIRGINIA BLUEBELL *(Mertensia virginica)*   Borage Family

Also known as the Virginia Cowslip and Roanoke-bells, this is one of our most beautiful wild flowers of spring. It is a smooth and pale green plant 1 to 2 feet high, with elliptic or egg-shaped leaves 2 to 5 inches long. The nodding, trumpet-shaped flowers are about an inch long, pink when in the bud but becoming a bright lavender blue or bright blue when fully open. It grows in rich moist woods, on rocky slopes, or along streams; blooming between March and May.

RANGE: Ont. to Minn. south to Va., Ala., Ark. and Kan.

GREEK-VALERIAN *(Polemonium reptans)*   Phlox Family

This is a native plant with branching, smooth or sparsely hairy stems 6 to 15 inches long. Its leaves are divided into from 3 to 15 lance-shaped or elliptic leaflets. The flowers are about ½ inch across, light blue-violet; with their stamens included within the somewhat bell-shaped, deeply 5-lobed corolla. It grows in rich woods and bottomlands, blooming between April and June.

RANGE: N.Y. to Minn. south to Ga., Miss., Mo. and Okla.

MOSS-PINK *(Phlox subulata)*   Phlox Family

This is a low and mat-forming plant with trailing or creeping stems; and numerous pairs of very narrow, almost needle-like leaves ½ to 1 inch long. Its flowers are about ½ inch across and usually rose-pink or purplish (rarely white), the spreading corolla lobes commonly being deeply notched at the tip. It grows in dry, rocky or sandy, open woods and rocky slopes; blooming between April and June. The plant is widely cultivated, in the South generally under the name of Thrift.

RANGE: N.Y. and Ont. to Mich. south to N.J., w. N.C. and e. Tenn.

WILD BLUE PHLOX *(Phlox divaricata)*   Phlox Family

This phlox has slender, upright, more or less hairy stems 6 inches to 1 foot tall; with widely-spaced pairs of lance-shaped or narrowly egg-shaped leaves 1 to 2 inches long. The pale bluish to lilac flowers have a slender corolla tube with 5 spreading lobes which are often notched at the tip; and the stamens are completely within the tube. Often called the Wild Sweet-William, it is often common in open woods and on rocky slopes; blooming from April to June. Often cultivated as a border plant.

RANGE: Vt. and Que. to Minn. and Neb. south to Fla. and Tex.

ERECT SILKY LEATHER-FLOWER *(Clematis ochroleuca)*   Buttercup Family

Instead of being a vine, this leather-flower is an erect branching plant from 1 to 2 feet tall. It has pairs of simple, egg-shaped, stalkless leaves ranging from 1½ to 2 inches in length. New growth and the lower surfaces of the leaves are silky-hairy but they eventually become smooth. The flowers are bell-shaped, dull yellowish or purplish, silky on the outside, and about an inch long. Each one nods at the end of a slender stalk. It grows in woods, thickets, and on rocky slopes, blooming during April or May. Another name for it is Curly-heads.

RANGE: Se. N.Y. and se. Pa. south to Ga.

SPRING FLOWERS OF THE WOODLANDS, Continued

EARLY MEADOW-RUE *(Thalictrum dioicum)*   Buttercup Family

The Early Meadow-rue is a smooth, slender-stemmed plant from 1 to 2 feet tall. Its drooping flowers are yellowish-green, or often tinged with purplish, and are borne in a loose terminal cluster. The stamens and the pistils are not only in different flowers but on different plants. The leaves are divided into a number of thin, delicate, roundish leaflets which have from 5 to 9 rounded teeth on their margins. The upper ones are not usually fully expanded at flowering time in April or May. It is quite common in rich, rocky woods and shady ravines.

RANGE: Me. and Que. to Ont., Minn., and S.D. south to Ga., Ala., and Mo.

BLUE COHOSH *(Caulophyllum thalictroides)*   Buttercup Family

The leaves of the Blue Cohosh resemble those of the meadow-rues, being divided into a number of leaflets with from 3 to 5 lobes. It is a smooth and more or less whitened plant from 1 to 3 feet tall. About midway on the stem there is a leaf divided into 3 stalked divisions, each of which bears about 9 leaflets. Above this is the stalked cluster of purplish-green flowers. Each flower is about ½ inch across and it has 6 sepals, 6 small gland-like petals, 6 stamens and a single pistil. The 2 ovules within the ovary of the pistil burst the ovary wall as they grow; and they mature as a pair of large, stalked, blue, and berry-like seeds which look like small blue grapes. Another name for the plant is Papoose-root. It grows in rich, moist woods; blooming in April or May.

RANGE: N.B. to Man. south to S.C., Tenn., and Mo.

DWARF LARKSPUR *(Delphinium tricorne)*   Buttercup Family

At the time of flowering, in April or May, the stems of this plant are usually 6 to 12 inches high, but later they become much taller. The larkspurs are unusual among the members of this family in that their flowers have a bilateral symmetry. Those of this species are 1 to 1½ inches long, usually a deep blue-violet or variegated with white, and arranged in a rather loose, cylindrical cluster. As in other larkspurs there are 5 small, irregular, petal-like sepals and the uppermost one is prolonged into a hollow spur. There are also 4 petals but they are quite small, the upper pair having spurs which are enclosed within the spur of the sepal. The leaves are cut into 5 radiating divisions which are themselves cleft and sharply toothed. The Dwarf Larkspur grows in rich woods and on rocky slopes, blooming in April or May.

RANGE: Pa. to Minn. and Neb. south to Ga., Ala., Ark., and Okla.

ROUND-LEAF RAGWORT *(Senecio obovatus)*   Composite Family

This species has a rather smooth and slender stem 1 to 1½ feet tall. The basal leaves are usually more top-shaped than round, bluntly toothed, and 1 to 3½ inches long. Those upward along the stem are small, narrow, and more or less cut. The flower heads are about ⅔ inch across with 8 to 12 bright yellow rays. It grows on wooded slopes and in ravines, blooming between April and June.

RANGE: N.H. to Ont. and Mich. south to Fla. and Tex.

VIOLET WOOD-SORREL *(Oxalis violacea)*   Wood-sorrel Family

Both leaves and flower stalks of this species arise from scaly-coated bulbs. Usually 3 to 12 flowers are clustered on leafless stalks from 4 to 8 inches high. They are about ⅜ inch across and have rose-purple or violet petals. The leaves have shorter stalks than the flowers. It grows in rich or alluvial woods, thickets, meadows, and on slopes; blooming in April and May and August to October.

RANGE: Mass. to Minn. south to Fla. and N. Mex.

188

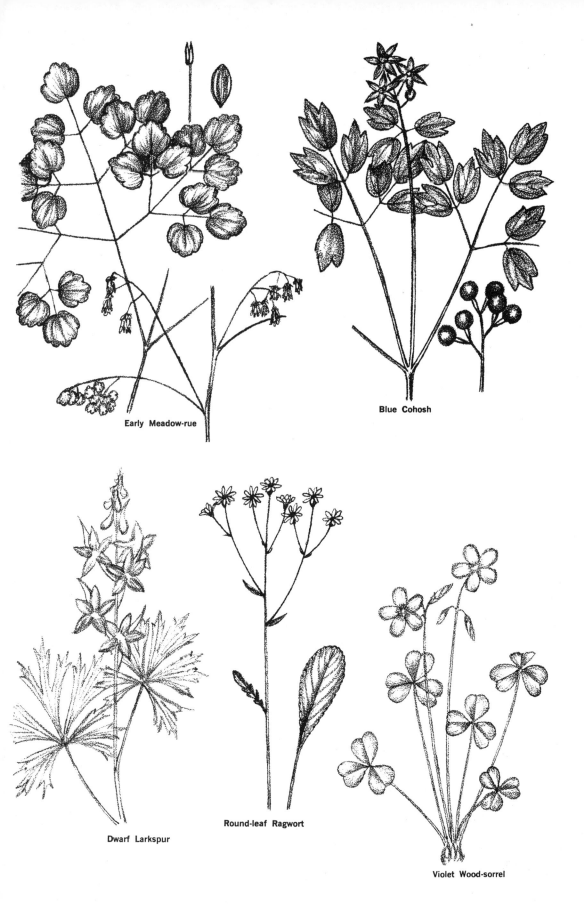

Early Meadow-rue

Blue Cohosh

Dwarf Larkspur

Round-leaf Ragwort

Violet Wood-sorrel

Golden-star

Goat's-beard

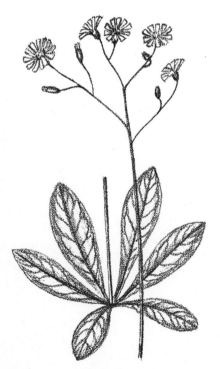

Rattlesnake-weed

Bowman's-root

GOLDEN-STAR *(Chrysogonum virginianum)*   Composite Family

In early spring, when the Golden-star begins to bloom, it appears to be a stemless, low, hairy plant; but it later becomes from 3 to 12 inches high through the growth of branches. It has pairs of oblong or egg-shaped leaves which are 1 to 3 inches long, bluntly toothed, and rather long-stalked. The attractive flower heads are about 1¼ inches across, with usually 5 broad and bright yellow rays. It grows in sandy or rocky woodlands and on banks, blooming between late March and June.
RANGE: Pa. and W. Va. south to Fla. and La.

GOAT'S-BEARD   *(Aruncus dioicus)*   Rose Family

FIELD MARKS: The Goat's-beard is a plant from 3 to 6 feet tall; with large leaves sometimes 2 feet across, divided 2 or 3 times into a large number of leaflets which are 2 to 5 inches long, more or less egg-shaped or often heart-shaped, and with sharply-toothed margins. The small, 5-petalled white flowers are in a large, showy, plume-like cluster; blooming between May and July; the stamen-bearing and the pistil-bearing flowers are on separate plants. It grows in rich moist woods and in ravines.
RANGE: Pa. to Iowa south to Ga., Ala. and Okla.

RATTLESNAKE-WEED *(Hieracium venosum)*   Composite Family

This native species is often common in dry open woods and clearings, and is sometimes called Poor Robin's-plantain. It is quite a smooth plant with a basal rosette of elliptic to narrowly top-shaped leaves from 1 to 4 inches long. They are beautifully veined or mottled with purple above and are pale to purplish and somewhat hairy beneath. The heads of bright yellow flowers are little more than ½ inch across and are in a loose cluster at the summit of a leafless or few-leaved stalk usually 1 to 2 feet high. It blooms between May and September. RANGE: Me. to Ont. south to Fla. and La.

BOWMAN'S-ROOT *(Gillenia trifoliata)*   Rose Family

The Bowman's-root, or Indian-physic, is often conspicuous in rich, open woods and thickets when it is in flower between May and July. It grows from 2 to 3 feet high and its slender and often somewhat twisted branches terminate in loose clusters of showy flowers. They are about an inch across, with a reddish calyx cup and 5 strap-shaped white or pale pinkish petals. The leaves are stalkless and divided into 3 sharply toothed leaflets 2 to 3 inches in length. There is a pair of small stipules at the base of each leaf.
RANGE: N.Y. to Ont. and Mich. south to Ga. and Ala.

FLY-POISON *(Amianthum muscaetoxicum)*   Lily Family

Between May and July this plant sends up a practically leafless flower stalk from 1 to 3 feet tall. On it is a dense cylindrical cluster of flowers which are at first white but later become greenish or purplish. Both leaves and flower stalk arise from a very poisonous bulb-like base. Another name for the plant is Crow-poison. Whether or not flies and crows are affected by it we cannot say, but cattle and sheep are often poisoned by eating the leaves. It grows in a variety of places: dry to moist open woods, mountain balds, bogs, and savannahs.

RANGE: N.Y. and Pa. south to Fla., Miss. and Okla.

COMMON WOOD-BETONY *(Pedicularis canadensis)*   Figwort Family

This is a hairy plant with a cluster of simple stems 6 to 18 inches high. The lance-shaped leaves are so deeply cut into toothed lobes that they appear almost fern-like, the larger ones being 3 to 5 inches long. Its flowers are about ¾ inch long, the corolla yellow and reddish and with a long and arching upper lip, and are borne in short, densely-bracted end clusters. It grows in open woods, thickets, and clearings; blooming between April and June. Another name is Lousewort.

RANGE: Me. to Que. and Man. south to Fla. and Tex.

ROBIN'S-PLANTAIN *(Erigeron pulchellus)*   Composite Family

Between April and July, the attractive flowers of this fleabane may be seen on the wooded slopes and banks, or even along roadsides. The heads are an inch to 1½ inches broad and have about 50 narrow lavender or violet rays. They are usually arranged in a loose cluster of between 2 and 6 heads. The whole plant is quite hairy, with a simple stem from 1 to 2 feet high. The basal leaves are narrowly top-shaped or spoon-shaped, toothed, and 1 to 3 inches long. Those of the stem are few and widely spaced, smaller, lance-shaped, and untoothed or very nearly so.

RANGE: Que. to Ont. and Minn. south to Fla., La. and Kan.

AMERICAN ALUMROOT *(Heuchera americana)*   Saxifrage Family

This is our most common and widespread species of alumroot, being found quite generally in dry woods and on rocky slopes. It has a smooth or sparingly hairy, rather stout stem from 1 to 3 feet tall. The leaves are chiefly basal. They are roundish heart-shaped with from 7 to 9 rounded and bluntly toothed lobes, smooth or nearly so, 3 to 4 inches wide; and have long, slender stalks. The small purplish or reddish-tinged flowers have a cup-like calyx. 5 minute petals, and 5 stamens which extend well beyond the calyx cup. They are very numerous and arranged in a long, loose, several-branched cluster which overtops the leaves. The flowering season extends from April to June. It is often called the Rock-geranium.

RANGE: Conn. to Ont. and Mich. south to Ga., Ala., and Okla.

Common Wood Betony

Fly-poison

Robin's-plantain

American
Alumroot

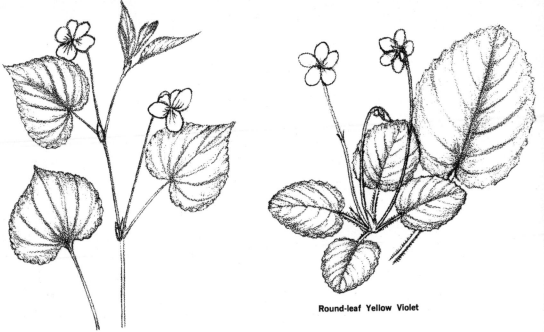

Round-leaf Yellow Violet

Smooth Yellow Violet

Early Blue Violet

Halberd-leaf Violet

Canada Violet

SMOOTH YELLOW VIOLET *(Viola pensylvanica)*   Violet Family

This violet has smooth, leafy stems 6 to 12 inches tall with from 1 to 3 basal leaves. The latter, and the few stem leaves are smooth, heart-shaped, and from 2 to 4 inches wide. The yellow flowers are about ¾ inch across, their 3 lower petals being veined with purple. It grows in moist woods and on cool rocky slopes; blooming in April or May.
    RANGE: Conn. to Minn. south to Ga., Ala., Ark. and Okla.

ROUND-LEAF YELLOW VIOLET *(Viola rotundifolia)*   Violet Family

This is our only "stemless" violet with yellow flowers. It has roundish or oval leaves with a wavy-toothed margin. At flowering time, between March and May, they are only about an inch wide and are finely hairy. Later they become 2 to 4 inches broad, thickish, quite smooth, and lie flat on the ground. The flowers are about ½ inch across, bright yellow, the 3 lower petals being veined with brown. Both leaves and flowers arise from a long, stout, jagged rootstock. Look for it in cool, moist, rich woods or on banks; southward in the mountains.
    RANGE: Me. to Ont. south to Del., Pa., n. Ga. and e. Tenn.

EARLY BLUE VIOLET *(Viola palmata)*   Violet Family

From March to May this violet blooms on dry but rich wooded hillsides. It is best distinguished by its leaves which have from 5 to 11 lobes or segments, the middle one being largest and all variously toothed and cleft. The violet-purple flowers are about an inch across. Both they and the leaves arise from a thick, erect, fleshy rootstock and both have stalks which are somewhat hairy.
    RANGE: N.H. to Ont. and Minn. south to Fla. and Miss.

HALBERD-LEAF VIOLET *(Viola hastata)*   Violet Family

On a slender stem 4 to 10 inches tall, this violet has from 2 to 4 narrowly triangular, taper-pointed leaves. Its yellow flowers are about ½ inch across and on slender stalks arising from the axils of the leaves. The petals are tinged with violet on the back. It grows in rich, often rocky woods; blooming late March to May.
    RANGE: Pa. and Ohio south to Fla. and Ala.

CANADA VIOLET *(Viola canadensis)*   Violet Family

This is a smooth or slightly hairy plant with 1 or more leafy stems usually between 8 and 14 inches tall. The flowers have white petals which are tinged with lilac on the back. They are about ¾ inch across and on slender stalks arising from the axils of the heart-shaped leaves. This violet grows in cool, moist, rich woodlands; blooming between April and July.
    RANGE: N.H. and Que. to Mont. south to Md., nw. S.C., n. Ga., Tenn., Iowa, S.D., Colo. and Utah.

WILD STRAWBERRY (*Fragaria virginiana*)   Rose Family

Like our cultivated strawberries, the Wild Strawberry is a low plant with a very short stem. From it grow the leaves, the flower clusters, and the slender runners on which new plants are produced. The long-stalked leaves are divided into 3, elliptic or oval shaped, sharply toothed leaflets which are usually 2 to 4 inches long. The flowers are about ¾ inch across and have 5 oval-shaped white petals, a large number of stamens with yellow anthers, and numerous pistils on a cone-shaped receptacle in the center of the flower. This receptacle develops into an egg-shaped red "berry" with the small fruits (achenes) imbedded in pits on its surface. This native species grows in open woods, fields, and on grassy slopes; blooming between April and June.
RANGE: Nfd. to Alb. south to Ga., La., and Okla.

COMMON BLUETS (*Houstonia caerulea*)   Madder Family

Often called Innocence or Quakerladies, this is a smooth little plant with thread-like tufted stems 3 to 6 inches high. It has narrowly top-shaped leaves about ½ inch long in a basal rosette, and pairs of smaller ones on the flower stems. Its bright pale blue to whitish flowers have a yellow "eye". It is common in open woods, meadows and clearings; blooming between April and June.
RANGE: N.S. to Ont. and Wis. south to Ga., Ala. and Mo.

LYRE-LEAF SAGE (*Salvia lyrata*)   Mint Family

The Lyre-leaf Sage is a somewhat hairy plant with a simple or sparingly branched and erect stem 1 to 2 feet tall, on which are pairs of small bract-like leaves and a terminal flower cluster. The basal leaves are stalked, 3 to 8 inches long, and vary from ones with merely wavy-toothed margins to others which are pinnately lobed, usually with a large terminal segment. Its bright blue flowers are about an inch long and occur in several whorls along the upper part of the stem, blooming between April and June. It grows in rather dry but rich open woods, pinelands, and along roadsides.
RANGE: Conn. to Ill., Mo. and Okla. south to Fla. and Tex.

COMMON WINTER-CRESS (*Barbarea vulgaris*)   Mustard Family

The Winter-cress, or Yellow Rocket, is a common weed which is often abundant in fields, meadows, and wet woods. It is a smooth, branching plant with leafy stems from 1 to 2 feet tall. The lower leaves are stalked and have a terminal segment much larger than the 1 to 4 pairs of side ones. Those along the upper portion of the stem are stalkless and often have clasping bases. The bright yellow, 4-petalled flowers are about ⅓ inch across; and are borne in rather dense, cylindrical clusters at the end of the stem and its branches; blooming from April to June or later. It is a native of Europe.

COMMON CINQUEFOIL (*Potentilla canadensis*)   Rose Family

A large number of cinquefoils occur in eastern North America. Many are native plants and a few have been introduced from Europe. Some are erect plants with leafy stems and they have leaves which are variously divided. None are more common or better known than this creeping plant of dry open places. Its leaves are divided into 5 radiating and wedge-shaped leaflets which are sharply toothed on the margin, at least above the middle. The flowers are about ⅓ inch across and have 5 broadly top-shaped, bright yellow petals and a number of stamens. They are borne singly on slender stalks which arise from the axils of the leaves. Another name for the plant is Five-finger. It blooms between March and June.
RANGE: N.S. to Ont. south to Ga., Tenn., and Mo.

196

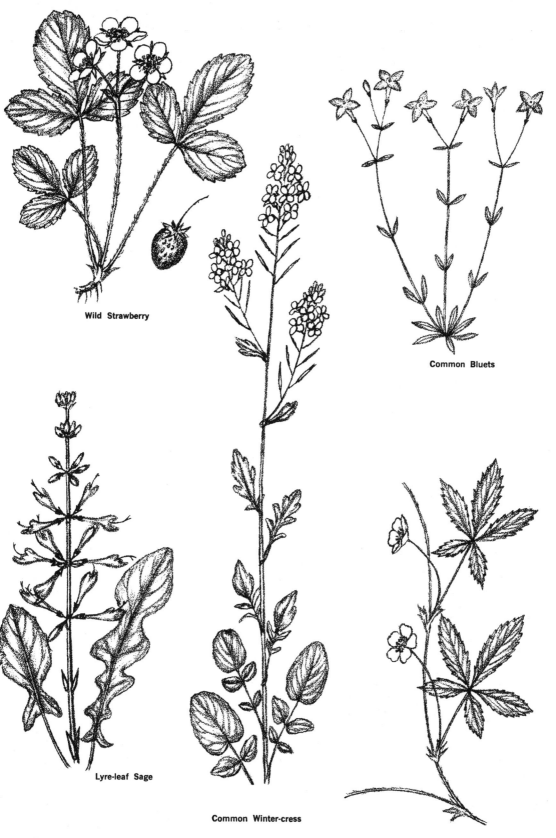

Wild Strawberry

Common Bluets

Lyre-leaf Sage

Common Winter-cress

Common Cinquefoil

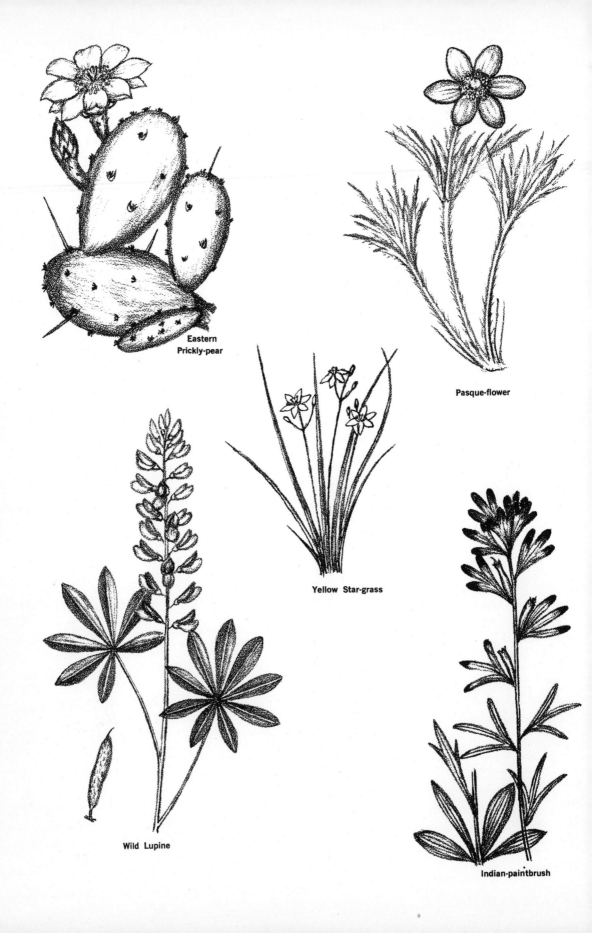

Eastern
Prickly-pear

Pasque-flower

Yellow Star-grass

Wild Lupine

Indian-paintbrush

EASTERN PRICKLY-PEAR *(Opuntia compressa)*   Cactus Family

Prickly-pears have fleshy, flat, jointed stems which are green. The leaves are small and scale-like and are soon shed; but in their axils there are clusters of barbed hairs and occasional slender spines. The flowers are 2 to 3 inches across, yellow sometimes with a red star-shaped "eye", and have from 8 to 12 petals. They are followed by pear-shaped, dull purplish-red, fleshy fruits 1 to 1½ inches long. It grows in dry sandy and rocky places, blooming between May and July. Another name for it is Indian-fig, the fruits being edible.

RANGE: Mass. to Minn. south to Fla., Ala., Mo. and Okla.

PASQUE-FLOWER *(Anemone patens)*   Buttercup Family

The beautiful Pasque-flower has a silky-hairy stem from 4 to about 16 inches tall, but at flowering time it is considerably shorter. Its leaves are basal, cut into numerous narrow divisions, and also covered with silvery-silky hairs. The flower is about 2 inches across and has from 5 to 7 large petal-like sepals varying from white to lavender-blue or purple in color. It grows on prairies and on dry, exposed slopes; blooming between April and June. May be grown in a sunny or lightly shaded spot in the flower garden.

RANGE: Mich. to B.C. south to Ill., Mo., Tex., N.Mex., Utah, and Wash.

WILD LUPINE *(Lupinus perennis)*   Pea Family

This is the only lupine found north and west of the Carolina coastal plain. Usually it has several erect or ascending stems from 1 to 2 feet tall. Between April and June these terminate in elongate clusters of showy flowers which are about ⅔ inch long and usually lavender-blue to purplish-blue in color. Occasional plants have flowers which are pinkish or white. The leaves are divided into from 7 to 11 leaflets which radiate from the summits of the long leaf stalks like the spokes of a wheel. The leaflets are narrowly top-shaped and from 1 to 2 inches in length. This plant grows in dry open woods, thickets, and on sandhills. It is often called the Sundial Lupine.

RANGE: Me. to Ont. and Minn. south to Fla. and La.

YELLOW STAR-GRASS *(Hypoxis hirsuta)*   Amaryllis Family

Yellow Star-grasses are small plants with clusters of from 2 to 7 flowers at the summit of a hairy stalk from 2 to 6 inches long. The six-parted perianth is smooth and bright yellow above but usually greenish and hairy beneath, opening to about the size of a dime. Both flower stalks and the narrow grass-like leaves arise from a hard corm. This species grows in dry open woods and meadows, blooming between March and September. Several other species are more commonly found in the southeastern coastal plain.

RANGE: Me. to Man. south to Fla. and Tex.

INDIAN-PAINTBRUSH *(Castilleja coccinea)*   Figwort Family

Also known as the Scarlet Painted-cup, this is a somewhat hairy, simple-stemmed plant 8 to 15 inches tall; with the upper stem leaves, or bracts, deeply 3- to 5-cleft and tipped with brilliant red (sometimes pink or white). The flowers are not very conspicuous, about an inch long, greenish-yellow, and in the axils of the colored bracts. It grows in moist meadows, thickets, along roadsides and on prairies; flowering between April and July. A parasite on the roots of other plants.

RANGE: N.H. to Man. south to Fla., La. and Okla.

YELLOW THISTLE *(Carduus spinosissimus)*   Composite Family

This thistle has a very stout, leafy, branching stem 2 to 5 feet tall which is somewhat woolly when young. Its leaves are 2 to 5 inches long, green on both sides, and cut into triangular lobes which have many yellowish prickles. The flower heads are 2 to 4 inches across, with numerous pale yellow to purple flowers. The involucre is surrounded by narrow, spiny, bract-like leaves but the true bracts of the involucre have soft and unarmed tips. It grows in sandy fields, savannahs, roadsides and waste places; blooming between late March and June.
    RANGE: Me. to Pa. south to Fla. and Tex.

COMMON BLUE VIOLET *(Viola papilionacea)*   Violet Family

This is undoubtedly the commonest of our blue violets; growing in open woods, meadows, door-yards, and along roadsides everywhere. Its rich violet-colored flowers are about an inch across, whitish toward the center, and are on smooth stalks no longer than the leaves. Both of the side petals are "bearded" but none of the hairs are club-shaped. Its smooth leaves are broadly heart-shaped and by midsummer may become 5 inches wide. Both flowers and leaves arise from a thick and fleshy rootstock. It blooms between late February and June. Also called Hooded Blue Violet.

BIRDFOOT VIOLET *(Viola pedata)*   Violet Family

This is certainly one of our most striking species of violet, and one that is very easy to recognize. Its showy flowers are often an inch or more across. Usually all 5 petals are lilac-colored but in one variety the 2 upper petals are dark violet. The stamens are a bright orange-yellow. Its name comes from the leaves which are deeply cut into narrow and radiating segments. Both leaves and flowers arise from a short, erect, fleshy rootstock. It grows on dry, sunny, sandy, rocky, or clayey banks and open woods; blooming between March and June.
    RANGE: Mass. to Ont., Minn. and Kan. south to Ga. and Tex.

SMALL'S RAGWORT *(Senecio smallii)*   Composite Family

This species has several stems 1½ to 2½ feet tall which are loosely woolly toward the base. The basal leaves are lance-shaped or narrowly oblong, bluntly toothed and 3 to 6 inches long. Those upward along the stem become progressively smaller and deeply cut into many segments. The numerous flower heads are about ½ inch across, with 8 to 10 bright yellow rays. It grows in open woods, fields and roadsides; blooming from May to early July.
    RANGE: N.J. to Pa. and Ky. south to Fla. and Ala.

HAIRY BEARD-TONGUE *(Penstemon hirsutus)*   Figwort Family

Beard-tongues are so-called because their flowers have 5 stamens, the fourth one lacking an anther but having a hairy, or bearded, filament. This species has a slender, grayish-downy stem 1 to 3 feet tall, often with gland-tipped hairs in the flower cluster. It has pairs of lance-shaped, elliptic, or narrowly top-shaped leaves 2 to 4 inches long, with sharply toothed margins; the upper ones being stalkless, the lower ones with stalks. The flowers are about an inch long, the slender, dull purple or violet corolla having whitish lobes, and its throat closed by an upward arching lower lip. It grows in dry, rocky, open woods and in fields; blooming between May and July.
    RANGE: Que. to Ont. and Wis. south to Va. and Tenn.

200

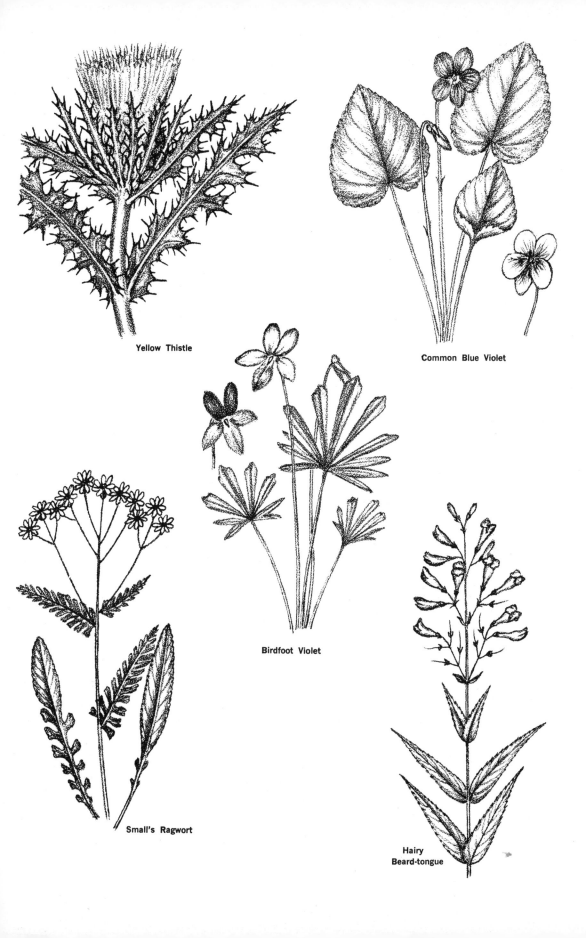

Yellow Thistle

Common Blue Violet

Birdfoot Violet

Small's Ragwort

Hairy
Beard-tongue

Golden-club

Green Dragon

Skunk-cabbage

Sweetflag

Wild Calla

GOLDEN-CLUB *(Orontium aquaticum)*   Arum Family

A plant of swamps, pond margins, bogs, and slow-moving streams. The "club" is a spa-dix from 4 to 8 inches long, tipped with closely packed yellow flowers. Near its base is a small bract-like spathe. The bluish-green leaves are 6 to 12 inches long and often float on the water. When emersed they show a silvery or coppery iridescence and come out perfectly dry. For this reason the plant is locally known as the Never-wet. The bright yellow clubs are produced between late March and May.

RANGE: Mass. to Ky. south to Fla. and Tex.

GREEN DRAGON *(Arisaema dracontium)*   Arum Family

A unique plant with usually but one leaf which is divided into from 7 to 15 lance-shaped leaflets or leaf segments. The spadix is prolonged into a long, pointed tail-like portion which projects upward through an opening in the spathe. Less common and much less familiar than the Jack-in-the-pulpit, the Green Dragon grows in low wet woodlands or on flats along streams. The plants are from 1 to 3 feet high, and may be found in flower between May and July.

RANGE: N.H. to Ont. and Minn. south to Fla. and Tex.

SKUNK-CABBAGE *(Symplocarpus foetidus)*   Arum Family

All parts of this plant have a characteristic skunk-like odor when bruised or broken. The large hood-like spathes vary from yellowish-green to reddish-brown and are streaked and spotted with purple. They often appear above the half-thawed ground in late February or March, in wet meadows or swampy woods. These flower spathes are soon followed by big veiny leaves which have heart-shaped bases. They unfurl from tightly wrapped cones as the spathes wither and are very conspicuous throughout the summer.

RANGE: Que. to Man. south to w. N.C., n. Ga. and Tenn.

SWEETFLAG *(Acorus calamus)*   Arum Family

Rootstocks of the Sweetflag are pleasantly aromatic and in bygone days were often boiled in syrup and eaten as a candy. The spathe in this plant looks very much like the long, narrow, and flattened leaves, being prolonged upward 2 or 3 inches above the out-wardly pointing spadix. It grows in wet open places and the flowering season is between May and July.

RANGE: N.S. to Ore. south to S.C., Tenn., Miss., and Tex.

WILD CALLA *(Calla palustris)*   Arum Family

The Wild Calla or Water-arum grows in cold northern bogs and swamps. It is small plant seldom a foot high; with beautiful dark green, heart-shaped leaves from 2 to 4 inches wide. The nearly flat, snow-white spathe is sometimes 2 inches across and stands behind the spadix on which the real flowers are clustered. It blooms from late April to June or sometimes later. A good plant for bog gardens in regions with cool summers but it must have an acid soil.

RANGE: Nfd. to Alaska south to n. N.J., n. Pa. and Great Lakes region.

ROSE POGONIA *(Pogonia ophioglossoides)*   Orchid Family

The Rose Pogonia, or Snake-mouth, usually has 1, but sometimes 2, leafy-bracted pink flowers at the top of a slender stem from 10 to 20 inches tall. The flower is an inch to 1½ inches broad, and it has a spoon-shaped lip which is beautifully bearded with yellow-tipped hairs. A solitary and usually broadly lance-shaped leaf 2 to 4 inches long is located about midway on the stem. This orchid grows in wet to moist meadows, thickets, pinelands, and bogs; blooming between May and August.

RANGE: Nfd. to Ont. south to Fla. and Tex.

GRASS-PINK *(Calopogon pulchellus)*   Orchid Family

Several rose-pink to magenta flowers are produced along the 8 to 24 inch tall stem of this plant. As in all grass-pinks the spoon-shaped lip is uppermost and has a tuft of yellow, crimson-tipped, club-shaped hairs. The flowers are an inch or more across and open successively up the stem. There is but one broad grass-like leaf, from 6 to 12 inches long, toward the base. This attractive orchid is quite common in wet meadows, bogs, and southward in the wet pinelands. It blooms between April and August.

RANGE: Nfd. to Que. and Minn. south to Fla. and Tex.

ARETHUSA *(Arethusa bulbosa)*   Orchid Family

Arethusa has a solitary flower at the summit of a 5 to 10 inch stem; along which are a few, loose, sheathing bracts. Not until the flower matures does the single grass-like leaf protrude from one such sheath, later growing to a length of about 6 inches. The broad tongue-like lip is whitish with conspicuous purple spots, and on it is a crest consisting of 3 rows of fleshy, yellow- and purple-tipped hairs. The other petals and the sepals are magenta-pink. In most places Arethusa is a bog orchid, but nowhere does it grow so abundantly as in the salt marshes along the northern New England coast. It blooms in May or June. It is also known as the Dragon's-mouth and Bog-pink.

RANGE: Nfd. to Ont. and Minn. south to Md., nw. S.C., and the Great Lakes region.

SPREADING POGONIA *(Cleistes divaricata)*   Orchid Family

At the summit of a 1 to 2 foot stem, this orchid has a solitary, leafy-bracted pink flower an inch to 2 inches long. The trough-shaped lip is veined with purple, lobed at the tip, and crested but not bearded. The other 2 petals lie forward over the lip, while the 3 narrow brownish sepals widely spread. About midway on the stem is a lance-shaped leaf from 2 to 5 inches long. It grows in moist woods, wet meadows and swamps; blooming May to July. Also called Rose Orchid, Rosebud Orchid, and Lady's-ettercap.

RANGE: N.J. south to Fla.; Ky. south to Ga., Tenn. and La.

SHOWY LADY'S-SLIPPER *(Cypripedium reginae)*   Orchid Family

Often called the Queen Lady's-slipper, this species has a stout, leafy stem from 1 to 2½ feet tall. The large corrugated leaves range up to 7 inches in length and resemble those of the White Hellebore. The flowers are usually solitary and have a pouch-like lip 1½ to 2 inches long which is white but strongly suffused with rose or magenta. The 2 other petals and 2 sepals are white. Hairs of the plant may produce a dermatitis in sensitive persons. It grows in swamps, bogs, and moist wooded slopes; blooming between April and July.

RANGE: Nfd. to Man. south to Pa., w. N.C., e. Tenn., Mo. and N.D.

CALYPSO *(Calypso bulbosa)*   Orchid Family

The solitary and oddly beautiful flower of Calypso is borne atop a sparsely bracted 3- to 6-inch stem; at the base of which is a broad but pointed, plaited leaf which withers soon after the plant flowers. The lance-shaped sepals and 2 side petals are purplish and spread or ascend over the slipper-shaped, inflated lip. The latter bends downward; its white surface is streaked and spotted with cinnamon-brown and purple within, and in front there are 3 double rows of golden yellow hairs. By many it is considered to have the most beautiful flower of any of our native orchids, and it is often called the Fairy-slipper. It grows in cool, damp, mossy woods and blooms in May or June.

RANGE: Nfd. to Alaska south to N.Y., Mich., Wis., and in mts. to Ariz. and Calif.

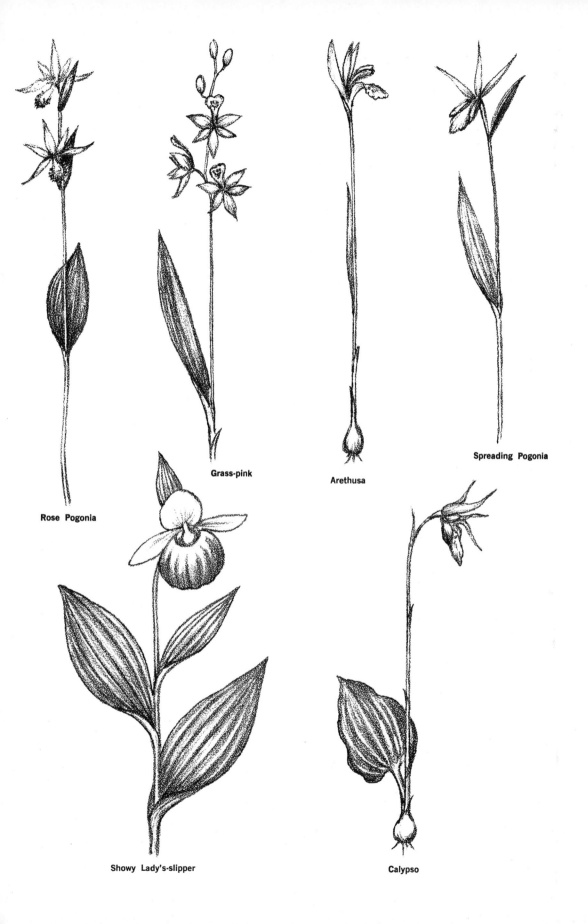

Grass-pink

Arethusa

Spreading Pogonia

Rose Pogonia

Showy Lady's-slipper

Calypso

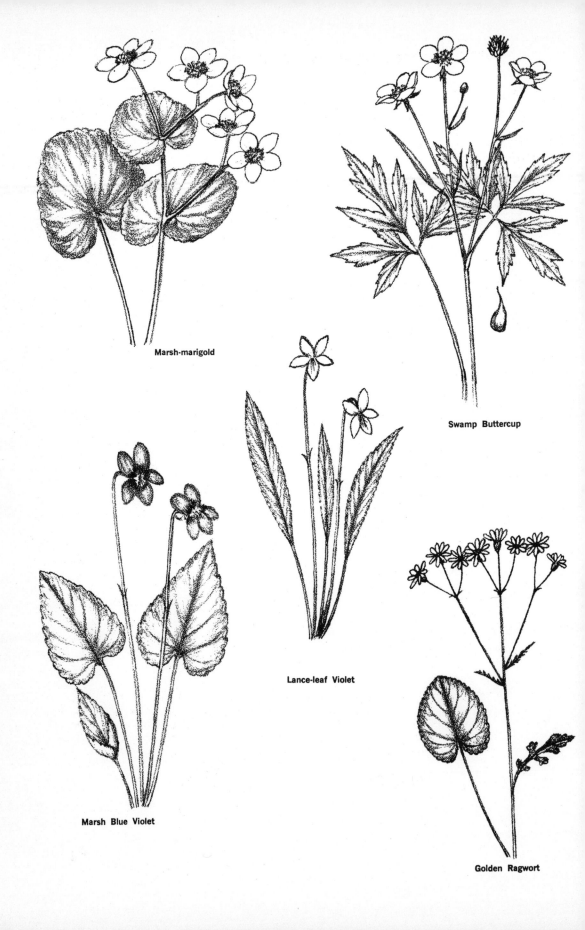

Marsh-marigold

Swamp Buttercup

Lance-leaf Violet

Marsh Blue Violet

Golden Ragwort

SPRING FLOWERS OF WET PLACES, Continued

MARSH-MARIGOLD *(Caltha palustris)*   Buttercup Family

The Marsh-marigold, or Cowslip, is a smooth plant with a stout, hollow, forking stem from 1 to 2 feet tall. It has flowers an inch to 1½ inches broad, which have 5 or 6 petal-like sepals of the brightest yellow. The roundish, heart-shaped leaves are 2 to 6 inches across and have low teeth on their margins. The young leaves are very popular as spring greens, and in the Northeast they are often sold in the markets. As its name implies, the plant grows in swamps and in wet open woods and meadows. The flowering season is between April and June, or even later in the Far North.
RANGE: Lab. to Alaska south to N.C., Tenn., Iowa, and Neb.

SWAMP BUTTERCUP *(Ranunculus septentrionalis)*   Buttercup Family

As its name indicates, the Swamp Buttercup grows in wet or swampy places; and there it may be found in bloom between late April and July. It is a branching plant with smooth to somewhat hairy stems ranging from 1 to about 3 feet tall. The flowers are about an inch across and they have 5 bright yellow petals. Its leaves are long-stalked and divided into 3 lobed and sharply toothed divisions.
RANGE: Que. to Man. south to Md., Ky. and Mo.

MARSH BLUE VIOLET *(Viola cucullata)*   Violet Family

As its name implies, this violet grows in wet meadows, bogs, and springy places. Its violet-blue flowers are darker toward the center, about an inch broad, and are on long stalks which overtop the leaves. The side petals have hairy tufts containing many club-shaped hairs. The leaves are heart-shaped with rather bluntish teeth on the margin, and they are smooth or very nearly so. The plant is usually tufted with several crowns; and both flowers and leaves arise from a thick, erect, fleshy rootstock. It blooms between April and July.
RANGE: Nfd. to Ont. and Minn. south to Va., n.Ga., Ark. and Neb.

LANCE-LEAF VIOLET *(Viola lanceolata)*   Violet Family

This violet can be recognized very easily by its long and narrow, lance-shaped leaves which have low and rounded teeth on the margin. The leaves are commonly from 2 to 6 inches long, but sometimes as much as a foot in length. The white flowers are a half inch or a little more across, the 3 lower petals having conspicuous purple veins. Both leaves and flowers arise from a slender rootstock, and the plants spread by means of runners. Look for this violet in wet meadows, marshy places, and bogs. It blooms between March and July.
RANGE: N.S. to Que., Minn. and Neb. south to Fla. and Tex.

GOLDEN RAGWORT *(Senecio aureus)*   Composite Family

Also called Squaw-weed, this is a rather smooth plant with usually several slender stems 6 inches to 2½ feet tall. The basal leaves are oblong-heart-shaped, bluntly-toothed, slender-stalked, often purplish beneath and 1 to 6 inches long. Those upward along the stem are small, narrow, and more or less deeply cut. The many flower heads are about ¾ inch across, with 8 to 12 bright yellow rays. It grows in rich moist woods, wet meadows, swamps and bogs; blooming late March to July.
RANGE: Nfd. to Que. and Wis. south to Fla., Tenn. and Mo.

SWAMP SAXIFRAGE *(Saxifraga pensylvanica)*   Saxifrage Family

As its name indicates, the Swamp Saxifrage grows in swamps, bogs, and wet meadows. It has a stout and somewhat sticky-hairy flower stalk from 1 to 3½ feet tall, with a ro-sette-like cluster of leaves at its base. The leaves are oval to narrowly top-shaped, thick and somewhat leathery in texture, and from 4 to about 12 inches long. Its small flowers vary from greenish-white to yellowish or purplish and have 5 narrow petals. The flower-ing season is between April and June.
RANGE: Me. to Minn. south to Va., w. N.C., Ill., and Mo.

PURPLE PITCHER-PLANT *(Sarracenia purpurea)*   Pitcher-plant Family

This pitcher-plant really has pitcher-shaped leaves which are 4 to 10 inches long, with a rather broad wing and an erect hood which is covered with backward-pointing bristles. The reclining or ascending pitchers are often beautifully veined with purple. Its flower is more or less globe-shaped, about 2 inches across, usually a deep purplish-red, and stands on a stalk 10 to 20 inches tall. It is the only species of pitcher-plant found north of the southern part of Virginia. It blooms between April and August. Sometimes it is called the Huntsmans-cap or Sidesaddle-flower.
RANGE: Nfd. to Sask. south to Fla. and La.

ATAMASCO-LILY *(Zephyranthes atamasco)*   Amaryllis Family

Also known as the Zephyr-lily and Wild Easter-lily, this plant has rather large lily-like flowers that are usually borne solitary on a naked stalk 8 to 15 inches tall. The flowers are white when they first open but later turn pink. Both the flower stalks and the long, narrow leaves arise from an onion-like bulb. It grows in rich moist woods, swamps, and meadows; blooming between March and May.
RANGE: Va. south to Fla. and west to Miss.

BULBOUS CRESS *(Cardamine bulbosa)*   Mustard Family

This smooth, leafy-stemmed plant has a knobby tuber at the base of its 6- to 18-inch stem, hence the name Bulbous Cress. It is also known as the Spring Cress. Between March and June it produces quite showy clusters of white flowers which are about a half-inch across. The leaves along the stem vary from lance-shaped to roundish and they may or may not have wavy-toothed margins. The basal ones are roundish to heart-shaped, often angled, and long-stalked. It is quite common in wet woods and meadows.
RANGE: N.H. to Ont. and Wis. south to Fla. and Tex.

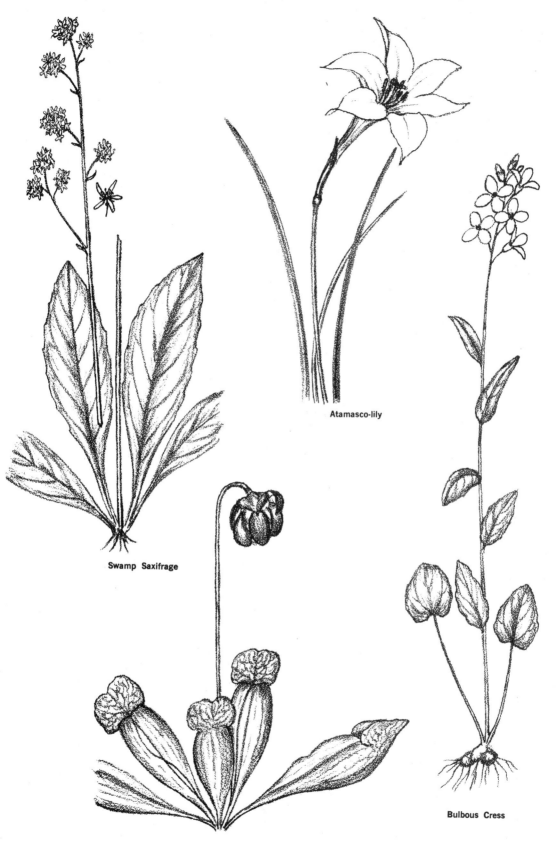

Atamasco-lily

Swamp Saxifrage

Purple Pitcher-plant

Bulbous Cress

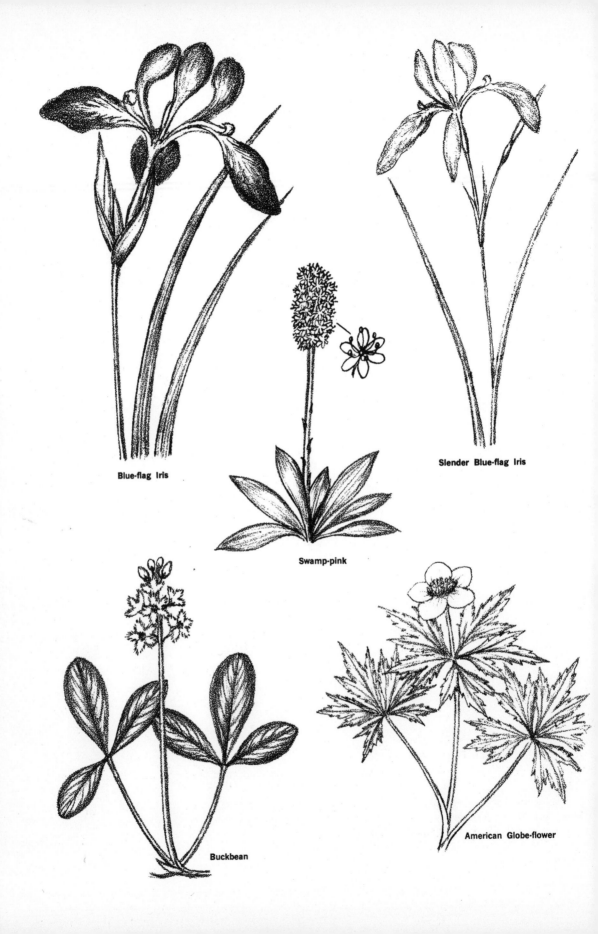

Blue-flag Iris

Slender Blue-flag Iris

Swamp-pink

Buckbean

American Globe-flower

BLUE-FLAG IRIS (*Iris versicolor*)   Iris Family

Flowers of the Blue-flag are often seen in wet meadows and marshes between May and August. The violet-blue sepals are whitish toward the base and beautifully veined with a darker purple, while the base of each one shows a yellow or greenish-yellow spot. The 3 petals are about half as large and plain blue-violet.

RANGE: Lab. to Man. south to Va., Ohio, Wis. and Minn.

SOUTHERN BLUE-FLAG IRIS (*Iris virginica*)   Iris Family

This species is quite similar to the preceding but the sepals usually have a brighter yellow and usually downy spot at the base. It is the most common of the tall blue-flowered irises in the South and is often abundant in the borders of swamps, marshes, and roadside ditches. It blooms between April and June, and its range extends from Va. northwestward to Minn. and south to Fla. and Tex. (Not illustrated)

SLENDER BLUE-FLAG IRIS (*Iris prismatica*)   Iris Family

This iris has slender flower stalks 1 to 2 feet tall and very narrow leaves. Its pale lavender-blue flowers are about 3 inches across, and the 3 sepals have a yellowish spot at the base. The sharply 3-angled capsules are helpful in distinguishing it. It grows in wet meadows, marshes and on shores; blooming between April and June.

RANGE: Along coast from Me. south to S.C.; in mountains from Va. and Ky. south to n. Ga. and Tenn.

BUCKBEAN (*Menyanthes trifoliata* var. *minor*)   Gentian Family

The Buckbean has a thick, scaly, creeping stem from which its leaves and flower stalks arise. The former are divided into 3 elliptic or narrowly top-shaped, untoothed leaflets 1½ to 3 inches long; on leaf stalks 2 to 10 inches in length. Its white flowers are about ½ inch across, and the 5 petals have glistening hairs on their upper surface. They are clustered on stalks 3 to 12 inches long and bloom between May and July. Bogbean and Marsh-trefoil are other names often given this plant of shallow waters and boggy places.

RANGE: Lab. to Alaska south to Del., W.Va., the Great Lakes region, Mo., Neb. and Wyo.

SWAMP-PINK (*Helonias bullata*)   Lily Family

The Swamp-pink, as its name indicates, grows in swamps and bogs. It has a stout, hollow flower stalk from 6 to 15 inches tall with almost scale-like bracts toward the base. Towards the top is a short but dense cluster of pink flowers with lavender-blue stamens. The true leaves are flat, dark green, broadest above the middle, and form a rosette at the base of the flower stalk. It blooms in April and May.

RANGE: Se. N.Y. and N.J. south to Va. and in mts. to n. Ga.

AMERICAN GLOBE-FLOWER (*Trollius laxus*)   Buttercup Family

Like the preceding species, the Globe-flower grows in swamps and wet meadows or thickets, but it is rather rare and local in occurrence. It has a slender, smooth stem 1 to 2 feet tall. The leaves are divided into from 5 to 7 radiating and cut-toothed segments. They are from 2 to 4 inches wide and all but the uppermost ones are stalked. The flowers are usually solitary, 1 to 1½ inches across, and have from 5 to 7 pale greenish-yellow petal-like sepals. It blooms in April or May.

RANGE: Conn. to Pa. and Mich.

TURKEY-BEARD *(Xerophyllum asphodeloides)* Lily Family

This plant has a dense basal cluster of slender leaves which might easily be mistaken for a tuft of wiry grass or the needles of a young Longleaf Pine. Sometime in May or June it sends up a flower stalk from 2 to 3 feet tall. Along it are a few scattered leaves and at the top there is a densely cylindrical cluster of white flowers. It grows in dry woodlands, southward chiefly in the mountains.
RANGE: Coastal plain N.J. and Del. south to Va.; mountains Va. to Ga.

FALSE BUGBANE *(Trautvetteria carolinensis)* Buttercup Family

This plant has a branching stem from 2 to 3 feet tall along which are alternate, deeply-lobed, and sharply toothed leaves. The basal ones are 6 to 8 inches across, 5- to 11-lobed, and long-stalked. The white flowers are borne in clusters at the ends of the branches. They have 3 to 5 sepals which drop off as the flowers open, thus each flower consists of a tassel of white stamens and a head of several pistils. The False Bugbane is also known as Tassel-rue. It grows along the banks of streams and in ravines, flowering between June and August.
RANGE: Sw. Pa. to Mo. south to nw. Fla.

GALAX *(Galax aphylla)* Galax Family

Galax has long-stalked, roundish heart-shaped, thickish, shiny leaves 1 to 3 inches across, with small bristly teeth on their margins. Bright green in summer, they become bronzed or reddish during the winter. The small white flowers are arranged in a narrow cluster on a naked flower stalk 10 to 18 inches tall, blooming May to July. It grows chiefly in mountain and upland woods. Another name for it is Beetleweed.
RANGE: Va. and W. Va. south to n. Ga. and n. Ala.

SHORTIA *(Shortia galacifolia)* Galax Family

The Shortia, or Oconee-bells, is an interesting little plant which spreads by means of short runners and often forms large colonies. It has a very short stem with long-stalked, shiny, oval or roundish, wavy-toothed leaves ¾ to 2½ inches long. The white or pinkish flowers are about an inch across, with 5 irregularly toothed petals, and are on naked stalks 3 to 6 inches long; blooming during March and April. It grows in wooded ravines and along streams in the foothills and lower slopes of the mountains from sw. Va. south to n. Ga.

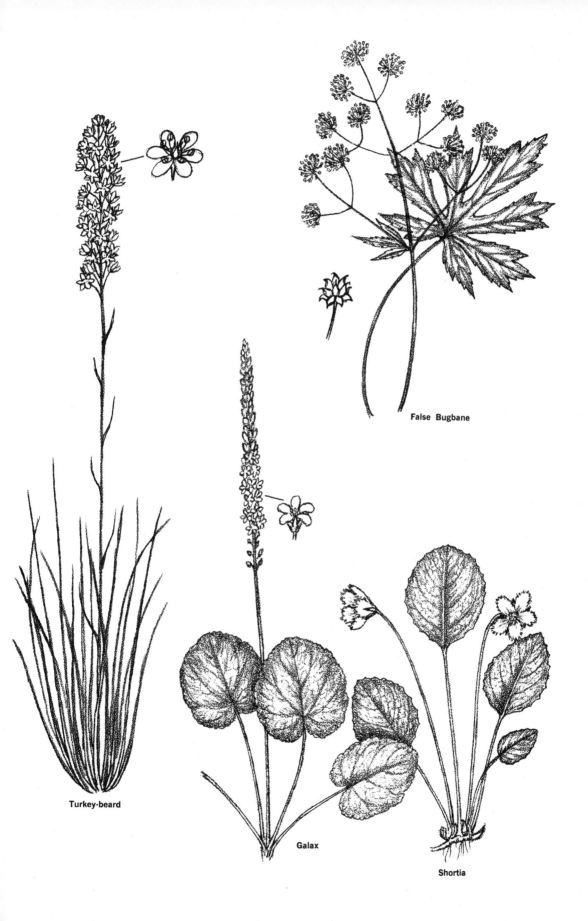

False Bugbane

Turkey-beard

Galax

Shortia

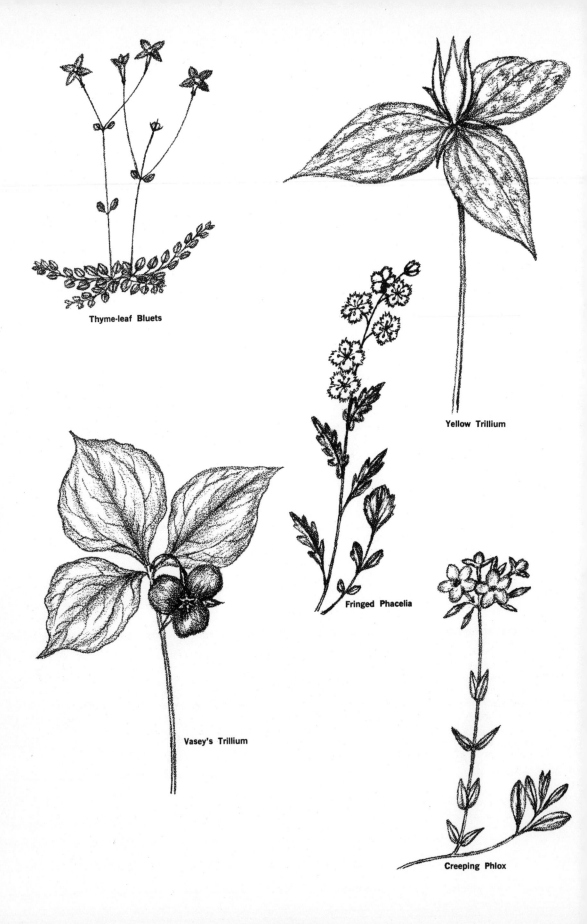

Thyme-leaf Bluets

Yellow Trillium

Fringed Phacelia

Vasey's Trillium

Creeping Phlox

THYME-LEAF BLUETS *(Houstonia serpyllifolia)*   Madder Family

This is a delicate little plant with creeping, leafy stems 4 to 10 inches long. The deep blue flowers resemble those of the Common Bluet. It grows in wet places, often along mountain streams; blooming between April and July.

RANGE: Pa. and W.Va. south to n. Ga. and e. Tenn.

YELLOW TRILLIUM *(Trillium luteum)*   Lily Family

This striking trillium has a stout stem 8 to 18 inches tall, with broadly oval, stalkless leaves which are beautifully mottled. The stalkless flower has erect lemon-yellow petals from 2 to 3 inches in length, and 3 yellowish-green sepals which spread horizontally. The flowers have a very pleasant odor which suggests that of lemons. It grows in rich moist woods and ravines, blooming in April or May.

RANGE: w. N.C., Ky. and Mo. south to n. Ga., Ala. and Ark.

VASEY'S TRILLIUM *(Trillium erectum* var. *vaseyi)*   Lily Family

By some botanists this is considered to be a distinct species. Its flowers have broad, deep maroon petals and pale anthers; and they are quite sweet-scented. It is sometimes called the Sweet Trillium or Sweet-Beth. A white-flowered form of this is called the Woodland White Trillium *(Trillium simile)* in some manuals. Both grow in rich moist woods from Tenn. and w. N.C. south to nw. S.C. and n. Ga. blooming between April and early June.

FRINGED PHACELIA *(Phacelia fimbriata)*   Waterleaf Family

The stems of this phacelia are weak, seldom over 6 inches tall, and have some spreading hairs. Its leaves are cut into 5 to 9 unequal, rather blunt-tipped segments. The lower ones are 2 to 4 inches long and slender-stalked but those along the stem are much smaller and stalkless. Its flowers are white to pale lilac, about ½ inch across, with lilac-colored anthers and the corolla lobes strongly fringed. It grows in rich woods and along streams in the mountains, blooming in April and May.

RANGE: w. Va. south to w. N.C. and e. Tenn.

CREEPING PHLOX *(Phlox stolonifera)*   Phlox Family

The Creeping Phlox produces creeping leafy stems which often form sizeable colonies of the plant. It has upright flowering stems 4 to 10 inches high with a few pairs of lance-shaped or narrowly oblong leaves up to ¾ inch long. Those of the sterile shoots are often 1 to 3 inches long, top-shaped, and taper into stalks. The flowers are bright pink or violet-purple, about ¾ inch across, and have rounded corolla lobes. A few of the orange-yellow anthers usually protrude from the summit of the corolla tube. It grows in moist woods and on flats along streams, chiefly in the mountain region; blooming between April and June.

RANGE: Pa. and Ohio south to n. Ga. and Tenn.

MOUNTAIN MEADOW-RUE *(Thalictrum clavatum)*   Buttercup Family

This little meadow-rue differs from all of our other species in that its flowers always contain both stamens and pistils. The flowers are white, long-stalked, and in a relatively few-flowered end cluster. Their stamens have club-shaped, petal-like filaments and the pistils stand on little stalks. The Mountain Meadow-rue is a smooth and very slender-stemmed plant from 6 inches to about 2 feet tall. Its leaves are biternately divided into 9 thin, oval- or egg-shaped leaflets which are pale beneath and usually 3-lobed, but they also have a few additional rounded teeth. It is found in wooded ravines and along streams in the mountains. Another name for it is Lady-rue. It blooms in May or June.
    RANGE: Va., W.Va. and Ky. south to n. Ga. and nw. Ala.

WILD BLEEDING-HEART *(Dicentra exima)*   Fumitory Family

The native Wild Bleeding-heart is sometimes called Turkey-corn and Staggerweed, and in cultivation it is known as the Plumy Bleeding-heart. It is a somewhat whitened, smooth plant from 10 inches to about 2 feet high. The pink to flesh-colored flowers are about ¾ inch long and they are produced between April and September. The leaves are all basal, ternately divided, and cut into numerous oblong segments. It grows in rocky woods and on rock cliffs in the mountains.
    RANGE: N.Y. and W.Va. south to n. Ga. and e. Tenn.

LILY-OF-THE-VALLEY **(Convallaria majalis** var. *montana)*   Lily Family

This native of our southern Appalachian Mountains is considered by most botanists to be a variety of the European Lily-of-the-valley, which is very common in cultivation and sometimes occurs as an escape. Unlike the European plant our native Lily-of-the-valley is not a colony-forming plant. It has nearly the same broad elliptic leaves, and long clusters of fragrant white flowers which resemble little globe-shaped bells. Our native plants grow on rich, rocky wooded slopes and bloom between April and June.
    RANGE: Va. and W.Va. south to w. N.C. and e. Tenn.

UMBRELLA-LEAF *(Diphylleia cymosa)*   Barberry Family

This plant gets its name from the single, large, umbrella-like leaf of the non-flowering plants. It is attached to the stem near the center of the leaf. Flowering plants have a pair of similar but smaller leaves which are deeply cleft into two divisions, coarsely toothed, and attached to their stalks near the leaf margin. The white flowers are about ¾ inch across and borne in clusters. They have 6 sepals which are soon shed, 6 oval-shaped petals, 6 stamens, and a pistil. The latter develops into a roundish or oval-shaped, blue berry about ½ inch long. It grows in rich woods, often along streams, in the southern mountains; blooming in April or May.
    RANGE: Western Va. south to n. Ga.

MOUNTAIN PHLOX *(Phlox ovata)*   Phlox Family

The flowering stalks of this phlox arise from reclining leafy stems. They are usually slender, quite smooth, 1 to 2 feet tall; and have from 3 to 7 pairs of leaves which are 1 to 2 inches long, rounded at the base, and pointed at the tip. The lower ones are somewhat larger and narrowed to a stalked base. The flowers are about ¾ inch across, pink to reddish-purple, and have rounded corolla lobes. It grows in moist to rather dry open woods, thickets, and meadows; blooming during May and June.
    RANGE: Pa. to Ind. south to S.C. and Tenn.

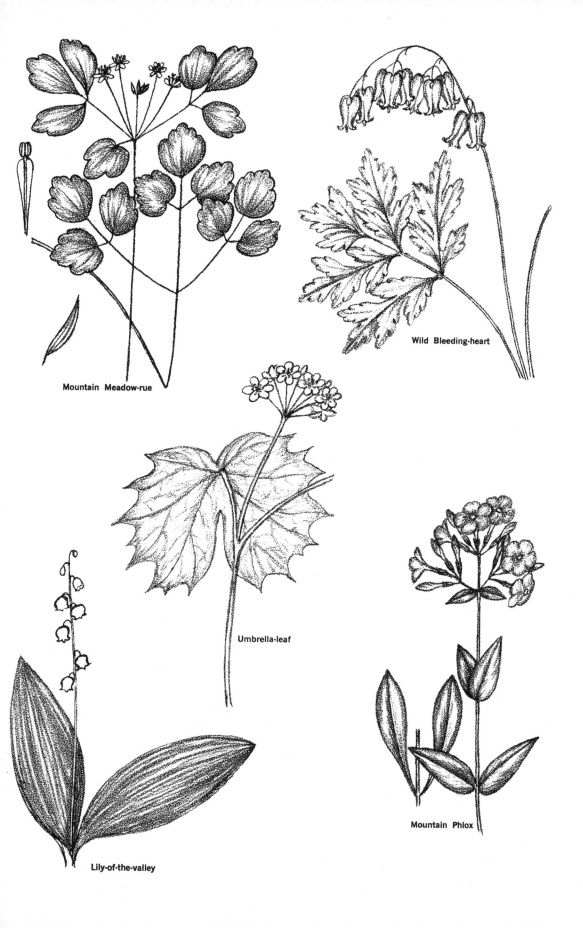

Mountain Meadow-rue

Wild Bleeding-heart

Umbrella-leaf

Lily-of-the-valley

Mountain Phlox

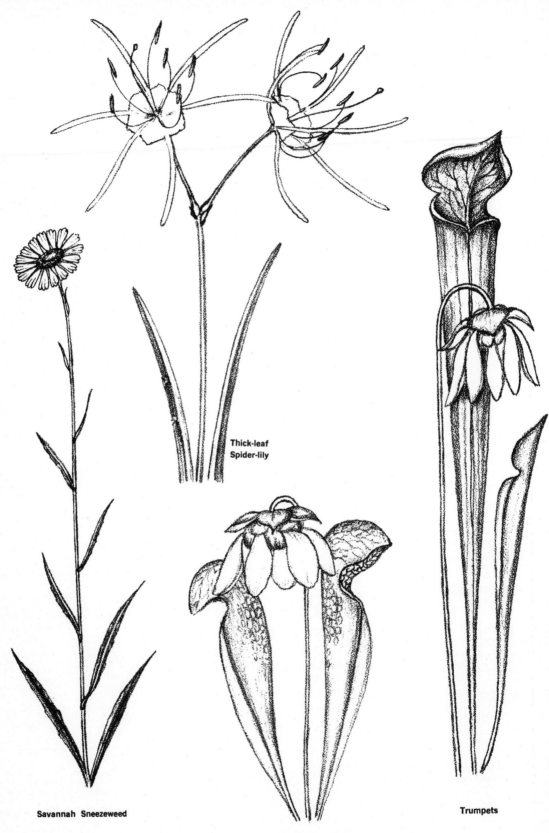

Thick-leaf Spider-lily

Savannah Sneezeweed

Hooded Pitcher-plant

Trumpets

THICK-LEAF SPIDER-LILY *(Hymenocallis crassifolia)*   Amaryllis Family

At the summit of a naked stalk from 1½ to 2 feet tall, this spider-lily has 2 or 3 large white flowers. The long, green, stalk-like perianth tubes suddenly flare into 6 long and very narrow, petal-like segments. Within them are the 6 stamens, the slender filaments of which are joined toward the base with a cup-shaped white membrane which adds immeasurably to the showiness of the flower. The leaves are all basal, strap-like and up to 20 inches in lenth. This species of spider-lily grows in coastal plain marshes and along the bank of tidewater streams; blooming in May or June.
    RANGE: N.C. south to Fla. and west to Ala.

SAVANNAH SNEEZEWEED *(Helenium vernale)*   Composite Family

This species has a simple, erect stem 1 to 2 feet tall. The lower and basal leaves are long and narrow, from 2 to 6 inches in length, and have sparingly wavy-toothed margins; but on the stem they are rapidly reduced in size upward. The solitary flower head is about 2 inches across; with 15 to 25 spreading bright yellow rays 3-lobed at the summit, and a large yellowish disk which is flattened and dome-shaped. It grows in wet coastal plain pinelands and savannahs, blooming in April or May.
    RANGE: S.C. south to Fla. west to Miss.

HOODED PITCHER-PLANT *(Sarracenia minor)*   Pitcher-plant Family

This species has erect, trumpet-shaped leaves 8 to 16 inches tall, with an arching dome-like hood which covers the open top of the trumpet-like leaf. Toward the summit they have numerous translucent, window-like spots; and they are often veined with purple. The yellow flowers are about 2½ inches across and stand on stalks 6 to 12 inches tall. It grows in wet coastal plain pinelands and bogs, blooming between April and June.
    RANGE: N.C. south to Fla.

TRUMPETS *(Sarracenia flava)*   Pitcher-plant Family

This distinctive species has trumpet-shaped leaves 1½ to 4 feet tall, which have a narrow wing and an erect hood 3 to 4½ inches broad. The latter is often yellow or strikingly veined with red or purple. Its yellow flowers are 3 to 4½ inches across and stand on stalks from 1½ to 3 feet tall. It grows in bogs and savannahs, chiefly in the coastal plain; blooming in March or April. Also known as the Trumpet-leaf or Huntsman's-horn.
    RANGE: Se. Va. south to Fla. and west to Ala.

WHITE-TOPPED SEDGE (*Dichromena latifolia*)   Sedge Family

This is a conspicuous plant in the wetter pinelands and savannahs of the Southeast from May until after mid-summer. What appear to be petals are really the white leaf-like bracts which surround the cluster of true flowers. They are 1½ to 3 inches long, mostly white but with green tips, and usually more than 7 in number.
RANGE: N.C. south to Fla. and west to Texas.

BLUE BUTTERWORT (*Pinguicula caerulea*)   Bladderwort Family

Butterworts got their name from the fact that the European species have been used as rennin in curdling milk. They have basal rosettes of shiny, sticky, pale green leaves. Insects stick to them as to flypaper, and the edges of the leaves roll up as their bodies are digested. This one has leaves ½ to 2 inches long. Its flowers are pale violet, almost an inch across, the corolla having 5 deeply notched lobes and a spur. They are solitary on sticky-hairy stalks 4 to 10 inches tall. It grows in wet coastal plain pinelands, blooming during April and May. RANGE: N.C. south to Fla.

OBOVATE-LEAF BARBARA'S-BUTTONS (*Marshallia obovata*)   Composite Family

Unlike the preceding species, this one grows in old fields and open woods chiefly in the piedmont region. It is also a smooth plant, usually with a slender and simple stem from 6 inches to about 2 feet tall, which is leafy chiefly below the middle or only toward the base. Its leaves are mostly narrowly top-shaped and from 1 to 4½ inches long. The flower heads are about an inch across; made up of a number of whitish to pale pink flowers with slender tubes. It blooms during April and May.
RANGE: N.C. and Mo. south to Fla. and Ala.

SUN-BONNETS (*Chaptalia tomentosa*)   Composite Family

This little daisy-like composite is one of the first flowers to appear in the spring in the coastal plain pinelands. The plant has a basal rosette of leaves which are bright green and smooth above but densely white-woolly beneath, the new ones not being fully grown at the time the plant blooms. Its flower heads are almost an inch across when fully expanded, and they have a number of marginal rays which are white or creamy-white on the upper surface and violet-tinged on the back. Each head nods at the summit of a slender, naked, woolly-coated stem from 4 to 12 inches tall. It grows in moist places, blooming between late February and May.
RANGE: N.C. south to Fla. and west to Tex.

YELLOW MILKWORT (*Polygala lutea*)   Milkwort Family

The bright orange-yellow flower heads of this milkwort are conspicuous in coastal plain bogs and wet pinelands between April and October. It is the only milkwort having flowers of this color, which makes its identification easy. It is a smooth plant with several erect or ascending stems from 6 to about 12 inches high. Along them are numerous narrow leaves from ¾ to 1½ inches long. Other names for it are Orange Milkwort and Yellow Bachelor's-button.
RANGE: se. N.Y. south to Fla. and west to La.

OAK-LEAF FLEABANE (*Erigeron quercifolius*)   Composite Family

This fleabane resembles the preceding one but it is usually a smaller plant from 6 inches to 1½ feet tall. The lower and basal leaves are quite distinctly lobed, hence the name of Oak-leaf. Its flower heads are about ½ inch across and have a number of narrow bluish or violet rays. It grows in fields and along roadsides, generally in sandy soils of the coastal plain; blooming April to June.
RANGE: Va. and Tenn. south to Fla. and Tex.

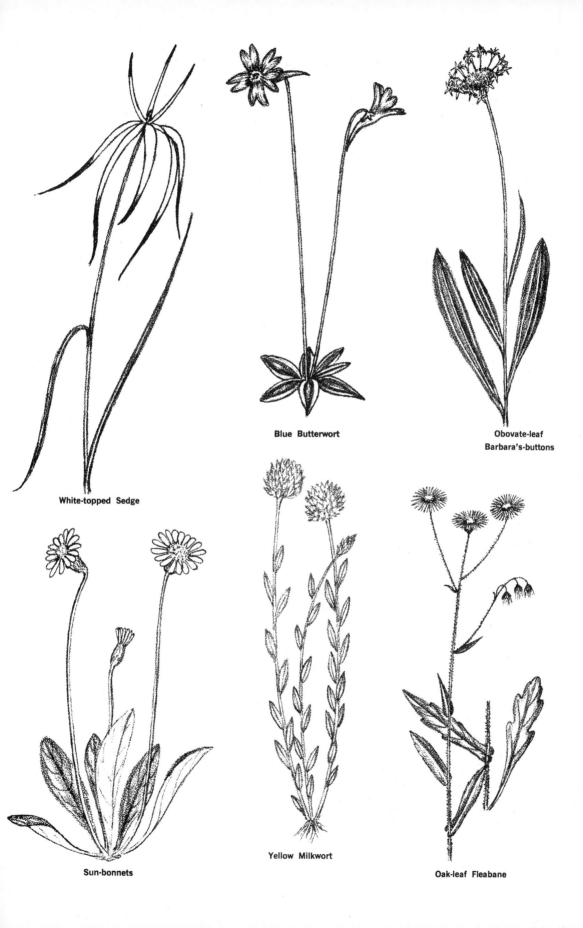

White-topped Sedge

Blue Butterwort

Obovate-leaf
Barbara's-buttons

Sun-bonnets

Yellow Milkwort

Oak-leaf Fleabane

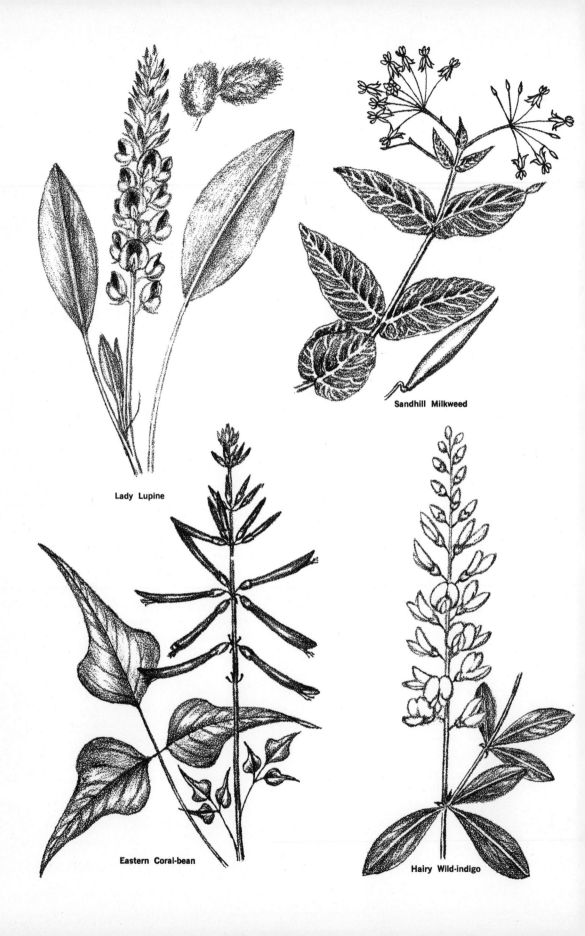

Lady Lupine

Sandhill Milkweed

Eastern Coral-bean

Hairy Wild-indigo

LADY LUPINE *(Lupinus villosus)*   Pea Family

This is a striking plant of the dry pinelands and sandhills of the southeastern coastal plain. The stalked leaves are 1-foliate with lance-shaped or elliptic blades from 2 to 6 inches long, and are so densely covered with silky hair that they appear quite a grayish-green. The plant has several radiating stems or branches which are more or less prostrate, but turn up at the ends and terminate in dense clusters of flowers from 4 to 7 inches in length. The flowers are about ¾ inch long and are deep lilac to purple, with a very dark purple or red spot in the center of the standard petal. They are followed by pods so densely covered with silvery-gray hairs that they suggest pussy willows. It blooms in April or May.
RANGE: e. N.C. south to Fla. and west to Miss.

SANDHILL MILKWEED *(Asclepias humistrata)*   Milkweed Family

This unusual milkweed grows in the driest of sandy places: chiefly in coastal plain pine and oak woods, and on sandhills. It is a pale green and smooth plant which is whitened by a bloom. The often purplish stem is prostrate, 1 to 3 feet long, and the paired leaves stand almost vertically. They are egg-shaped, pointed at the tip, stalkless, and from 2 to 5 inches long. Both surfaces of the leaves are alike—pale green and strikingly veined and bordered with white or coral-pink. The flowers are about ⅓ inch long and have grayish or greenish-purple corolla lobes and white hoods. They are arranged in rather loosely-flowered umbels and bloom in May or June. It cannot possibly be mistaken for any other species of milkweed.
RANGE: e. N.C. south to Fla. and west to Miss.

EASTERN CORAL-BEAN *(Erythrina herbacea)*   Pea Family

Between May and July, the brilliant red flowers of this plant are conspicuous in coastal plain pinelands, thickets, and the borders of woods; the long and open clusters being held aloft on leafy stems from 2 to 4 feet tall. Its flowers are slender-looking and about 2 inches long, consisting of a long and narrow standard which turns up only toward the tip. Stamens protrude slightly beyond the end of the standard but the wing and keel petals are quite small. These flowers are followed by bean-like pods which have conspicuous constrictions between the bright red seeds. The leaves are long-stalked and divided into 3 rather triangular leaflets. At the base there is a broad and roundish lobe on each side, above which they taper to a long-pointed tip. Some of the other names given this plant are Cardinal-spear, Cherokee-bean, and Firecracker-plant; the latter because the color and shape of its flowers suggest firecrackers.
RANGE: e. N.C. south to Fla. and west to Tex.

HAIRY WILD-INDIGO *(Baptisia cinerea)*   Pea Family

This is an erect, branching plant 2 to 3 feet tall which may be softly hairy or merely downy on the younger growth. It has many inch-long yellow flowers arranged in narrow clusters up to 10 inches in length. Its leaves are stalkless or nearly so and divided into 3 lance-shaped to narrowly top-shaped leaflets 2 to 4 inches in length; with a pair of prominent stipules at the base of each leaf. It grows in dry sandy pinelands and on sandhills in the coastal plain blooming in April or May.
RANGE: se Va. south to S.C.

WILD SARSAPARILLA *(Aralia nudicaulis)*   Ginseng Family

This plant has but one long-stalked leaf which is divided into 3 parts; each of which are again divided into usually 5 egg-shaped or oval, sharply toothed leaflets 2 to 5 inches long. The naked flower stalk usually has 3 clusters of small greenish-white flowers; which are followed by round, purplish-black berries. Beneath the ground the plant has a creeping aromatic rootstock. It grows in rich moist woods, blooming from May to July.

RANGE: Nfd. to Man. south to Va., n. Ga., e. Tenn. and Mo.

DWARF GINSENG *(Panax trifolium)*   Ginseng Family

Dwarf Ginseng has a stem 3 to 8 inches tall which bears 3 leaves and a solitary umbel of small white flowers. Each leaf is divided into 3 to 5 stalkless leaflets which are 1 to 1½ inches long and blunt at the tip. The flowers are followed by yellowish berries. The plant grows from a roundish pungent tuber about ½ inch in diameter, which gives it the common name of Groundnut. It grows in rich moist woods and blooms between May and August.

RANGE: N.S. to Minn. south to n. Ga., Tenn., Iowa and Neb.

TWINFLOWER *(Linnaea borealis* var. *americana)*   Honeysuckle Family

The Twinflower is a slender-stemmed, trailing or creeping plant which grows in cold woods and bogs in the northern portions of both the Old and the New Worlds. Between June and August it sends up 3- to 10-inch stalks bearing pairs of stalked, roundish or oval, obscurely toothed leaves ⅓ to ⅔ of an inch wide. At their tips they have a pair of nodding, bell-shaped, pink flowers about ⅓ of an inch long. The genus was named for the immortal Linnaeus who was especially fond of this dainty little plant.

RANGE: Lab. to Alaska south to Md., W.Va., the Great Lakes region, S.D., Colo., Utah and Calif.

SHINLEAF *(Pyrola elliptica)*   Wintergreen Family

The Shinleaf has an erect, naked flower stalk 5 to 10 inches tall; on which is a narrow cluster of nodding, white, fragrant flowers about ⅔ inch across. At the base of this stalk are several leaves which are oval or elliptic, rather thin in texture, dull green above, obscurely toothed, and from 1 to 3 inches in length. It grows in dry to fairly moist, rich woods; blooming between June and August.

RANGE: Nfd. to B.C. south to W. Va., Ohio, Ill., Iowa, S.D. and N. Mex.

INDIAN-PIPE *(Monotropa uniflora)*   Wintergreen Family

This is a strange and ghostly-looking plant which grows in dimly lighted, rich, moist woodlands. Containing no chlorophyll, the entire plant is waxy-white, or sometimes pinkish, and in drying becomes blackish. A solitary flower about ¾ inch long, with 4 or 5 petals and 10 stamens, nods at the end of a scaly stalk from 4 to 10 inches tall. The flower stalks are usually in clusters, arising from a ball-like mass of roots. The plant is a saprophyte, obtaining its nourishment from the decaying vegetable matter in the soil. Also known as the Corpse-plant, it blooms between June and October.

RANGE: Nfd. to Alaska south to Fla., Tex. and Calif.

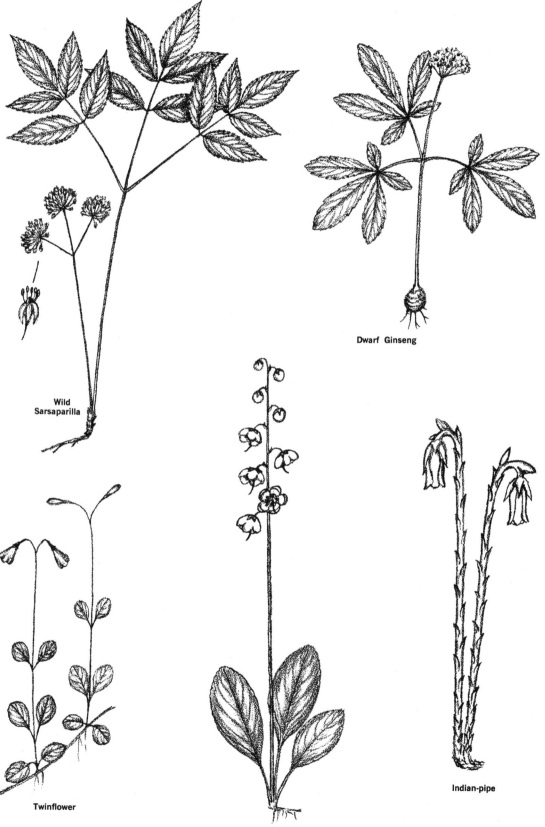

Dwarf Ginseng

Wild
Sarsaparilla

Twinflower

Shinleaf

Indian-pipe

Partridge-berry

Cranefly Orchid

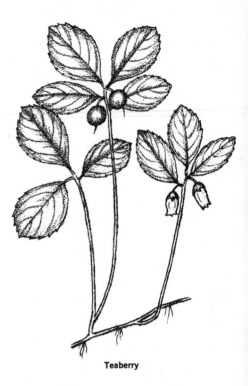

Teaberry

Pipsissewa

Spotted Wintergreen

PARTRIDGE-BERRY *(Mitchella repens)* Madder Family

Also known as Twinberry, this is a smooth plant with trailing slender stems 6 to 12 inches long; with pairs of lustrous, evergreen, roundish and stalked leaves usually ½ to ¾ inch long. The white or pinkish, fringed flowers are in pairs and have their bases united. They are followed by bright red, double berries about ⅓ inch across; which often persist until the next flowering time between May and July.

RANGE: Nfd. to Ont. and Minn. south to Fla. and Tex.

TEABERRY *(Gaultheria procumbens)* Heath Family

The Teaberry has slender stems which creep on or beneath the surface of the ground, sending up erect branches 2 to 6 inches high which bear the leaves and flowers. Its urn-shaped white flowers are about ⅜ inch long and usually solitary in the leaf axils. They are followed by globular, bright red, berry-like fruits about ⅜ inch in diameter. The leaves are elliptic, oval, or top-shaped, ¾ to 2 inches long, somewhat leathery, and have low bristle-tipped teeth on their margins. The plant has an oil of wintergreen odor and taste. It grows in woods and thickets, blooming between June and August. Other names for it are Mountain-tea, Checkerberry, and Spicy Wintergreen.

RANGE: Nfd. to Man. south to Ga., Ala., Wis. and Minn.

CRANEFLY ORCHID *(Tipularia discolor)* Orchid Family

During the fall this orchid produces a single broadly egg-shaped leaf 2 to 3 inches long, which is purple beneath. By flowering time, in July or August, this leaf withers and disappears. The bronzy or tawny flowers have a long slender spur, and they stand on slender stalks which gives the impression of a long-legged insect. A number of the flowers are arranged in a long cluster on a leafless, smooth, tawny stalk 1 to 2 feet tall. It grows in rich woodlands.

RANGE: Mass. to Ind. and Mo. south to Fla. and Tex.

PIPSISSEWA *(Chimaphila umbellata)* Wintergreen Family

Our Pipsissewa, or Prince's-pine, is a variety of a plant found throughout the northern portion of the Northern Hemisphere. It is a little plant with erect leafy flowering stems 6 to 12 inches high, arising from extensively creeping underground stems. Its leaves are nearly whorled, 1 to 2½ inches long, bright green and shining, sharply toothed, and distinctly broadest toward their tips. The white or pale pinkish flowers are ½ to ⅔ inch across and in an umbel-like end cluster. The Pipsissewa grows in dry woodlands, blooming between May and August.

RANGE: N.S. to Ont. south to Ga., Ohio, Ill. and Minn.

SPOTTED WINTERGREEN *(Chimaphila maculata)* Wintergreen Family

The Spotted Wintergreen, or Spotted Pipsissewa, is similar in habit and stature to the preceding species. Its leaves, however, are broadest toward the base, egg-shaped or lance-shaped, from 1 to 3 inches long and have sharp but rather widely spaced teeth on the margin. Even in winter, the plant is brought to our attention by the white mottling along the veins of its otherwise dark green leaves. Between May and August a few white or pinkish flowers, about ¾ inch across, are borne in an end cluster. It usually grows in rather dry rich woodlands.

RANGE: N.H. to Ont. and Mich. south to Ga., Ala. and Tenn.

BLACK COHOSH *(Cimicifuga racemosa)*   Buttercup Family

The Black Cohosh, or Black Snakeroot, is one of the most conspicuous plants in our
wooded areas during the summer months; for it is then that it displays its long, slender,
candle-like clusters of small white flowers. On close inspection, one will find that each
flower consists largely of a tassel-like group of white stamens with a pistil in the center.
Some of the outermost stamens resemble small petals but there are no true petals, and
the sepals drop off as the flowers open. The pistil develops into a small dry pod. The
Black Cohosh has a somewhat slender stem from 3 to 6 feet tall, on which are 2 or 3
large compound leaves. The leaflets are mostly egg-shaped, rounded or somewhat pointed
at the base, and are cleft or sharply toothed on the margin. It blooms between June
and September. The rootstocks are used medicinally.
    RANGE: Mass. to Ont. south to Ga., Tenn., and Mo.

DWARF CORNEL *(Cornus canadensis)*   Dogwood Family

Often called the Bunchberry, this plant has a slender stem which runs underground and
sends up erect branches from 2 to 10 inches tall. On them is what appears to be a whorl
of usually 6 oval-shaped leaves, from 1 to 3 inches long, and what appears to be a solitary flower. Actually it is a dense little cluster of small greenish-yellow or sometimes
purplish flowers, and the flower cluster is surrounded by usually 4 petal-like white bracts.
Roundish bright red fruits follow the flowers which bloom between May and July. It
grows in cool moist woods and bogs.
    RANGE: Lab. to Alaska south to Md., W.Va., the Great Lakes region, S.D., N.Mex.
and Calif.

ROUND-LEAF ORCHID *(Habenaria orbiculata)*   Orchid Family

This woodland orchid has a pair of large, round, shiny, pad-like leaves which are 4 to 8
inches wide and usually lie flat on the ground. The flower stalk is 8 to 20 inches tall and
usually has several small, bract-like leaves below the narrow flower cluster. Its greenish-
white flowers are about an inch long and they have slender dangling spurs. It blooms between June and August.
    RANGE: Nfd. to Ont. south to n. Ga., Tenn. and Ill.

TALL ANEMONE *(Anemone virginiana)*   Buttercup Family

This is one of several species of *Anemone* popularly called Thimbleweeds because their
achenes are crowded on a long and thimble-shaped receptacle. The Tall Anemone has a
stout and hairy stem from 2 to 3 feet tall. On it is a whorl of usually 3 stalked and 3-
parted leaves, which are variously cleft and sharply toothed. From this whorl of leaves
arise the long stalks which end in a solitary flower. The flower is a little more than an
inch across and has 5 greenish-white, petal-like sepals. The basal leaves are long-stalked
but similar to those of the flower stem. In this species the achenes are crowded in a
woolly, cylindrical head an inch or more long. The Tall Anemone grows in usually dry
and rocky open woods and thickets; blooming between June and August.
    RANGE: Me. to Minn. south to Ga., Tenn., and Kan.

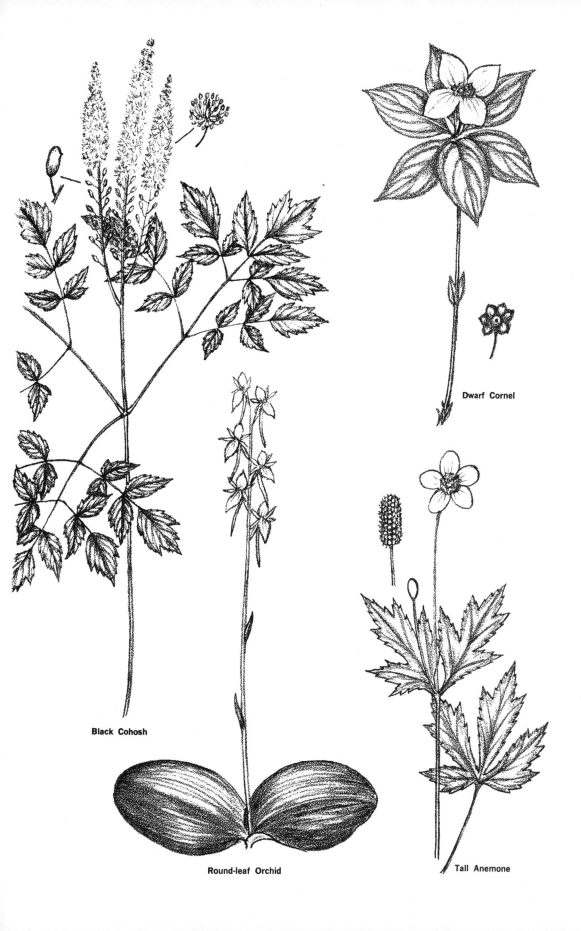

Black Cohosh

Round-leaf Orchid

Dwarf Cornel

Tall Anemone

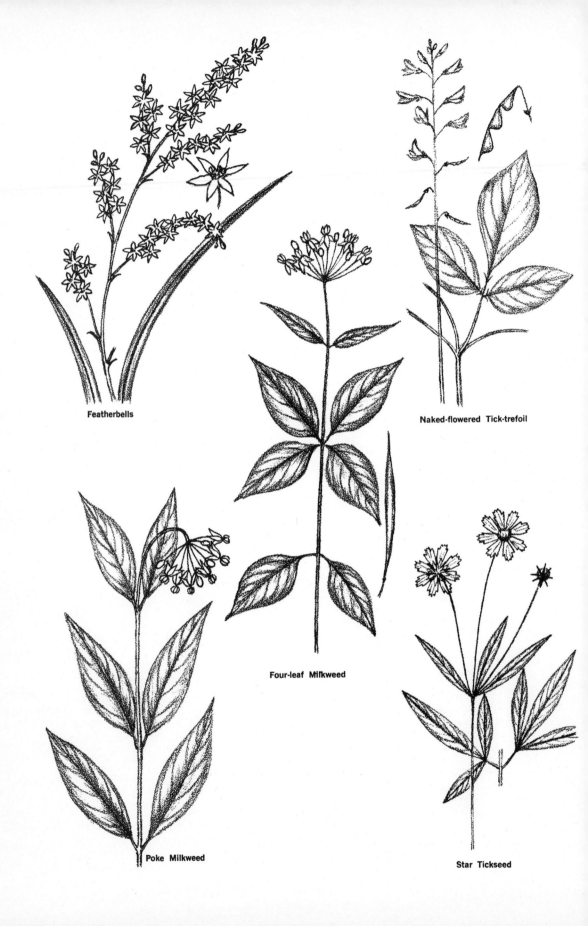

Featherbells

Naked-flowered Tick-trefoil

Four-leaf Milkweed

Poke Milkweed

Star Tickseed

FEATHERBELLS *(Stenanthium gramineum)*   Lily Family

Often called Feather-fleece, this is an attractive plant with large and more or less drooping clusters of small, starry, white flowers. It grows to a height of 3 to 6 feet and has
long, narrow, grass-like leaves which are more numerous and larger toward the base of
the plant. This attractive plant grows in moist open woods, meadows, and bogs; and
blooms between June and September.
RANGE: Pa. to Ill. and Mo. south to N.C., nw. Fla. and e. Tex.

NAKED-FLOWERED TICK-TREFOIL *(Desmodium nudiflorum)*   Pea Family

This tick-trefoil gets its name from the fact that there are no leaves on the flowering
stem which usually overtops the one bearing the leaves. The leaves are clustered at the
summit of a stem generally less than a foot high. They have 3 leaflets from 1 to 3 inches
long; the end one usually somewhat diamond-shaped, the others rather unevenly egg-
shaped. Its rose-purple flowers are about 1/3 of an inch long. The fruits are 2- to 4-joined
and are not constricted along the top edge. It grows in rather dry but rich woodlands,
blooming between June and August.
RANGE: Me. to Que. and Minn. south to Fla. and Tex.

POKE MILKWEED *(Asclepias exaltata)*   Milkweed Family

The Poke or Tall Milkweed is a smooth plant, usually with a simple stem 3 to 6 feet
tall; and pairs of rather thin, egg-shaped to broadly lance-shaped leaves 4 to 9 inches
long, which taper at both ends and are long-stalked. Its flowers are about 2/3 inch long,
with greenish or greenish-purple corolla lobes and white hoods. They are in rather large
but loosely-flowered and usually nodding umbels; blooming between June and August. It
grows in rich open woods and thickets.
RANGE: Me. to Minn. south to Ga., Ky., Ill. and Iowa.

FOUR-LEAF MILKWEED *(Asclepias quadrifolia)*   Milkweed Family

This dainty little milkweed grows in dry open woods, blooming between May and July.
On a usually unbranched, slender stem 1 to 2 feet tall, it has 1 or 2 whorls of leaves
near the middle and a pair of leaves both above and below the whorled ones. All are
quite thin, egg-shaped to lance-shaped, definitely stalked and from 2 to 6 inches long.
The flowers have pale pink corolla lobes and white hoods. They are in from 1 to 4 rather
small terminal umbels.
RANGE: N.H. to Ont. and Minn, south to n. Ga., Ala., Ark., and Kan.

STAR TICKSEED *(Coreopsis pubescens)*   Composite Family

The Star Tickseed has a slender and downy stem 2 to 4 feet tall, which may have a few
branches. The upper leaves are short-stalked or stalkless, lance-shaped, or sometimes cut
into 3 to 5 segments, and 2 to 3 inches long. The lower ones are top-shaped and taper
into slender stalks. Its flower heads are about 1¼ inches across, with 8 to 10 yellow rays
which are lobed at the summit and a yellowish disk. The spreading narrow outer bracts
of the involucre are star-like and about as long as the inner ones. It grows in dry open
woods and on slopes or cliffs, blooming between July and September.
RANGE: Va. to s. Ill. and Mo. south to Fla. and La.

SMOOTH FALSE FOXGLOVE *(Aureolaria flava)* Figwort Family

The yellow-flowered false foxgloves are parasitic on the roots of oak trees. This species is characterized by usually branched and often purplish stems 3 to 6 feet tall, which are more or less whitened with a bloom. Its leaves are elliptic to lance-shaped; the lower ones 4 to 6 inches long and pinnately cleft, the upper ones smaller and either toothed or untoothed. The flowers have a slightly bilateral, trumpet-shaped corolla 1½ to 2 inches long, with roundish lobes. It grows in dry to moist woods, blooming between July and September.

RANGE: Me. to Minn. south to Fla. and La.

LARGER SKULLCAP *(Scutellaria integrifolia)* Mint Family

Skullcaps get their name from a peculiar little cap-like projection on the upper side of the calyx. A dozen or more species of them occur in the eastern United States north of Florida, and this species is one of the more showy ones. It is a somewhat hoary-downy or hairy plant with an erect, simple or branched stem from 6 inches to 2 feet high. The leaves of the upper part of the stem are narrow, untoothed, 1 to 2 inches long, and stalkless or very short-stalked. Those toward the base are slender-stalked, egg-shaped to roundish, and have toothed margins. Its purplish-blue flowers are often whitish underneath and almost an inch long. Also known as the Hyssop Skullcap, it grows in open woods, thickets, and clearings; blooming between May and July.

RANGE: Mass. to Ky. and Mo. south to Fla. and Tex.

OSWEGO-TEA *(Monarda didyma)* Mint Family

Often called the Bee-balm, this plant is well known for its bright red or scarlet flowers which are borne in showy heads at the summit of the stem or its branches. They are 1½ or 2 inches long and have a narrow, ascending upper lip and a somewhat drooping and broader lower one with 3 short lobes. It grows from 2 to 3 feet tall and has lance- to egg-shaped, sharply-toothed, stalked leaves 3 to 6 inches in length. It is often common in rich moist woods and bottomlands, blooming July to September.

RANGE: N.Y. to Mich. south to n. Ga. and Miss.

TALL BELLFLOWER *(Campanula americana)* Bluebell Family

The Tall or American Bellflower usually has a simple, more or less hairy stem, from 2 to about 6 feet tall; along which are scattered lance-shaped to narrowly egg-shaped, toothed leaves 3 to 6 inches long, most of them tapering at the base into short stalks. Its flowers are star-shaped rather than bell-like, with 5 long and pointed lobes. They are about an inch across, light violet-blue, and are in the axils of leaf-like bracts; forming a long and slender end cluster. It grows in rich moist woods and thickets, blooming between June and August.

RANGE: Ont. to Minn. south to Fla., Ala. and Mo.

STARRY CAMPION *(Silene stellata)* Pink Family

Atop a stem from 2 to 3 feet tall, the Starry Campion has a loose cluster of white flowers. Along the stem below them are whorls of 4 lance-shaped leaves 2 to 4 inches long and minutely downy beneath. The flowers are about ¾ inch across and have an inflated, bell-shaped, usually downy calyx. The 5 petals are delicately fringed at the end. Often common in open woods, clearings, and thickets; it blooms between July and September.

RANGE: Mass. to Minn. south to Ga., Ala., Ark., Okla., and Tex.

232

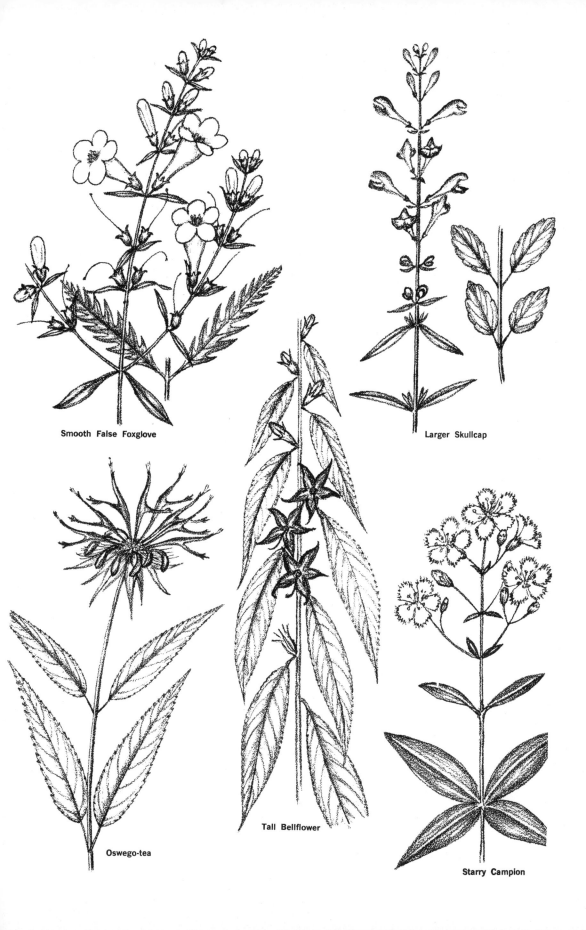

Smooth False Foxglove

Larger Skullcap

Oswego-tea

Tall Bellflower

Starry Campion

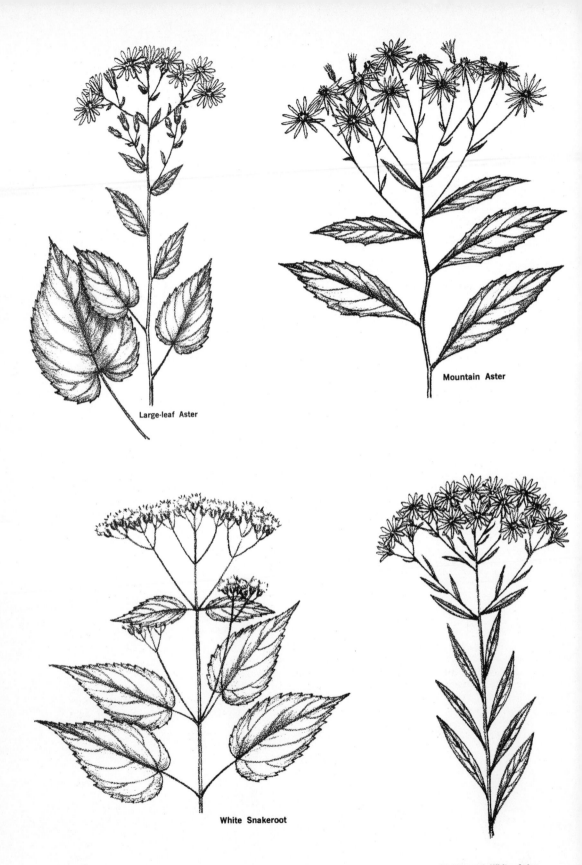

Large-leaf Aster

Mountain Aster

White Snakeroot

Flat-topped White Aster

LARGE-LEAF ASTER *(Aster macrophyllus)*   Composite Family

Very large, thickish, rough, sharply toothed, and heart-shaped basal leaves characterize this aster of the open woodlands. The flower heads have white to lavender or bluish rays, and the branches of the flower cluster have small stalked glands. It blooms from July to September.

RANGE: Que. to Minn. south to Md., n. Ga., n. Ala., Ohio and Ill.

MOUNTAIN ASTER *(Aster acuminatus)*   Composite Family

The Mountain or Whorled Aster has a somewhat zig-zag and minutely downy stem 1 to 3 feet high, branching toward the summit. Its leaves are thin, broadly lance-shaped or elliptic, 3 to 6 inches long, pointed at both ends, and rather coarsely toothed. Those on the upper part of the stem are often so close together that they appear to be whorled. The flower heads are about 1¼ inches across and have 12 to 18 narrow white or purplish-tinged rays. It grows in dry to moist woods and clearings, blooming between July and November.

RANGE: Nfd. to Que. south to N.J., Pa., n. Ga. and Tenn

WHITE SNAKEROOT *(Eupatorium rugosum)*   Composite Family

The White Snakeroot usually has a smoothish and much-branched stem 1 to 4 feet high. The pairs of egg-shaped leaves are 3 to 6 inches long, sharply toothed on the margin, heart-shaped at the base, and have taper-pointed tips. They are rather thin in texture and have slender stalks usually 1 to 2½ inches long. The heads contain from 15 to 30 bright white, tubular flowers and they are arranged in rather dense flat-topped clusters; blooming between July and October. It grows in rich woods, thickets, and clearings. This plant is the principal cause of "milk sickness", which is transmitted to humans through the milk of cattle which have eaten it.

RANGE: N.B. to Sask. south to Va., n. Ga. and Tex.

FLAT-TOPPED WHITE ASTER *(Aster umbellatus)*   Composite Family

This is a rather smooth plant with leafy stems from 1 to 8 feet tall. The leaves are lance-shaped to very narrowly egg-shaped, untoothed, pointed at both ends, up to about 6 inches long, and stalkless or very short-stalked. They are roughish on the upper surface and sometimes downy beneath. Its heads of flowers are ½ to about an inch across, with from 2 to 15 white rays; and are arranged in a broad, flat-topped cluster. It grows in both moist or dry open woodlands, thickets, and meadows; blooming between July and October.

RANGE: Nfd. to Ont. and Minn. south to Ga., Ky., Iowa and Neb.

ENCHANTER'S-NIGHTSHADE *(Circaea lutetiana* var. *canadensis)* Evening-primrose
Family

The Enchanter's-nightshades are woodland plants with opposite, rather long-stalked, wavy-toothed, egg-shaped leaves. The small white flowers are in long and narrow end clusters. They have but 2 petals which are so deeply notched that they appear to be four, and a pair of stamens. The fruits are oval-shaped pods covered with hooked bristles, and they often hitch a ride on one's clothing. This species has leaves from 2 to 4 inches long, rather firm in texture, dark green, and usually rounded at the base; and the stem is 8 inches to 3 feet tall. It blooms between June and August.
RANGE: N.S. to s. Ont. and N.D. south to Ga., Tenn., Mo. and Okla.

BUTTERFLY-PEA *(Clitoria mariana)* Pea Family

The showy, 2-inch long, pale lavender-blue or violet flowers of the Butterfly-pea are really impressive. They owe their beauty, however, to the large, rounded standard which is notched at the tip, for the keel and wing petals are quite short and far from conspicuous. From 1 to 3 such flowers are borne on stalks arising from the axils of the leaves between June and August. Late in the season, small and bud-like flowers are produced; and, although hardly noticeable they form pods with viable seeds. The Butterfly-pea has trailing but seldom climbing stems from 1 to 3 feet in length; and stalked leaves which are divided into 1-to 2-inch egg-shaped or lance-shaped leaflets. It grows in dry open woods, thickets, and pinelands.
RANGE: se. N.Y. to W. Va. and Iowa south to Fla. and Tex.

CANADA LILY *(Lilium canadense)* Lily Family

On a stem 1 to 4 feet tall this lily usually has several nodding, bell-shaped, red to yellow flowers which are spotted with purplish-brown. The 6 perianth parts of its flowers have spreading or slightly recurved tips. It usually has several whorls of lance-shaped leaves with roughish margins. This northern species is often common in wet woods and meadows and is found southward along the mountains. It blooms in June or July. Another name for it is Wild Yellow Lily.
RANGE: N.S. to Que. south to Va., n. Fla. and Ala.

HAIRY RUELLIA *(Ruellia ciliosa)* Acanthus Family

The Hairy Ruellia is a somewhat variable plant. It has a more or less hairy, simple or branched stem 6 inches to 2½ feet tall. The egg-shaped, lance-shaped, or elliptic leaves have short stalks and are 1½ to 4 inches long ;usually being rather crowded toward the tips of the stems. The lavender or lilac-blue flowers are 1 to 2 inches long, the united sepals being prolonged into bristle-like and usually hairy-fringed tips. They are nearly stalkless and several usually occur together in the leaf axils. It grows in dry sandy woods and clearings, blooming between May and September.
RANGE: N.J. to Ind. south to Fla. and Tex.

NORTHERN RED LILY *(Lilium philadelphicum)* Lily Family

Often called the Wood Lily, this species has a stem 1 to about 3 feet tall on which are from 2 to 6 whorls of lance-shaped leaves. At its summit there may be from 1 to 5 flowers which stand upright. Their 6 perianth parts are distinctly stalked, bright orange-red, and purple-spotted. It grows in dry open woods and clearings and southward in mountain meadows and balds, blooming between June and August.
RANGE: Me. to s. Que. and s. Ont. south to Del., n. Ga. and Ky.

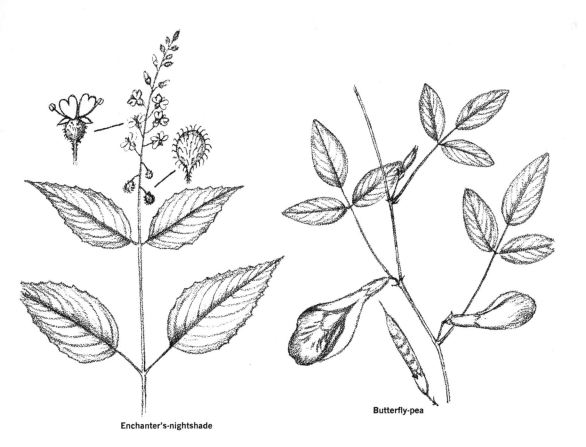

Enchanter's-nightshade

Butterfly-pea

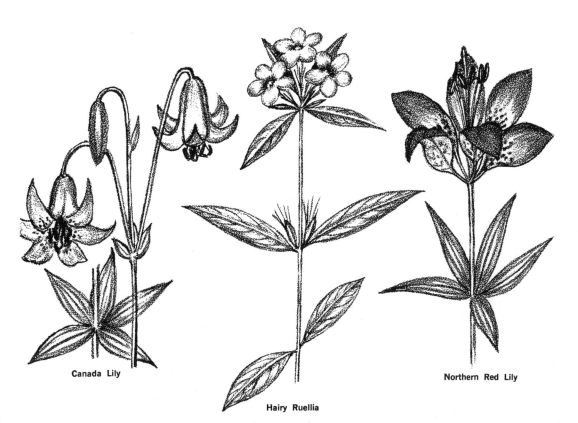

Canada Lily

Hairy Ruellia

Northern Red Lily

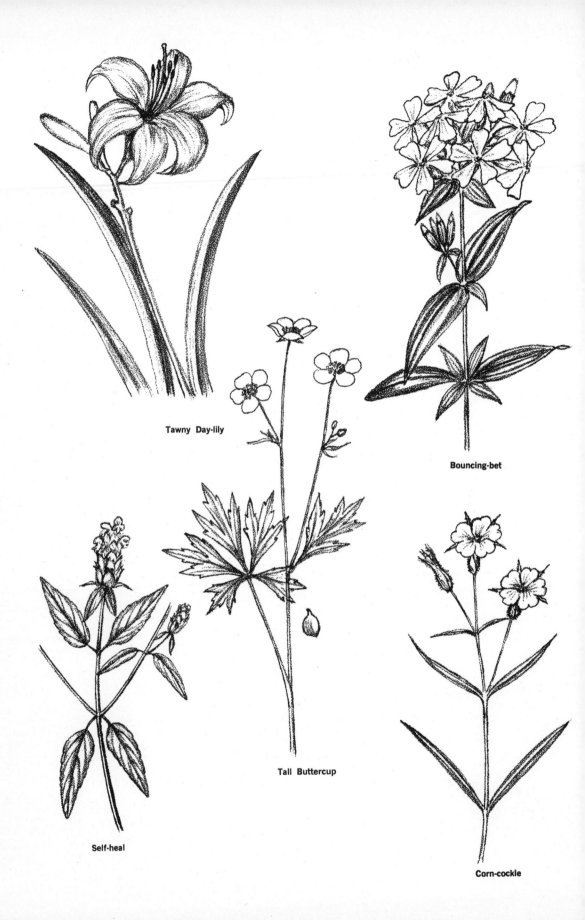

Tawny Day-lily

Bouncing-bet

Tall Buttercup

Self-heal

Corn-cockle

SUMMER FLOWERS OF FIELD AND WAYSIDE

TAWNY DAY-LILY *(Hemerocallis fulva)*   Lily Family

This native of Eurasia long ago escaped from American flower gardens, and it is now so widely naturalized that many think it has always been here. It is often very common along roadsides and in the borders of fields and woods; in fact, it has become a real weed. Unlike the true lilies, the day-lilies have a leafless flower stem which forks repeatedly. Although each flower lasts but a few hours, the plant produces a succession of them from May to about mid-summer. At the base of the plant is a cluster of long, strap-shaped, and channeled leaves. The flowers of this species are quite large and have 6 tawny-orange perianth segments.

TALL BUTTERCUP *(Ranunculus acris)*   Buttercup Family

The Tall Buttercup, which is also known as the Common or Meadow Buttercup, is a native of Europe which is now widely naturalized in America. It is the common and weedy buttercup so often seen in fields and meadows or along roadsides, especially in the northeastern United States and Canada. A branching and usually hairy plant from 2 to 3 feet tall, it has deeply 3- to 5-parted leaves in which the divisions are again cut into narrow and toothed lobes. The basal leaves are long-stalked. It has numerous flowers with 5 bright yellow petals, and it blooms between May and August.

BOUNCING-BET *(Saponaria officinalis)*   Pink Family

The Bouncing-bet is a native of Europe but it is now widely naturalized in America. A weed, but a very pretty one, it is often abundant along roadsides, on railroad beds, and in waste places generally. It is a rather coarse but smooth plant from 1 to 2 feet tall; with pairs of broadly lance-shaped, strongly 3- to 5-ribbed leaves which are 2 to 3 inches long. The pale pink or whitish flowers are grouped in quite dense end clusters, and are produced between July and September. Another name for the plant is Soapwort for its juice makes a lather in water.

SELF-HEAL *(Prunella vulgaris)*   Mint Family

This plant which is also known as Heal-all or Carpenter's-weed, is common everywhere in open places. It is a low plant commonly with several branches and may be but a few inches to nearly 2 feet high. The egg-shaped to lance-shaped leaves are 1 to 4 inches long, slender-stalked, and often have some low teeth on the margin. Its small, bluish to lavender or whitish flowers are in cylindrical-shaped heads; in the axils of large, greenish or purplish-tinged, bristly-fringed bracts and bloom between May and October. The narrow-leaved variety found from Nfd. to Alaska south to se. N.Y., w. N.C., Tenn., Kan., N. Mex., Ariz. and Calif. is believed to be a native plant. The broad-leaved form has evidently been introduced from Europe.

CORN-COCKLE *(Agrostemma githago)*   Pink Family

This plant is another immigrant from the Old World which has become widely naturalized here. It is a quite slender and silky-hairy plant a foot to nearly 3 feet tall, with pairs of narrowly lance-shaped leaves from 2 to 4 inches long. The showy purplish-pink flowers are 1½ to 2½ inches across. It is frequently found along roadsides, in waste places, and in grain fields; blooming between June and September. The small black seeds often become mixed with grain but must be removed before it is ground into flour as they are poisonous.

RED CLOVER *(Trifolium pratense)*   Pea Family

Although introduced from Europe as a forage plant, the Red Clover is now widely naturalized in North America. It is a more or less hairy, usually branched plant, from 6 to about 24 inches tall. The purplish-pink flowers are in dense, roundish to somewhat egg-shaped heads about an inch in diameter, with a pair of leaves at the base. Each of the 3 oval or top-shaped leaflets have toothed margins and have a prominent pale V-shaped spot. It is common in fields, waste places and along roadsides; blooming between April and October.

YELLOW SWEET-CLOVER *(Melilotus officinalis)*   Pea Family

The two sweet-clovers are smooth and branching plants from 3 to 6 feet tall; with numerous, small, flowers arranged in long and narrow clusters arising from the axils of the leaves. They get their name of "sweet-clover" from the sweet-scented, vanilla-like odor the plants give off when they are crushed or dried. Both species are natives of Europe which have become widely naturalized here in America; being found in fields, waste places, and along roadsides. They bloom almost continuously between May and October. This species is distinguished by its yellow flowers. The leaves are divided into 3 narrowly top-shaped leaflets which are toothed on the margin and rounded at the tip.

WHITE SWEET-CLOVER *(Melilotus alba)*   Pea Family

This species is practically identical to the preceding one but it is readily distinguished by its white flowers. The 3 leaflets of its leaves are also notched at the tip. (Not illustrated)

PENNSYLVANIA SMARTWEED *(Polygonum pensylvanicum)*   Buckwheat Family

A number of smartweeds similar to this one are found in eastern North America, but this is one of the most common and widespread species. It grows to a height of 1 to 3 feet, usually branches freely, and has lance-shaped leaves from 2 to 10 inches long. Showy clusters of pink flowers are produced from July until late fall. The gland-tipped hairs on the stalks of the flower cluster help to distinguish it from similar smartweeds.
RANGE: N.S. to N.D. south to Fla. and Tex.

ALSIKE CLOVER *(Trifolium hybridum)*   Pea Family

Often called the Alsatian Clover, this European species is now widely naturalized in fields and along roadsides throughout much of North America. A smooth plant, it has erect or ascending, branched stems often 1 to 2 feet tall. Its flowers are white or pink-tinged but turn brown when old, very fragrant; and in long-stalked, globe-shaped heads about ¾ inch across. The broadly oval to top-shaped leaflets have minutely toothed margins. It blooms between April and October.

WHITE CLOVER *(Trifolium repens)*   Pea Family

This is another immigrant from Europe which is now common in fields, lawns, and along roadsides throughout most of North America. It is a creeping plant with long, smooth, mat-forming stems. The inversely heart-shaped leaflets are minutely toothed on their margins; and the white or pinkish flowers are in globe-shaped, long-stalked heads about ¾ inch in diameter. It blooms between April and October.

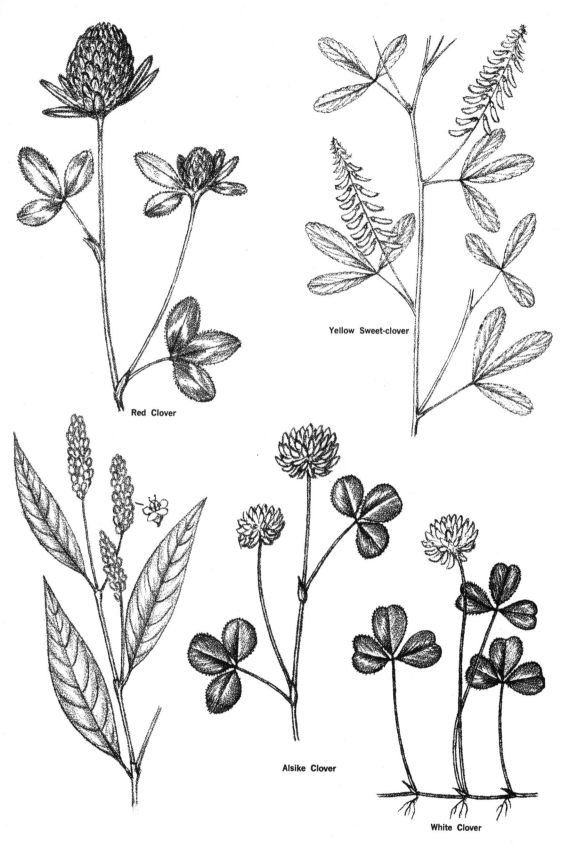

Red Clover

Yellow Sweet-clover

Alsike Clover

White Clover

Pennsylvania Smartweed

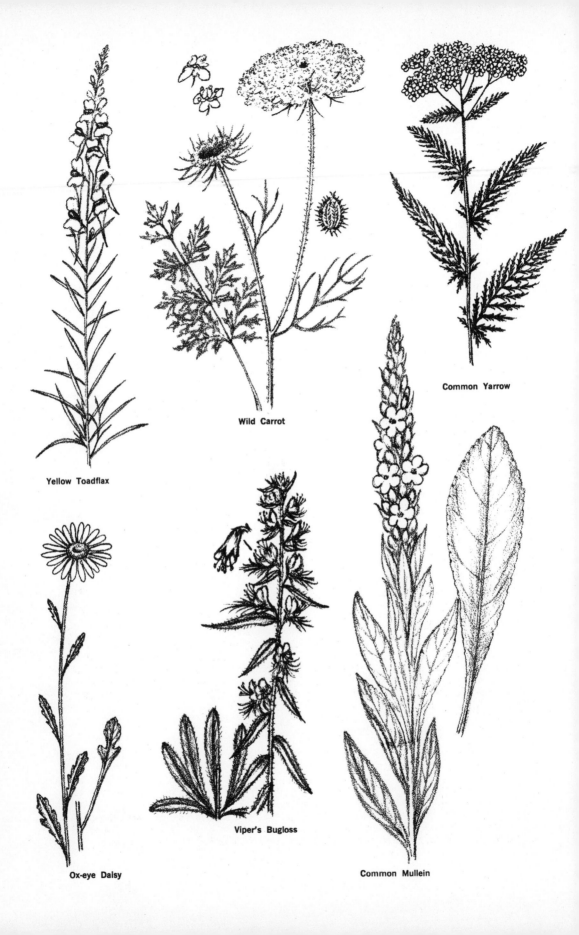

Common Yarrow

Wild Carrot

Yellow Toadflax

Ox-eye Daisy

Viper's Bugloss

Common Mullein

YELLOW TOADFLAX (*Linaria vulgaris*)   Figwort Family

Butter-and-eggs is another name often given this plant, which was originally introduced into this country from Europe as a garden flower. It now grows in fields, waste places, and along roadsides almost everywhere. Usually it has several, smooth, very leafy stems from 1 to 2 feet high, which end in a long cluster of flowers. The scattered leaves are very narrow, stalkless, and ½ to 1½ inches long. The attractive flowers are about an inch long, bright yellow, and have a prominent orange protuberance or palate on the lower lip; as well as a long, slender, and curved spur. The flowering season is between May and October.

WILD CARROT (*Daucus carota*)   Parsley Family

This weedy ancestor of our cultivated carrots is a native of Europe which is now widely naturalized here in North America. It is frequently abundant in old fields, waste places, or along roadsides; blooming between May and September. The plant has a very bristly-hairy stem from 1 to 3 feet tall, and leaves which are pinnately divided and deeply cut into innumerable narrow segments. Its many umbels of small white flowers are disposed into a lacy-looking and flat-topped cluster usually 3 or 4 inches broad, most often with a solitary and deep purple floret in its center. Before the flower cluster is in full bloom, and again as the fruits form, it is hollow and its shape suggests that of a bird's nest. In fact it is often called the Queen Anne's-lace or Bird's-nest.

COMMON YARROW (*Achillea millefolium*)   Composite Family

Often called Milfoil, this European plant is now widely naturalized in old fields, waste places and along roadsides. It is a smoothish to cobwebby plant with a very strong and distinctive odor, with a simple or branched stem 1 to 2 feet tall. The narrowly oblong to lance-shaped leaves are finely dissected into numerous and very slender segments, the lower ones often as much as 10 inches long and tapered at the base into stalks. The numerous small flower heads are arranged in a dense, flat-topped, terminal cluster. Each head has 4 to 6 small white or occasionally pink or purplish rays. It blooms from late April to September or October.

OX-EYE DAISY (*Chrysanthemum leucanthemum*)   Composite Family

This common and well-known plant, often called the White or Field Daisy, is a native of Europe which is now widely naturalized in fields, meadows, waste places and along roadsides. It is a smooth or slightly hairy plant with a simple or sparingly branched stem 1 to 3 feet tall. The basal leaves are top-shaped or spoon-shaped, toothed or often lobed, and rather long-stalked. Those along the stem are narrow, stalkless, toothed or often cut-lobed, and 1 to 3 inches long. The flower heads are 1 to 2 inches across, with 20 to 30 bright white rays and a somewhat flattened yellow disk. It blooms from April to July or August.

VIPER'S BUGLOSS (*Echium vulgare*)   Borage Family

Blueweed is another name for this bristly-hairy European immigrant which is now thoroughly at home here in America. Between June and September, its bright blue, ¾-inch long flowers with their long red stamens are very conspicuous in old fields, waste places, and by the wayside. The plant grows from 1 to 2½ feet tall and has many narrowly oblong or lance-shaped leaves 1 to 6 inches long, the ones on the upper part of the stem being small and stalkless.

COMMON MULLEIN (*Verbascum thapsus*)   Figwort Family

During the first year this plant produces a large rosette of big, grayish-green, flannel-like leaves which are often conspicuous in fields, waste places, and by the wayside. The second year it sends up a wand-like leafy stem from 2 to 7 feet tall, which ends in a dense and cylindrical flower cluster. Stem and leaves alike are densely woolly-hairy; the leaves being elliptical, pointed at both ends, 4 to 12 inches long, and tapering into winged stalks. The flowers are about ¾ inch across, the 5-lobed yellow corolla being almost regular. It blooms between June and September, only a few flowers being open at any time. A native of Europe, it is widely naturalized in America.

GREAT WILLOW-HERB *(Epilobium angustifolium)* Evening-primrose Family

The Great Willow-herb, or Fireweed, is one of some 20 species found in northeastern North America. It is an erect, smooth, leafy-stemmed plant 2 to 6 feet tall; with inch-wide, 4-petalled, bright purple or magenta flowers in a long terminal cluster. The leaves are almost stalkless, willow-like and 2 to 6 inches long. It grows in open woods, clearings, and in burned-over areas; blooming between July and September. The slender pods which follow the flowers contain numerous seeds with a tuft of silky hairs at one end.

RANGE: Lab. to Alaska south to Md., w. N.C., the Great Lakes region, S.D., Ariz. and Calif.

COMMON EVENING-PRIMROSE *(Oenothera biennis)* Evening-primrose Family

This common plant has an erect, stout, more or less hairy, often red-tinged, leafy stem 2 to 6 feet tall. The flowers, which open in the evening and close the following morning, are 1 to 2 inches across; with 4 pale yellow petals atop the long and slender calyx tube. The lance-shaped leaves are stalkless, elliptic or lance-shaped, wavy-toothed on the margin and 1 to 6 inches in length. It grows in dry open places and along roadsides, blooming between June and September.

RANGE: Lab. to Alaska south to Fla. and Tex.

COMMON SUNDROPS *(Oenothera fruticosa)* Evening-primrose Family

This is quite a variable plant and botanists recognize several varieties. As a rule it has erect or ascending and usually branched stems from 1 to 3 feet high which may be hairy or nearly smooth. Its leaves range from narrowly lance-shaped or narrowly egg-shaped to oblong, and the margins may be untoothed or wavy-toothed. They are usually 1 to 4 inches long. The flowers are an inch to 2 inches across and have 4 inversely heart-shaped, bright yellow petals and a slender calyx tube; the ovary being distinctly club-shaped. As the flowers open during the daytime, the name "sundrops" is quite appropriate. It is common in dry to moist open woods, fields, and meadows; blooming between April and August.

RANGE: N.H. to Mich. south to Fla., La. and Okla.

BUTTERFLYWEED *(Asclepias tuberosa)* Milkweed Family

This is the beautiful orange-flowered milkweed so often seen in dry fields, on rocky open slopes, and along the roadside. It is a roughish-hairy plant with reclining, ascending, or even somewhat erect stems 1 to 2 feet high, which usually branch toward the summit. The numerous leaves are lance-shaped or narrowly egg-shaped, stalkless or very short-stalked, 1 to 4 inches long, and usually scattered singly along the stems. The flowers are orange-yellow to orange-red but vary considerably in their brilliance. Although it is a milkweed, the plant does not have a milky juice. It blooms between May and September. Other names for it are Yellow Milkweed and Pleurisy-root.

RANGE: Vt. and Ont. to Minn., Neb. and Colo. south to Fla., Tex. and Ariz.

DOTTED ST. JOHN'S-WORT *(Hypericum punctatum)* St. John's-wort Family

This is a smooth and sparingly-branched plant from 1½ to 3 feet tall, with a crowded flower cluster at the summit. The flowers are about ½ inch across and the 5 yellow petals have several rows of small black dots. The pistil has 5 styles. Its leaves are 1 to 3 inches long, oblong in shape, rounded at the tip, and more or less clasping at the base. They are liberally sprinkled with both translucent and black dots. This is a common plant in open woods, thickets, and fields; blooming between June and September.

RANGE: Que. to Ont. and Minn. south to Fla. and Tex.

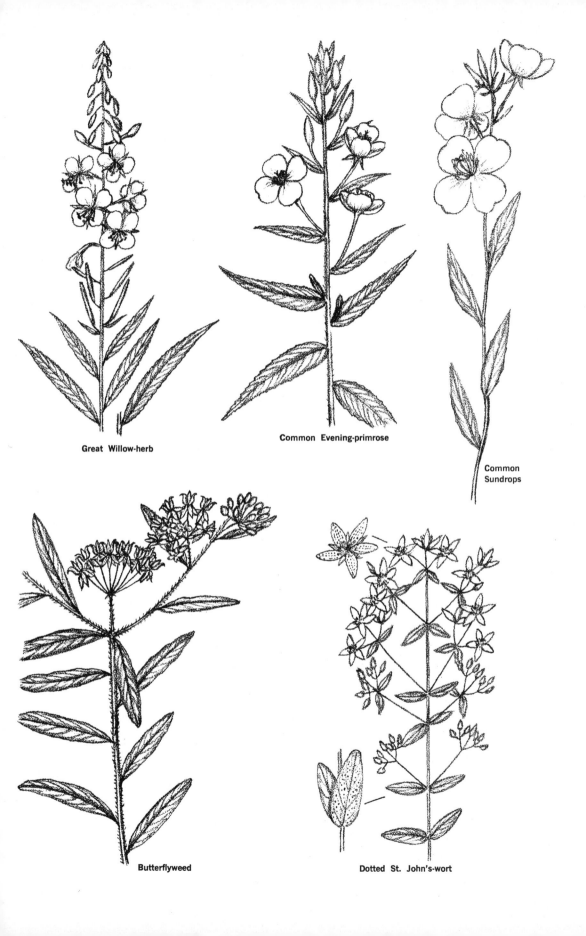

Great Willow-herb

Common Evening-primrose

Common
Sundrops

Butterflyweed

Dotted St. John's-wort

Common Milkweed

Common Thistle

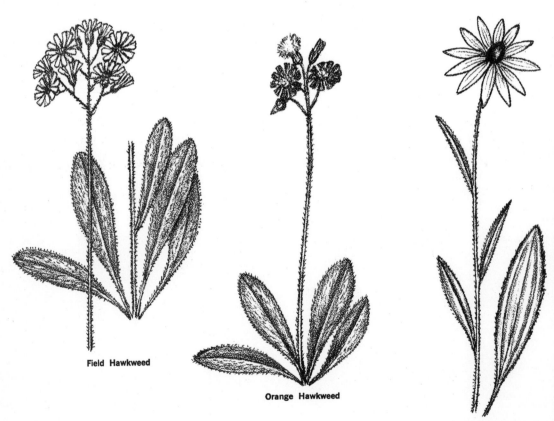

Field Hawkweed

Orange Hawkweed

Black-eyed Susan

COMMON MILKWEED *(Asclepias syriaca)*   Milkweed Family

The Common Milkweed has a stout, usually simple stem from 3 to 5 feet in height. Its paired leaves are oblong or oval, more or less rounded at both ends or abruptly pointed at the tip, softly downy beneath, and from 3 to 8 inches long. The dull lavender to greenish-white flowers are about ⅓ inch long and in rather densely crowded umbels a few inches across. This is our commonest species of milkweed, growing in dry fields, thickets, and along roadsides everywhere. It blooms between June and August.
RANGE: N.B. to Sask. south to Ga., Tenn., Mo. and Kan.

COMMON THISTLE *(Carduus lanceolatus)*   Composite Family

Often called the Bull Thistle, this native of Europe is now widely naturalized in fields, pastures, and along roadsides. It has a stout, branching, leafy stem 3 to 6 feet tall which is more or less wooly and has prickly wings running down from the leaf bases. Its leaves are green above, pale or with a web-like wool beneath, 3 to 6 inches long, and pinnately cut into a number of spiny segments. The flower heads are 1½ to 2 inches across, with numerous purple flowers; and all of the involucral bracts are tipped with a prickle. It blooms between June and October.

FIELD HAWKWEED *(Hieracium pratense)*   Composite Family

Our most common and weedy species of hawkweeds, such as this one, are naturalized immigrants from Europe. The Field Hawkweed, or King-devil, is a hairy plant with a cluster of basal leaves and a simple stem 1 to 2 feet high, which has but 1 or 2 small leaves. The basal leaves are oblong or narrowly top-shaped, 2 to 5 inches long, mostly untoothed, and tapered into winged stalks. The flower heads are borne in a more or less compact terminal cluster and contain a number of yellow-rayed flowers. It is often common in fields, clearings, and along roadsides as far south as w. N.C. and n. Ga.; blooming between May and August. Some of the hairs on the upper part of the stem are blackish.

ORANGE HAWKWEED *(Hieracium aurantiacum)*   Composite Family

Also known as the Devil's-paintbrush, this plant is quite similar to the preceding species, but it has heads of bright orange-red flowers. A very pretty but often extremely troublesome weed, it is also a native of Europe. It and the preceding species often occur together, blooming at the same time.

BLACK-EYED SUSAN *(Rudbeckia hirta)*   Composite Family

Often called the Yellow Daisy, this is one of our best known wild flowers. It grows very commonly in fields, on banks, and along the roadsides; blooming between May and September. A roughish-hairy plant, it has simple or few-branched stems from 1 to 3 feet tall; and lance-shaped or narrowly top-shaped leaves which are 2 to 7 inches long, with untoothed or indistinctly toothed margins. The larger, lower ones taper into rather long stalks. Its flower heads are 2 to 4 inches broad and have from 10 to 20 bright orange-yellow rays; and an egg-shaped disk which is dark purplish-brown.
RANGE: Ont. to Man. south to Fla. and Tex.

VIRGIN'S-BOWER *(Clematis virginiana)*   Buttercup Family

The Virgin's-bower is a vine that commonly climbs over other vegetation on the borders of swamps, along streams, and in moist wayside thickets. Between July and September, it produces numerous, showy clusters of white flowers. Each one is a half to ¾ of an inch broad, with 4 or 5 petal-like sepals and tassel-like stamens. In the autumn the clusters of achenes with their long and plume-like tails are just as attractive as the flowers which preceded them. The opposite leaves are divided into 3 egg-shaped leaflets which have a few sharp teeth on their margins. Like other species of *Clematis*, it climbs by means of its leafstalks which act like tendrils. It can be grown in the garden on a fence or trellis.
    RANGE: N.S. to Man. south to Ga., La., and Kan.

WILD POTATO-VINE *(Ipomea pandurata)*   Morning-glory Family

The slender, smooth or minutely downy trailing or slightly twining stems of this plant arise from an enormous root often weighing as much as 15 to 30 pounds. Its leaves are heart-shaped, 2 to 6 inches long; and often have a purplish midrib, stalks, and margin. The flowers are white with a purple blotch in the center and are about 3 inches across. It grows quite commonly in dry fields, thickets, and along roadsides; blooming between June and September. Another name frequently given it is Man-of-the-earth.
    RANGE: Conn. to Ont. and Mich. south to Fla. and Tex.

COW-PARSNIP *(Heracleum maximum)*   Parsley Family

This is a conspicuous woolly-hairy plant 4 to 8 feet tall, with a stout grooved stem and very large leaves. Between June and August it displays umbels of white or purple-tinged flowers 6 inches to nearly a foot across. Although it has a rank odor the plant is not poisonous. It grows in moist open places and thickets.
    RANGE: Lab. to Alaska south to n. Ga., Tenn., Mo., N. Mex. and Calif.

TALL MEADOW-RUE *(Thalictrum polygamum)*   Buttercup Family

The Tall Meadow-rue has a stout, smooth or somewhat hairy stem 3 to 8 feet tall, with white flowers in rather large clusters at the top. Some of the flowers have only stamens, while others have both pistils and a few stamens. The stamens have club-shaped filaments. Its leaves are large and ternately divided into a number of leaflets which usually have 3 lobes. It is the common tall meadow-rue of moist meadows, thickets, and sunny swamps; flowering between June and August.
    RANGE: Nfd. to Ont. south to Ga. and Tenn.

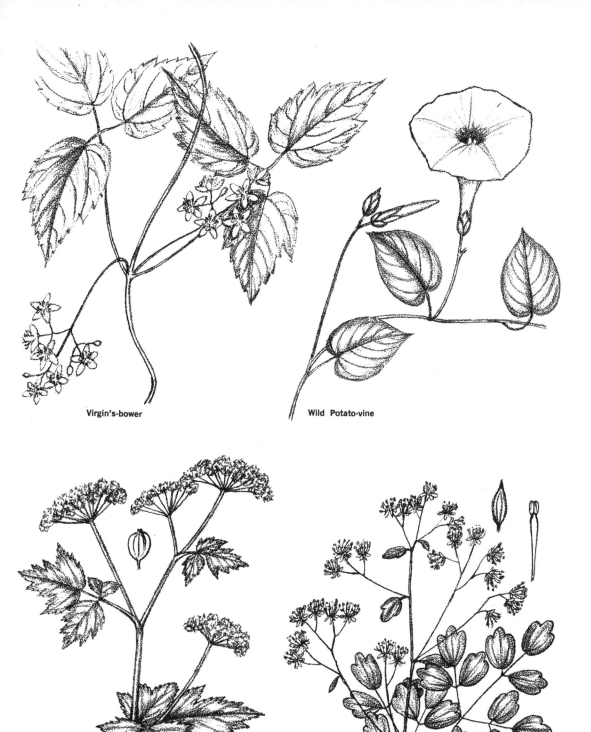

Virgin's-bower

Wild Potato-vine

Cow-parsnip

Tall Meadow-rue

Maypop

Spurred Butterfly-pea

Goat's-rue

**Cat-claw
Sensitive-brier**

MAYPOP *(Passiflora incarnata)*   Passionflower Family

Also known as the Purple Passion-flower, this trailing or climbing vine grows abundantly in open woods, thickets, and dry fields in the South. Its leaves are 3-lobed, toothed on the margin, from 3 to 5 inches wide, and have stalks 1 to 2 inches long with a pair of prominent glands at their summits. The odd-looking lavender flowers are 2 to 3 inches broad and have a very striking fringed "crown". They bloom between May and August and are followed by egg-shaped fruits about 2 inches long. When ripe they are yellowish and edible. Passion-flowers get their name from a fancied resemblance of the flower parts to various implements of the crucifixion.

RANGE: Md. to s. Ohio, Ill., Mo. and Okla. south to Fla. and Tex.

SPURRED BUTTERFLY-PEA *(Centrosema virginianum)*   Pea Family

This is a trailing or climbing plant with minutely rough-hairy stems from 2 to 4 feet in length. It has clusters of from 1 to 4 flowers on stalks which arise from the axils of the leaves. They are violet colored and have a big, broad standard an inch or more across. On its back, and near the base, is a spur-like projection from which the plant gets its name. The leaves are divided into 3 narrowly egg-shaped to lance-shaped leaflets from 1 to 2 inches long. It grows in dry sandy open woods and fields; blooming between June and August.

RANGE: N.J. to Ky. and Ark. south to Fla. and Tex.

GOAT'S-RUE *(Tephrosia virginiana)*   Pea Family

Among the other names given to this plant are Devil's-shoestring, Cat-gut, Wild Sweet-pea, and Dolly Varden. It is quite an attractive, more or less whitish silky-hairy plant with an erect stem 1 to 2 feet tall. The showy flowers are about ¾ inch long. They have a yellow standard petal which is commonly flushed with pink, and a rose-pink keel. The leaves are pinnately divided into from 14 to 28 narrowly oblong leaflets. It grows in dry open woods, thickets, or fields in usually sandy soils; blooming between May and August.

RANGE: Mass. to Ont., Wis. and Okla. south to Fla. and Tex.

CAT-CLAW SENSITIVE-BRIER *(Schrankia nuttallii)*   Pea Family

Sensitive-briers have long, slender, trailing or sprawling stems often 2 to 4 feet in length. They, as well as the leaf stalks and those of the flower clusters—and even the fruit pods —are well-armed with small and hooked prickles. The small pink to rose-purple flowers are in puffy ball-shaped heads which are borne on long stalks arising from the leaf axils. The sensitive leaves are doubly compound, each of the primary leaf divisions being divided again into from 8 to 16 small leaflets. In this species the leaflets show conspicuous veins on the lower surface. It has a densely prickly and narrow pod 2 to 3½ inches long which is short-pointed at the tip. Quite common in dry fields, open woods, and pinelands; it blooms between June and September.

RANGE: Ill., Neb. south to Ala. and Tex.

SMALL-LEAF SENSITIVE-BRIER *(Schrankia microphylla)*   Pea Family

This eastern species is very similar to the preceding one but it has somewhat smaller and narrower leaflets without obvious veins on the lower surface. The slender and prickly pods are 3 to 6 inches long and have long-pointed tips. It grows in dry sandy open woods, thickets, or fields; flowering between June and September.

RANGE: Va. and Ky. south to Fla. and Tex.

251

JIMSONWEED *(Datura stramonium)*   Nightshade Family

Also known as the Thorn-apple and Stramonium, this is a smoothish plant with a stout, forking, widely branched, often purple-tinged stem 1 to 5 feet tall. The rather thin, egg-shaped, irregularly toothed leaves are 3 to 8 inches long. It has trumpet-shaped white, lavender or violet flowers 3 to 4 inches long, with 5 pointed lobes on the corolla rim. The flowers are followed by erect spiny capsules. It is a native of Asia now widely naturalized in fields and waste places, blooming from July to September.

PARTRIDGE-PEA *(Cassia fasciculata)*   Pea Family

Also known as the Golden Cassia or Large-flowered Sensitive-plant, this is a branching plant 1 to 2 feet high. Its leaves are pinnately divided into 10 to 15 pairs of small leaflets which fold together when the leaf is touched. The flowers are 1 to 1½ inches across and have 5 bright yellow petals often with reddish-purple spots at the base. Four of the 10 stamens have yellow anthers and 6 have purple ones. It grows in open thickets, meadows, and along roadsides; blooming between July and September.
RANGE: Mass. to Ont. and Wis. south to Fla. and Tex.

HEDGE BINDWEED *(Conolvulus sepium)*   Morning-glory Family

The Hedge Bindweed has smooth or somewhat hairy, trailing or twining stems up to 10 feet long; and triangular or arrow-shaped leaves from 2 to 5 inches long, the 2 basal lobes being rather short and blunt. The white or pink trumpet-shaped flowers are 2 to 3 inches across, and on long stalks arising from the leaf axils. At the base they have a pair of large, heart-shaped bracts. It is often abundant in fields, thickets, waste places, and along roadsides; blooming between May and September. It is often called the Wild Morning-glory.
RANGE: Nfd. to B.C. south to Fla., Tex. and N.Mex.

COMMON TEASEL *(Dipsacus sylvestris)*   Teasel Family

This native of Europe is widely naturalized in waste places, old fields, and along roadsides in eastern North America. It has a stout prickly stem 3 to 6 feet tall. The pairs of lance-shaped or oblong leaves are 6 to 12 inches long, the upper ones clasping the stem at the base. The flowers are very small, with a tubular lilac or pinkish-purple corolla; and are crowded in an egg-shaped or cylindrical head, intermixed with prickly bristles. It blooms between July and October.

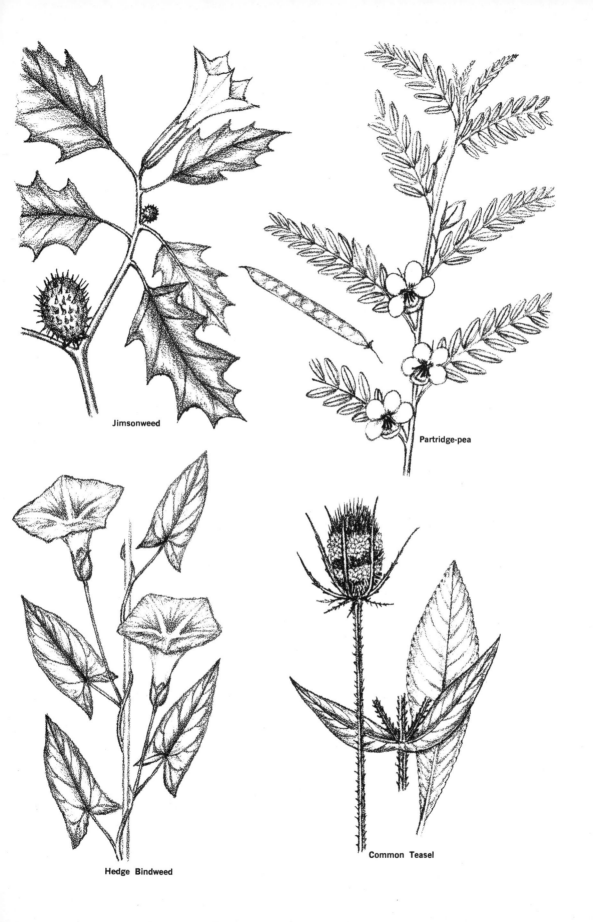

Jimsonweed

Partridge-pea

Hedge Bindweed

Common Teasel

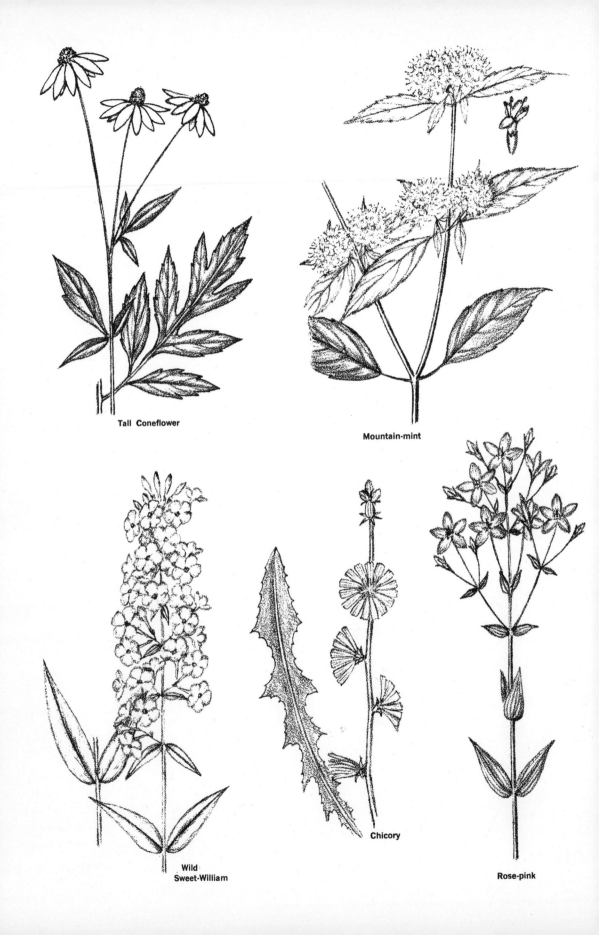

Tall Coneflower

Mountain-mint

Wild
Sweet-William

Chicory

Rose-pink

TALL CONEFLOWER *(Rudbeckia laciniata)*   Composite Family

The Tall Coneflower has a smooth, whitened, and branching stem from 2 to 9 feet high. Its lower leaves are stalked, usually divided into 5 to 7 deeply cut or 3-lobed leaflets, and often a foot wide. Those upward along the stem are often similar but stalkless; or sometimes 3- to 5-parted, or merely toothed. The long-stalked flower heads are quite numerous, 2½ to 4 inches across; with 6 to 10 bright yellow rays and a greenish-yellow, dome-shaped disk. It grows in rich, moist, open woods and thickets; blooming between July and October. A form with more numerous ray flowers is cultivated as the Goldenglow.

RANGE: Que. to Mont. south to Fla., Tex. and Ariz.

MOUNTAIN-MINT *(Pycnanthemum incanum)*   Mint Family

A number of species of mountain-mints occur in the eastern United States, some of them in the coastal region. This wide-spread species is apt to attract attention by the conspicuously whitened leaves or bracts associated with the flower clusters. It is a more or less downy plant with a branching stem 1½ to 3 feet tall. The egg-shaped to broadly lance-shaped leaves are 1½ to 3 inches long, with rather widely spaced marginal teeth. Its flowers, about ¼ inch long, are whitish to rose-pink or purple and have small purple spots. It grows in dry open woods, thickets and field; blooming between June and August.

RANGE: N.H. to Ill. south to Ga. and Miss.

WILD SWEET-WILLIAM *(Phlox maculata)*   Phlox Family

This phlox has fairly smooth and usually purple-spotted stems 1 to 3 feet tall; with 7 or more pairs of lance-shaped or narrowly egg-shaped leaves, rounded at the base, and 2 to 5 inches long. Its flowers are about ⅔ inch across, pinkish-purple or rarely white, and are in narrowly cylindrical end clusters. It grows in moist meadows, bottomlands, and along the banks of streams; blooming between June and September.

RANGE: Conn. and N.Y. to Que. and Minn. south to Md., w. S.C., Tenn. and Mo.

CHICORY *(Chicorium intybus)*   Composite Family

The Chicory, or Succory, is a common but quite pretty weed which also came from Europe. It is now common in fields and along roadsides throughout much of eastern North America except in the Deep South. It is an erect plant often 3 feet or more high, and on its upright and rigid branches it produces a procession of flower heads a bit more than an inch across, their numerous rays being a most beautiful bright blue color. Its flowering season often extends from late May to October. The lower leaves are 3 to 6 inches long, variously toothed, cut, or lobed, and taper into long stalks. Those upward along the stem are smaller and have clasping bases. Some of its varieties are cultivated either as a leafy vegetable or for the roots which are used as a substitute or adulterant for coffee. Endive is a closely related species, *Chicorium endivus*.

ROSE-PINK *(Sabatia angularis)*   Gentian Family

This is our most common and best known species of *Sabatia* for it grows in open woodlands, thickets, meadows and marshes over a wide range. Known also as the Bitterbloom, it has a much branched and sharply 4-angled stem from 1 to about 3 feet tall. The paired leaves are egg-shaped, ¾ to 1½ inches long, and have heart-shaped clasping bases. The numerous flowers are rose-pink, rarely white, about an inch across, with 5 petal-like corolla lobes and a greenish-yellow star-shaped "eye". The branching of the flower cluster is opposite. This is one of our more attractive mid-summer wild flowers. It blooms in July and August.

RANGE: N.Y. and Ont. to Wis. and Mo. south to Fla., La. and Okla.

JOE-PYE-WEED *(Eupatorium fistulosum)*   Composite Family

This species of Joe-Pye-Weed has a rather slender, smoothish, hollow, green to purplish-tinged and often somewhat whitened stem 3 to 10 feet tall. The lance-shaped leaves are in whorls of 4 to 7. They are bluntly toothed and 4 to 12 inches long. There are 5 to 8 tubular, purplish- to lilac-pink flowers in each head; and the heads are arranged in round-topped or dome-like clusters; blooming between July and September. It grows in moist meadows and thickets.
RANGE: Me. to Que., Ill., Iowa and Okla. south to Fla. and Tex.

NEW YORK IRONWEED *(Vernonia noveboracensis)*   Composite Family

The New York Ironweed has a smoothish stem 3 to 6 feet tall; and scattered, lance-shaped, rather finely toothed leaves from 3 to 10 inches long. The numerous heads of deep purple, tubular flowers are in a big flat-topped cluster. Each head contains from 30 to 50 flowers which have a ring of purple or purplish-tinged bristles at the base of the corolla tube. The bracts of the involucre are also purplish and their tips are prolonged into slender and spreading "tails". It grows in moist thickets and fields, and along the banks of streams; blooming between July and September.
RANGE: Mass. to W.Va. and Ohio south to Ga. and Miss.

PEARLY EVERLASTING *(Anaphalis margaritacea)*   Composite Family

This plant gets its common name from the pearly-white involucral bracts of its flower heads. It is a snowy-white, woolly plant with an erect leafy stem 1 to 3 feet tall which branches toward the summit. Its leaves are all very narrow, white-woolly beneath and often also above, 1 to 4 inches long, with the margins rolled inward beneath. The flower heads are close to ½ inch across and contain many tubular flowers. It grows in dry fields and pastures, blooming between July and September.
RANGE: Nfd. to Alaska south to W. Va., Ohio, Wis., S.D., Colo. and Calif.

EARLY GOLDENROD *(Solidago juncea)*   Composite Family

The Early Goldenrod is a quite smooth plant with a rather stout and light green stem from 1 to 4 feet high; branching toward the summit into several ascending, spreading, or recurved flower-bearing branches. Its leaves are quite firm; the lower and basal ones 4 to 12 inches long, broadly lance-shaped to oval, sharply toothed, and tapering into winged and usually hairy-fringed stalks. The upper ones are gradually reduced in size upwards becoming lance-shaped stalkless, and untoothed. It grows in dry and rocky open places, blooming from June to October.
RANGE: N.B. to Sask. south to N.C., Tenn. and Mo.

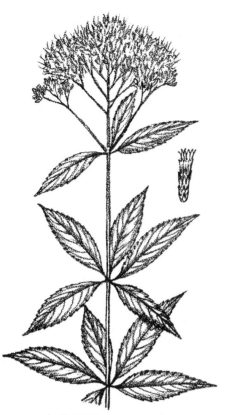

Joe-Pye-weed

New York Ironweed

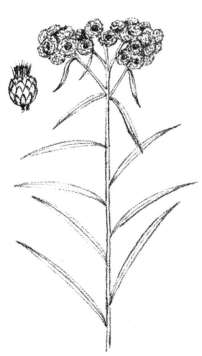

Pearly Everlasting

Early Goldenrod

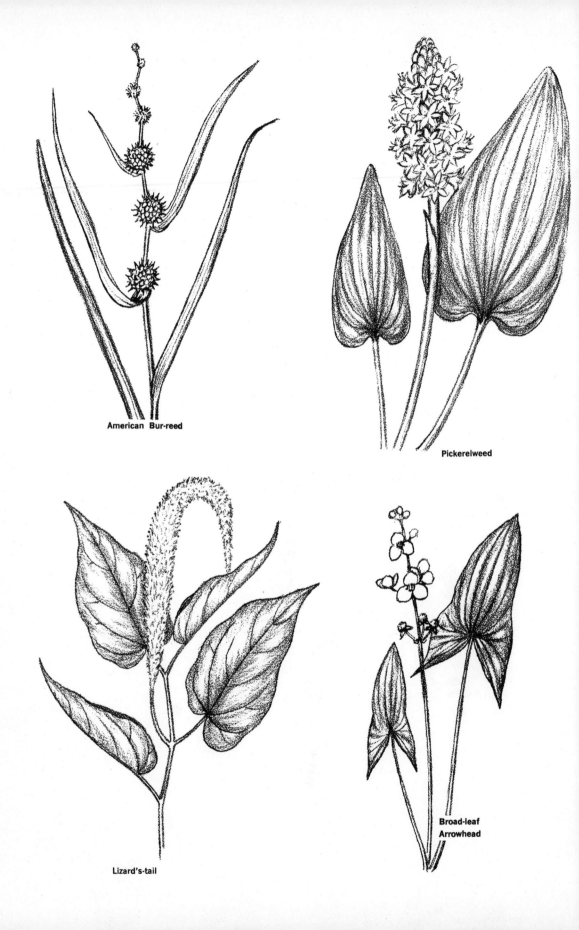

American Bur-reed

Pickerelweed

Lizard's-tail

Broad-leaf
Arrowhead

AMERICAN BUR-REED (*Sparganium americanum*)   Bur-reed Family
This is the most widely distributed species of bur-reed. It is often common on mucky or peaty shores and in the shallow water of marshes. The plants grow from 1 to about 3 feet tall and have ball-like fruit heads from ¾ to about an inch in diameter. It blooms between May and September.
RANGE: Nfd. to Minn. south to Fla. and Mo.

PICKERELWEED (*Pontederia cordata*)   Pickerelweed Family
The bright lavender-blue flowers of this plant may be seen from May to September, or even later in Florida. There are 2 yellow spots on the middle upper lobe of the corolla but these can be seen only at close range. The leaves vary from egg-shaped to lance-shaped and they may have heart-shaped or wedge-shaped bases. It grows quite commonly on muddy shores and in shallow waters.
RANGE: N.S. to Ont. south to Fla. and Tex.

LIZARD'S-TAIL (*Saururus cernuus*)   Lizard's-tail Family
The Lizard's-tail is a plant of swamps and shallow waters. It has heart-shaped leaves 3 to 6 inches long which are scattered along the more or less zig-zag 1½ to 3 foot tall stem. The small, fragrant, white flowers are in a long, slender, tapering, and gracefully drooping cluster; blooming between May and September. The extensively creeping rootstocks are aromatic.
RANGE: Que. and Ont. south to Fla. and Tex.

BROAD-LEAF ARROWHEAD (*Sagittaria latifolia*)   Water-plantain Family
This is the commonest, best known, and most widely distributed of all the arrowheads. The leaves are quite variable in width but are usually arrow-shaped. Its 3-petaled white flowers with clusters of golden stamens are quite attractive and may be seen from June to September. They are subtended by thin papery bracts. Also called Wapato or Duck-potato, the tubers of the plant were a food of the Indian.
RANGE: N.S. to B.C. south throughout most of the U.S.

WATER-PARSNIP *(Sium suave)*   Parsley Family

The Water Parsnip has an erect, branching stem 2 to 6 feet tall which is longitudinally furrowed. Its leaves are pinnately divided into 5 or more very narrow, lance-shaped, sharply and evenly toothed leaflets 1½ to 5 inches long. The lower ones are long-stalked and submersed leaves are often finely dissected. Its small white flowers are in umbels 2 to 4 inches across. It grows in swamps, wet meadows, and on muddy shores; blooming between June and September.
RANGE: Nfd. to B.C. south to Fla., La. and Calif.

WATER-HEMLOCK *(Cicuta maculata)*   Parsley Family

The roots of water hemlocks resemble small sweet-potatoes, have an odor similar to parsnips, and are deadly poisonous. This species, often called the Spotted Cowbane, Musquash-root and Beaver-poison, has a stout erect stem 3 to 6 feet tall which is usually streaked or spotted with purple. The lower leaves are often a foot long and pinnately divided, or redivided, into a number of lance-shaped, sharply toothed leaflets 1 to 5 inches long. The small white flowers are in umbels 2 to 5 inches across. It grows in swamps, wet meadows and thickets; blooming between May and August.
RANGE: N.B. to Man. south to Fla. and Tex.

SWEET-SCENTED WHITE WATERLILY *(Nymphaea odorata)*   Waterlily Family

Both the leaves and the flowers of the white waterlily float on the surface of the water. Its flowers are white or pinkish, fragrant, and from 3 to 5 inches across. Their petals are broadest at or near the middle. The leaves are roundish with a V-shaped notch at the base, usually purplish beneath, and from 4 to 10 inches in diameter. It is quite common in ponds and slowly moving streams, blooming between June and September.
RANGE: Nfd. to Man. south to Fla. and Tex.

YELLOW PONDLILY *(Nuphar advena)*   Waterlily Family

This plant of pond margins, swamps, and slow-moving streams is often called Spatterdock. The flowers and leaves float on the water surface or are raised slightly above it. The leaves are egg-shaped or oval with a deep V-shaped notch at the base, and are 5 to 12 inches long. The bright yellow, globe-shaped flowers are 2 to 3 inches across and produced between April and October.
RANGE: Mass. to Wis. and Neb. s. to Fla. and Tex.

AMERICAN LOTUS *(Nelumbo lutea)*   Waterlily Family

The lotus raises its flowers, and usually its leaves, above the surface of the waters of ponds and slowly moving streams. Its pale yellow flowers are 4 to 8 inches across. The numerous pistils are in pits on the disk-like and elevated receptacle. Later their ovaries become acorn-like fruits which are imbedded on the surface of the disk. The leaves are circular, 1 to 2 feet in diameter, and attached to the leaf stalk in the center. It blooms between July and September. Also called Yellow Lotus and Water-chinquapin.
RANGE: N.Y. and Ont. to Minn. and Iowa south to Fla. and Tex.

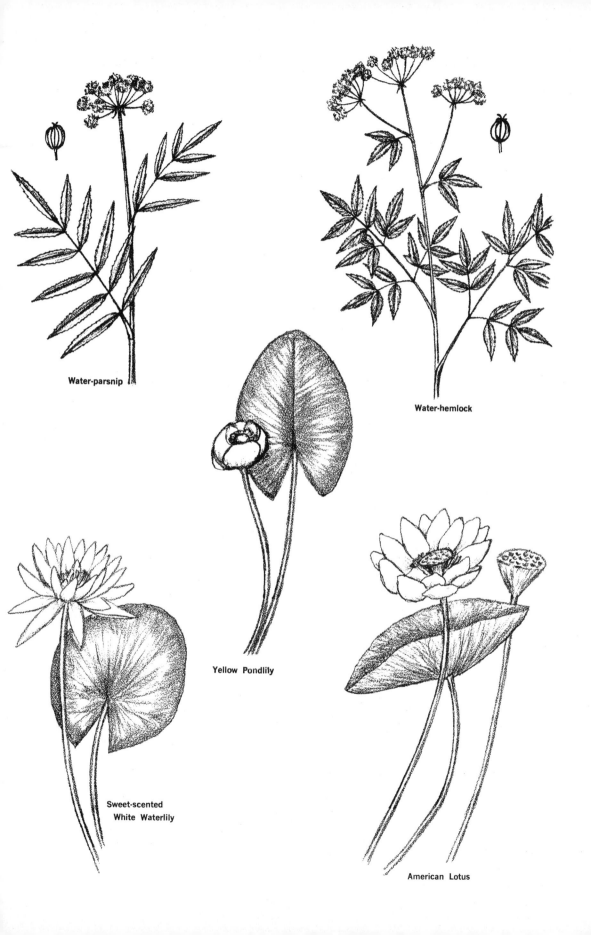

Water-parsnip

Water-hemlock

Yellow Pondlily

Sweet-scented
White Waterlily

American Lotus

American
White Hellebore

Spotted Touch-me-not

Swamp Milkweed

Slender Marsh-pink

AMERICAN WHITE HELLEBORE *(Veratrum veride)*   Lily Family

This is often a common and conspicuous plant in swamps and on moist wooded slopes. It has a stout, leafy, more or less downy stem from 2 to 5 feet tall. The large leaves are broadly elliptic, prominently veined and plaited, and have bases which clasp the stem. They are often mistaken for the leaves of some of the lady's-slipper orchids. A large branched cluster of small, downy, yellowish-green flowers is produced between June and August. It is also known as the False Hellebore and Indian-poke.

RANGE: N.B. to Minn. south to Md., n. Ga. and Tenn.

SPOTTED TOUCH-ME-NOT *(Impatiens capensis)*   Jewelweed Family

This is the smooth, branching, watery-stemmed plant so often met with in moist woods, swamps, and in springy places. It grows from 2 to 5 feet tall and has alternate, thin, elliptic to egg-shaped leaves with coarsely toothed margins. They are from 1½ to about 3½ inches long and are noticeably stalked. The orange flowers are more or less spotted with red, about ¾ inch long, and have a tail-like spur. Usually they are in pairs on slender stalks arising from the leaf axils and are produced continuously between June and September. Other names for it are Jewelweed and Snapweed.

RANGE: Nfd. to Alaska south to Fla., Ala., Ark., and Okla.

PALE TOUCH-ME-NOT *(Impatiens pallida)*   Jewelweed Family

This species is quite similar to the preceding one but somewhat larger and stouter; the canary-yellow to creamy-white flowers being about an inch long, and either unspotted or sparingly spotted with reddish-brown. It is often common in wet or springy woods and in moist, shaded ravines; blooming between July and September. Pale Snapweed or Pale Jewelweed are other names sometimes given to it.

RANGE: Nfd. to Sask. south to Ga., Tenn., Mo., and Kan.

SWAMP MILKWEED *(Asclepias incarnata)*   Milkweed Family

This is another common milkweed and, as its name indicates, it grows in swamps and other wet places. It has a slender and often branched stem from 2 to 4 feet in height; and numerous pairs of leaves which are lance-shaped, taper-pointed, from 3 to 6 inches long and either smooth or downy beneath. They are very short-stalked or practically stalkless. Its flowers are about ¼ inch long, pink or rose-colored, and in many-flowered umbels. The flowering season extends from July to September.

RANGE: N.S. to Man. and Wyo. south to Ga., Tex. and N.Mex.

SLENDER MARSH-PINK *(Sabatia campanulata)*   Gentian Family

The Slender Marsh-pink has pale crimson, pink, or occasionally white flowers about an inch across, with 5 petal-like corolla lobes and a yellow "eye". It is a smooth plant with a very slender stem, or stems, from 1 to 2 feet high; with pairs of often very narrow leaves 1 to 1½ inches long, tapering to the tip from below the middle. The flowers are generally numerous and the flower cluster has alternate branching. It grows in savannahs and wet sandy or boggy places, blooming between June and August.

RANGE: Coast from Mass. south to Fla. and La.; inland from Va. and Ind. south to Ga. and Ala.

VIRGINIA MEADOW-BEAUTY *(Rhexia virginica)*   Meadow-beauty Family

Deergrass is another name often given this attractive plant of bogs and moist, open, sandy places. It is a more or less hairy plant 1 to 2 feet tall, with a simple or branched stem which is 4-sided and has narrow wings. The leaves are oval or egg-shaped, 1 to 2 inches long, and have small bristly teeth on their margins. Its bright purple flowers are an inch or so across and have a glandular-hairy calyx tube. They bloom between May and September.

EASTERN GRASS-OF-PARNASSUS *(Parnassia glauca)*   Saxifrage Family

This is a smooth plant with a basal cluster of roundish leaves which are often slightly heart-shaped at the base, 1 to 2½ inches long, and long-stalked. Like other species of *Parnassia* the solitary flower is on a long stalk on which there is a stalkless leaf between the middle and the base. The flower is 1 to 1½ inches across and has 5 sepals, and 5 broadly oval white petals with greenish veins. There are 5 anther-bearing stamens which alternate with the petals; and 5 sterile stamens (staminodia) with 3 prongs usually shorter than the stamens, and placed at the bases of the petals. It grows in wet meadows and thickets, blooming between July and October.

RANGE: Nfd. to Man. south to Pa., the Great Lakes region, Iowa, and S.D.

GREAT LOBELIA *(Lobelia siphilitica)*   Lobelia Family

Sometimes the Great Lobelia is called the Blue Cardinal-flower. It has a nearly smooth, erect, rather stout, and simple stem from 1 to 3 feet tall. The many leaves are lance-shaped to egg-shaped, stalkless, untoothed or irregularly toothed on the margin, and from 2 to 6 inches long. Its bright blue flowers are about an inch long and often have white marks on the lower corolla lobes. They are borne in the axils of crowded leaf-like bracts toward the summit of the stem; blooming between July and October. It grows in wet or swampy places.

RANGE: Me. to Minn. south to Va., nw. S.C., n. Ala., La. and Tex.

CARDINAL-FLOWER *(Lobelia cardinalis)*   Lobelia Family

Also known as the Red Lobelia, this plant always attracts one's attention by its terminal clusters of brilliant red flowers. Each flower is about 1½ inches long and the tube of stamens projects upward through the cleft in the corolla. It usually has a simple stem from 1 to 3 feet tall. The numerous leaves are 2 to 6 inches long, lance-shaped to narrowly egg-shaped, and are toothed on the margin. It grows in moist meadows, thickets, swamps, and along the banks of streams; blooming between July and October.

RANGE: N.B. to Ont. and Minn. south to Fla. and Tex.

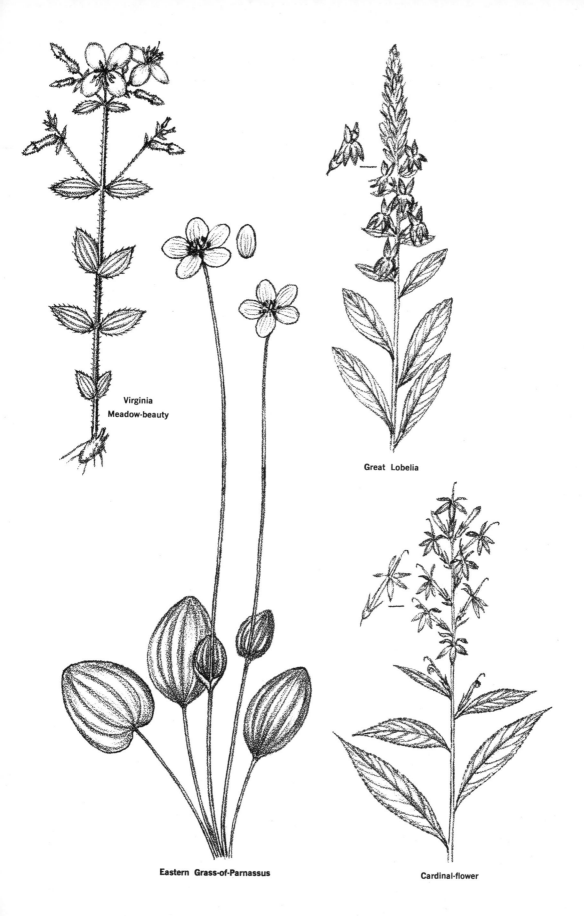

Virginia
Meadow-beauty

Great Lobelia

Eastern Grass-of-Parnassus

Cardinal-flower

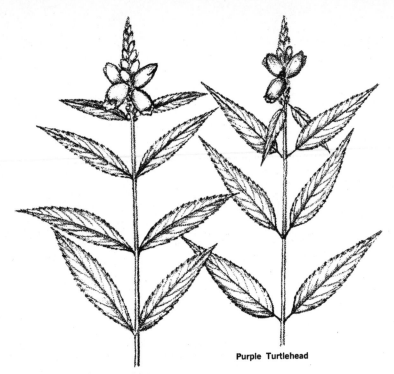

Purple Turtlehead

White Turtlehead

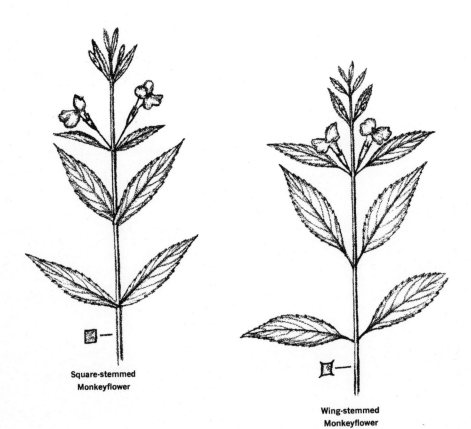

Square-stemmed Monkeyflower

Wing-stemmed Monkeyflower

WHITE TURTLEHEAD *(Chelone glabra)*   Figwort Family

The turtleheads get their name from a fancied resemblance of their flowers to the head of a turtle. Those of this species are about an inch long and usually white, though they are quite often tinged with pink or purple near the tip. It is a smooth plant with a slender erect stem 1 to 3 feet tall; and the opposite leaves are lance-shaped, sharply toothed, stalkless or nearly so, and from 3 to 6 inches long. The flowers of this, and other species, are arranged in narrow but dense end clusters; blooming between August and October. It grows in swamps, along streams, and in other wet places.

RANGE: Nfd. to Ont. and Minn. south to Ga., Ala. and Mo.

PURPLE TURTLEHEAD *(Chelone obliqua)*   Figwort Family

This is also a smooth plant 1 to 2 feet tall; with sharply toothed and rather broadly lance-shaped leaves 2 to 6 inches long. They taper at the base into slender stalks ¼ to ½ inch long. The flowers are about an inch long, deep pink to rose-purple and the lower lip is bearded with yellow hairs. It grows in wet woods and swamps; blooming between August and October.

RANGE: Md. to Tenn. south to Ga. and Miss.; Ind. to s. Minn. south to ark.

SQUARE-STEMMED MONKEYFLOWER *(Mimulus ringens)*   Figwort Family

The monkeyflowers received their name from the fancied resemblance of their 2-lipped corollas to a grinning face. This species is a smooth plant with a branching 4-sided or square stem 1 to 3 feet tall. The lance-shaped to narrowly oblong leaves are 2 to 4 inches long, sharply toothed, and stalkless. Its flowers are about an inch long and have slender stalks usually 1 to 2 inches in length; the corolla being a light violet-blue. It grows in wet meadows, swampy places, and along streams; blooming between June and September.

RANGE: N.S. to Man. south to Ga., La., Tex. and Colo.

WING-STEMMED MONKEYFLOWER *(Mimulus alatus)*   Figwort Family

This species is similar to the preceding one but the 4-sided stems are more or less winged on the angles. Its leaves have very evident stalks and its pale blue-violet or pinkish flowers have stalks which are shorter, or no longer than the leaf stalks. It grows in similar situations, blooming between July and October.

RANGE: Conn. to s. Ont., Iowa and Neb. south to Fla. and Tex.

267

CLIMBING HEMPWEED *(Mikania scandens)*   Composite Family

This plant is quite unusual among our composites as it is a climbing and twining vine, with smoothish stems from 5 to 15 feet long. Its leaves are somewhat triangular, heart-shaped at the base, taper-pointed at the tip, sometimes toothed, 2 to 4 inches long, and have long stalks. The whitish to pale purplish, tubular flowers number about 4 in each head; and they are clustered at the ends of long stalks arising from the leaf axils. It grows in swamps, moist thickets, and along the banks of streams; blooming between July and October.

RANGE: Me. to N.Y. and Ont. south to Fla. and Tex.

TURK'S-CAP LILY *(Lilium superbum)*   Lily Family

The showy Turk's-cap is the tallest of our native lilies, being from 3 to about 5 feet in height. Along its stem are several whorls of leaves and some scattered ones near the summit. They are broadest about the middle and pointed at both ends. Between June and August the plants produce anywhere from a few to as many as 40 handsome flowers. These are orange-red thickly spotted with purple and the 6 perianth parts are curved backward so their tips often touch. It grows in wet meadows and moist woods, southward chiefly in the mountains.

RANGE: Mass. to Ind. south to N. Fla. and Ala.

SWAMP ROSE-MALLOW *(Hibiscus moscheutos)*   Mallow Family

Between June and September, this plant of marshes and wet spots produces a succession of showy flowers along its 4- to 7-foot tall stem. They are 4- to 6-inches across and their white or creamy white petals have purplish or dark crimson bases. The flower stalks are united for part of their length with the leaf stalks, thus appearing to grow out of the latter. Its leaves are 3 to 8 inches long, narrowly egg-shaped or lance-shaped, and toothed on the margin. It is also known as the Mallow-rose and Wild-cotton.

RANGE: Md. and W.Va. to Ohio and Ind. south to Fla. and Ala.

FALSE DRAGONHEAD *(Dracocephalum virginianum)*   Mint Family

This plant has a smooth, erect, often branching stem 1 to 4 feet tall; with sharply-toothed lance-shaped leaves 1½ to 5 inches long. The pale purple or rose flowers are about an inch long, and borne in showy terminal spikes. The corolla is swollen at the throat, the upper lip being domed and the lower one spreading and 3-lobed. It is often called the Obedient-plant as the flowers tend to stay put when bent from their normal position. It grows in wet meadows, bogs, and along streams; blooming July to October.

RANGE: Que. to Minn. south to Fla. and La.

Climbing Hempweed

Turk's-cap Lily

Swamp Rose-mallow

False-dragonhead

Common Sneezeweed

Purple-stemmed Aster

Larger Bur-marigold

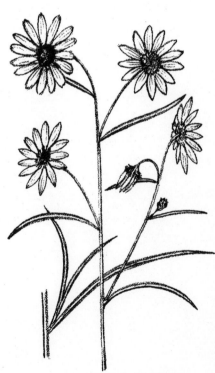

Narrow-leaf Sunflower

COMMON SNEEZEWEED *(Helenium autumnale)* Composite Family

The conspicuously wing-angled stem of this plant is 2 to 6 feet tall and branches toward the summit. Its narrowly oblong to lance-shaped leaves are stalkless, usually toothed, and 2 to 5 inches long. The usually numerous flower heads are 1 to 2 inches across; with from 10 to 18 drooping bright yellow rays which are 3-lobed at the summit, and a large ball-shaped yellowish disk. It grows in swamps, wet meadows and thickets; blooming in September and October.

RANGE: Que. to Minn. and Neb. south to Fla., Tex. and Ariz.

PURPLE-STEMMED ASTER *(Aster puniceus)* Composite Family

This is another common but variable aster. It usually has a stout stem which is reddish- or purplish-tinged, often rough-hairy, much-branched, and from 3 to 8 feet high. The leaves are more or less lance-shaped, sharply toothed, tapering gradually both to the tip and to the somewhat "eared" and clasping base. Those on the main part of the stem are 3 to 6 inches long, and they may be quite smooth or roughish-hairy. The flower heads are almost an inch across and have from 20 to 40 lilac, blue-violet, pinkish, or even whitish rays. It grows quite abundantly in moist meadows, thickets, and in swampy places; blooming between August and October. Also known as the Red-stalked Aster and Early Purple Aster.

RANGE: Nfd. to Man. south to Ga., Ala., Tenn. and Iowa.

LARGER BUR-MARIGOLD *(Bidens laevis)* Composite Family

Also known as the Smooth Bur-marigold, this species is a smooth plant with a branching stem 1 to 3 feet high; and lance-shaped, toothed leaves 3 to 8 inches long. Its flower heads are much more showy than those of the preceding species, 1 to 1½ inches across, with 8 to 10 rather large and bright yellow rays. It grows in swamps, wet meadows, or along streams; blooming between September and November.

RANGE: N.H. to W.Va. and Ind. south to Fla. and Mex.

NARROW-LEAF SUNFLOWER *(Helianthus angustifolius)* Composite Family

This sunflower of the wet pinelands and swampy thickets has a slender stem 2 to 6 feet tall. It may be simple or branched above and is more or less rough, at least on the lower part. Its leaves are all very narrow, stiff, rough, untoothed, stalkless, 2 to 7 inches long, and often have clusters of smaller leaves in their axils. The flower heads are 2 to 3 inches across, with a dark purplish-brown disk and from 12 to 20 bright yellow rays. It blooms between July and October.

RANGE: se. N.Y. to s. Ind. and Mo. south to Fla. and Tex.

271

SUMMER AND FALL COASTAL PLAIN SPECIALTIES

LANCE-LEAF SABATIA *(Sabatia difformis)*　　　　　Gentian Family

This is a smooth plant with a somewhat 4-angled and slender stem from 1 to about 3 feet tall. On it are pairs of narrowly lance-shaped leaves 1 to 2 inches long. Its flowers are white, ¾ to an inch across, and have 5 petal-like corolla lobes. They are quite numerous and arranged in a terminal flower cluster which has opposite, or forking branches. It is often exceedingly abundant in the wet coastal plain pinelands and savannahs, blooming between July and September.

RANGE: N.J. south to Fla.

LARGE MARSH-PINK *(Sabatia dodecandra)*　　　　　Gentian Family

Also known as the Sea-pink, this plant has attractive flowers 1½ to 2½ inches across, usually pink but sometimes white with a bright yellow "eye", and from 8 to 12 petal-like corolla lobes. They bloom between July and September. The plant has a simple or sparingly branched stem 1 to 2 feet high, on which are pairs of lance-shaped or narrower leaves and the terminal flowers. The basal leaves are larger, 1½ to 3 inches long, and are rather spoon-shaped. It grows on the sandy borders of pools and in brackish or salt marshes, blooming between June and August.

RANGE: Conn. south to Fla. and west to La.

SOUTHERN RED LILY *(Lilium catesbaei)*　　　　　Lily Family

This beautiful lily grows in the wet pinelands and savannahs of the southeastern coastal plain. It is 1 to 2 feet tall and along the stem are small, scattered, lance-shaped leaves which point upward. Between July and September each stem bears a solitary flower in which the 6 perianth parts have long and slender stalks. Their blades are yellow toward the base but bright scarlet above, thickly spotted with purple, and the long-pointed tips curve gracefully outward. Also called the Pine Lily, Leopard Lily, and Catesby's Lily. It was named for Mark Catesby (1679-1749), one of the earliest southern naturalists.

RANGE: Va. south to Fla. and west to La.

SAVANNAH MEADOW-BEAUTY *(Rhexia alifanus)*　　　　Meadow-beauty Family

This, the largest and certainly the most beautiful of our meadow-beauties, is often abundant in the wetter coastal plain pinelands and savannahs of the Southeast. There it blooms between May and September. It is a smooth plant, more or less whitened by a waxy bloom, with roundish, slender, simple or sparingly branched stems from 1 to about 3 feet tall. The pairs of 1- to 3-inch lance-shaped leaves point upward. Its flowers are a bright rose-purple, about 2 inches across, and have a calyx tube bristling with reddish glandular hairs.

RANGE: e. N.C. south to Fla. and west to La.

GREEN-FLY ORCHID *(Epidendrum conopseum)*　　　　　Orchid Family

This is the only epiphytic orchid to be found north of Florida. It grows on the trunks or branches of live oaks and other trees, along with the Spanish-moss and the resurrection fern. The plant has a bulb-like base and thick roots which serve as holdfasts; and a basal cluster of thickish, leathery, narrow leaves up to 3 inches in length. The flowers are about ¾ inch across, greenish or tinged with purple, and have a delicate fragrance. Several are borne in a cluster on a stalk from 2 to 8 inches long, between July and September.

RANGE: se. N.C. south to Fla. west to La., near the coast.

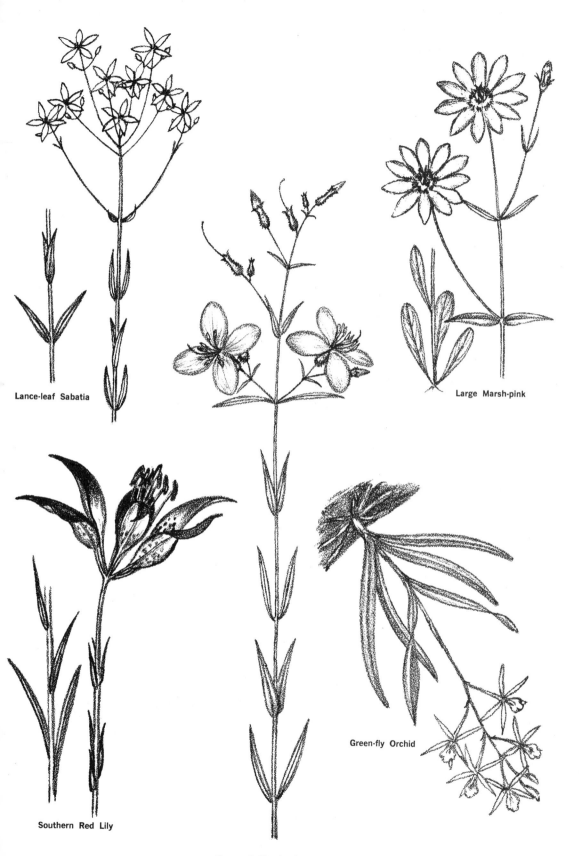

Lance-leaf Sabatia

Large Marsh-pink

Southern Red Lily

Green-fly Orchid

Savannah Meadow-beauty

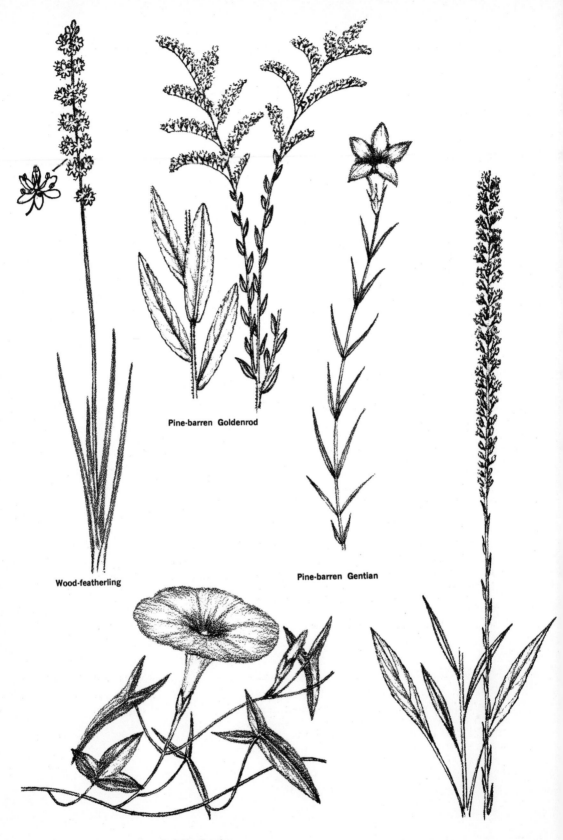

Wood-featherling

Pine-barren Goldenrod

Pine-barren Gentian

Arrow-leaf Morning-glory

Wand-like Goldenrod

WOOD-FEATHERLING *(Tofieldia racemosa)* Lily Family

In June or July the flowers of this plant often whiten the wet pinelands and savannahs of the southeastern coastal plain. The long, narrow, grass-like leaves are all at the base of the plant. Its flower stalk is from 1 to 2 feet tall and bears a long, narrow, more or less interrupted cluster of small white flowers. Both the upper part of the flower stalk and the pedicels of the individual flowers are roughened by minute glandular hairs.
RANGE: N.J. south to Fla. and west to Tex.

PINE-BARREN GOLDENROD *(Solidago fistulosa)* Composite Family

This goldenrod has a rather stout, simple or branched stem 2 to 6 feet tall; with numerous, ascending, broadly lance-shaped or oblong leaves which are stalkless and have clasping bases. The lower ones are 1 to 4 inches long, broad at base, and sparingly toothed; the upper ones smaller and untoothed. Its small heads of flowers are in a terminal cluster which has several arching or spreading branches. It grows in low, moist, coastal plain pinelands; blooming between August and October or later.
RANGE: N.J. south to Fla.

PINE-BARREN GENTIAN *(Gentiana autumnalis)* Gentian Family

This is a distinctive plant which has a solitary flower at the tip of a slender, simple or few-forked stem 6 to 18 inches tall. Along the stem are a number of pairs of rather thick and very narrow leaves from 1 to 2 inches in length. The flower has an almost lily-like, funnel-shaped corolla about 2 inches long, which is bright indigo-blue or rarely lilac or whitish, and is often spotted with greenish or brown within. The corolla lobes are much longer than the small fringed lobes between them. It grows in savannahs and moist, sandy coastal plain pinelands; blooming from September to early December. It is also known as the One-flowered Gentian.
RANGE: N.J. south to S.C.

ARROW-LEAF MORNING-GLORY *(Ipomea sagittata)* Morning-glory Family

This native morning-glory has attractive rosy-pink flowers about 3 inches across. Its leaves are quite variable but most often arrow-shaped with the 2 basal lobes pointing outward, and usually 1½ to 3 inches long. It creeps over the ground or climbs in bushes on the borders of coastal sand dunes, swamps, and marshes; blooming between July and September.
RANGE: e. N.C. south to Fla. and west to Tex.

WAND-LIKE GOLDENROD *(Solidago stricta)* Composite Family

This unique goldenrod is a smooth plant with a simple, slender, wand-like stem 2 to 8 feet tall; along which are numerous small, narrow, erect leaves. The basal leaves are lance-shaped or broadest near the tip, inconspicuously toothed, stalked and 3 to 8 inches long. It grows in wet coastal plain pinelands, meadows and savannahs; blooming in September or October.
RANGE: N.J. south to Fla. and west to Tex.

HAIRY TRILISA *(Trilisa paniculata)*   Composite Family

This is a common and conspicuous plant in the low, wet cosatal plain pinelands which blooms from August to October. It has a stiffly erect, sticky-hairy stem from 1 to 2 feet tall along which are numerous, scattered, small, lance-shaped leaves which tend to stand erect. The basal leaves are either lance-shaped or narrowly oblong and from 3 to 10 inches in length. Its numerous ¼ inch heads of tubular, rose purple flowers are arranged in a narrowly cylindrical cluster along the upper portion of the stem.
RANGE: N.C. south to Fla. and west to La.

CATESBY'S GENTIAN *(Gentiana catesbaei)*   Gentian Family

This gentian of the wet coastal plain pinelands and savannahs is readily identified by its bell-shaped, deep blue or violet-purple flowers which are about 2 inches long. It has a simple or sparingly branched stem 8 inches to 2 feet tall, with pairs of egg-shaped or lance-shaped leaves 1 to 2½ inches in length. It blooms from September to November.
RANGE: Del. south to Fla.

SANDHILL BLAZING-STAR *(Liatris secunda)*   Composite Family

This species and the similar *Liatris pauciflora* are unique blazing-stars of dry coastal plain pinelands and sand-hills in the Southeast. Both have narrowly cylindrical heads about ¾ inch long which are all turned to the upper side of the arching stems; the heads having relatively few but large flowers. The plants are 1 to 2½ feet high and have narrow leaves. *Liatris secunda* has downy stems while those of *Liatris pauciflora* are smooth. The former ranges from N.C. south to Fla. and west to Ala.; the latter, from Ga. south to Fla.

LOW PINE-BARREN MILKWORT *(Polygala ramosa)*   Milkwort Family

This plant is very conspicuous in the low, wet, coastal plain pinelands when it blooms between June and September. It has a smooth, erect stem, or stems, from 6 to about 16 inches high, along which are numerous small and narrow leaves. At the top it has a flat-topped cluster of small sulfur-yellow flowers which may be from 3 to 6 inches across. At the base of the plant there is a rosette of broader, top-shaped leaves up to about an inch in length.
RANGE: Del. south to Fla. and west to La.

VANILLA-LEAF *(Trilisa odoratissima)*   Composite Family

Unlike the Hairy Trilisa, this is a smooth plant with an erect stem 2 to 3 feet tall, along which are scattered small leaves. The basal ones are smooth, thickish, usually broader above the middle but rather narrow, and from 4 to 10 inches long. When bruised they emit a characteristic vanilla-like odor. The numerous heads of small, tubular, rose-purple flowers are in a rather flat-topped terminal cluster. It grows in dry to wet coastal plain pinelands; blooming from August to October. Also known as Deer's-tongue, Hound's-tongue, and Carolina-vanilla; large quantities of its leaves are used in the flavoring of tobacco.
RANGE: N.C. south to Fla. and west to La.

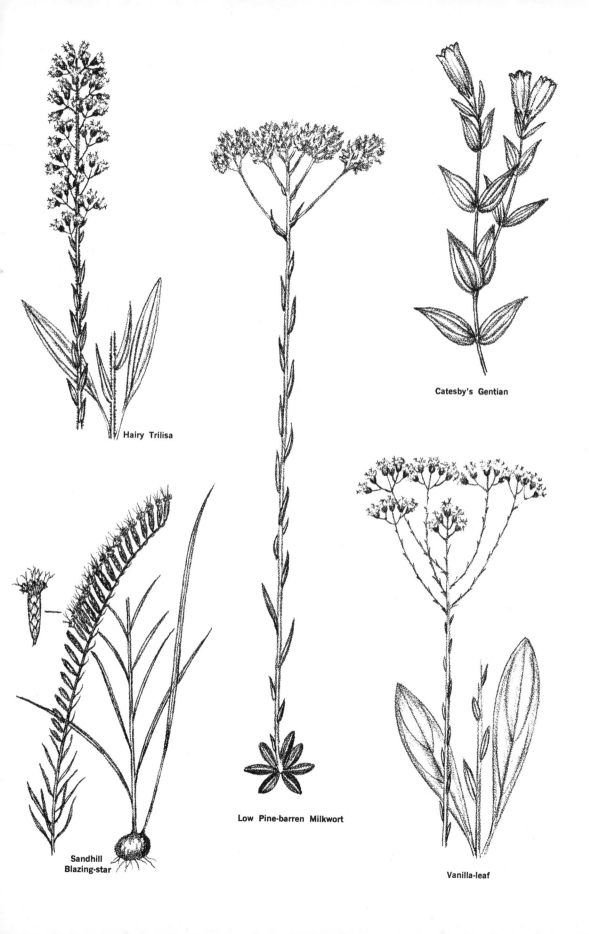

Hairy Trilisa

Catesby's Gentian

Sandhill
Blazing-star

Low Pine-barren Milkwort

Vanilla-leaf

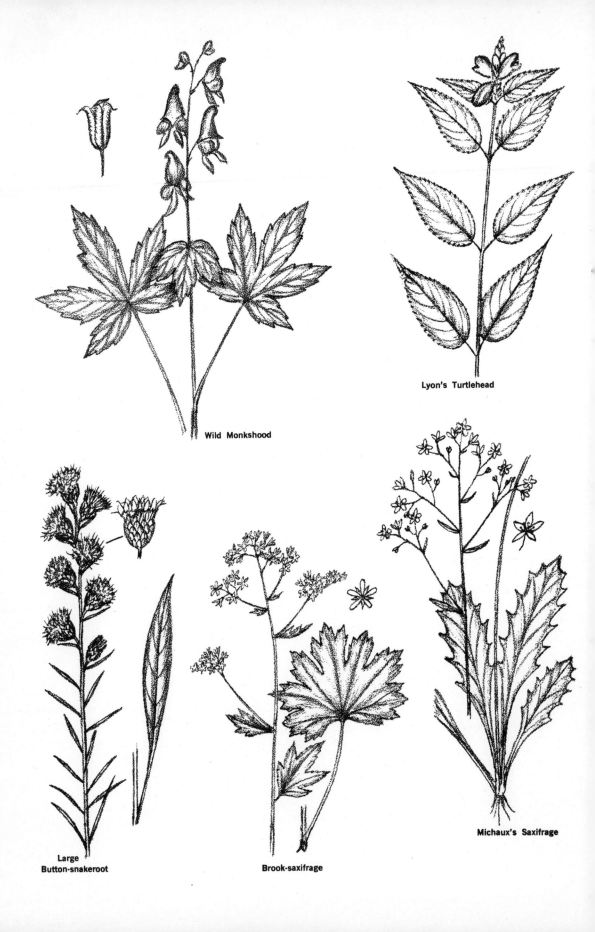

Wild Monkshood

Lyon's Turtlehead

Large
Button-snakeroot

Brook-saxifrage

Michaux's Saxifrage

WILD MONKSHOOD *(Aconitum uncinatum)*   Buttercup Family

The Wild Monkshood has a slender, leafy, rather weak, branching stem from 2 to about 3 feet tall; with violet-blue flowers clustered at the ends of the branches. The flowers are about 1 inch across and have a bilateral symmetry. They have 5 very irregular, petal-like sepals, the upper one being much larger and shaped like a hood or helmet. The petals are small and inconspicuous, 2 of them being covered by the hooded sepal. The leaves are deeply divided into from 3 to 5 cut-toothed lobes and they, like the rest of the plant, are smooth or nearly so. The Wild Monkshood is also known as the Wild Wolfsbane. It grows in moist woods, thickets, and on rocky slopes; blooming between August and October.

RANGE: Pa. to Ind. south to Ga. and Ala.

LYON'S TURTLEHEAD *(Chelone lyoni)*   Figwort Family

This turtlehead can be distinguished by its egg-shaped leaves which are 3 to 7 inches long, rounded at the base, taper-pointed at the tip, sharply toothed, and have slender stalks up to 1½ inches long. Its flowers are about an inch long, deep pink to rose-purple; the corolla having a sharp ridge on its back and a lower lip bearded with deep yellow hairs. It grows in wet woods and along streams in the southern mountains; blooming between July and September.

RANGE: Va. south to w. N.C., nw. S.C. and e. Tenn.

LARGE BUTTON-SNAKEROOT *(Liatris scariosa)*   Composite Family

This beautiful blazing-star has flower heads which are bowl-shaped, up to an inch across, and contain from 25 to 60 flowers. Its stem is from 1 to 5 feet tall, finely downy at least above, and the leaves are hairy and often roughish. The basal ones vary from lance-shaped to slenderly top-shaped, up to a foot long, and ½ to 2 inches broad. It grows in dry woods and clearings chiefly in the mounain region.

RANGE: Pa. and W.Va. south to Ga. and Miss.

BROOK-SAXIFRAGE *(Boykinia aconitifolia)*   Saxifrage Family

The Brook-saxifrage is a rather stout-stemmed, erect plant from 1 to 2 feet tall. Most of its leaves are basal and they, as well as the ones on the lower part of the stem, are 5- to 7-lobed, cut-toothed, and long-stalked. Both the stem and the leaf stalks are glandular-hairy. The small flowers clustered at the upper part of the stem have 5 white petals and 5 stamens. It grows in rich woods, on wet rocks, and along the banks of streams, chiefly in the mountains. The flowering season is during June and July. Another name often given it is Aconite-saxifrage, due to the resemblance of its leaves to those of the monkshoods.

RANGE: Va., W.Va., and Ky. south to Ga. and Ala.

MICHAUX'S SAXIFRAGE *(Saxifraga michauxii)*   Saxifrage Family

Michaux's Saxifrage grows in crevices on the face of rocky cliffs and on sunny, wet rocks in the southern Appalachians. In typical saxifrage fashion, it has a sticky-hairy flower stalk from 6 to about 20 inches tall with a rosette-like cluster of leaves at the base. Its leaves are narrowly top-shaped, from 3 to 7 inches long, and have coarse, sharp teeth on their margins. Among saxifrages, the flowers of this one are unusual in that the white petals are not all alike. There are 3 large ones which are heart-shaped at the base and have a pair of yellow spots, and 2 smaller ones which have tapering bases and no spots. It blooms between June and August.

RANGE: Western Va. and W.Va. south to n. Ga. and e. Tenn.

LATE SUMMER AND FALL FLOWERS OF THE WOODLANDS

BLUE-STEMMED GOLDENROD *(Solidago caesia)*   Composite Family

The Blue-stemmed or Wreath Goldenrod has slender, smooth, roundish stems 1 to 3 feet high, which are commonly purplish and usually coated with a whitish bloom. It has narrowly oblong or lance-shaped leaves which are stalkless, narrowed at both ends, sharply toothed, and 2 to 5 inches long. Its heads of flowers are in the axils of the leaves, blooming during September and October. It grows chiefly on wooded slopes or banks.

RANGE: N.S. to Ont. and Wis. south to Fla. and Tex.

WHITE-LETTUCE *(Prenanthes alba)*   Composite Family

Also called Rattlesnake-root, this is a smooth whitened plant, usually with a purplish stem 2 to 5 feet tall. Its leaves are variable but commonly egg-shaped, heart-shaped or triangular; and coarsely toothed, lobed or divided. Most of them are stalked and the lower ones may be as much as 8 inches long. The usually numerous flower heads are in an open cluster. They contain 8 or more whitish flowers with a cinnamon-brown pappus, and the purplish involucre is whitened with a bloom. It grows on wooded slopes and roadbanks; blooming from August to October.

RANGE: Me. to Que. and Sask. south to N.C., Tenn. and Mo.

BROAD-LEAF GOLDENROD *(Solidago flexicaulis)*   Composite Family

This is a well-marked goldenrod with a slender, zig-zag, somewhat angled green stem 1 to 3 feet high. The broad, egg-shaped, sharply toothed leaves are 2 to 7 inches long and are pointed at the tip and abruptly narrowed into winged stalks. Its heads of flowers are also clustered in the axils of the leaves, blooming between late August and October. It grows in rich woods and in ravines. Some know it as the Zig-zag Goldenrod.

RANGE: N.S. to N.D. south to Ga., Tenn. and Kan.

WHITE GOLDENROD *(Solidago bicolor)*   Composite Family

Silver-rod is another name often given to this pale-flowered goldenrod, the short outer rays of the heads being white or cream-colored. It is a grayish-downy plant up to 2 feet tall. The basal leaves are stalked, top-shaped, shallowly toothed, and 2 to 4 inches long. Those of the stem gradually decrease in size upward and are stalkless. It grows in dry open woods, thickets, and on slopes; blooming during September and October.

RANGE: N.B. to Ont. south to Ga. and Ark.

WHITE WOOD ASTER *(Aster divaricatus)*   Composite Family

This aster grows in dry open woods and clearings, blooming from August to October. It has a slender, often zig-zag, smoothish stem 1½ to 2½ feet tall. The thin heart-shaped leaves are smooth or sparingly hairy, mostly stalked, and at least the lower ones are very coarsely but sharply toothed. The flower heads are almost an inch across. They have from 6 to 10 white rays and the disk flowers soon become brownish.

RANGE: Me. to Ohio south to Ga., Ala. and Tenn.

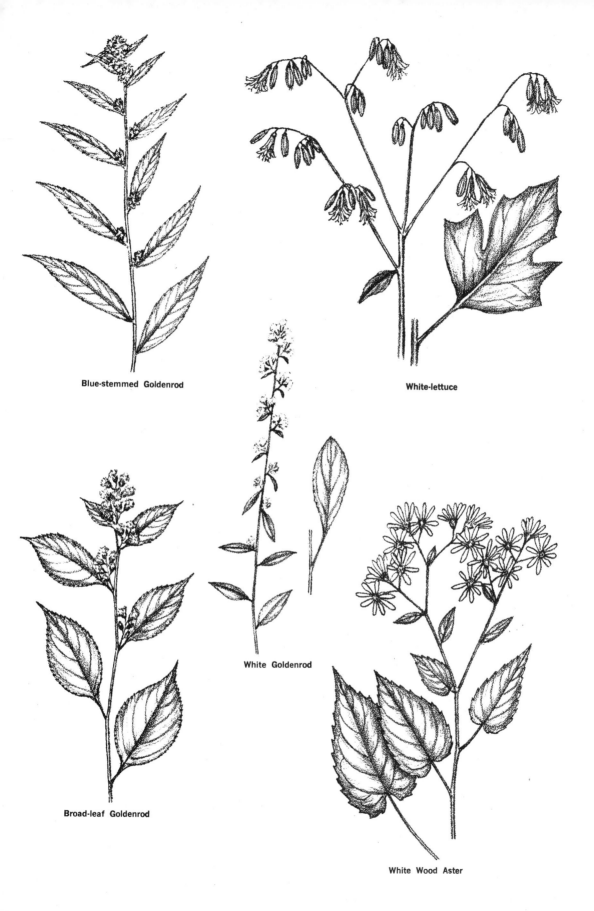

Blue-stemmed Goldenrod

White-lettuce

White Goldenrod

Broad-leaf Goldenrod

White Wood Aster

Common Blue Wood Aster

Crooked-stemmed Aster

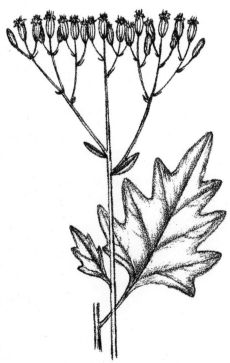

Pale Indian-plantain

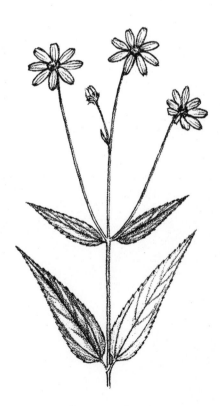

Small Wood Sunflower

COMMON BLUE WOOD ASTER *(Aster cordifolius)*   Composite Family

This is a common but quite variable woodland aster. It usually has smoothisn and branching stems 1 to 5 feet high. Most or all of the lower leaves are heart-shaped, coarsely toothed, 2 to 5 inches long, and have slender stalks. The ones on the stem above are smaller, shorter stalked, less toothed, and often taper at the base. It usually has numerous flower heads about ⅓ inch across, with 10 to 20 whitish, pinkish, or pale blue-violet rays; and often a reddish disk. It flowers between August and October.

RANGE: N.S. to Que. and Wis. south to Ga., Ala., Mo. and Kan.

CROOKED-STEMMED ASTER *(Aster prenanthoides)*   Composite Family

Usually this aster has a stout, somewhat zig-zag, branched stem 1 to 2 feet high, which may be smooth or have finely hairy lines. The leaves are lance-shaped to narrowly egg-shaped, taper-pointed at the tip, sharply toothed, and abruptly contracted into a broad and untoothed stalk-like portion expanding into 2 "ears" at the clasping base. The middle and lower ones are 3 to 8 inches long, usually roughish above but smooth beneath. Its flower heads are almost an inch across and have from 20 to 30 pale blue-violet rays. It grows in rich woods, damp thickets, and along streams; blooming between August and October.

RANGE: Mass. to Minn. south to Va., Ky. and Iowa.

PALE INDIAN-PLANTAIN *(Cacalia atriplicifolia)*   Composite Family

This striking plant has a smooth, round, whitened stem 3 to 6 feet tall. The leaves are somewhat triangular or fan-shaped with a broad base and angular lobes. They are thin, pale green above, whitened beneath, and up to 6 inches across. It numerous heads have a cylindrical involucre about ⅓ inch high and contain several tubular white flowers; and they are arranged in a large, loose, more or less flat-topped cluster. It grows in dry open woods and thickets, blooming between June and September.

RANGE: N.Y. to Minn. south to Ga., Tenn. and Okla.

SMALL WOOD SUNFLOWER *(Helianthus microcephalus)*   Composite Family

This woodland sunflower has a slender, smooth stem from 3 to 6 feet high which is branched above. Its leaves are lance-shaped to narrowly egg-shaped, thin, roughish above, pale and downy beneath, sharply toothed, stalked, and from 3 to 7 inches long. The flower heads are numerous, about an inch across, and have 5 to 10 yellow rays and a yellowish disk. It usually grows in moist places, blooming from August to October.

RANGE: Pa. to Ill. south to Fla., Miss. and Mo.

YELLOW FRINGED ORCHID *(Habenaria ciliaris)*   Orchid Family

The bright orange-yellow plumes of this common orchid make it one of our most conspicuous wild flowers, and have earned it the name of Orange-plume. It blooms between July and September. The plant has a leafy stem from 1 to 2½ feet tall, the larger leaves toward the base being 4 to 8 inches in length. The flowers have an oblong-shaped lip which is deeply fringed about the margin; and a slender spur as long as, or longer than, the colored and stalk-like ovary. It grows in moist open places, on slopes, and in thickets from the coast to the mountains.

RANGE: Vt. to Ont. and Wis. south to Fla. and Tex.

SLENDER LADY'S-TRESSES *(Spiranthes gracilis)*   Orchid Family

About a dozen species of lady's-tresses occur in eastern North America. All of them have rather small white, greenish-white, or yellowish flowers arranged in a more or less spirally twisted spike. This one has small white flowers which have a green spot on the lip. They are arranged in a single and strongly spiraled row on a leafless stalk 8 to 24 inches tall. The leaves are egg-shaped, stalked, and about 1 to 2½ inches long but they may not be present at flowering time. It grows in dry to moist open woods and fields, blooming from late July to October.

RANGE: N.H. to Wis. and Okla. south to Fla. and Tex.

NODDING LADY'S-TRESSES *(Spiranthes cernua)*   Orchid Family

This is a widespread and common little orchid; growing in moist to dry fields, thickets, and open woods. It has white flowers about ⅓ of an inch long, which are arranged in 3 or 4 somewhat twisted rows on stalks 6 to 18 inches tall. The grass-like leaves are basal, several inches long, and narrower downward. It blooms from August to October, and the flowers are sweet-scented.

RANGE: N.S. to Que. and Wis. south to Fla. and Tex.

284

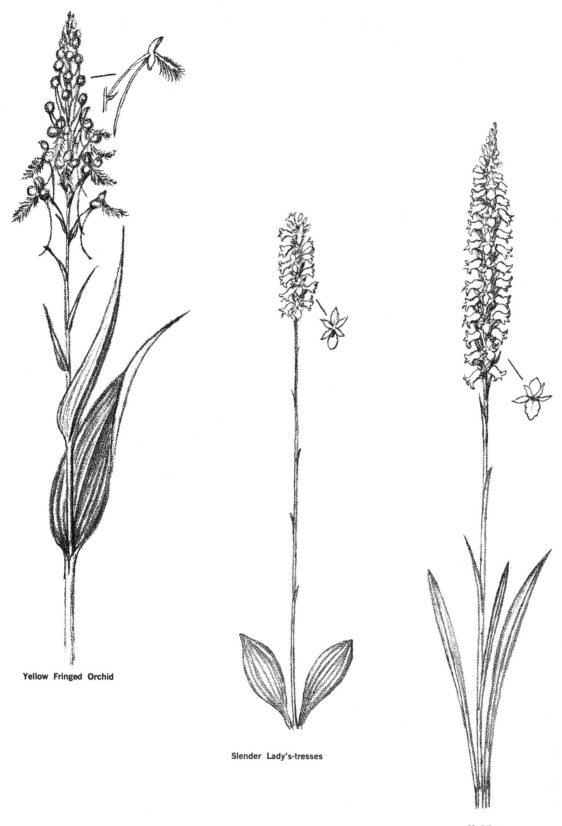

Yellow Fringed Orchid

Slender Lady's-tresses

**Nodding
Lady's-tresses**

Boneset

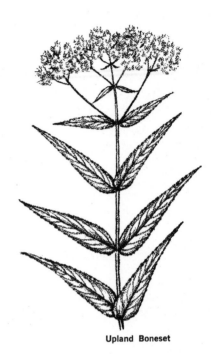

Upland Boneset

Jerusalem-artichoke

Ox-eye

BONESET *(Eupatorium perfoliatum)* Composite Family

The Boneset or Thoroughwort is a hairy plant with a stem 2 to 4 feet tall, usually branching above. The pairs of wrinkled-looking, lance-shaped, finely toothed leaves are 3 to 6 inches long; and are joined together at the base so that the stem appears to pass through them. The heads contain 10 to 20 small, white, tubular flowers; and they are arranged in flat-topped clusters. It grows in low moist thickets, open woods, and meadows; blooming between August and October. The plant was a favorite home remedy for colds and other afflictions.

RANGE: Que. to Man. south to Fla. and Tex.

UPLAND BONESET *(Eupatorium sessilifolium)* Composite Family

This is a rather smooth plant 2 to nearly 5 feet tall, usually branching above. It has pairs of lance-shaped, sharply toothed leaves 3 to 6 inches long, which are stalkless but not united at the base. The heads have about 5 tubular white flowers and are arranged in a flat-topped cluster. It grows in rather dry woods, thickets, and on hillsides; blooming between July and October.

RANGE: Mass. to Minn. south to Ga., Ala. and Mo.

JERUSALEM-ARTICHOKE *(Helianthus tuberosus)* Composite Family

In spite of its common name, this is a native American sunflower. Its thick and fleshy rootstocks bear edible tubers which were once much used by the Indians, and still sometimes cultivated. It has a very roughish-hairy stem 6 to 10 feet tall which is branched above. Its leaves are thick and hard, very rough-hairy above, downy beneath, and prominently 3-veined. Those along the main part of the stem are 4 to 8 inches long, egg-shaped, coarsely toothed, and contracted into broadly winged stalks. The flower heads are quite numerous, 2 to 3 inches across, with from 12 to 20 bright yellow rays and a yellowish disk. It grows in moist thickets and open places, blooming between July and October.

RANGE: Ont. to Sask. south to Ga., Tenn. and Ark.; and more widely naturalized.

OX-EYE *(Heliopsis helianthoides)* Composite Family

The Ox-eye is a sunflower-like plant with a smoothish stem 3 to 5 feet tall which may be simple or branched above. Its leaves are paired, egg-shaped or broadly lance-shaped, sharply toothed, slender-stalked, often more or less rough on the upper surface, and from 3 to 6 inches long. The heads of flowers are about 2 inches across and have 10 yellow rays which, unlike the rays of the true sunflowers, have pistils. It grows in open woods, thickets, and on dry banks; blooming between May and October. Also called False Sunflower.

RANGE: N.Y. to Ont. and Minn. south to Ga. and Tex.

FRINGED GENTIAN *(Gentiana crinita)*   Gentian Family

The Fringed Gentian has violet-blue flowers about 2 inches long, with the 4 petals united below into a bell-shaped tube and with the free ends conspicuously fringed. It has a stem 1 to 3 feet tall, with pairs of lance-shaped leaves 1 to 2 inches long on the stem and spoon-shaped ones at the base. It grows in cool, moist, open woods and meadows; blooming in September and October.

RANGE: Me. to Man. south to Ga., Ind. and Iowa.

CLOSED GENTIAN *(Gentiana andrewsii)*   Gentian Family

The club-shaped flowers of this and the next species do not open, nor do they show prominent corolla lobes at the tip. If spread open, the pale appendages between the narrower corolla lobes show a fringed margin in this species. The deep violet-blue (rarely white) flowers are 1 to 2 inches long, and clustered in the axils of the upper leaves. It grows in moist open places and thickets, blooming between August and October. Often called the Blind or Bottle Gentian.

RANGE: Mass. and Que. to Man. south to Ga. and Ark.

STRIPED GENTIAN *(Gentiana villosa)*   Gentian Family

This species has slender, smooth stems 6 inches to 2 feet tall; with pairs of egg-shaped leaves ½ to 2 inches long, which are stalkless and have clasping bases. Its flowers are 1 to 3 inches long, club-shaped, greenish-white to purplish-green with purple stripes, and have 5 corolla lobes which become erect. It grows on wooded slopes and stream banks, blooming from August to November. Also called Samson's Snakeroot.

RANGE: N.J. and Pa. south to Fla. and La.

STIFF GENTIAN *(Gentiana quinquefolia)*   Gentian Family

Also called Agueweed and Gall-of-the-earth, this species has stiffly erect, wing-angled stems 6 inches to 2 feet tall. The paired leaves are egg-shaped, ½ to 2 inches long, stalkless, and with clasping bases. Its flowers are about ¾ inch long, funnel-shaped, violet-blue to lilac, and have no pleats between the 5 triangular lobes. They are borne in both end and axillary clusters and bloom between August and October. It grows in dry to moist open woods, and along stream banks and roadsides.

RANGE: Me. to Ont. south to Fla., La. and Mo.

WING-STEM *(Verbesina alternifolia)*   Composite Family

The Wing-stem, or Yellow Ironweed, has a stem from 4 to 9 feet tall which is winged along the upper portion, usually branched above, and often somewhat hairy. The leaves are scattered, or the lower ones may be opposite or in whorls of 3. They are mostly broadly lance-shaped, toothed, pointed at both ends, 4 to 12 inches long, and stalkless or short-stalked. The flower heads are numerous, 1 to 2 inches across, and the 2 to 10 yellow rays often differ quite a bit in size. It grows in the borders of moist woods and thickets, blooming during August or September.

RANGE: N.Y. to Ont. and Iowa south to Fla. and La.

THIN-LEAF SUNFLOWER *(Helianthus decapetalus)*   Composite Family

Also known as the Ten-petalled Sunflower, this species has a smoothish stem 1 to 5 feet tall which is branched and may be slightly roughish above. Its thin textured leaves are smooth or but slightly roughish above and are rather indistinctly 3-veined. The larger and lower ones are egg-shaped, 3 to 8 inches long, sharply toothed, and slender stalked. Those of the upper part of the stem are smaller, lance-shaped, and taper into short stalks. The flower heads are 2 to 3 inches across, with from 8 to 15 light yellow rays and a yellowish disk. It grows in open woods, thickets, and often along streams; blooming between August and October.

RANGE: Me. to Que., Minn. and Neb. south to Ga., Ky. and Mo.

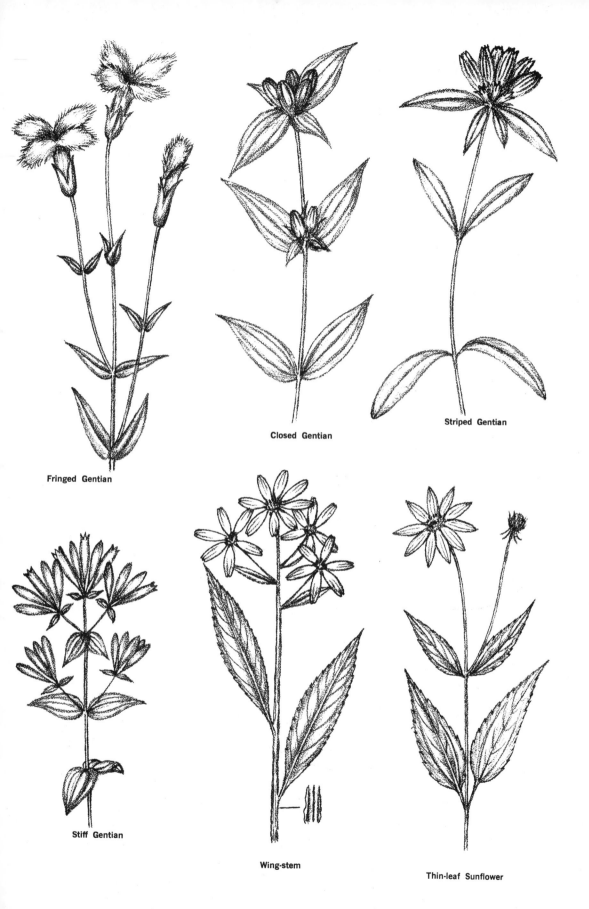

Fringed Gentian

Closed Gentian

Striped Gentian

Stiff Gentian

Wing-stem

Thin-leaf Sunflower

New England Aster

Tall Thistle

White Old-field Aster

Calico Aster

TALL THISTLE *(Carduus altissimus)*   Composite Family

Often called the Roadside Thistle, this species has a fairly stout, branching, woolly, and leafy stem 3 to 10 feet tall. Its leaves are undivided but have shallowly lobed or bristly-toothed margins, and they are densely felted with white wool beneath. The flower heads are about 2 inches across, with numerous rose-purple flowers; while the outer involucral bracts have a dark glandular spot and also a weak prickle. It grows in open woods, fields, pastures and thickets; blooming from August to late fall.
RANGE: N.Y. to Mich. and Minn. south to Fla. and Tex.

NEW ENGLAND ASTER *(Aster novae-angliae)*   Composite Family

This is a very attractive wild aster which is sometimes cultivated. It is a hairy plant 2 to 8 feet high with a rather stout stem which is branched above and very leafy. The leaves are lance-shaped, untoothed, mostly 2 to 4 inches long, and clasp the stem by their heart-shaped or "eared" bases. The numerous flower heads are about 1½ inches across and have about 40 or 50 narrow violet-purple rays. Both the stalks of the heads and the involucres are covered with minute and sticky glands, and the involucral bracts have rather long, spreading tips. It grows in moist thickets, fields, swamps, and along roadsides; blooming between August and October.
RANGE: Que. to Alb. south to Md., w. N.C., e. Tenn., Kan. and Colo.

WHITE OLD-FIELD ASTER *(Aster pilosus)*   Composite Family

Sometimes this aster is pilose—meaning hairy—but just as often, it is smooth. It grows in dry thickets, clearings, and along roadsides; and it is often very abundant in abandoned fields. It grows from 2 to about 5 feet tall and has several slender branches which are ascending or stiffly spreading. Its leaves are all narrow or lance-shaped, stalkless, stiffish, slightly if at all toothed, and 1 to 3 inches long. The numerous flower heads are about ¾ inch across, with 15 to 25 white or sometimes pale purplish rays, and grow along the upper side of the branches; blooming between August and November.
RANGE: Me. to Minn. and Kan. south to Ga., Ala. and Ark.

CALICO ASTER *(Aster lateriflorus)*   Composite Family

The Calico or Starved Aster differs from the preceding species in having thinner and flexible leaves which are usually broader, 2 to 6 inches long, sharply toothed as a rule, and quite roughish. Its flower heads are about ½ inch across, with from 10 to 20 white rays and purplish disk flowers. The bracts of the involucre have a prominent green midrib. The heads are usually very numerous and borne in a branching flower cluster; blooming between August and November. It grows in dry to moist open woods, thickets, fields, and along roadsides.
RANGE: Que. to Minn. south to Ga. and Tex.

TALL GOLDENROD *(Solidago altissima)*   Composite Family

The Tall or Canada Goldenrod has a stout grayish-downy or sometimes roughish stem 2 to 8 feet tall; with numerous. crowded, lance-shaped, sharply toothed, stalkless or short-stalked leaves 3 to 6 inches long. They are thickish, 3-veined, and rough on the upper surface. Involucres of the flower heads vary from less than ⅛ inch to ¼ inch in height; and the numerous heads are arranged in a large pyramid-shaped terminal cluster, with many spreading or recurved branches. It grows in old fields, meadows and thickets; blooming in September and October.

RANGE: Nfd. to Sask. south to Fla. and Tex.

WRINKLED-LEAF GOLDENROD *(Solidago rugosa)*   Composite Family

This is a common but variable goldenrod with a usually stout stem 2 to 6 feet high, crowded with leaves and often with lines running down from the leaf bases. The leaves, like the stem, may be either smooth or hairy but they present a very wrinkled appearance above and are very veiny beneath. They are 1 to 4 inches long, lance-shaped to oval, sharply toothed, and are often rough above. The flower cluster has a number of spreading or recurved branches. It grows in dry to moist open woods, clearings, and thickets; blooming between August and October.

RANGE: Nfd. to Ont. and Mich. south to Fla. and Tex.

SWEET GOLDENROD *(Solidago odora)*   Composite Family

The crushed leaves of this goldenrod have an anise-like odor. It has a slender smooth or slightly downy stem 2 to 4 feet tall; and numerous narrowly lance-shaped leaves 2 to 4 inches long which are stalkless, untoothed, and marked with tiny translucent dots. The flower heads are in a loose, 1-sided, plume-like cluster. It grows in dry open woods, fields, and thickets; blooming between July and October. Also called the Anise-scented Goldenrod.

RANGE: N.H. to Ohio, Ky., Mo. and Okla. south to Fla. and Tex.

BUSHY GOLDENROD *(Solidago graminifolia)*   Composite Family

This is a bushy-branched plant 2 to 4 feet tall, with numerous narrowly lance-shaped leaves 1 to 5 inches long which show 3 prominent veins. The small flower heads are in flat-topped end clusters. It grows in wet fields and stream bottoms, blooming between July and October. Also called Fragrant or Flat-topped Goldenrod.

RANGE: Nfd. to Sask. south to N.C. and Mo.

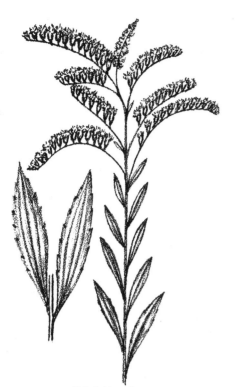

Tall Goldenrod

Wrinkled-leaf Goldenrod

Sweet Goldenrod

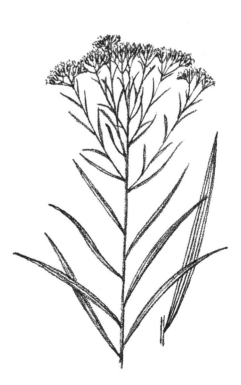

Bushy Goldenrod

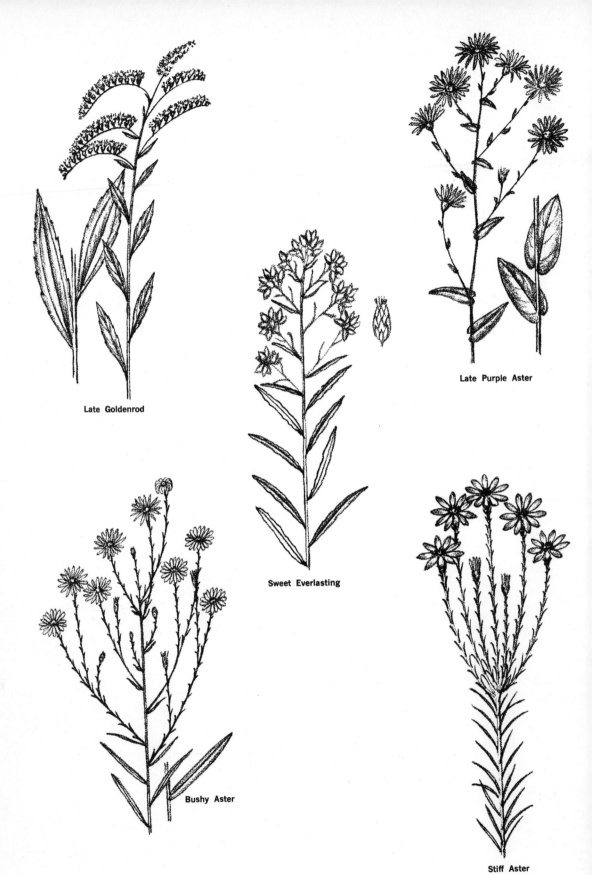

Late Goldenrod

Sweet Everlasting

Late Purple Aster

Bushy Aster

Stiff Aster

LATE PURPLE ASTER *(Aster patens)*   Composite Family

The stems of this aster are slender, roughish-hairy, 1 to 3 feet tall, and are branched above. Its leaves are oblong or oval, mostly 1 to 2 inches long, untoothed, rather thickish and somewhat rigid, and roughish or hairy. They clasp the stem by their heart-shaped bases. The uppermost leaves in the flower cluster are small and often almost bract-like. It has beautiful flower heads about ⅔ inch across, with from 20 to 30 deep violet or bluish-purple rays, produced between August and October. This species also grows in dry open woods, thickets, and fields.
RANGE: Me. to Minn. south to Fla. and Tex.

LATE GOLDENROD *(Solidago gigantea)*   Composite Family

This species has a stout, smooth stem from 2 to 8 feet tall which is usually whitened with a bloom. The leaves are lance-shaped or narrowly oblong, stalkless, sharply toothed at least above the middle, 3 to 6 inches long, conspicuously 3-veined, and somewhat hairy on the veins beneath. The small flower heads are arranged along the spreading or re-curved branches of the terminal flower cluster, blooming between July and October. It often forms extensive colonies in the borders of damp woods and thickets.
RANGE: N.B. to B.C. south to Fla. and Tex.

BUSHY ASTER *(Aster dumosus)*   Composite Family

This is a slender-stemmed and usually minutely downy plant 1 to 3 feet high, with spreading or ascending branches. Its heads of flowers are about ½ inch across, with 15 to 25 pale lavender or bluish rays. They terminate slender branchlets 2 to 4 inches long, on which are crowded, small, bract-like leaves. The larger leaves are quite narrow and from 1 to 3 inches long. Also known as the Rice-button Aster, it grows in dry to moist sandy fields and thickets; blooming between late August and October.
RANGE: Me. to Ont. and Mich. south to Fla. and Tex.

SWEET EVERLASTING *(Gnaphalium obtusifolium)*   Composite Family

This plant has pleasantly fragrant, wavy-margined, narrow leaves which are smooth and green above but white-woolly beneath, and 1 to 3 inches long. It is a whitish-cobwebby plant from 1 to 3 feet tall, often with a branched stem. The bracts of the involucres are pale yellowish. It grows abundantly in dry fields, clearings, and along roadsides; blooming August to October.
RANGE: Nfd. to Alaska south to W. Va., Ohio, Wis., N. Mex., and Calif.

STIFF ASTER *(Aster linariifolius)*   Composite Family

Savory-leaf Aster and Pine-starwort are other names given to this aster. It has a tuft of stiff, roughish, minutely hairy stems 6 inches to 2 feet high which are branched above. On them are numerous and rather closely crowded, very narrow, stiff, rough-margined leaves. The larger ones are ¾ to 1½ inches long, the upper ones being reduced to rigid bracts. The flower heads are solitary at the ends of the erect or ascending branches; each one about an inch across, with from 10 to 15 bright lavender rays. It grows in dry sandy or rocky open places, blooming between September and November.
RANGE: N.B. to Que. and Minn. south to Fla. and Tex.

EASTERN SILVERY ASTER *(Aster concolor)*   Composite Family

Also called the Lilac-flowered Aster, this species has a slender and usually minutely downy stem 1 to 2½ feet tall, which is simple or with a few almost erect branches. The numerous leaves are minutely silvery-silky, stalkless, and untoothed; the lower ones being elliptic to lance-shaped and 1½ to 2 inches long. Those upward on the stem are very much smaller or even bract-like. The pretty flower heads are about ¾ inch across, with from 10 to 15 lilac to violet-purple rays, and arranged in a long and narrow cluster. It grows in dry and sandy open woods and pinelands, chiefly in the coastal plain. Its flowering season is during September and October.

RANGE: Mass. and Ky. south to Fla. and La.

DENSE BUTTON-SNAKEROOT *(Liatris spicata)*   Composite Family

This species has smoothish stems 1 to 6 feet tall with crowded, very narrow, smooth leaves gradually becoming larger toward the base. The lower ones are still narrow, ¾ inch or less across, but often 5 to 15 inches long. The upper portion of the stem has crowded heads of flowers which bloom progressively downward from the tip. Each head is usually about ⅓ inch across, containing between 5 and 15 flowers. It grows in wet open woods and fields.

RANGE: Del. to W.Va., Ohio and Neb. south to Fla. and Tex.

SCALY BLAZING-STAR *(Liatris squarrosa)*   Composite Family

The large heads of this species have spreading or recurving, thickish, and stiff bracts; and they usually contain from 25 to 40 rather large flowers. The plant has rather stout stems 1 to 3 feet high; and numerous narrow, rigid, resin-dotted leaves. It grows in dry open woods and fields.

RANGE: Del. to W.Va., Ohio. and Neb. south to Fla. and Tex.

WAVY-LEAF ASTER *(Aster undulatus)*   Composite Family

The Wavy-leaf Aster has a stiffly erect stem which is usually somewhat minutely roughish-hairy, branched above, and from 1 to 3½ feet tall. Its lower leaves are lance-shaped or egg-shaped, heart-shaped at the base, and 2 to 6 inches long. They are wavy on the margin, or sometimes with some low and blunt teeth, and have winged leaf-stalks which broaden at the clasping base. The ones upward along the stem are smaller and stalkless or nearly so. All of the leaves are roughish on the upper surface and downy underneath. The flower heads are about ½ inch across and have from 8 to 15 pale violet or bluish rays. It grows in dry open woods and thickets; blooming between August and November.

RANGE: N.S. to Ont. and Minn. south to Fla., La. and Ark.

SMOOTH ASTER *(Aster laevis)*   Composite Family

This is a smooth plant with a rather stout and whitened stem 2 to 4 feet tall, which is often more or less branched. Its leaves are thick, lance-shaped to elliptic or egg-shaped, 1 to 3 inches long, and mostly untoothed. The ones on the upper part of the stem are stalkless but the lower and basal ones taper into winged stalks. Its flower heads are almost an inch across and have 15 to 30 violet or bluish rays; blooming between August and October. It grows on the borders of woods and in thickets or dry fields.

RANGE: Me. to Sask. south to Ga., La. and Kan.

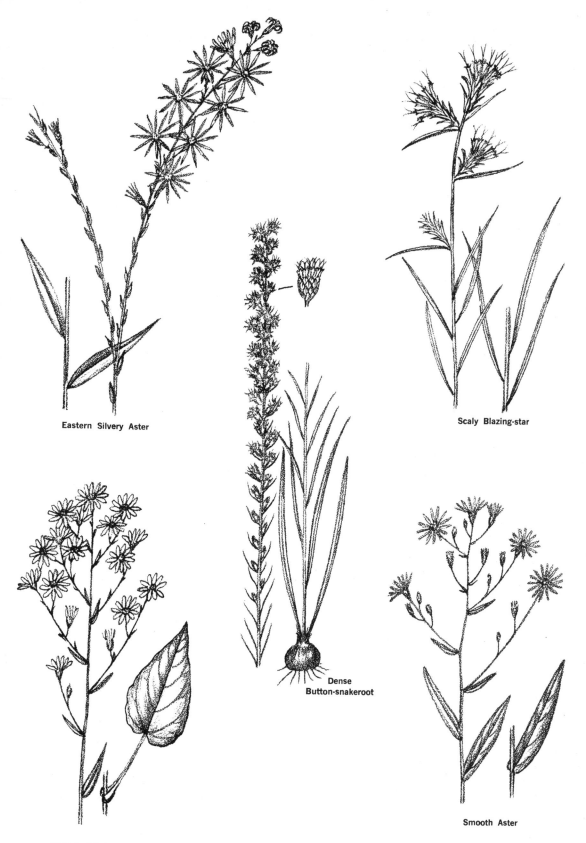

Eastern Silvery Aster

Scaly Blazing-star

Dense
Button-snakeroot

Wavy-leaf Aster

Smooth Aster

GLOSSARY

ACHENE   A small, hard, dry, one-seeded fruit which does not split open when ripe.

AERIAL ROOTLETS   Small root-like structures on the stems of some climbing vines.

ALTERNATE   Spaced singly at intervals along the stem.

ANGLED   With several edges or evident ridges.

ANTHER   The part of a stamen which produces pollen.

AQUATIC   Living in water.

ARMED   Provided with prickles, spines, or thorns.

AROMATIC   Having a pleasant spicy smell.

ASCENDING   Growing upward at an angle.

AWL-LIKE   Narrow and tapering to a sharp point.

AXIL   The upper angle formed by a leaf with the stem; the similar angle formed by a vein with the midrib of a leaf.

AXILLARY   Situated in the axil of a leaf or bract.

BEAK   A long and prominent point.

BEARD   A group of long or stiff hairs.

BERRY   A fruit derived from a single ovary which is fleshy or pulpy throughout.

BERRY-LIKE   Resembling a berry but not a true berry in the botanical sense.

BILATERAL   A flower which can be divided into two like halves only by dividing it vertically through the center.

BLADE   The flat or expanded portion of a leaf.

BLOOM   A white powdery or waxy substance which is easily rubbed off.

BRACT   A small or scale-like leaf beneath a flower or a flower cluster.

BRANCHLET   A small branch of the current season; a twig.

BRISTLE   A stiff-hair or weak outgrowth less formidable than a prickle.

BUD   An undeveloped leafy stem, flower, or flower cluster.

BULB   A kind of underground bud with fleshy scales.

BUNDLE SCARS   Dot-like scars within a leaf scar which represent the broken ends of ducts which led into the leaf stalk.

CALYX   The outer circle of organs in a flower; a collective term for the sepals.

CAPSULE   A dry pod formed by two or more carpels which splits open into two or more parts at maturity.

CARPEL   A simple pistil or one of the parts of a compound pistil.

CATKIN   A group of small, scaly-bracted flowers arranged in a long and often drooping cluster.

CHAFF   Small, thin, dry scales associated with the disk flowers in many composites.

CHAFFY   Covered with small, bran-like scales.

CHAMBERED PITH   Pith divided crosswise by woody plates or partitions.

CLAW   The narrow or stalk-like base of a petal.

CLEFT   Deeply cut but not divided.

COMPOUND LEAF   A leaf in which the blade is divided into smaller leaf-like parts or leaflets.

CONTINUOUS PITH   Pith which is not divided into compartments by cross plates.

CORM   The enlarged base of a stem which is bulb-like but solid.

COROLLA   A collective name for the petals of a flower whether separate or joined together.

CORYMB   A more or less flat-topped flower cluster in which the outer or marginal flowers open first.

CRESTED   Having elevated ridges or projections.

CYME   A more or less flat-topped flower cluster in which the central flowers open first.

DIAPHRAGM   A zone of denser or woody tissue in the pith.

DISK FLOWER   The tubular flowers in the center of the heads of some composites such as daisies, sunflowers, and asters.

DIVIDED   Separated to the base.

DOUBLE-TOOTHED   Having large teeth which in turn have smaller teeth on them.

DOWNY   Coated with short fine, soft hairs.

DRUPE   A fleshy fruit with the seed enclosed in a hard and bony covering often called a pit.

DRUPELET   A very small drupe.

EGG-SHAPED   Shaped like a bird egg or broadest below the middle.

ELLIPTIC (ELLIPTICAL)   Having the outline of an ellipse; widest in the middle and about equally narrowed at both ends.

ELONGATE   Very much longer than broad.

ENTIRE   A leaf which is neither lobed nor toothed on the margin.

EVERGREEN   With leaves remaining more or less green throughout the year.

EYE   A prominent mark in the center of a flower.

FEATHER-VEINED   A leaf with veins arising along the sides of the midrib.

FILAMENT   The stalk of a stamen.

FLAKY   Having loose scales.

FLORET   A small flower, especially one which is in a dense cluster.

FRUIT   The seed-bearing portion of a plant; botanically a ripened ovary together with parts of the flower united with it.

GLAND   A small organ having the function of secretion.

GLANDULAR   Having or bearing glands.

HEAD   A dense cluster of stalkless or nearly stalkless flowers.

HEART-SHAPED   Shaped like a Valentine heart.

HOARY   Grayish-white with fine and close hairs.

IMPERFECT FLOWER   A flower lacking either stamens or pistils.

INFERIOR OVARY   An ovary which is surrounded by and more or less united with the calyx of the flower.

INFLATED   Seeming to be blown up; bladdery.

INFLORESCENCE   A group or cluster of flowers.

INVOLUCRE   A circle or group of bracts below a flower or flower cluster.

IRREGULAR FLOWER   A flower in which the parts are not of the same size or shape.

KEEL   The two lower petals of a pea-like flower; having a central ridge like the keel of a boat.

LANCE-SHAPED   Long and narrow, broadest below the middle and tapering to a point at the tip.

LATERAL   Situated along the side.

LEAFLET   One of the small leaf-like parts of a compound leaf.

LEAF SCAR   The scar left on a twig when a leaf falls.

LEAF STALK   The stalk supporting a leaf.

LENTICEL   A corky spot on the bark which permits air to enter the stem.

LINEAR   Long and narrow with the sides parallel or nearly so.

LIP   One of the parts of an unequally divided calyx or corolla; in orchids a petal, usually the lowest, which differs in size, shape, and often in color from the other petals.

LOBE   A more or less rounded extension of an organ; the projecting part of a leaf, or calyx or corolla of a flower.

MIDRIB   The central or main vein of a leaf, the extension of the leaf stalk.

NAKED BUD   A bud which is not covered with scales.

NEEDLE-LIKE   Very slender and pointed at the tip.

NODAL   Pertaining to or situated at a node.

NODE   The point on a stem where a leaf or leaves is attached.

NUT   A hard-shelled, one-seeded fruit which does not split open at maturity.

NUTLET   A very small and nut-like hard fruit.

OBLONG   Longer than wide and with the sides nearly parallel.

OPPOSITE   In pairs and directly across from each other on the stem.

OVAL   Broadly elliptic; widest at the middle and about equally narrowed at the ends.

OVARY   The basal portion of a pistil which contains the ovules.

OVULE   A small body in the ovary which develops into a seed.

PALMATE   With veins, or lobes, or leaflets radiating from one point like the spread fingers of a hand.

PAPPUS   Hairs, bristles, or scales that form the calyx limb in composites.

PARTED   Cleft nearly but not quite to the base.

PERFECT   A flower which possesses both stamens and pistils.

PERIANTH   The parts of a flower surrounding the stamens and pistils.

PETAL   One of the flower parts immediately outside the reproductive organs and commonly white or colored other than green.

PINNATE   Arranged along the sides of a stalk or midrib.

PISTIL   The female organ of a flower which develops into the fruit.

PITH   Soft or spongy tissue in the center of a stem or twig.

POD   A dry fruit which splits open at maturity.

POLLEN   The minute grains produced in anthers and containing the male reproductive cells.

PRICKLE   A small, sharp, needle-like outgrowth of the bark.

RADIALLY SYMMETRIC   A flower which can be divided in many ways through the center into two similar halves.

RAY (RAY FLOWER)   In composites the flowers with strap-shaped, petal-like corollas.

RECEPTACLE   The enlarged or expanded end of a stem to which the parts of a flower are attached; in composites the enlarged stem end to which the flowers of the head are attached.

RECURVED   Curving downward or backward.

REFLEXED   Abruptly bent or turned downward.

REGULAR FLOWER   A flower in which the sepals (and petals) are alike in size and shape.

RIB   A primary or prominent vein of a leaf.

ROOTSTOCK   A more or less horizontal underground stem.

ROSETTE   A circle of leaves lying more or less flat on the ground.

RUNNER   A slender more or less trailing stem which takes root at the nodes.

SCALE   A small modified leaf such as those usually covering a bud.

SCURFY   Covered with small bran-like scales.

SEPAL   One of the outermost series of organs of a flower, usually green in color.

SIMPLE LEAF   A leaf in which the blade is not divided.

SINUS   The indentation between the lobes of a leaf blade.

SPADIX   A thick stalk bearing small, stalkless, crowded flowers.

SPATHE   A large bract enclosing or surrounding a flower cluster.

SPIKE   An elongate cluster of stalkless flowers.

SPINE   A sharp-pointed, rigid, thorn-like outgrowth.

SPUR   A short, slow-growing branch; a hollow tubular or sac-like projection of a petal (or sepal).

STAMEN   The male element of a flower which produces pollen.

INDEX

INDEX TO SCIENTIFIC NAMES

316

Gentiana catesbaei 276
Gentiana crinita 288
Gentiana quinquefolia 288
Gentiana villosa 288
Geranium maculatum 183
Gillenia trifoliata 191
Gleditsia triacanthos 104
Gnaphalium obtusifolium 295
Gordonia lasianthus 59

Habenaria ciliaris 284
Habenaria orbiculata 228
Halesia carolina 156
Hamamelis virginiana 88
Helenium autumnale 271
Helenium vernale 219
Helianthus angustifolius 271
Helianthus decapetalus 288
Helianthus microcephalus 283
Helianthus tuberosus 287
Heliopsis helianthoides 287
Helonias bullata 211
Hemerocallis fulva 239
Hepatica americana 164
Heracleum maximum 248
Heuchera americana 192
Hibiscus moscheutos 268
Hieracium aurantiacum 247
Hieracium pratense 247
Hieracium venosum 191
Houstonia caerulea 196
Houstonia serpyllifolia 215
Hydrangea arborescens 108
Hymenocallis crassifolia 219
Hypericum densiflorum 107
Hypericum galioides 63
Hypericum hypericoides 79
Hypericum punctatum 244
Hypericum spathulatum 107
Hypoxis hirsuta 199

Ilex ambigua var. montana 119
Ilex cassine 52
Ilex glabra 160
Ilex opaca 139
Ilex verticillata 32
Ilex vomitoria 160
Impatiens capensis 165
Impatiens pallida 165
Ipomea pandurata 248
Ipomea sagittata 275
Iris cristata 183
Iris prismatica 211
Iris verna 183
Iris versicolor 211
Iris virginica 211
Itea virginica 59

Jeffersonia diphylla 164
Juglans cinerea 128
Juglans nigra 100
Juniperus communis 24
Juniperus virginiana 24

Kalmia angustifolia 39
Kalmia latifolia 83
Kalmia polifolia 47

Larix laricina 23
Ledum groenlandicum 40
Leiophyllum buxifolium 79
Leucothoë fontanesiana 155
Leucothoë racemosa 59
Leucothoë recurva 155
Liatris scariosa 279
Liatris secunda 276
Liatris spicata 296
Liatris squarrosa 296
Lilium canadense 236
Lilium catesbaei 272
Lilium philadelphicum 236
Lilium superbum 268
Linaria vulgaris 243
Lindera benzoin 27
Linnea borealis var. americana 224
Liquidambar styraciflua 143
Liriodendron tulipifera 95
Lobelia cardinalis 264
Lobelia siphilitica 264
Lonicera canadensis 132
Lonicera oblongifolia 48
Lonicera sempervirens 147
Lonicera villosa 48
Lupinus perennis 199
Lupinus villosus 223
Lyonia ligustrina 84
Lyonia lucida 51
Lyonia mariana 76

Magnolia acuminata 116
Magnolia fraseri 151
Magnolia grandiflora 159
Magnolia tripetala 136
Magnolia virginiana 51
Maianthemum canadense 180
Malus angustifolia 140
Malus coronaria 91
Medeola virginica 172
Melilotus alba 240
Melilotus officinalis 240
Menispermum canadense 92
Menyanthes trifoliata var. minor 211
Menziesia pilosa 151
Mertensia virginica 187
Mikania scandens 268

Rhamnus caroliniana 139
Rhexia alifanus 272
Rhexia virginica 264
Rhododendron calendulaceum 148
Rhododendron canadense 40
Rhododendron catawbiense 148
Rhododendron maximum 116
Rhododendron minus 148
Rhododendron nudiflorum 28
Rhododendron viscosum 27
Rhus aromatica 71
Rhus copallina 100
Rhus glabra 100
Rhus radicans 99
Rhus toxicodendron 79
Rhus typhina 100
Rhus vernix 36
Ribes americanum 115
Ribes cynosbati 127
Ribes glandulosum 127
Ribes lacustre 47
Ribes rotundifolium 127
Robinia hispida 143
Robinia pseudoacacia 104
Robinia viscosa 155
Rosa carolina 99
Rosa palustris 36
Rubus allegheniensis 131
Rubus canadensis 131
Rubus hispidus 131
Rubus idaeus var. strigosus 128
Rubus occidentalis 128
Rubus odoratus 127
Rudbeckia hirta 247
Rudbeckia laciniata 255
Ruellia ciliosa 236

Sabal palmetto 156
Sabatia angularis 255
Sabatia campanulata 263
Sabatia difformis 272
Sabatia dodecandra 272
Sagittaria latifolia 259
Salix bebbiana 115
Salix discolor 43
Salix humilis 67
Salix interior 43
Salix lucida 43
Salix nigra 31
Salix sericea 31
Salix serissima 43
Salvia lyrata 196
Sambucus canadensis 112
Sambucus pubens 135
Sanguinaria canadensis 164
Saponaria officinalis 239
Sarracenia flava 219

Sarracenia minor 219
Sarracenia purpurea 208
Sassafras albidum 95
Saururus cernuus 259
Saxifraga michauxii 279
Saxifraga pensylvanica 208
Saxifraga virginiensis 167
Schrankia microphylla 251
Schrankia nuttallii 251
Scutellaria integrifolia 232
Sedum ternatum 167
Senecio aureus 207
Senecio obovatus 188
Senecio smallii 200
Serenoa repens 156
Shepherdia canadensis 75
Shortia galacifolia 212
Silene stellata 232
Silene virginica 183
Sium suave 260
Smilacina racemosa 180
Smilax bona-nox 80
Smilax glauca 80
Smilax hispida 80
Smilax laurifolia 55
Smilax rotundifolia 80
Smilax walteri 55
Solidago altissima 292
Solidago bicolor 280
Solidago caesia 280
Solidago fistulosa 275
Solidago flexicaulis 280
Solidago gigantea 295
Solidago graminifolia 292
Solidago juncea 256
Solidago odora 292
Solidago rugosa 292
Solidago stricta 275
Sorbus americana 128
Sparganium americanum 259
Spiraea alba 119
Spiraea tomentosa 32
Spiranthes cernua 284
Spiranthes gracilis 284
Staphylea trifolia 111
Stellaria pubera 167
Stenanthium gramineum 231
Stewartia ovata 152
Streptopus amplexifolius 171
Streptopus roseus 171
Styrax americana 59
Symplocarpus foetidus 203
Symplocos tinctoria 136

Taenidia integerrima 180
Taxodium distichum 23
Taxus canadensis 23

319